Indian Place-Names

INDIAN

PLACE-NAMES

THEIR ORIGIN, EVOLUTION, AND MEANINGS, COLLECTED IN KANSAS FROM THE SIOUAN ▲ ALGONQUIAN ▲ SHOSHONEAN CADDOAN ▲ IROQUOIAN ▲ AND OTHER TONGUES ▲ ▲ ▲

BY JOHN RYDJORD

UNIVERSITY OF OKLAHOMA PRESS ▲ NORMAN

By John Rydjord

Foreign Interest in the Independence of New Spain (Durham, N. C., 1935)

Indian Place-Names (Norman, 1968)

Library of Congress Catalog Card Number: 68-10303

 Composed and printed at Norman, Oklahoma, U.S.A., by the University of Oklahoma Press. First edition.

Preface

My interest in place-names began some forty years ago when I was called upon to give a lecture on Kansas. In preparing the lecture, I examined a map of Kansas and became impressed by the great variety of its place-names. Not only does Kansas have names descriptive of its flora and fauna and its geography, but it also has biblical names, Greek and Roman classical names, names from Spain, France, Germany, and England, a few Oriental names, an occasional African name, and it has names of local, state, and national politicians. The names of Kansas counties read like a "Who's Who in the Civil War," explaining why Kansas is called "The Soldier State." Equally conspicuous are the Indian names.

Not until I retired in 1958 did I start a serious study of Kansas place-names. In spite of the accumulation of a vast amount of material, it soon became obvious that a more specialized study was essential before attempting the broad survey originally planned. The area which was in the greatest need of further study was Indian place-names. Not only did Kansas have its native Indian tribes, but it also became the temporary home for tribes from other areas. Many Indian place-names came to Kansas with the migrating Indians; others were brought to Kansas by white settlers who had lived in towns which had Indian names. From Maine to Florida, from the Carolinas to California, and from Alaska to Peru in Spanish America, native names were chosen for place-names in Kansas.

Much of the material on the Indian place-names was inadequate or superficial. Stating that Kiowa was named for an Indian tribe seemed to be sufficiently obvious to be unnecessary and quite insufficient to be informative. In this study a very brief account of each tribe, a thumbnail sketch, has been included as an essential background. Each tribe has been identified geographically and linguistically in so far as this is possible.

Enough examples of native names have been included to indicate the difficulty of transferring the gutteral and nasal sounds of Indian words into the phonetics of a European language. After all, the natives did not give us the seemingly atrocious orthography for their outlandish names. Americans had a way of modifying and simplifying these unpronounceable and seemingly unspellable names until the names were sufficiently simplified to become acceptable and often attractive place-names in America. Many of the names lost their meaning in their transition from one language to another and on their way to becoming Americanized. A number of names of places which no longer exist have been included since the primary interest has been in the preservation of a name and not in perpetuating a town. Non-Indian names have been included if they have been associated with Indian names.

There is much doubt and considerable disagreement among professional students regarding the origin, evolution, and meaning of Indian names. Recognizing this, one becomes increasingly sympathetic to, rather than harshly critical of, others who have tried to solve the mysteries of Indian names. I have therefore included a wide variety of interpretations, even contradictory ones. Legends and folklore have been included as an important and interesting phase of place-name studies.

Many names have been quite ephemeral, most of them have gone through an interesting evolution in spelling, and pronunciations have become provincial. In a *Pronunciation Guide to Kansas Place Names*, the William Allen White School of Journalism at the University of Kansas concluded that Kansas names have now become "thoroughly Americanized, yea, even Kansanized."

JOHN RYDJORD

Wichita, Kansas
February 12, 1968

Acknowledgments

MANY YEARS AGO Dave Leahy, a colorful Wichita journalist, expressed the hope that I would write on Kansas history. George R. Stewart over a cup of coffee in Berkeley gave a word of encouragement for undertaking a study of Kansas place-names. The interest in this project shown by many of my former students and friends has also been stimulating. I owe a great deal to those who have given me aid and encouragement.

The Kansas State Historical Library in Topeka has been used extensively, and I wish to express my appreciation for the co-operation of the staff under the competent direction of Lyle H. Miller. Downing P. O'Harra, librarian, and his staff at the Wichita State University Library have been most helpful and co-operative. John W. Ripley of Topeka, former president of the Kansas State Historical Society, provided a set of the Shawnee County Historical Society bulletins. Stephen B. Lee of Wichita loaned me a set of the Kansas Historical Society publications. Wayne E. Corley of Denver sent me a mimeographed copy of his study on "County and Community Names in Kansas." For all such aid I wish to express my thanks.

I am grateful to the administration of Wichita State University for providing a study in Ablah Library. For special aid I wish to thank President Emory K. Lindquist, Fred Sudermann, Ross M. Taylor, and Henry Malone, and for technical help on the maps, Arthur Risser and Jim Harvey. My son John L. Rydjord and his wife Sylvia read most of the manuscript and gave helpful suggestions. My wife Lillian copied much of the material collected on our trips to the State Library at Topeka. Most helpful were the criticism and suggestions of Professor Robert W. Mood, Jr., who read the whole manuscript. However, there may be omissions, and errors have surely crept in, and for these only the author can be held responsible.

JOHN RYDJORD

Contents

Illustrations

Maps

Indian Place-Names

▲ I

Introduction

OVER A HUNDRED YEARS AGO Lewis H. Morgan in his book on the Iroquois made a statement which may well serve as an introduction to this study. In his chapter on names he said:

> The features of nature were first christened by the red man. These baptismal names, the legacy of the Indian, it was prodigality to cast away. To the future scholar this subject will commend itself, when perchance, the dusky mantle of obscurity has enshrouded it, and research itself cannot penetrate the covering.[1]

It has been a challenge to uncover this "legacy of the Indian" and to search for light to bring these place-names from their "dusky mantle of obscurity."

Only Oklahoma can equal Kansas in the variety of Indians, Indian languages, and Indian names. Indians had converged on Kansas from all sides before the coming of the white man. After the white man had settled the eastern part of the United States, he made Kansas a part of the Indian Territory as the new home for the Indians from the eastern states. These immigrant Indians have added not only variety but complexity to the study of Indian place-names in Kansas. Back of the Americanized Indian names are the interesting but obscure names in their original and varied languages. "They suggest little or nothing to us by their sound," said one writer on the Indians, "but it gratifies us to find on investigation that they had their origin in some happy Indian phrase or romantic legend."[2]

[1] *League of the Ho-de-no-sau-nee or Iroquois*, II, 78.
[2] J. L. Sanborn, "American Town Names," *Kansas Magazine*, III, 167.

A brief survey of the resident Indians and of the eastern immigrant Indians will serve to introduce the tribes and linguistic groups which contributed the most to the Indian place-names of Kansas. The Pawnees were in Kansas before the Sioux, and their hunting areas once covered most of the state. Among the Pawnees were the Republican Pawnees, the Tapage Pawnees, and the Panis piqués or Wichitas. Then out of the East came the Kansa and Osage Indians, Siouan tribes which moved up the Missouri and entered Kansas by its western tributaries. From the West and North came first the Comanches and then the Kiowas, Arapahos, and Cheyennes. The Pawnees were squeezed between the two with a battleground along both borders. This is where the Spaniards and French found them.

There were seventeen tribes which were settled in Kansas, according to some estimates. But there were so many divisions and bands which were separated at one time and united at another that it is difficult to give an exact number. For example, the Sac and Fox Indians might be listed as two divisions or one. According to William E. Connelley's listing, there were many more than seventeen tribes in Kansas. Among the immigrant tribes he listed fifteen units of Algonquians, each with its distinctive name: the Chippewas, Delawares, Kaskaskias, Kickapoos, Miamis, Munsees, Ottawas, Peorias, Piankashaws, Potawatomis, Sac and Foxes, Shawnees, Stockbridges, Weas, and Brothertons. Almost all of these left place-names in Kansas. In the Iroquoian group Connelley listed seven: the Cayugas, Cherokees, Oneidas, Onondagas, Senecas, St. Regis, Tuscaroras, and Wyandots. All of the names in this group became Kansas place-names except St. Regis. In addition to the Kansa and Osage, four other Siouan tribes were listed: the Iowas, Missouris, Otos, and Quapaws.[3] The early resident Indians of Kansas left a proportionately larger number of names on the map than did the immigrant Indians.

Like the barbarian invasions of Europe during the decline of the Roman Empire, there were great migrations of natives in North America before the coming of the white man. The Iroquois had

[3] *A Standard History of Kansas and Kansans*, I, 180–81. (Hereafter referred to as *Kansas and Kansans*.)

Tribes Contributing Place-Names to Kansas

put pressure on the Algonkins, and the Algonkins had put pressure on the Sioux, and the Sioux had pushed against the Pawnees and others on the plains. When the white man settled on the Atlantic seaboard, he had a base from which he pushed the natives westward with a seemingly irresistible force, and eventually Kansas was occupied by Algonkins, Iroquois, additional Sioux, and a few Shoshonis.

The natives took sides in the colonial wars, in the American Revolution, and in the War of 1812, hoping to stem the tide of white expansion. It was a futile struggle and most of the wars ended in defeat and disaster for the natives. Each defeat of the natives by great Indian fighters such as Mad Anthony Wayne, Andrew Jackson, and William Henry Harrison resulted in loss of lands by the Indians. King Phillip, Pontiac, Tecumseh, and Black Hawk tried desperately but futilely to stem the white tide.

Treaties were made, to be sure, but the native had little understanding of land ownership and of personal or political boundaries. Wild game–fish, fowl, or four footed–recognized no legal barriers, and the Indian in pursuit of his food could see no more sense in an imaginary line stopping him than in such a line stopping a fish in a stream or a deer in the woods. Yet the white man had his papers, deeds, and treaties that made "legal" restrictions by imaginary and invisible lines. This made no sense to most Indians. Treaties were frequently signed by native chiefs who had been given personal rewards and payments for their accommodations. Few would consider such diplomatic gifts by such crude names as bribes or the treaties as frauds. There were numerous chiefs, however, who refused to put an "X" back of their names as a sign of their approval. Treaty-making was poorly understood by the natives. Yet treaty by treaty and state by state the Indians were dispossessed of their lands and were moved westward towards the Mississippi and beyond.

Let us examine briefly the reason or explanation for the choice of Kansas as the final home for the eastern Indians. The frontier had stopped along the western border of the first tier of states west of the Mississippi. Beyond this line the timbered lands seemed to disappear; so there, it was assumed, the pioneers lacked even the essential materials for making a home. This dependence on timber was called by Walter Prescott Webb the "wooden psychology" of the pioneer. This psychology, supported by those who described the Great Plains as the Great American Desert, delayed the westward movement on the Missouri-Kansas border. There were good reasons to believe that the white man would never settle more than one tier of states west of the Mississippi.

The High Plains had been described by the first American explorers as semidesert to desertland. Zebulon M. Pike referred to them as "a hopeless reach of desert" which was quite untenable by the white man. As for the Indians, Pike considered "the borders of the Arkansaw . . . the paradise (terrestrial) of our wandering savages. . . . I believe," he added, "there are buffalo, elk, and deer sufficient on the banks of the Arkansas alone, if used without waste, to feed all the savages in the United States territory one century."[4] "Our citizens will," he concluded, "through necessity, be constrained to limit their extent on the west to the border of the Missouri and Mississippi, while they leave the prairies incapable of cultivation to the wandering and uncivilized aborigines of the country."[5]

One man's opinion may not have been enough to create the Great American Desert in the minds of the American public, but Pike's opinions were soon supported by others. Major Stephen H. Long, who traveled across the West in 1819, found the land to be "almost wholly unfit for cultivation." H. M. Brackenridge described the desolation of the western plains as becoming "more dreary" as one approached the Rocky Mountains. "It combines within its frightful and extensive territory," he said, "the Steppes of Tartary, and the moving sands of the African deserts."[6] Out of such opinions grew the Great American Desert, a desert whose boundary lines were

[4] Leverett W. Spring, *Kansas, The Period to the War for the Union*, 22.

[5] LeRoy R. Hafen and Carl Coke Rister, *Western America*, 284.

[6] Frederic L. Paxson, *History of the American Frontier*, 216.

left vaguely to the imagination of those who lived in the East. It would take a lot of rain and a lot of travel before the desert image was removed.

What to do about the West became a serious political issue in the 1820's. Senator Benton of Missouri favored developing it. Daniel Webster opposed him, and with his usual oratorical flare he condemned the area in these words: "What do we want with this vast and worthless area, of this region of savages and wild beasts, of deserts, of shifting sands and whirlwinds, of dust, of cactus and prairie dogs; to what use could we ever hope to put these great deserts." The answer was not long in coming. In the very year when Webster was debating the issue, others were making plans to move the Indians from the East into the Great American Desert beyond Missouri.[7]

The policy of Indian removal was much simpler on paper and in the minds of politicians than it was in reality. The Rev. Isaac McCoy came to Kansas to check its suitability for Indian settlement, and he found it to be reasonably satisfactory. Kansas had an abundance of food from the buffalo and other game. But a double problem confronted the promoters of the removal policy. Indians in Kansas, especially along the eastern border, would have to be induced to give up much of their land and accept limited reserves and restrictions to make room for the eastern Indians. Secondly, the eastern Indians would have to be induced to give up their lands and homes in the East for Kansas lands whose merits were generally unknown. They were reluctant to leave their homes yet happy to get away from thieving whites and whisky-dealing traders. It frequently took both bribes and whisky to induce the Indian chiefs to agree to abandon their homes.[8]

A few representatives of eastern Indians crossed the Mississippi to see for themselves what chance they had of making a living in the West. They found the population pressure too great to remain even in Missouri and Iowa. By 1825 the removal policy became official with the promise that the Indians could retain their new

[7] Federal Writers' Project, *Kansas, A Guide*, 45.

[8] For a general account see Grant Foreman, *The Last Trek of the Indians*.

lands as long as the grass grew green in springtime and as long as the sun continued to shine—in one word, forever. Then the Indian learned an important lesson in the theory of relativity: that "forever" was a relatively short time.

It took about twenty-five years to settle the northern and eastern Indians in Kansas. By the time the last ones had been brought in, negotiations were already under way to move them out. Travelers across Kansas had come to the conclusion that much of the Kansas soil could be cultivated. If the grass could keep millions of buffalos alive, then farmers and cattlemen could feed their stock in Kansas. Furthermore, Kansas was on the highway to the Far West. So once again the Indians had to move on, this time into the smaller Indian Territory south of Kansas, where Oklahoma became the Indian melting pot. Many of the eastern Indians accepted the ultimatum and moved on.

But on the High Plains the Indians made a last desperate effort to stop the invasion. It was too late. Trails were being followed by rails, and both trails and rails were being protected by forts and soldiers. Earlier there had been a line of forts forming an arc along the "permanent" Indian frontier, from Fort Snelling, Fort Dodge, Fort Leavenworth, Fort Scott, and Fort Smith to Fort Towson near the Red River, for the purpose of protecting the Indians from any further invasion by the white frontiersman. But later a new line of forts followed the trails across Kansas to protect the white man's penetration of the Indian country.

The Indian problem loomed large in the nation, and it was highly concentrated in Kansas. Though the Indians who resisted were generally defeated, there were great chiefs who won fame and distinction during the conflicts. The Americans who defeated the Indians had enough respect for their tribal names and their chiefs to adorn the map with their historical names. The natives also had descriptive names all over Kansas, and many of these were retained in modified form as understood by the French, English, or Americans. Others were translated, correctly or incorrectly, and left with questionable meanings and often with little indication of their sources.

The name by which a tribe is known is not generally from the language of that tribe; it is more likely to be the name given by other tribes. Such names might be descriptive, but they were frequently derogatory names of enemies. The descriptive names could refer to the appearance of the people or their dress. Indians were also known by location or even by direction, as the *Abnakis* or "easterners" in the Pennsylvania–New York area and the *Shawanoes* or "southerners." Others were known by a chief's name, especially if he had led his own band away from the main tribe. The division and desertion of tribes was not uncommon.

No Indian is supposed to have given himself a name. Indian children's names were not important, but as a man grew to adulthood, he won a name by some unusual act. He could, however, be named for some personal peculiarity or distinction. A name with prestige could be given by a chief to his son or to another who seemingly deserved it. For example, there were several chiefs with the name of White Cloud and White Hair.

One might also have his name changed, but that was left to the approval of a tribal council. This may be illustrated by the Indian whose name was Johnny-Belches-When-He-Eats. His name caused derisive laughter by the Americans who knew its meaning. Annoyed by this ridicule and laughter, Johnny-Belches-When-He-Eats went to the tribal council and asked if he could have his name changed. The chiefs told him to furnish the food for the council meeting and then they would consider his request. He complied and furnished a scrawny calf for the stew. The council met and deliberated, and when they came out of the meeting, Johnny-Belches anxiously asked them if they had agreed to change his name. He was told that they had acted favorably, and henceforth his name would be Johnny-Does-Not-Belch-When-He-Eats. How could they have come to a more logical conclusion than to reverse the meaning of an obnoxious name?

Many native names suffered from a failure to understand the native thought or circumstances under which a name was chosen. Chief Stinking Saddle Blanket had a name whose malodorous implication was not pleasing to the white man. But to his own people the name meant that this Kiowa chief was a hard-riding hunter and in battle a hard-riding warrior. When he returned to camp, his horse blanket had the most powerful smell of horse's sweat. Far from belittling this leader, the name of Stinking Saddle Blanket was a name with prestige. This is somewhat like the brave who was known as Young-Man-Whose-Very-Horses-are-Feared, which by a poor translation became Young-Man-Afraid-of-His-Horse.[9]

Another good illustration of a poor translation was the name of the Indian who was known as Hole-in-the-Sky. The name is meaningless, but its origin makes good sense. At the time of his birth the parents rejoiced and expressed the feeling that the occasion was like a dark, cloudy day when there was a rift in the clouds and the clear blue began to show with a sunbeam breaking through. What a fine sentiment! Yet in English this became Hole-in-the-Sky.

There were people in the East, such as Washington Irving, who had a high regard for the Indians and their names, but wars always aroused mixed emotions in the public. In World War I, Americans were sufficiently aroused to change German names of towns as a result of war psychology and opposition to names that memorialized the enemy. Yet in Kansas, where Indian wars became serious after the Civil War, there were towns, counties, and creeks with the names of the enemy tribes and their chiefs. In spite of popular hostility, there were those who showed some respect for the Indians. Whatever the public's opinion might have been regarding the Indian, it considered Indian names worthy of preservation. A certain kind of respect is well illustrated by "Uncle Jack" Langley's inscription on a tombstone for an Indian for whom he also gave the funeral sermon.[10] One should, perhaps, keep in mind that this was a dead Indian. The tombstone inscription read:

Here, under the sod, lies Johnnie Cunkapod.
God bless Johnnie Cunkapod;
I would if I were God and you
were Johnnie Cunkapod.

[9] Eldon C. Smith, *The Story of Our Names*, 118.
[10] *Hill City Times*, Aug. 22, 1940.

Washington Irving was a strong advocate of Indian names for place-names. He found some English names glaringly objectionable, and in such cases he proposed substituting a more suitable Indian name, especially a name which was "striking and euphonious." In most cases, he thought, these names would be "infinitely superior to the trite, poverty-stricken names which had been given by the settlers."[11] Aside from any strong opinions regarding the preference of Indian names over other names, the fact remains that Kansas was once all Indian country, and even after the white man's occupation of Kansas, Indian names survived as reminders of its Indian background.

It has been said that the Indian names were the "most appropriate" and the "most picturesque." Walt Whitman was of the opinion that "all aboriginal names sound good." This may vary greatly with the names and the tastes of those who hear them. Whitman added, however, that "they all fit." The better the translation, the more truth there is in the latter statement.[12] Some of the Indian names were simple and euphonious and others were complex and seemingly unpronounceable. However, the frontier had a way of simplifying the complex names to make them acceptable. Instead of Whitman's generous opinions about the Indian names, one might better judge that their variety and suitability were as widely divergent as those in other languages. As one writer said, they were "significant or meaningless, pretty or ugly, gracefully flowing or roughly jawbreaking, and with all their faults, perhaps, still the best we have."[13]

[11] "National Nomenclature," *Works*, IV, 438.
[12] "An American Primer," *Atlantic Monthly*, XCIII, 65.
[13] Sanborn, *Kansas Magazine*, III, 159.

▲ II

Kansa, Kaw, and Kansas

KANSAS AS A NAME may mean different things to different people. The name may create an image, as names frequently do. To some it may be only the image of a rectangular map with the ragged, upper right-hand corner torn off.[1] Some people may know the topography of Kansas and think of its rolling hills and wooded valleys in the east, its prairies in the cattle country of the Flint Hills, its high plains cut by eroded valleys in the west, or its limestone formations from which were made limestone fence posts and limestone buildings. Kansas may be thought of as a territory of immigrant trails to the Far West and of cattle trails from the South. The name of Kansas may arouse the image of a person: Wyatt Earp, John Brown, Carry Nation, or William Allen White. Few would think of Kansas as a word associated with Indians. Yet Kansas is one of twenty-six states in the Union which has an Indian name.

While exploring the Mississippi River in 1673, Father Jacques Marquette, a Jesuit missionary, and Louis Joliet, his companion, heard about a tribe of Indians living some distance up the Missouri River, whose name was something like "Kansa." They put the name on the map in 1673.[2] It was then only the name of an Indian tribe.

Who were the Kansas? They were Siouan Indians, closely re-

[1] This trans-Missouri triangle, called the "Platte Purchase," had been ceded to Missouri by the Indians in 1821.

[2] For Marquette's map see Alfred T. Andreas and W. G. Cutler, *History of the State of Kansas*, 46; and Kansas State Historical Society *Transactions*, X, facing page 80. (Andreas and Cutler is hereafter referred to as *History of Kansas*, and *Transactions and Collections* of the Kansas State Historical Society as *KHC*.)

lated to the Omahas, Quapaws, Osages, and Poncas. Linguistically these were all related to the Dhegiha or Dakota Sioux. During the westward migration of the Siouan tribes along the Great Lakes and the valley of the Ohio, the Kansas with their associates crossed the Mississippi and migrated up along the Missouri River. The Quapaws went down the Mississippi until they reached the mouth of the Arkansas River. Each of the other related Siouan tribes picked its own stream or tributary of the Missouri as its new home. The French generally named the stream for the tribe which lived in the area.[3]

Tribes were seldom known by what they called themselves; what the Kansas called themselves, *Hútañga*, had little significance. In Riggs's Dakota dictionary, the word which most nearly resembles *Hútañga* is *hu-tam-ya*, and this was said to mean "by the edge of the shore." It is their Kansa name which needs clarification, a name which the natives had themselves accepted, although they may have pronounced it something like "Kauzau."

Even though Marquette, a Frenchman, was the first to put the name of the Kansas on the map, efforts have been made to discover a Spanish source for the name. Since Kansa resembles the Spanish word *cansar*, it has been assumed that *cansar* was its source. In Spanish, *cansar* means "to tire" or "to molest" or possibly "to bore" or "to disturb." Any of these terms might apply to the Kansa Indians, but the similarity of sounds of words, especially in different languages, is no valid proof of relationship or of a common origin. Spanish names for the tribes which Coronado found living beyond the Pawnees of the Quivira country were *Harahey* and *Guaes*. But as early as 1720, Governor Antonio Valverde of New Mexico spoke of "having come to the river Cances," where the Comanches lived.[4] So by this time the Spaniards had accepted the French name.

Since Kansa is an Indian name, we must find its meaning from

[3] Gerard Fowke, "Some Notes on the Aboriginal Inhabitants of Missouri," Missouri Historical Society *Collections*, IV, 96; George P. Morehouse, "History of the Kansa or Kaw Indians," *KHC*, X, 329.

[4] Morehouse, *KHC*, X, 335; *Wilson County Citizen*, June 4, 1909; *Pichardo's Treatise on the Limits of Louisiana and Texas* (ed. by Charles W. Hackett), I, 206. (Hereafter referred to as *Pichardo's Treatise*.)

the Indians. When the Osages, linguistically akin to the Kansas, were asked what Kansa meant, they readily replied "cowards." This was not, however, the meaning of Kansa; it was merely what the Osages called them when the Kansas refused to participate in a war against the Cherokees. Names do evolve occasionally from such an incident but not this one.[5]

Kansa as a name has been subject to a wide variation of translations and interpretations. It has been associated with "wind," but even when "wind" was accepted as the meaning of the name, there was no agreement on what sort of wind this might be. And Kansas, like most other states, has a great variety of winds, varying from a gentle breeze to a terrific tornado, a soft zephyr from the south being the most common. There were other interpretations, however, and some of these may be considered first.

The Kansa name has frequently been associated with "smoke." Albert Richardson, the Boston journalist traveling in Kansas in 1854, said that Kansa meant "smoky."[6] J. M. Holloway, one of the early historians of Kansas, accepted this definition and concluded that it "derived from the chief river running . . . through the centre of the state."[7] Instead of giving the Indian name to the river, he gave the river name of the Smoky Hill to the Indians. The suggestion that the name meant smoky because of the battles over "Bleeding Kansas" is, of course, far fetched and chronologically wrong. Nor need there be any connection between Kansa Indians being called "smoky" and "fire people," unless one accepts the old saying that where there is smoke there must be fire. There was still an association with the river when it was said that Kansa meant "smoky water." There was a transition from water to wind when Kansa was said to mean "smoky wind."

Professor John B. Dunbar of Washburn University informed Giles of Topeka that Kansa meant "swift." In support of this, William Hamilton listed *Kantha* as the Iowa name for the Kansa Indians, also interpreting it to mean "swift." The word "swift"

[5] Ed Blair, *History of Johnson County, Kansas*, 17.
[6] *Beyond the Mississippi*, 29.
[7] *History of Kansas*, 87.

CHEYENNE RAWLINS DECATUR NORTON PHILLIPS SMITH JEWELL REPUBLIC WASHINGTON MARSHALL NEMAHA BROWN DONIPHAN
SHERMAN THOMAS SHERIDAN GRAHAM ROOKS OSBORNE MITCHELL CLOUD CLAY RILEY POTTAWATOMIE ATCHINSON LEAVENWORTH JEFFERSON
WALLACE LOGAN GOVE TREGO ELLIS RUSSELL LINCOLN OTTAWA GEARY WABAUNSEE SHAWNEE WYANDOTTE DOUGLAS JOHNSON
ELLSWORTH SALINE DICKINSON MORRIS LYON OSAGE FRANKLIN MIAMI
GREELEY WICHITA SCOTT LANE NESS RUSH BARTON RICE MC PHERSON MARION CHASE COFFEY ANDERSON LINN
HAMILTON KEARNY FINNEY HODGEMAN PAWNEE STAFFORD RENO HARVEY GREENWOOD WOODSON ALLEN BOURBON
EDWARDS GREY FORD BUTLER
STANTON GRANT HASKELL KIOWA PRATT KINGMAN SEDGWICK ELK WILSON NEOSHO CRAWFORD
MORTON STEVENS SEWARD MEADE CLARK COMANCHE BARBER HARPER SUMNER COWLEY CHAUTAUQUA MONTGOMERY LABETTE CHEROKEE

Kansas Counties

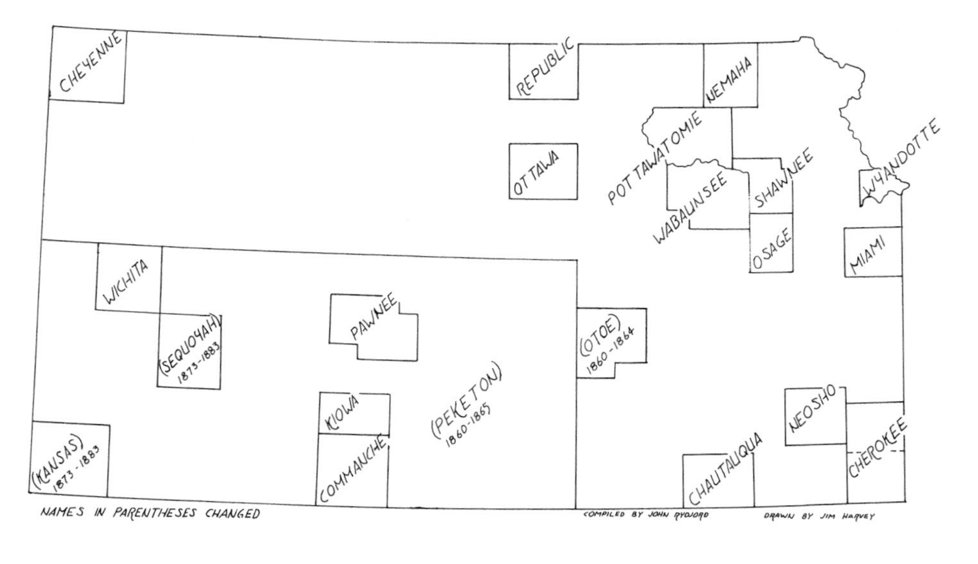

Kansas Counties with Indian Names

should describe something, and in this case it was assumed that Kansa meant "swift wind."[8]

Among the varied interpretations for Kansa are the following: "wind people," "swift wind people," "swift," "south wind people," "small wind," "windy," and more elaborately, "makes-a-breeze-near-the-ground." With such a wide variety from which to choose, one can see why W. J. McGee said cautiously of Kansa or "Kanze" that it "refers to winds, though precise significance is unknown."[9] But more commonly accepted is the one that called the Kansas the "south wind people." This has been based on the assumption that the Sioux Indians in the North might speak of their Kansa cousins as the people who lived in the land from which the south wind came. William Connelley finally concluded also that "south wind people" was the correct interpretation, "as every schoolboy knows." The name of the Kansas may not specify the direction from which the wind may blow, but it was logical to associate the name with the wind. The Kansas were the "keepers of the rites pertaining to the wind." Among the Siouan tribes, it was the Kansas who performed the ceremony for the *Wakon* or spirit of the four winds. By this rite they could be identified by their neighbors.[10]

The sources for several of the interpretations which have been given for Kansa are to be found in the names of the gens or smaller divisions of the Kansa tribe. "Camp-behind-all" is a rather vague interpretation for the name of a Kansa gens whose name was *Tci hacin qtci* or *Real Tci hacin*. The important part of this name is the *Tci hacin* which was the "lodge in the rear," and that was only

[8] F. W. Giles, *Thirty Years in Topeka*, 55; Morehouse, *KHC*, X, 333n.; *Kansas City Times*, Jan. 17, 1950.

[9] "The Siouan Indians," *Bureau of American Ethnology Fifteenth Annual Report* (1893–94), 162; Connelley, *Kansas and Kansans*, I, 193–205; G. E. Shankle, *State Names*, 70; George Remsburg, *Scrapbook*, I, 315; F. H. Barrington, *Kansas Day*, 62. (Bureau of American Ethnology is hereafter referred to as BAE.)

[10] Frank Haucke, "The Kaw or Kansa Indians," *Kansas Historical Quarterly*, XX, 36; Connelley, *Kansas and Kansans*, I, 184; "Names," MS, Kansas State Historical Society Archives; Alice C. Fletcher and Francis La Flesche, "The Omaha Tribe," *BAE Twenty-seventh Annual Report* (1905–1906), 38 and 66. (*Kansas Historical Quarterly* is hereafter referred to as *KHQ*, and Kansas State Historical Society as KSHS.)

another way of locating the "camp-behind-all" or the "last lodge."

James Dorsey and W. J. McGee of the Bureau of American Ethnology have given us this interpretation and a list of the names of the other gens or tribal subdivisions with their translations. It is from this list that we get the various interpretations for supposing that Kansa meant "wind people." The *Tadje unikacinga* was said to mean "wind people." Another group was called the *Man Nan hindje*, which was interpreted to mean "Makes-a-breeze-near-the-ground." Finally there was the *Ak'a unikacinga*, the "south wind people." The *Tadje jinga* meant "small wind." The *jinga* and *cinga* and possibly *hindje* for "small" was like the Siouan word *zhinga* or *shinka* for small. In some way, Dorsey made *Kanze* the equivalent of *Tadje* when he wrote "Tadje or Kanze (Wind) gens."[11] One may assume that *tadje jinga*, "small wind," was a soft southerly breeze or south wind which "Makes-a-breeze-near-the-ground." It is not unusual for the name of a subdivision to be applied to the larger division or tribe. This had been fairly common practice in naming the European states. So Kansa means the "wind people."

The variation in the interpretation of the name of Kansas is not anywhere nearly as great as the variation in its spelling. It took a long time to learn how to spell Kansas. Orthography, it is said, is "the art of writing words with the proper letters," and in accordance with the "standard usage." Yet the seemingly simple name of Kansas baffled all efforts of conformity and correct usage for nearly two hundred years. However, it is by popular adoption or use that a name becomes correct.

The phonetics of the Indians and the phonetics of the French did not always coincide, and the Anglo-Americans, who frequently "played it by ear," as did the French, showed orthographic ingenuity but little consistency in transferring the Indian-French names into English or "Americanese." The Americanized version of a French version of a poorly understood Indian language could become fantastic and even absurd.

[11] "Siouan Sociology," *BAE Fifteenth Annual Report* (1893–94), 231–33; McGee, "The Siouan Indians," *BAE Fifteenth Annual Report* (1893–94), 157 and 189–92.

When "Sockless" Jerry Simpson was running for Congress, he was accused of misspelling Medicine Lodge, the name of his home town. He pled guilty; "and I tell you further," he added, "I wouldn't give a tinker's dern for a man who can't spell a word more than one way."[12]

Robert Hay in 1882 made a list of 24 ways in which to spell Kansas. Sixty years later Cecil Howes, addressing a Kiwanis Club, said that there were 44 different ways of spelling Kansas. More recently it has been reported that there were 80 different ways of spelling Kansas. The figure has now been raised to a total of 120.[13] The last figure is based upon the questionable assumption that Kansas and Arkansas had the same origin and that the Indians who were called *Escansaques* were also Kansa Indians.

George P. Morehouse and others have assumed that the *Escansaques*, who accompanied Juan de Oñate in 1601 to the Quivira or Panis piqué settlements in southern Kansas, were also a Kansa tribe. Oñate, he said, had named them *Escansaques* because they were "the disturbers" or "the troublemakers." "From this it is easy to see," he added, "how the 'wind people' might have been used in referring to the tribe." Some have enlarged this definition to mean "those who come like the winds sweeping across the prairies" as a disturbance. In going back to Oñate's own record, we find a different version. His campmaster had met these natives whom they called "Escanxaques, because they stretched out one hand toward the sun and then placed it on the chest saying loudly 'escanxaques' which was their sign for peace." So perhaps they were not the "disturbers."[14]

Alfred B. Thomas, a noted authority on the borderlands Indians, has pointed out that when the *Escansaques* came to the border of Kansas, they refused to go on because their enemies lived there.

[12] Debs Myers, "The Exciting Story of Kansas," *Holiday*, IX, 63.

[13] Robert Hay, "Kaw and Kansas," *KHC*, IX, 523; Cecil Howes, in *Topeka Journal*, Jan. 5, 1942; Morehouse, *KHC*, X, 333; "The Name 'Kansas,'" *KHQ*, XX, 450.

[14] George P. Hammond and Agapito Rey (eds.), *Oñate, Colonizer of New Mexico*, I, 25, and II, 854; Morehouse, KHC, X, 335; *Pichardo's Treatise*, II, 368 and 456.

Both by location in the Oklahoma area and by description the *Escansaques* were most likely a division of the Apaches. In fact, they were said in Oñate's report to have "the same characteristics as the Apaches."[15]

It seems as if the similarity of the name of the *Escansaques* and Cansas could have been the reason for assuming that these were only different ways of spelling Kansas. By dropping a syllable from each end of *Escansaques*, one does get "cansa," but even this is insufficient evidence to make *Escansaques* a source for Cansa or Kansa. Furthermore, the name had at first been spelled *Escanjaques* and *Escanxaques*. We may therefore drop *Escansaques* from the many ways in which to spell Kansas.

With the name of Arkansas we have the same problem; it looks like Kansas, but these names need not have the same origin. Kansas already had twice as many variations as Arkansas, which is more than enough without being confused with "Arkansaw," over which we are still confused. Surely, eighty different ways of spelling Kansas will be sufficient.

First we should follow the French in search of the evolution of Marquette's Kansa name. The 1717 Vermale map of *Louisiane ou du Micisipi* listed the name of the river as *R. des canzes*. In 1718, Guillaume de l'Isle (or Delisle) used the term *Grande Rivière des Cansez*. Benard de la Harpe in 1720 called the natives *Canci* and *Cannecis*. Four years later Sieur de Bourgmont came to Kansas on a peace mission. There he came upon "a beautiful river" which he called *Quans*, seemingly for the Kansa Indians, but he also used the name *Kanzes* for the natives. Governor Iberville of Louisiana referred to the natives as *Les Canses*, as did Vaugondy, the geographer. Émile Lauvrière, a Frenchman who wrote *Histoire de la Louisiane*, spelled the name a half-dozen different ways in one volume. Charlevoix wrote it *Cansez* in 1766 and Le Page du Pratz wrote it *Canzez* and *Canzas*, as well as

[15] Alfred B. Thomas, *After Coronado*, 8; George E. Hyde, *Pawnee Indians*, 19 and map facing page 18; Waldo R. Wedel, "The Kansas Indians," Kansas Academy of Science *Transactions*, XLIX, 8; Hammond and Rey, *Oñate, Colonizer of New Mexico*, II, 854.

Canchez and *Canchaz.* Spelling varied from one person's choice to another but Du Pratz gave us four choices, and Lauvrière, six.[16]

The following will illustrate a few of the Anglo-American variations. Lewis and Clark, who had access to both Spanish and French maps, spelled Kansas both Kansez and Kances. Sergeant Ordway with Lewis and Clark spoke of the "old village of the Kansers." Patrick Gass, also with Lewis and Clark, said that they had spent the Fourth of July on the site of the "Old town de Caugh," referring to a Kansa village site. But Gass also spelled the name Kanzau and 'Kanzas.[17] Captain Pike used the short form of Kans. Major Sibley in 1811 spoke of his arrival "on the Konsee River." Major Long and his men used both Konza and Konzas, as did George Catlin, the artist. Parkman's Kanisse resembled La Harpe's French name of *Cannecis.* T. J. Farnham in 1839 illustrated the continued confusion when, like Gass, he gave the reader a choice of three names: "Konzas, Kausaus, or Caws." An interesting distinction between the name of the land and the people is seen in the statement, "The country of the Kauzaus lies on the Konzas River."[18] One of the most popular names for the river was Konzas. "Different persons have, at various times, written the name of this tribe differently, as suited the fancy of each," said Isaac McCoy who knew the Indians well in the 1830's.

The variations in pronunciation were naturally closely associated with the variations in spelling. McCoy also had a sensible suggestion about how the name should be pronounced. "We have chosen," he said, "to adhere to the pronunciation of the natives themselves, which is Kau-zau." Bliss Isely, an authority on Kansas history, said

[16] Carl I. Wheat, *Mapping the Trans-Mississippi West*, passim; Charles O. Paullin, *Atlas of the Historical Geography of the United States*, plates 23, 24, and 33; Connelley, *Kansas and Kansans*, I, 192; Morehouse, *KHC*, X, 334; Edgar Langsdorf, "A Review of Early Navigation on the Kansas River," *KHQ*, XVIII, 140.

[17] Cora Dolbee, "The Fourth of July in Early Kansas," *KHQ*, VIII, 116; *The Journals of Captain Meriwether Lewis and Sergeant John Ordway* (ed. by Milo M. Quaife), 399. (Hereafter referred to as *The Journals of Lewis and Ordway.*)

[18] Connelley, *Kansas and Kansans*, I, 193; Connelley "Note on the Early Indian Occupancy of the Great Plains," *KHC*, XIV, 459; "Extracts from the Diary of Major Sibley," *Chronicles of Oklahoma*, V, 196–97; Reuben Gold Thwaites (ed.), *Early Western Travels*, XVIII, 138, and XXVIII, 57, 64, and 87.

that the "n" and the "s" were barely audible and that the name was therefore pronounced "Kausa" or "Ka-a." A. W. Stubbs was of the opinion that the Kansa Indians pronounced the name as if it were "Konza," with a scarcely audible second syllable. Even McCoy allowed for a slight variation when he informed the War Department that the name was pronounced "Kaw saw." In spite of all the fancy variation, we are finally back to Father Marquette's Kansa with the addition of a final "s," as it was used by Antoine de Bougainville in 1757.[19]

It seems human nature to abbreviate long names, and even a two-syllable name can be reduced to one. The French followed the normal trend when they abbreviated Kansa or Kansas to *Quans*, *Caugh*, *Caw*, *Kaw*, and *Kah*, and the Americans imitated all of these, some with variations. The abbreviated or short form of the name met with considerable criticism from those who refused to go along with the evolution of a name. "To cap all absurdity," said Max Greene, "the Indians scarcely know themselves by any other word than Kaw."[20] However, to speak of it as an "absurdity" was as unfair to the Indians as it was to the French. Another writer, more critical of the Indians than of the name, said that it was easy for the French to drop a syllable from "Kauzau." Then he added the comment, "the degraded Kaw would accept it." It was evidently not degrading to call the Kansas by the shorter name of Kaw but only degrading to accept it. Supposing the name of the tribe had been that of one of their worthy chiefs, Cayagettsazesheengaw, would it then have been degrading to reduce it to "Cay" or "Gaw," not unlike Kaw?

One may be critical of the use of the abbreviated Kaw, since it fails to distinguish between the Indians and the popular name for the Kansas River, more often called the Kaw than the Kansas. "It may be wise to preserve this French-Canadian name Kaw, in re-

[19] Isaac McCoy, "Shawnee Baptist Mission," *Annual Register of Indian Affairs* (May, 1837), 27; McCoy to Sec. of War, Jan. 3, 1831, 22 Cong., 1 sess., *Exec. Doc. No. 172*, 13; Bliss Isely, in *Wichita Beacon*, April 14, 1929; *Lewis H. Morgan: The Indian Journals, 1859–1862* (ed. by Leslie A. White), 16; A. W. Stubbs to F. G. Adams, "Names," MS, KSHS Archives. (Morgan is hereafter referred to as *Morgan: The Indian Journals.*)

[20] *The Kanzas Region*, 23.

ferring to the Kansas river," said Morehouse, "but it is a nickname, a misnomer, means nothing, has no good foundation, and it should not be applied to the tribe, for it was not their name." He preferred Kansa. Yet Joseph Whitehouse with the Lewis and Clark expedition wrote "River de Caugh."[21] It was confusing to have one name for three objects, the Indians, the river, and the state, and the change from Kansa to Kaw for the first two was a popular step towards greater clarification. Charles Curtis, most famous of the Kansa Indians and Vice President of the United States, referred to his Indian ancestors as the Kaws.[22]

Having abbreviated the name of the Indians as well as the name of the Kansas River to Kaw, one might assume that even the name of the state might also become Kaw. This was suggested, not seriously one may assume, but only as satire. "Should the territory be erected into a slave State," said Max Greene, "it might be advisable to adopt this latter as the title—being the ominous croak of the raven."[23] The outcome of the Civil War and the freedom of the slaves have, according to this, justified the preservation of the full name of Kansas rather than the adoption of an abbreviated nickname like the croak of a crow or raven.

To transfer the name of the Kansa Indians to the river on which they lived was only a short step. By 1718, as we have seen, Delisle made it the *Grande Rivière de Cansez.* This name was too long. Zebulon M. Pike said that "The Kans are a small nation situated on a river of that name."[24] Many of the explorers and travelers used both the long and short form, Kansas or Kaw, for the river. Horace Greeley in his *Overland Journey* used both names but showed a preference for Kaw. Even Mrs. Charles Robinson, wife of the first state governor of Kansas, adopted this short form. Kaw gradually replaced the longer name of Kansas for the river. It was also used for the Little Kaw Creek in Leavenworth County.

21 Morehouse, *KHC*, X, 333–34; *The Journals of Lewis and Ordway*, 89n.

22 Hay, *KHC*, IX, 525; *Kansas City Star*, Aug. 5, 1940; Remsburg, *Scrapbook*, I, 159.

23 *The Kanzas Region*, 33.

24 Morehouse, *KHC*, X, 344 and n.; *The Expedition of Zebulon Montgomery Pike* (ed. by Elliot Coues), II, 536. (Hereafter referred to as *Expedition of Pike.*)

Nos-kah-noie and Wash-shun-gah, Kansa chiefs (Oklahoma Historical Society)

The United States Board on Geographic Names decided in 1891 that the river, as well as the state, should be Kansas and neither Kanzas nor Kaw.[25] In the minds of the people of Kansas, as well as elsewhere, the river was the Kaw. The public decides. In writing about the Kansas River in the *Rivers of America Series*, Floyd B. Streeter called his book *The Kaw*. So be it.

Kansa was first the name of the Indians, then the name of the river, and then it became the name of the land. In 1744 the land was referred to as the *Pays des Canses*, the "country of the Canses." In 1798, Vaugondy's map portrayed the Kansas lands as extending all the way from Missouri to the Rockies. This territory became known, however, not as Kansas but as Nebraska, although on one map it was actually included in the Oregon Territory. The name of Kansas was later back on a map as a restricted Indian territory called the Kansas Reservation. In 1846 the whole area was mapped as Indian Territory.[26]

In 1852, when Kansas and Nebraska were one, a bill was introduced to create the "territory of the Platte," embracing Kansas and Nebraska. Before 1853 the whole area was known as Nebraska, as it had been referred to in Congress for some time. In the same year, when Augustus Dodge proposed the organization of the Nebraska Territory, which included Kansas and a lot more, he referred to it simply as the Platte Country. Had the territory not been divided in 1854, it could have been called Platte, the French name for "flat," or Nebraska from *niobrara*, the Indian word for "flat."[27] Before 1854, David Atchison, senator from Missouri, had been a strong advocate for the organization of the Nebraska Territory and he used the term Nebraska consistently.[28]

A delegation of settlers, who lived south of the Platte and who considered the Platte to be a suitable boundary line, asked to be

[25] U.S. Board of Geographic Names *Sixth Report* (1933), 404.

[26] Morehouse, *KHC*, X, 345n.; Robert W. Baughman, *Kansas in Maps*, 21, 24–25, and 34.

[27] Lillian L. Fitzpatrick, *Nebraska Place Names*, I, 261–80.

[28] W. A. Phillips, "Kansas History," *KHC*, IV, 357; *The Weekly Highlander*, Jan. 1, 1859, quoted in *KHQ*, VI, 201; H. C. McDougal, "Historical Sketch of Kansas City, Missouri," *KHC*, XI, 589.

annexed to Kansas, since the Platte River with its quicksand bottom "could not be forded, it could not be bridged . . . and it could not be ferried." Kansas Republicans showed little interest in annexing the Democrats of the "South Platte" nor in making the Platte its boundary line, even though it was said that "Providence intended it for a natural boundary."[29] Rivers roam about too freely to make reliable boundaries, and the Platte has now been forded, ferried, and bridged.

Senator Atchison of Missouri has been given credit for having suggested the name of Kansas to Stephen A. Douglas.[30] The Kansas-Nebraska Bill of 1854 popularized the name of Kansas for a political unit. In the Senate debates the name had been spelled Kansas in 1854, and as Kansas Territory it became official, and doubly official as the name of the State of Kansas in 1861.[31]

Up to this time the spelling of Kanzas with a "z" was acceptable and seemingly correct. There were still a few who continued to spell the name with a "z" after 1854. Max Greene in 1856 named his book on Kansas, *The Kanzas Region.* In 1857, Preston B. Plumb called his Emporia newspaper *The Kanzas News.*[32] In the critical year of 1854, Edward E. Hale, distinguished New England author, published a book which he named *Kanzas and Nebraska.* He preferred Kanzas to Kansas, but he expressed a willingness to accept Kansas, which he referred to as "the more fashionable spelling of a few weeks past." It is worthy of note that a fashion in spelling could determine the name in a matter of "a few weeks." But there was no doubt, said Hale, that "the z best expresses the sound." While submitting to the popular trend, Hale regretted the change from Kanzas to Kansas, because Kansas "then will, at best," he said, "too much resemble the name Arkansas," which he thought derived from it. "To keep them by one letter apart," he concluded,

[29] P. Orman Ray, "The Genesis of the Kansas-Nebraska Act," American Historical Association *Annual Report* (1914), I, 261–80; G. Raymond Gaeddert, *The Birth of Kansas*, 58–60.

[30] Isely, in *Wichita Beacon*, April 14, 1929; E.B.D. Beachy, in *Kansas City Times*, Dec. 6, 1951; Walter H. Schoewe, "Political and Geographical Aspects of Territorial Kansas," *Territorial Kansas* (1954), 14.

[31] Hay, *KHC*, IX, 521.

[32] Laura M. French, *History of Emporia and Lyons County*, 5.

"is to gain something." It was not too late to lament, but it was too late to change. The die was cast and the name became Kansas.[33]

Lippincott's *Gazetteer of the United States*, published the year before Kansas became a territorial name, identified the "Kanzas, Kansas, or Konzas River," and in the next item the "Kanzas, Kansas, or Konzas Indians." Each of the two subjects had a choice of three names and both had the same three from which to choose.

It might have been well to have made a distinction in the names for the Kansa Indians, the Kansas River, and the state of Kansas, such as Konza, Kaw, and Kansas. Now the Kansas name brings to mind primarily the name of the state. It is a good name. William Connelley, who had a lot of ideas on Kansas history, said: "Kansas, as now accepted, written, and spoken, is one of the most beautiful words adapted to use in the English tongue. As a name for a state it is unequalled."[34] Citizens of other states with Indian names, we surmise, may have similar opinions about their own state names.

[33] Edward E. Hale, *Kanzas and Nebraska*, v; Dolbee, "First Book on Kansas," *KHQ*, II, 165.

[34] *Kansas and Kansans*, I, 193.

▲ III

Kansas City and Places Named Kansas

FOR THE FRONTIER TRADER AND TRAVELER the best known entrance to Kansas was at the mouth of the Kansas River. One need not go to the New Yorker's map of the United States, which lists Kansas as a city in Missouri, to appreciate the importance of Kansas City, Missouri. Since it bore the Kansas name and served the Kansas territory, even when that territory was known as Nebraska, the name of Kansas City east of the Missouri belongs to the story of Kansas City west of the river. When Kansas City, Kansas, was named, the sister city on the Missouri side was still technically the City of Kansas.

The Indians knew the Kansas City sites on both sides of the river. The Sauks or Sacs lived east of the river on the site which became Westport. The Kansas, Delawares, Wyandots, and Shawnees lived on the Kansas City site in Kansas. According to William E. Connelley, the Wyandots called the site of Kansas City, Missouri, where a steep cliff projects into the river, *Kyooh-rah-dooh-hih*, which means "the point where the cliff stands into the *Kyooh-tahn-deh-yooh-rah*," which was their name for the Missouri River.[1] The Delawares may have had something similar in mind when they called the river *Os-sen-see-poo*, meaning "rock river."[2]

Cyprian Chouteau recognized the importance of the site opposite the mouth of the Kansas or Kaw and established his trading post there. It had been known as West Bottoms and Kaw Bottom before it was settled. Then it was called Chouteau's Warehouse, but

[1] "The East Boundary Lines of Kansas," *KHC*, XI, 79.
[2] *Leavenworth Times*, Jan. 24, 1907.

Cyprian Chouteau called it the Kansas Landing, taking the name from the river. The flood of 1826 washed the warehouse away.[3] South of Chouteau's trading post, a nucleus for a town was started by Isaac McCoy and his son John. It was only a store on the deserted site of a Sac Indian village, but it was called Shawnee for the Indians across the border. Two years later, in 1834, John C. McCoy, the storekeeper, also became the postmaster, and then the town was named Westport since it was to be "the port of entry into the great western country." With a road cut down to the bank of the river, it became known as Westport Landing, as it was listed on some of the early maps. Locally it was spoken of as "the Landing."[4]

Above Westport lived "One-Eyed" Ellis in a log cabin where he kept his good and sharp eye open for business, part of which was the selling of whisky in tin cups, but also "with a sharp lookout for stray horses." Several Missouri speculators met in his cabin to promote a new town and to give it a name. Abraham Fonda, one of the promoters, thought the town should be named Port Fonda. But this ran into serious opposition, partly because of Fonda's attitude of superiority. He signed his name "Abraham Fonda Gentleman." This was not acceptable on the frontier even though a "gentleman" was considered to be only a man with no particular occupation. Henry Jobe, evidently not a "gentleman," was so vehement in his opposition to the use of Fonda's name that he implied that he would prevent it by the use of his shotgun. Such a strong feeling over the choice of a name may be explained in part by the strong drink served by "One-Eyed" Ellis. The name of Fonda was lost without the loss of life.[5]

Less serious than Henry Jobe was "Squire" Bowers who suggested the names of Rabbitville or Possum-Trot. The contents of the tin cups seemed to have affected him differently; he was in good humor. His names were not accepted, yet there is a Possum-Trot in the Kansas City area. The more serious-minded members

[3] Remsburg, *Scrapbook*, I, 97; Isely, in *Wichita Beacon*, April 14, 1929.

[4] Carry W. Whitney, *Kansas City, Missouri*, I, 55; McDougal, *KHC*, XI, 588.

[5] Whitney, *Kansas City, Missouri*, I, 91 and 98; Darrell Garwood, *Crossroads of America*, 30; Charles P. Deatherage, *Greater Kansas City*, I, 251 and 324.

of the group, and possibly more sober, recognized the value of a name which would appeal to the public, especially in real estate. Kawsmouth would be satisfactory. When the name of Kansas was proposed, McCoy said, "I did not like the name then," nor did he like it later. He preferred Port Fonda. Nevertheless, the town company agreed to name the place the Town of Kansas.[6]

It became better known by its popular name Port of Kansas. Either name could claim to be correct but both were cumbersome. Having changed from the Town of Kansas to the Port of Kansas, the public dropped the "Port" and called the place Kansas. So did the Wyandots who crossed the river to do business in Kansas, Missouri. Westport residents ridiculed the new Town of Kansas and belittled it by calling it Westport Landing. "Kansas City is a colony originally sent out by Westport to her steamboat landing," said John C. McCoy. Westport boosters had a temporary, technical advantage, since a flaw in the land title in 1839 prevented the incorporation of the Town of Kansas until 1850, and the incorporation was not legalized by the legislature until 1853, the year before Kansas had a territorial name of its own. That year the Town of Kansas changed its name to the City of Kansas.[7]

Few people had used the full name of Town of Kansas or City of Kansas, preferring, as Senator Benton did, to call it just Kansas. Even as late as 1854 residents of the City of Kansas continued to refer to their town as Kansas. "My address is Kansas, Missouri," wrote the Rev. S. Y. Lum in October, 1854. Another in the same month gave his address as "Kansas, Mouth of Kansas river."[8] The Morse and Gaston map of 1856 and the J. G. Wells map of 1857 also listed the City of Kansas as just Kansas.

After 1854, when the name of Kansas was given to the territory west of Missouri, the City of Kansas could no longer be called just Kansas without confusing it with the name of the territory. The

[6] Whitney, *Kansas City, Missouri*, I, 91; Garwood, *Crossroads of America*, 27; A. Theodore Brown, *Frontier Community*, I, 39.

[7] McDougal, *KHC*, XI, 589; *Kansas City Star*, April 29, 1945; Deatherage, *Greater Kansas City*, I, 365; Brown, *Frontier Community*, I, 61.

[8] "Names," MS, KSHS Archives; "Letters of John and Sarah Everett," *KHQ*, VIII, 4.

solution was to use the descriptive term of "City" which was technically correct after 1853. In a search for brevity and simplicity, the public switched "City" from its place preceding the name of Kansas and placed it after the name to make it Kansas City. Colton's map of 1855 actually listed the name as Kansas City. Long after the public had popularized the change from City of Kansas to Kansas City, the state legislature gave a belated recognition of the name by legalizing it in 1889.

The commercial center for Kansas was for a long time Kansas City, Missouri. Not only its business but its press and its politics had their influence on Kansas. A possible solution for its dependence on a city in another state might have been for Kansas to annex the Missouri city with the name of Kansas. This may seem unreasonable now, but Missouri did not think so then. We may recall that Missouri residents on the border had served in the Kansas legislature. The *Kansas City Times* of Missouri in 1878 even suggested that the city might be sold for a quarter of a million dollars.[9] It was a bargain.

A Missouri delegation which came to Topeka to consider the deal was given a grand reception by Governor John P. St. John. A committee from the Kansas legislature was appointed to plan the annexation. With the sympathy of men like David Atchison and Dr. John H. Stringfellow from Missouri, it was thought that the support of Congress could be won. A Kansas agent was sent to Washington to lobby for the plan. But when he arrived in Washington, he "fell in love with a lady with whom he took a trip to Europe, and was not heard from in these parts for over two years."[10] For the sake of this sudden love, Kansas City, Missouri, was lost by Kansas. The confusion of having two cities with the same name has continued, and, although they are neighbors, they are identified only by the name of a state. The metropolitan area which crossed both the Missouri and the Kaw has enough in common to share the stories of its name.

[9] George W. Martin, "The Boundary Lines of Kansas," *KHC*, XI, 73; *KHQ*, VII, 104.

[10] Martin, *KHC*, XI, 73.

The Chouteaus, who were the first to settle on the site of Kansas City, Missouri, were also the first to settle on the site of Kansas City in Kansas. "My brother Francis had built his home at Kansas City in 1828," said Frederick Chouteau. The trading post called by the Indians the Four Houses had been built as early as 1820, he added.[11] The Chouteaus had trading posts on both sides of the Kaw. The real beginning of the settlements which formed the foundations of Wyandotte City and neighboring towns was made by the Wyandot Indians.

The Wyandots sold their land in Ohio in 1842 and in the following year they came to Kansas and settled on land which they had purchased from the Delawares in that strategic triangle between the Kaw and the Missouri. They were more white than Indian and they had taken on the political and business ways of the white man. Under the leadership of men like Silas Armstrong and others they promoted Wyandotte City, Kansas City, Armstrong, and a number of other towns which were later to be absorbed by Kansas City.[12]

New towns were built on the periphery of Wyandotte City and Kansas City. One was built in 1879 on the bluffs overlooking the river and was named Riverview. It did not take much ingenuity to suggest such a name, but some of these early towns, like the cities of today, recognized the sales value of a view and a name. Riverview seemed to have little future as an independent town, so in 1881 it petitioned to be annexed to Kansas City. The petition was approved by the city council but rejected by the mayor. Wyandotte City did not scorn its appeal and annexed it, so when Wyandotte became a part of Kansas City, so did Riverview.[13]

Rosedale, located south of the Kaw, was named by railroad promoters who were impressed by "the mass of wild roses growing on

[11] F. G. Adams, "Reminiscences of Frederick Chouteau," *KHC*, VIII, 425; *KHC*, IX, 574; Whitney, *Kansas City, Missouri*, I, 88.

[12] Deatherage, *Greater Kansas City*, I, 687–89; Ray E. Merwin, "The Wyandot Indians," *KHC*, IX, 74; Andreas and Cutler, *History of Kansas*, 1231 and 1240. For the story of the Wyandot names see Chapter XXI.

[13] Grant W. Harrington, *Historic Spots or Mile-stones in the Progress of Wyandotte County, Kansas*, 24. (Hereafter referred to as *Historic Spots in Wyandotte County*.)

the townsite." Like Riverview, it later became a part of Kansas City, but not without a long political battle. It had voted to join Kansas City in 1913, but not until 1921 was the merger accomplished and then only by a special act of the legislature and the approval of the governor.[14]

Boston's interest in Kansas was not limited to Bibles, rifles, and freedom; there was also a strong business interest. Charles Francis Adams, Jr., of the politically prominent Adams family of Massachusetts, and some associates organized the Kaw Valley Town Site and Bridge Company. They started a town on the Kaw about a mile and a half above the Missouri in 1880, and they named it Armourdale for the Armour brothers who were listed as "bankers and pork packers."[15]

Business and industry were booming in the eighties. To make room for its shops, the Kansas City, Topeka, and Western Railway started a new town about three miles up the Kaw. Within a year the Consolidated Kansas City Smelting and Refining Company moved to this townsite and gave it the name of Argentine, not for the South American state of Argentina, but for its Latin root of *argentum* or *argenta*, meaning "silver." It was said that the Argentine smelter was "built for the purpose of refining gold and silver bullion shipped in from the other smelters, and for such other kindred work as they could profitably follow." The "kindred work" turned out to be the processing of some copper ore which was shipped in from Socorro, New Mexico, and lead ore from southern Kansas.[16]

Kansas City on the Kansas side was promoted by Silas Armstrong and his associates in 1868. It grew slowly on its narrow strip between the Kaw River and the Missouri border. Its connection with Wyandotte was by ferry; its separation from the town of Kansas in Missouri was only a street. The town was not incorporated

[14] *Ibid.*, 249–51; Holsinger to Martin, "Names," MS, KSHS Archives.

[15] Richard L. Douglas, "A History of Manufactures in the Kansas District," *KHC*, XI, 174; Andreas and Cutler, *History of Kansas*, 1242.

[16] Harrington, *Historic Spots in Wyandotte County*, 248; Douglas, "A History of Manufactures in the Kansas District," *KHC*, XI, 6.

Silas Armstrong, Wyandot chief, one of the founders of Armstrong and Kansas City (Kansas State Historical Society *Collections*, IX, 216)

until 1872, and even then it had no post office and received its mail conveniently from the City of Kansas in Missouri.[17]

For several years there was talk of combining several cities at the mouth of the Kaw into one municipality. It took a special session of the legislature in 1886 to legalize the consolidation of Wyandotte City, Armourdale, and Kansas City. "It was expected," said Harrington, "that the name of the consolidated city would be Wyandotte and it has never been satisfactorily explained what sort of a hocus pocus led to the switch in name." But Governor John A. Martin, who signed the incorporation papers, was of the opinion that the city bonds would sell better if the city were named Kansas City. This was similar to the argument used for the choice of the name for the Town of Kansas on the Missouri side in preference to a name like Possum-Trot.[18] Two of the three towns had Indian names; the Kansans chose to retain the better known Indian name of Kansas. By mergers and annexations eight towns were absorbed, but their names have generally been preserved in the names of streets, parks, and cemeteries. Ferries served as a means of communication across the two large rivers for a time, but bridges were planned and pictured long before they became a reality to bind the urban and suburban centers into the metropolitan community known today as Greater Kansas City.

In the outskirts of Kansas City and in the bottom lands and flood area of the Kaw were several little squatter towns, each identified by its descriptive name. Some of the freed Negroes called "exodusters" built shacks along the tracks and river bottom in a community called Mississippi Town. Another name was Juniper Bottoms, better known by its shorter name of Junika. One socially segregated settlement was called Rattlebone Flats. Most of these were destroyed by order of the city in 1924.[19]

As Governor Martin had suggested, Kansas as a name had value. The name was used for towns scattered throughout the state, and for a short time it was also the name of a county. Occasionally

[17] Harrington, *Historic Spots in Wyandotte County*, 256.

[18] *Ibid.*, 244 and 326.

[19] *Ibid.*, 209; Federal Writers' Project, *Kansas, A Guide; Kansas City Times*, Dec. 3, 1953.

only a part of the name, such as Kan, was used, being added to a part of another name to make a new name. Twice the name was used as a popular appeal for towns which were ambitious to become the state capital.

The location of the capital of Kansas was a political plum for which many a town was willing to change its name. Among the candidates for the distinction was the town named Delaware City. J. Butler Chapman, the promoter of the town, changed its name to Whitfield City when he discovered that there was another Delaware.[20] It was most likely named for General John W. Whitfield, a man who was deeply involved in Kansas politics during its hectic territorial days. Chapman spoke of Whitfield City as "one of the most central and commanding situations in the territory." It was only a few miles north of Topeka, and its central location could make it a logical candidate for the capital of Kansas, but for this it would need a name of special distinction.[21]

What could be more distinctive than Kansopolis, the "city of Kansas"? Kansopolis, like Minneapolis, was a combination of an Indian word for a Siouan tribe, *Kansa*, and a Greek word for city, *polis*. Some spelled it Kansapolis, and others made it more complete, if not more difficult, by calling it Kansasopolis. No matter how it was spelled, it lost the capital contest to Topeka, another town with an Indian name. Kansopolis had a brief boom and then it declined, changing its name to Rochester. The town has now disappeared, as well as its four names.[22]

Kansopolis in Shawnee County had been fairly near the center of the settlements of Kansas when it made its futile bid for the capital. But as the population moved westward, there were those who thought that the capital should also be moved to a more central site. With this in mind, a town was built in Ellsworth County, very near the center of the state. There was some interest in calling the town Centropolis to advertise its central location. But the promoters wanted to make it another Kansas City without repeating

[20] Fannie E. Cole, "Pioneer Life in Kansas," *KHC*, XII, 354n.

[21] Dolbee, "The Third Book on Kansas," *KHQ*, VIII, 254.

[22] *Ibid.*, 244; Andreas and Cutler, *History of Kansas*, 534; James L. King, *History of Shawnee County, Kansas*, 55.

the name, so they followed the example of Kansopolis and dropped the "s" which made the new name Kanopolis.[23] It was highly advertised, and its boosters laid out a town to accommodate 150,000 people. It came near reaching the first thousand before its decline. The name, still on the map, has become well known from the dam on the Smoky Hill River which created a beautiful lake known as the Kanopolis Reservoir.

The exact center of Kansas is in Rice County, directly south of Ellsworth. A trading post on the northern border of Rice County was appropriately named Kansas Centre. Near it was Golden City which failed to qualify for either part of its name and disappeared after its post office was transferred to Kansas Centre. Nor was the name of Kansas Centre good enough to preserve it. The post office which replaced it was named Frederic. The town named Frederic had the advantage of being on the railroad and it also took over the business of a little town named Lodiana. Having replaced all these places and names, Frederic might have expected considerable growth. The town has not grown much but it has added a letter to its name which changed it from Frederic to Frederick. Lyons County once had a township named Kanzas Center, a misnomer since it is far from the center of Kansas. It has now dropped the "Kanzas" part and is only Center Township, which, by the way, is not in the center of the county.[24]

Town promoters continued to exploit the name of Kansas. Dr. George W. Cooper, who planned the town of Garnett, first laid out a town on Ianthe Creek which he called Kansas City. Then the name was changed to Ianthe for Ianthe Creek, which had been named for the Greek goddess Ianthe, the daughter of Oceanus and the playmate of Persephone. Whatever its name, the town lacked stability since the site had been occupied with a movable cabin, and when the cabin moved, there was no more need for a name.[25]

[23] *KHC,* VII, 480; John Watson, in *Wichita Evening Eagle,* Sept. 13, 1954.

[24] Jones, *The Story of Early Rice County,* 97; *KHQ,* XX, 288; Andreas and Cutler, *History of Kansas,* 760.

[25] Johnson, *The History of Anderson County, Kansas,* 61 and 346.

Papan's Ferry, which became Topeka, was called Kansasville before it was given an official name.[26] No such name is now found in Kansas but there is a Kansasville in Wisconsin. The ford just west of Topeka, where the Oregon Trail crossed the Kaw, was known as Kansas Crossing.

The suggestion by Baptiste Peoria that Osawatomie be called City of Kansas was rejected by "Osawatomie" Brown, who, by the way, was not Old John Brown, but Orville C. Brown, the founder of the town.[27]

Kansas as a name was used all the way across the state, occasionally in combination with other names such as Kanorado for Kansas and Colorado. In Elk County, Kanola and Greenfield had to merge to survive, and both towns argued for the preservation of its own name. The argument ended in a compromise and a combination of the two names into the name of Grenola. The "Kan" part of the name was lost when the name was terminated with "ola." Kanwaka, also spelled Kanawaka, a post office in Douglas County, was located between the Kaw and the Wakarusa rivers and is made up from the combination of the two names. The name remains on a Douglas County township. There is still a Kanona in Decatur County, but Kansada in Ness County ended its postal service in 1900. There is a Kansas Falls above Junction City in Geary County.

Kanorado on the Kansas-Colorado border in Sherman County is a combination made from the names of the two states. The first syllable is of Indian origin, but the second is from *colorado*, a Spanish name meaning "red." Kanorado had once been a post office named Lamborn which may well have been named for Charles B. Lamborn, an eastern stockholder in the Union Pacific Railroad.[28] Cokan Spur and Kanado, also on the border, are names on the Missouri Pacific Railroad, which are made up from combinations of Colorado and Kansas. Colokan, promoted by Civil War veterans from Illinois, was on the western border in Greely County. This

[26] Irene D. Paden, *In the Wake of the Prairie Schooner*, 38.
[27] Ely Moore, Jr., "The Naming of Osawatomie," *KHC*, XII, 340 and 346.
[28] John D. Cruise, "Early Days on the Union Pacific," *KHC*, XI, 25 and 539n.

was made up from the reverse combination of Colorado and Kansas. It was to be the "Star of Western Kansas," but a little town called Towner in Colorado became the railway station and eclipsed the "Star of Western Kansas."[29] These combinations may be compared with Mexicali and Calexico on the California-Mexico border.

Kaw, a name now acceptable for both the river and the Indians, was also acceptable for town names in various forms. Kaw Point was the name of the attractive place just above the mouth of the Kaw River, where Lewis and Clark camped and enjoyed a "panoramic view." Settlements at the mouth of the Kaw, on either side of the Missouri, were called Kansasmouth or Kawsmouth. This name was soon replaced by the various names for Kansas City.[30] Kaw City was a small town and post office northeast of Topeka; the railroad referred to it as Kaw Station. Now it is neither a post office nor a station. Wyandotte County once had a post office named Kaw Valley, and Linn County still has a place named Kaw. In Leavenworth County, Little Kaw Creek flows into Wyandotte County. Only two Kansas townships have been named Kaw, one in Jefferson County and one in Wabaunsee County.

Like the Little Osages, who had a well-known hunting trail to the Little River near Wichita, the Kansa Indians had their own favorite hunting trail known as the Kaw Trail. George P. Morehouse knew the Kansas and he knew their trail.

> It started . . . near the Kaw village near the mouth of Big John creek, four miles southwest of Council Grove, and bore almost west, a little southwest, crossing Diamond creek within a few rods of the present site of the railway station at Diamond Springs. It entered Marion county, near the old post-office of Bethel, on the head of Middle creek, and not far from the present site of the town of Lincolnville. From there it passed westward through Marion county and almost through the center of McPherson county, and on the forks of Cow creek, about three miles south of the present

[29] Conner Sorensen, "Ghost Towns in Greeley County" (term paper, University of Kansas, 1966), 28–30.

[30] Paden, *In the Wake of the Prairie Schooner*, 21; Andreas and Cutler, *History of Kansas*, 1240; George A. Root, "Ferries in Kansas," *KHQ*, II, 347; *KHQ*, XII, 390.

town of Lyons, near the center of Rice county. This was its western terminus.[31]

After Bourgmont opened Kansas in 1724, the French established a trading post among the Kansas and defended it with a fort which has been referred to as "a fort named 'Kansas.' " This evidently was the French fort which was officially named Fort de Cavagnial but called Kansas because of its location among the Kansa Indians.[32] The name was used again, unofficially, for a fort farther west. When G. M. Harker was stationed at the fort which was later to bear his name, he gave his address as "Fort Kansas, May 18th, 1855."[33]

In the southwestern corner of Kansas there was also a county named Kansas. Several of the western counties had been named before they were organized, and when they were organized, their boundaries were easily altered and names were lost. The county named Kansas was put on the map in 1873, but a decade later it still lacked sufficient population for a political organization. So the county named Seward, the second one with the Seward name, was given jurisdiction over Kansas County and the boundary of Seward County was extended to the Colorado border. The corner county once named Kansas was, however, resurrected and organized in 1886, but its name of Kansas was replaced by the name of a former governor of Indiana, Oliver Hazard Perry Throck Morton. His five names gave ample choice for the county name. His family name had been Throckmorton, but because of a family disagreement he had separated Throck from Morton, and the county was conveniently given the abbreviated name of Morton.[34]

The pioneers of Kansas County must have had little to say about having the county name changed from Kansas to Seward to Morton. The editor of the *Richfield Leader* minced no words when it

[31] John Madden, "Along the Trail," *KHC*, VIII, 70; Morehouse, "Along the Kaw Trail," *KHC*, VIII, 206.

[32] Morehouse, *KHC*, X, 341; Charles E. Hoffhaus, "Fort de Cavagnial," *KHQ*, XXX, 425ff.

[33] Louise Barry (ed.), "Kansas Before 1854," *KHQ*, XXXI, 259.

[34] Helen Gill, "The Establishment of Counties in Kansas," *KHC*, VIII, 469 and 470; Joseph N. Kane, *The American Counties*, 194.

came to expressing his disdain for those Topeka politicians who were the perpetrators of this unpopular change. Kansas editors have been famous for their frankness, and the editor of the *Leader* was no exception, as we may see from the following excerpt:

> We take it, that there is not a school boy in the land but what can tell you where Kansas county is, or at least where it ought to be, but owing to "an act" of a fool legislature last winter Kansas county was merged into, and made a part of Seward county. These very fellows are the chaps that we of Western Kansas are after this winter at the special session, and we propose to demand our rights, and restore the old lines as they were prior to '81.[35]

The name of Kansas, which started as the name of a tribe of Sioux Indians, has been applied to the river, the state, a county, and in various forms to trails, towns, townships, stations, forts, and cities. Not only does Missouri have a Kansas City, but four other states have towns named Kansas. It has been said that Kansas tourists who pass through these towns will stop for sentimental reasons to send postcards with a Kansas postmark back to Kansas. The most recent adoption of the name is the town of Kansas in Chile, so named in recognition of the aid which Kansas gave to rebuild its earthquake-torn towns.

[35] Gaeddert, "The First Newspapers in Kansas," *KHQ*, X, 405.

IV

Missouri, Oto, and Iowa

FROM EARLY TIMES the Missouri River has been known as the "Big Muddy." "I have seen nothing more dreadful," said Marquette as he witnessed the "accumulation of large and entire trees, branches and floating islands . . . issuing from the mouth of the River Pekitanoui."[1] In July, 1965, the author stood on the bank of the Missouri River at Atchison, Kansas, watching its high waters carrying loads of logs, whole trees, and islands of debris. This is how Marquette and later explorers saw it and described it. However, in 1965 one of the larger islands of debris carried a brightly colored buoy which had once served civilization. It had now become a useless companion of dirty driftwood at the mercy of the muddy Missouri.

Much of the history of Kansas has been influenced by the floods and ferries, barriers, and bridges of the Missouri River. The river once cut across the corner of northeastern Kansas, creating a barrier rather than a border, and by the Platte Purchase this trans-Missouri land was acquired by the state of Missouri from the Indians.

The first French record of a name for the Missouri was made by Father Marquette. He called it the *Pekitanoui.* That the source of this name was from the Illinois is indicated by a statement of Émile Lauvrière in which he referred to "*du Missouri (ou Pekitanoui comme l'appelant les Illinois).*"[2] Other Algonquian tribes used similar names, such as *Pikitin*, *Peekitin*, and *Pi ki tan.* This name could mean a "foaming stream," but it has also been inter-

[1] Phil E. Chappell, "A History of the Missouri River," *KHC*, IX, 239.
[2] *Histoire de la Louisiane Francaise, 1673–1939*, 300.

preted to mean "muddy water."[3] So the Missouri could become the Big Muddy from a translation of *Pekitanoui.*

Another interpretation of *Pekitanoui* was the "river of mystery." That it was the river of mystery is supported by the statement of Henri Joutel, a survivor of La Salle's expedition, who said that the "Indians did not fail to make sacrifice" to the Missouri.[4] There is a consistency in calling it the river of mystery, since the Pawnees gave it a name with a similar meaning. In their language it was called the *Kits war uks ti* or *Kiz paruks ti,* which was said to mean "mysterious water" or "medicine water," and *Kits u te war uks ti,* which meant "It is wonderful." The Pawnees "greatly revered the Missouri River," said Grinnell. Such are the reasons why the Indians gave sacrifice to this river.[5]

The Wyandots had a long rollicking name for the Missouri. They called it the *Kyooh-tahn-deh-yooh-ray*, which some of the older ones pronounced *Kyooh-tehn-den-dooh-rih.* This name, said Connelley, meant "muddy water" or possibly "yellow water." The Delawares were evidently impressed by the bluffs or rock walls on the Missouri River, because they gave it the name of *Os-sen-see-poo*, meaning "rock river." The Delawares may have learned the descriptive name from the Wyandots who spoke of the Kansas City, Missouri, site as *Kyooh-rah-dooh-hih*, which meant "the point where rock projects into the *Kyooh-tahn-deh-yooh-rah.*"[6] And how could one better describe it?

William Keating, who traveled through the Siouan country in the 1820's, said that the Siouan name for the Missouri was *Katapan Mene Shoska*, which he translated to mean "the river of thick

[3] J. T. Link, *The Origin of the Place Names of Nebraska,* Nebraska Geological Survey, *Bulletin* 7, 73; Virgil J. Vogel, "The Origin and Meaning of 'Missouri,'" Missouri Historical Society *Bulletin,* XVI, 214; Deatherage, *Greater Kansas City,* I, 388.

[4] T. F. Morrison, "The Osage Treaty of 1865," *KHC,* XVII, 692; John J. Mathews, *The Osages,* 131.

[5] Hyde, *Pawnee Indians,* 281; George B. Grinnell, "Some Indian Stream Names," *American Anthropologist* (n.s.), XV, 331; Mathews, *The Osages,* 131.

[6] Connelley, "The East Boundary Lines of Kansas," *KHC,* XI, 79; *Leavenworth Times,* Jan. 24, 1907.

water."[7] A simpler Siouan name was *Mini Sose*, which should be pronounced "Min'ny So'say," said Stanley Vestal, who translated it to mean "water roiled" or "muddy." Similarly, Stephen R. Riggs spelled it *Mi'no-so-se*, which he defined as "turbid water" and listed as the name for the Missouri River. *Minisose* appears to be closer to Minnesota than to Missouri, but this name is another source for calling the Missouri the Muddy.[8]

The name which the Missouri Indians gave themselves was quite different from the names given them by other Indians. They called themselves *Niútachi*, which was interpreted to mean "People who dwell at the mouth of a river." It could also mean "Those who build a town at the mouth of a river." There were several ways to write *Niútachi.* W. H. Jackson, the photographer, wrote *Nu-darcha*; others wrote it *Ne-o-ta-cha* and *Ne-o-ge-he*.[9]

Lewis H. Morgan, a pioneer anthropologist, suggested that there was a relationship between the Omaha name of *Ne-shoda* or *Ne-sho-ja*, meaning "muddy" or "riled water," and Missouri. Another spelling was *Nishuda* interpreted to mean "smoke river" from *ni*, "water" or "stream," and *shuda*, "smoke." "Ne-shoda," said Morgan, "was possibly the radix of the word Missouri."[10] *Neshoda* or *Neshoja* could also be the source of such Kansas names as Neosho and Neodesha. W. J. McGee admitted that "the exact meaning of Ni-u't'a'tci," as he spelled it, was uncertain. He was of the opinion that it could be a "corruption of Ni-shu'dje," which he thought meant "smoky water," the name of the Missouri River.[11] According to the La Flesche dictionary, the Osage name for the

7 Vogel, "The Origin and Meaning of 'Missouri,'" Missouri Historical Society *Bulletin*, XVI, 216.

8 Stanley Vestal, *The Missouri River*, 70; Stephen R. Riggs, *A Dakota-English Dictionary*, 52 Cong., 1 sess., *House Misc. Doc.*, 316.

9 Thomas Donaldson, "The George Catlin Indian Gallery," *Annual Report* of the Board of Regents of the Smithsonian Institution to July 1885, Part V, 79; Edwin James, *Account of an Expedition from Pittsburg to the Rocky Mountains from the Notes of S. H. Long* (vol. XV of Thwaites' *Early Western Travels*), 132. (Hereafter referred to as *Account of Long's Expedition.*)

10 *Morgan: The Indian Journals*, 34 and 88; Gilmore, "Some Indian Place Names," Nebraska Historical Society *Publications*, XIX, 137.

11 "The Siouan Indians," *BAE Fifteenth Annual Report* (1893–94), 162.

Missouri was *Ni-sho-dse*, meaning "smoky river," a name which they gave it because of its muddy appearance. This was also the Omaha name. To them, Kansas City was *Ni-sho-dse ton-won* or the "muddy river town."[12]

The Missouri might be muddy, smoky, or even foamy. Among the legends out of the West is the one about how the Cheyennes named the Missouri when they first saw it. Intrigued by the foam on the river, which looked like froth on a boiling kettle of bones to extract the grease, they named the river *Eomitai.* This has been interpreted to mean "It gives fat," or just "greasy," or, possibly more accurately, "fatty foam."[13]

Marquette used *Pekitanoui* as the name of the river but *Ouemessourit* as the name of the Indian village located near its mouth. *Ouemessourit*, whatever its variation in spelling, is said to have had a "characteristic Algonquian prefix," but it seems to be as much French as it is Algonquian. The prefix was occasionally printed with the "u" on top of the "o," which the printer would set as a figure 8, making it "8miss8rit" for *Oumissourit.* Father Membré and Henri de Tonty, associates of La Salle, referred to the river as the *Emissourita* in 1682. Henri Joutel is given credit for modernizing it to Missouri when he said in 1687: "We . . . passed by the mouth of a river called Missouri, whose water is always thick, and to which our Indians did not fail to offer sacrifice."[14] Franquelin's map of 1688 gave the name as *La Grande Rivière des Missourits, ou Emissourittes.* Delisle's map of 1702 made it the *R. des Missouris.*[15]

Until the name of the river became fixed, Missouri had to share its name, first with *Pekitanoui* and later with Osage and other names. The Recollets called the Missouri "the River of Ozages." Father Douay, a member of La Salle's expedition, referred to the river as the "Massourites or Ozages." He already knew, however, that the Osages were living on a tributary of the Missouri "to which

12 *A Dictionary of the Osage Language*, 110.

13 Grinnell, *The Cheyenne Indians*, I, 5n.

14 Morrison, *KHC*, XVII, 694.

15 Wheat, *Mapping the Trans-Mississippi West*, I, 52.

the maps have extended the name of Ozages."[16] A greater choice was given by Matthew Sutter on his map of 1735. On the north side of the river he listed the name as *Le Missouri ou Riv. d. S. Philippe* and on the south side, *Le Riv. des Osages ou des Missouris.* The king of France in 1712 also referred to the river as "The River St. Philip, heretofore called Missouri." He might better have said hereafter called the Missouri.[17] The transition from one name to the other was a gradual one, and Father Marest in a letter of November 9, 1712, referred to "a large river called the Missouri—or more commonly Pekitanou; that is to say 'muddy water.' " Marest's statement is not quite clear, but one may assume that it was the *Pekitanoui* and not the Missouri that was made to mean "muddy water."[18]

The Illinois, Wyandot, Omaha, and the Osage names for Missouri have been translated to mean "muddy water," "smoky water," or "riled water," which perhaps should have been spelled "roiled" even though it was pronounced "riled." Missouri has been taken apart and made to be "big muddy" by translating *missi* as "big" and *oui* as "muddy" or *missi*, "great," and *uri*, "muddy." It is likely, however, that the translation of the names above has been transferred to the Missouri, whatever the name might be, partly because the descriptive name was unquestionably accurate and had long been in use. Muddy though the river is, the word Missouri may not mean "muddy."[19]

J. T. Link, writing on Nebraska place-names, Virgil J. Vogel, writing on Indian names of Illinois, and Robert L. Ramsey, writing on Missouri place-names, all agree that Missouri was a name which was associated with the word for "canoe." In Maine the Indian

[16] Edna Kenton (ed.), *Black Gowns and Redskins*, 375n.; Morrison, *KHC*, XVII, 694; Chappell, *KHC*, IX, 243.

[17] Vestal, *The Missouri River*, 71; Hale, *Kanzas and Nebraska*, 14.

[18] Thwaites (ed.), *Jesuit Relations and Allied Documents*, LXVI, 225; Vogel, "The Origin and Meaning of 'Missouri,'" Missouri Historical Society *Bulletin*, XVI, 216; see also Fowke, "Some Notes on the Aboriginal Inhabitants of Missouri," Missouri Historical Society *Collections*, IV, 96.

[19] J. A. C. Leland, "Indian Names in Missouri," *Names*, I, 269; O. D. Von Engeln and Jane McElway Urquhart, *Story Key to Geographical Names*, 49.

name for canoe was *amasui*. In the Peoria or Miami language the name for canoe was *missuli*. Even the Illinois, who are supposed to have introduced the name of *Pekitanoui*, as Marquette understood it, are also said to have called the Missouri Indians *Miss-sou-li-au*, meaning "canoe men," since they did their traveling by canoe. The interpretation, possibly from the Fox, was that Missouri meant "people with big canoes" or "people with wooden canoes." This interpretation does not appear to be well known, but E. B. D. Beachy, writing in the *Kansas City Times* for January 17, 1950, gave the meaning of Missouri as "town of large canoes" or "wooden canoe people." So the Missouri River may continue to be the Big Muddy, but the meaning of the name Missouri evidently refers to the native means of transportation in a canoe.[20]

It may be that Marquette's name of *Pekitanoui* for the Missouri was revived when a Kansas county was named Peketon. John Maloy stated that "Peketon was a name coined by Judge A. I. Baker from the Sac language" and that it meant "flat" or "low land." Asahel Beach and associates, including "Buffalo Bill" Mathewson, promoted Peketon County. Sam Wood, who introduced the bill to establish the county, said that Beach and his son suggested the name to Governor Medary. Wood did not seem to know the origin of the name but he was under the impression that it was from the name of an Indian chief. This is a typical impression when an Indian name is unknown, but it is probably wrong. The note on this name goes on to say: "Another supposition is that the name was derived from Pekitanoui, the name given to the Missouri river by Marquette, or Pekatonica, a branch of the rock river." This is likely the correct "supposition."[21]

In 1860, Peketon County included all of southwestern Kansas south of Saline County and west of Marion. It was so big that it was later carved into thirty-six counties. It was not organized but it was named. According to Andreas, "the reader has his choice

[20] Link, *The Origin of Place Names in Nebraska*, Nebraska Geological Survey *Bulletin* 7, 73; Vogel, *Indian Place Names in Illinois*, 77; Robert L. Ramsay, *Our Storehouse of Missouri Place Names*, 10.

[21] "Some of the Lost Towns of Kansas," *KHC*, XII, 463n.

of name" from "Peketon, Pekton or Pecktun."[22] In the act creating the county the name was spelled Peketon but others spelled it Pekton and Peckton, confusing rather than clarifying the origin of the name. The writer of a letter to Sam Wood, dated May 10, 1864, gave his address as "Kiowa, Peketon County, Kansas."[23] As the *Pekitanoui* name was abandoned for the Missouri, so the Peketon name was abandoned for the county and changed to Washington before it was carved into small counties. Peketon had been promoted by Beach from the center of Rice County. A corruption of the *Pekitanoui* name still appears in Illinois.[24]

The Missouri name was used as a place-name in Kansas but with no lasting success. If there could be a Kansas City in Missouri, then there could also be a Missouri City in Kansas, and there was. Missouri City was incorporated in Johnson County in 1857 but it soon disappeared. When Arapahoe County, Colorado, was still in Kansas, it also had a Missouri City. There was a place named Missouri Farm in Doniphan County, and Sumner County had a Missouri Flat. In each case Missouri was only a part of the name and attached to a "City," a "Farm," and a "Flat."

The Missouri Indians, while living in Missouri, had been deserted by their Iowa and Oto relatives. Under pressure from the advancing frontier of the white man, they, too, had gone upstream where they joined the Iowas and Otos, former members of the Chiwere confederation who lived on the Iowa-Nebraska border. They were outnumbered and became so thoroughly absorbed that they lost their identity as Missouri Indians.

Even though the Missouri Indians are no longer known by this name, the Missouri name is one of the great names on the American map. There are those who regret that the Missouri River name was not extended down the Mississippi to the Gulf of Mexico. With its fingers draining the eastern slope of the Bitter Root Range of the

[22] *History of Kansas*, 812.

[23] "Some of the Lost Towns of Kansas," *KHC*, XII, 463n.; Martin, "The Boundary Lines of Kansas," *KHC*, XI, 62; Gill, "The Establishment of Counties in Kansas," *KHC*, VIII, 452 and 453n.

[24] Vogel, *Indian Place Names in Illinois*, 107.

Rockies in western Montana, it has the greatest drainage and the greatest length of any river in North America. Early explorers, not knowing its source, assumed it to be somewhere near the Pacific Ocean and spoke of it as the "River of the West."

Daniel Coxe, with a sea-to-sea grant in Carolina, is reported to have described the river as "the great Yellow river, so named because it is yellowish, and so muddy that the Meschacebe [Mississippi] is very clear where they meet," yet the waters there are discolored "even unto the sea." By the time it comes to Kansas it has become a powerful carrier of cargo and a dreadful carrier of debris and damaging floodwaters. The river, serving as a state boundary, unpredictable and unreliable though it be, is a part of the Kansas story. "This diabolically whimsical river called the Missouri" has honestly earned its earlier Indian name of being the Muddy. With its fearful floods and its heavy load of silt, "the wild Miz-zou-rye" still remains in the popular mind the Big Muddy.[25]

In one of the early eighteenth-century documents we find a note on the breakup of the Chiwere confederation. "We were told," said Le Chevalier de Beaurain, "that the Ayavois and Octatas had gone to station themselves up on the side of the Missouri river, in the neighborhood of the Maha."[26] The Otos were settled between the Iowas and the Omahas on the Iowa-Nebraska border.

The name of the Otos was the result of a gradual evolution of a much longer name. Their Siouan name was *Watohtata*. Swanton suggested that the Oto name came from *Octoctatas*, as used by the French. Hodge listed a shorter name, *Wato'ta*. The name started with five syllables; it was cut to four and then to three, and as Otoe it had but two left. Even that short name has been shortened by the deletion of the final vowel. Swanton and Hodge used the short form of Oto. However, as a Kansas place-name it was written Otoe. Its meaning was said to be "lechers" or, as McGee interpreted it, "aphrodisian."[27]

The "wild Otoes," as an agent called them, roamed into Mis-

[25] Morrison, "The Osage Treaty of 1865," *KHC*, XVII, 694; Mathews, *The Osages*, 4; Eric Thane, *High Border Country*, 19.

[26] Chappell, *KHC*, IX, 250.

[27] "The Siouan Indians," *BAE Fifteenth Annual Report* (1893–94), 162.

souri occasionally to raid the white settlements and to steal livestock in a country which was once their own. By 1833 they had joined the other tribes in the area in a general treaty of peace. Twenty years later they were approached by George Mannypenny about accepting a restricted reservation in order to make way for the white man. Their reservation was a little strip of land, ten miles wide and twenty-five miles long, on the borders of Nebraska and the Big Blue. It was good land, and it was not long before the aggressive and greedy white man moved in and settled on their lands without paying rent, taxes, or a purchase price. By 1881 the Otos gave up their Kansas homes for a promised land and protection in Indian Territory.[28]

In 1860 a county was named Otoe by the territorial legislature. It was only a small county, and, as the neighboring counties were organized, each acquired a portion until Otoe County was completely absorbed and obliterated by Marion, Butler, Harvey, and the ephemeral county named Irving.[29] The name disappeared with the county. Nebraska is the only other state to have a county named Otoe, and that was a result of a change from the name of Pierce. There is also a Nebraska town that had been named Berlin and was renamed Otoe during World War I. In early-day Kansas there was an Otoe stage station on the Oketo cutoff in Marshall County.[30]

The town of Oketo in Marshall County was said to be an English corruption of *Arkaketah*, the name of an Oto chief. The name was supposed to mean "Stands by It." On a treaty his name was listed as "Ar-ke-kee-tah, or Stay By It." The postmaster at Oketo explained to George Martin of the state historical society that the settlers "could not talk the Indian language and the nearest they could get to the name was Oketo." A short cut on the Oregon-California Trail north of Marysville was called the Oketo cutoff.[31]

[28] Foreman, *The Last Trek of the Indians*, 182 and 233.

[29] *Kingman Journal*, March 22, 1935; Gill, "The Establishment of Counties in Kansas," *KHC*, VIII, 452.

[30] Fitzpatrick, *Nebraska Place-Names*, 109; Emma E. Forter, *History of Marshall County, Kansas*, 179.

[31] "Names," MS, KSHS Archives; Frank A. Root and William E. Connelley, *The Overland Stage to California*, 200; Forter, *History of Marshall County, Kansas*, 179; *KHC*, XVI, 763.

There is still an Oketo railway station in Marshall County, and there is also an Oketo Township.

The Iowa Indians had left the Missouri tribe only to be reunited, and after 1833 they were quite thoroughly merged. One of their names was *Nadouessioux Maskoutens*, meaning "Dakotas of the prairies" or, as another wrote it, "Mascoutin or Prairie Nadouessi." We should recall that *Nadouessioux* came from their being called "snakes" as "enemies." Pleasing yet questionable are the translations which assumed that Iowa meant "beautiful" or a "beautiful place" or even "This is the Place."[32] Riggs's Dakota dictionary lists *i-o-wa* as "of owa," which was translated as "something to write or paint with, a pen or pencil." But Iowa, as we know the name today, may not have come from such a Siouan word.

Both Swanton and Hodge accepted the interpretation that Iowa meant the "sleepy ones." The Iowas were also called the "dusty noses," an interpretation that came from their being called *Pahodja* or *Pahucha*. McGee wrote it *Pa'go-tce*, which he translated to mean "dusty heads." It was also spelled *Pa'xo-dse*. Not only were they called "dusty heads" and "dusty men," but they were also called "snow heads," a name they were given, according to the Osages, when they separated from the other bands and "walked off with snow on their heads."[33]

The name Iowa, as we know it today, had several French forms before it became Americanized. Sieur de Bourgmont, French peacemaker among the prairie Indians in 1724, spelled the name *Iyovois*. Among the French variations were *Iyowois*, *Ayuhwa*, and *Aiaouex*; these may be of Siouan origin. Father Pichardo, a Spaniard, also spelled it *Aiaouez*.[34] Lewis and Clark followed a French pronunciation of the name when they spelled it *Ayauwais*. A few years later, Stephen H. Long retained the French pronunciation but gave

[32] Donaldson, "The George Catlin Indian Gallery," *Annual Report* of the Board of Regents of the Smithsonian Institution to July 1885, Part V, 153; Kenton (ed.), *The Indians of North America*, II, 294n.

[33] Mathews, *The Osages*, 128; McGee, "The Siouan Indians," *BAE Fifteenth Annual Report* (1893–94), 162.

[34] *Pichardo's Treatise*, II, map.

it an English spelling, Ioways.[35] A book published in 1834 bore the title, *Elementary Book of the Ioway Language*, leaving no doubt about the pronunciation. Frank H. Vizetelly as late as 1931 insisted that Iowa should be pronounced "I'oway, not Io'way." It is still not uncommon to pronounce the name as if it were Ioway even though the preferable pronunciation may follow the French of *Iyowois* rather than *Aiaouez.*[36]

The Iowas were settled in the northeastern corner of Kansas where a narrow strip of land was made a reservation for the Iowas and Sac and Foxes. It was from this reservation that the town of Reserve in Brown County received its name.[37] There the Iowas called Wolf River, *Shun-To-Nesh-rang-a*, which meant "wolf." On the Kansas side of the Missouri was the familiar landmark known as Iowa Point or simply "the Point." Major Wharton said that he had started for "*Jeffrey's*, or *Iowa Point*" on September 7, 1844. He had also camped on a small creek which he called Iowa Creek.[38] "I stopped at the Point," said Lewis H. Morgan a few years later, indicating that the Point was so well known that it needed no identification with Iowa.[39] When the Iowa Point Town Company established a town on this site in 1857, the town was conveniently named Iowa Point. The town is located in Iowa Township in Doniphan County.

From 1874 to 1902 there was an Iowaville post office in Sedgwick County, and for less than two months there was an Iowa City post office in Crawford County. Several towns were being promoted near the center of Ness County, each with a post office name and with ambitions to become the county seat. Ross Calhoun, one of the most active promoters, established a post office which he

[35] James, *Account of Long's Expedition* (vol. XV of Thwaites' *Early Western Travels*), 33.

[36] Lela Barnes, "Notes on Imprints from Highland," *KHQ*, VIII, 140; Deatherage, *Greater Kansas City*, I, 56, 69, and 141; Frank H. Vizetelly, "A Matter of Pronunciation," *Atlantic Monthly*, CXLVII, 150.

[37] Missouri Pacific Railroad Company, *The Empire that Missouri Pacific Built*, 141; *Atchison Daily Globe*, May 24, 1907.

[38] "The Expedition of Major Wharton in 1844," *KHC*, XVI, 295 and 302.

[39] *Morgan: The Indian Journals*, 137.

named Iowa. But it had to compete with neighboring towns named Schoharie, Clarinda, and Ness. The central location of Ness gave it an advantage, and when it won, it expressed its ambition by being renamed Ness City. Iowa was no longer a post office after 1881.[40] The three post offices with the Iowa name in three counties were most likely named by Iowa settlers. This would logically be true also of the three counties having Iowa townships: Kiowa, Rooks, and Sherman counties. But in Doniphan County, Iowa Township was named for the Iowa Indians who lived there.

In addition to the name of Iowa, there were other Indian names from Iowa which were adopted as place-names in Kansas. The town of White Cloud in northeastern Kansas was named for one of the most distinguished of the Iowa chiefs, the son of Old White Cloud who had been murdered in Iowa. It was White Cloud II who led the Iowa Indians to their reservation in Kansas in 1837. His Indian name was *Mew-hu-she-kaw*, which became *Mahushka* and then *Mohoska* and *Mohaska* and was finally adopted as *Mahaska*.[41] The founders of White Cloud planned to honor the Iowa chief by naming the town Mahushkah, but they decided that White Cloud was easier to pronounce and simpler to spell.[42] White Cloud's Indian name of Mahaska is the name of a station on the Burlington Railroad in Washington County. White Cloud was once a place-name in Dickinson County.

Mahaska also left his Indian name on an Iowa county whose county seat was Oskaloosa, and Oskaloosa became another source for a Kansas name. When Iowa settlers from Mahaska County came to Jefferson County in Kansas, they settled at a place called Newell's Mills, named for Jesse Newell, a Free State settler who actually survived a hanging by Border Ruffians. To continue their sentimental connection with their home town, the Iowa settlers changed the name of Newell's Mills to Oskaloosa, a name which was then also given to the local township. It has been said that

[40] Minnie D. Millbrook, *Ness: Western County, Kansas*, 85–86.

[41] Pryor Plank, "The Iowa, Sac and Fox Indian Mission and its Missionaries," *KHC*, X, 323; Thomas L. McKenney and James Hall, *The Indian Tribes of North America*, II, 114n.

[42] *Kansas City Star*, Sept. 25, 1942.

Mahaska or White Cloud, Iowa chief, for whom White Cloud in Doniphan County was named (McKenney and Hall, *The Indian Tribes of North America*, I, 302)

Oskaloosa was the wife of Mahaska. The geographical association of Oskaloosa as the county seat of Mahaska County in Iowa may be the reason for associating the two as man and wife. That Oskaloosa was the combination of *Oska*, the name of a chief, and *Loosa*, his squaw, has been a popular interpretation but should be told with tongue in cheek.[43] The Oskaloosa name is so much like such Muskogean names as Tuscaloosa and Ocaloosa that it may fit better in the story of the Five Civilized Tribes.

The well-known Iowa name of Ottumwa was a name of Indian origin and it may mean "tumbling water," "rippling water," or "rapids." But it has also been interpreted to mean the "place of the lone chief." The name was brought to Coffey County, Kansas, by Thomas Bowen, an ordained minister from Ottumwa, Iowa. He was also a Kansas politician who served as a member of the Topeka constitutional convention. An English Quaker, taking a look at Kansas in 1858, said that he had passed through "the little town of Autumia." That was, perchance, how Ottumwa sounded to him. The women of Ottumwa gave this town special distinction when they were the first women in the nation to vote in a presidential election; they all voted for Grant.[44]

43 Andreas and Cutler, *History of Kansas*, 502; *Atchison Daily Globe*, Oct. 15, 1910; *Topeka Capital*, July 31, 1956.

44 *Burlington Daily Republican*, Dec. 10, 1945; *The Gridley Light*, April 26, 1934; George Throckmorton, *First Hand Historical Episodes of Early Coffey County*, 94; Andreas and Cutler, *History of Kansas*, 647; Sheldon Jackson (ed.), "English Quakers Tour Kansas in 1858," *KHQ*, XIII, 47.

▲ V

More Siouan Names

EASTERN KANSAS naturally acquired place-names from the Kansa and Osage Indians with their Siouan language source. Minnesota, long a Sioux stronghold, was also a source for several Siouan names in Kansas. Most of these names now have no other meaning than the name of a white man's town or former post office, but they do have their native origins, interesting but elusive. Among the names originating with the Kansas were names left by their chiefs and some descriptive names in the Siouan language of the Kansas. Some of these names were quite transitory, not only from Indian to English, but also from one Americanized name to another.

Frederick Chouteau had a great deal of influence over the Indians. He would either establish a post among the Indians or he would persuade them to move their whole village to the site he selected for a trading post. When he moved up the Kaw River beyond Topeka, he established a trading post on a little creek on the south side of the Kaw in Shawnee County and named it "American Chief creek for the chief who established his village on its banks."[1] In 1805 the head of this village had visited Washington where President Jefferson made him a chief, which explains why he was called American Chief. His father was chief *E-ya-no-sa*, "Big both ways," and it was said that he "well became his name." American Chief was also a big man.[2]

The Methodists under William Johnson established a mission at

[1] Connelley, *Kansas and Kansans*, I, 199.

[2] Morehouse, *KHC*, X, 346; James M. Jameson, in *Western Christian Advocate*, Sept. 10, 1841, quoted in *KHC*, XVI, 264.

American Chief's village, and as a result of this the name of the creek was changed from American Chief Creek to Mission Creek. When Chouteau wrote in his "Reminiscences" about his experiences there, he continued to call the creek American Chief Creek and referred to Mission Creek only in parentheses.[3]

The Kansa village and the mission became the site for a town and a post office with the interesting name of Plow Boy or Plowboy. Among the farmers who were assigned to the Kansa Indians was Daniel M. Boone, grandson of the famous Daniel Boone. "I broke twenty acres of the land . . . on Mission creek," said Boone, and this seems to be the most likely source for the name of Plowboy.[4] In 1882 the descriptive name of Plowboy was changed to Redpath, probably for James Redpath, the journalist who was a defender of John Brown.

Menoken, also spelled Menokin, is located near the site of Fool Chief's village, a short distance above Topeka and across the Kaw from American Chief's village.[5] Fool Chief's name was *Ka-he-ga-wa-ta-ne-ga*, also spelled *Ca-ega-wa-tan-nin-ga*. The chief was not bad when he was sober, which was seldom, but he was crazy when he was drunk, and he evidently deserved his denigrating name. Menoken, the name of a town near the site of Fool Chief's village, was of Kansa origin, and was said to mean "a growing place" or "a fine growth" or even "a muddy place."

Menoken has a resemblance to both *moneka* and *monecato*. Since *monecato* meant "blue earth," it was likely that Menoken could also have in it a meaning associated with earth. Closely resembling Moneka is the word *mon-in-ka*, which, according to the La Flesche dictionary, meant "earth; soil; clay; mud." Similarly, *mon-hin-xa* meant "the clearing of a field of old stalks and dead weeds in preparing the soil for planting." But pioneers have referred to Moneka as "the little town with the Indian maiden's name." In support of this, the Osage dictionary, which defines *mon-hin-ci* as

[3] Adams, *KHC*, VIII, 425 and 428–31.

[4] J. J. Lutz, "Methodist Missions Among the Indian Tribes in Kansas," *KHC*, IX, 198n.; *Kansas City Star*, Nov. 12, 1942.

[5] Adams, *KHC*, VIII, 432; Morehouse, *KHC*, X, 348; Anna A. Ingleman, "Indian Place Names in Kansas" (thesis, University of Kansas, 1929), 348.

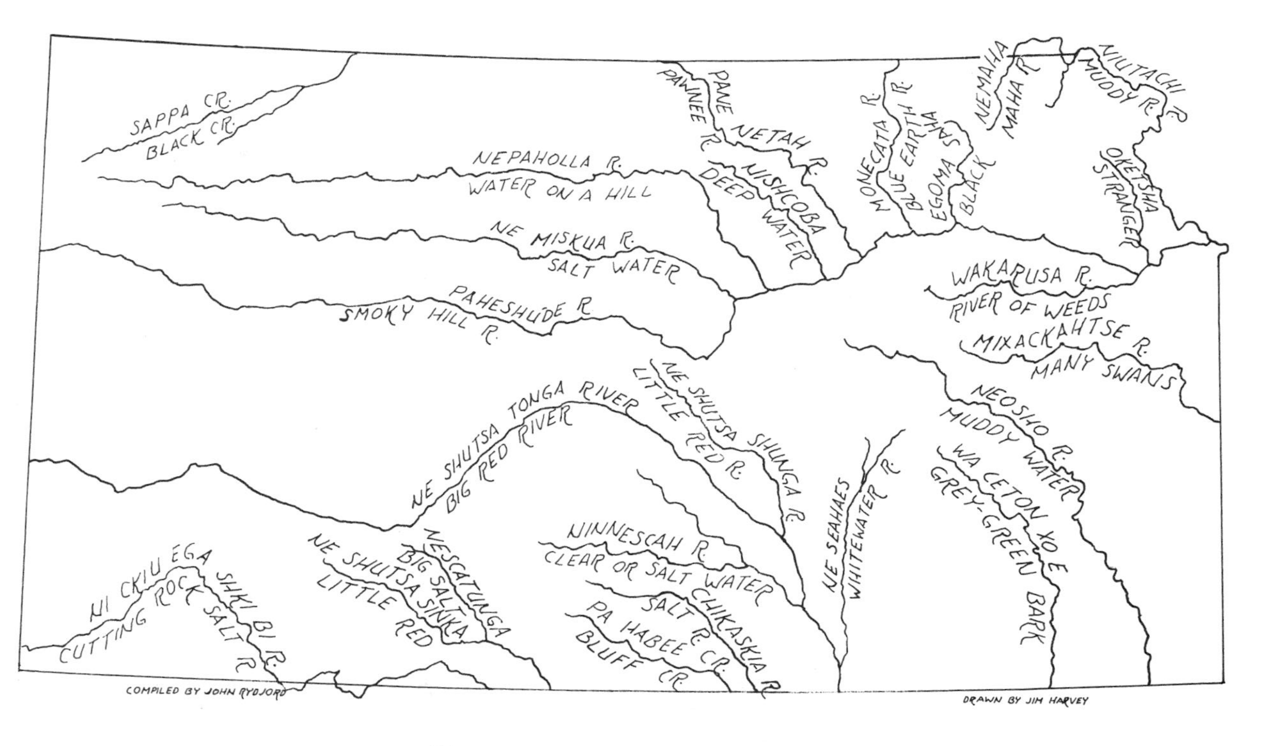

Rivers Named by Siouan Tribes

"flint" or "fire-flint," adds the suggestion that it may be a personal name. *Mi-na* is used by parents as a name for a first-born daughter, as is also *Wenonah*.

Andrew Stark of Connecticut was the "patron and promoter of Moneka." The town named Moneka or Moneca was founded in 1857 in Linn County where it flourished a few years, then declined.[6] In 1866 its post-office name was changed to Mansfield, which disappeared a decade later. Mansfield, named for an Ohio town, was unable to compete with Mound City and died. Similar to Moneka was Moniquee, once a town in Shawnee County.

Nearly all of the Minnesota names which were transferred to Kansas were of Indian origin. Minneapolis was, however, not pure Indian; it was part Sioux and part Greek. This strange combination of *minne* for "water" and *polis* for "city," made it simply "Watertown," a rather common name in the United States. Captain A. D. Pierce of Minneapolis, Minnesota, probably impressed by the three streams converging at his chosen townsite, gave his Ottawa County town the name of Minneapolis. It was located on the banks of the Solomon where Pipe Creek and Salt Creek converge. "By these streams," said Andreas, "the name Minneapolis, the City of Waters, was suggested." Before being named Minneapolis, it had been known as Markley's Mill.[7]

Mankato is another Siouan name from Minnesota. In regard to its meaning one local writer said, "We don't know what the deuce it does mean," but "as near as we can determine," it meant "green pastures."[8] Although its meaning has long been known, it is best to go back to its Minnesota origin for its use and interpretation. There Mankato is near the confluence of the Minnesota and Blue Earth rivers. The accepted meaning of Mankato is "blue earth." One of the chiefs of the Mdewakanton Sioux, said Hodge, was also known as Old Mankato. One of his successors was given the same name but it was spelled Makawto. Whatever the variations in spelling, the name was corrupted to Mankato.

[6] Theodore Botkin, "Among the Sovereign Squats," *KHC*, VII, 425; J. H. Stearns, "Moneka," *KHC*, XII, 429.

[7] Gaeddert, *KHQ*, III, 237; Andreas and Cutler, *History of Kansas*, 1426.

[8] *The Western Advocate*, July 25, 1940.

The Big Blue which flows from Nebraska into Kansas and enters the Kaw below Manhattan was called *Mon-eca-to* or *Mah-e-ca-te* by the Kansas. In translation it meant "blue earth."[9] The Indians had used the blue-gray earth along the river as a pigment and so they named it *Monecato*. Both McCoy and Hodge, as well as Thomas Say, knew that the Blue was properly named the Blue Earth. On Long's map it is also listed as the Blue Earth River. Lieutenant Tidbal, in reporting to Washington as late as 1853, used the correct translation and called the Monecato the Blue Earth River.[10] Unfortunately, the Big Blue from the north has occasionally and mistakenly been called Blue Water River.

By dropping the "Earth" part of the name and calling the river merely the Blue, the typical but incorrect assumption was made that the Blue referred to the water. This would fit the eastern Big Blue which McCoy described as "clear" and of a "bluish-green appearance where it is deep."[11] On Soulard's map of 1795 the northern Blue was called *R. Agua Azul* in Spanish. Perrin du Lac called it the *R.d'(e)l'Eau Bleue*. So in both Spanish and French it became known as the "blue water" river. This was unfortunate, because it lost its connection with the Siouan name Mankato or Monecato, and it caused no end of confusion by failure to distinguish it from the Blue River flowing into the Missouri below Kansas City. Reuben G. Thwaites illustrated the confusion when he said, "Hay Cabin Creek and Blue Water are known respectively as the Little Blue River and the Big Blue River." Then he warned the reader that this Blue River was "not to be confounded with the Big Blue of Kansas."[12] It might have been better had the Big Blue Fork of the Kaw retained its Indian name of Monecato, its Americanized form of Mankato, or, at least, its correct translation of Blue Earth.

Kansas might have established a town to be named Mankato on

[9] John F. McDermott (ed.), "Isaac McCoy's Second Exploring Trip in 1828," *KHQ*, XIII, 443; John C. McCoy, "Survey of Kansas Indian Lands," *KHC*, IV, 305.

[10] Langsdorf, "The First Survey of the Kansas River," *KHQ*, XVIII, 149ff.

[11] McDermott, *KHQ*, XIII, 443.

[12] *Early Western Travels*, XIV, 184n.

its own Blue Earth River, but it borrowed the name from Mankato, Minnesota. Mankato in Kansas was located in Jewell County some distance west of the Blue Earth River where it replaced the name of Jewell City. It was named by H. R. Hill who had attended school at Mankato, Minnesota, and who came to Kansas with a group of Minnesota settlers.[13]

To the other Siouan names starting with *minne* one might add the name of Mineola or Minneola, "the town that lived for a day" in Franklin County. When John Conner, lieutenant colonel of the Eighth Kansas Regiment, left Leavenworth to find Minneola, the capital of Kansas, most people from whom he asked direction said they had never heard of it, and those who had heard of it did not know where it was. However, it did exist.[14] "The town was well laid out on a map, all the roads in the United States pointing in that direction," and there were meetings held in the "capitol" building. The constitutional convention met there but its first business was a motion to adjourn.[15] The town had been promoted by politicians to become the capital of Kansas, but the political speculators aroused such a flurry of criticism that the bill to make it the territorial capital was vetoed by Governor Denver. The public "condemnation was swift as the lightning and as destructive as the cyclone," said C. K. Holliday. And Minneola, he concluded, "melted into air, into thin air and left not a rack behind."[16]

The name of Minneola was suggested by E. N. Morrill without any comment as to its source.[17] As in Minnesota, the *minne* would mean "water" and the *ola* could mean "little." However, one writer on Minnesota names has defined Mineola as meaning "much water." It appears to be a Siouan name, and therefore it seems strange to find a Mineola on Long Island, New York. This Mineola could

[13] *The Western Advocate*, July 25, 1940; Federal Writers' Project, *Kansas, A Guide*, 317; Isely, in *Wichita Beacon* (1929), Scrapbook, Wichita State University Library.

[14] Henry Shindler, "The First Capital of Kansas," *KHC*, XII, 337.

[15] *Kansas City Times*, April 17, 1947; "Some of the Lost Towns of Kansas," *KHC*, XII, 433; Cyrus K. Holliday, "The Cities of Kansas," *KHC*, III, 400.

[16] *KHC*, III, 396.

[17] Andreas and Cutler, *History of Kansas*, 605.

have had a different origin, possibly Algonquian, and it has been translated to mean "pleasant and palisaded village" or, if Muskogean, "good prairie."[18]

Minneola in Clark County, Kansas, has a completely different origin; there the name was created by the combination of the names of two women—Minnie Davis and Ola Watson—with the result that it looks like a Siouan name.[19]

F. W. Giles of Topeka became quite eloquent when he wrote about the many little streams which he cited in the neighborhood of Topeka. Said Giles: "The Shunganunga, past Burnett's Mound, and joined by Willit's creek, coursed its sinuous way through rich alluvial meadows. Martin's, Deer, Stinson's and Tecumseh from the south; Soldier, Muddy, Half-Day and Indian from the north—silent little rivulets, by wooded borders made conspicuous on the scene—at equal distances bisected by the broad valley of the Kaw, to confluence with its gulf-bound waters." Most of these names are Indian names or have an Indian association. Giles might also have mentioned Cross Creek which flows into the Kaw a short distance upstream on the north side. The Indians called it *Metsepa*, which meant "cross," for the way it joins the Kaw.[20]

Shunganunga Creek, which borders Topeka on the south and enters the Kaw at Tecumseh, has a name with a poetic appeal. It is most likely a Siouan name given by the Kansa Indians. That the name referred to some sort of "horse" is generally accepted, but there is a wide variation as to what sort of horse the name described. It has been said to be a "little" horse or a "pony," a "stud" horse or a "stallion," or a "race" horse. It must be the latter association that made Andreas suggest that Shunganunga meant a "race course."[21] Since *shunga* may mean "little," the name could refer to a pony by reversing the *shunga* and *nunga*, as the natives generally did. The Otos said it meant "no horse."

The Osage dictionary of La Flesche lists *Ka-wa zhi n-ga* as

[18] Vogel, *Indian Place Names in Illinois*, 74.
[19] *Kansas City Star*, Nov. 6, 1942; *Ashland Clipper*, Oct. 18, 1934.
[20] *Thirty Years in Topeka*, 411; Andreas and Cutler, *History of Kansas*, 589.
[21] Stubbs to Adams, and John B. Dunbar to W. W. Cone, "Names," MS, KSHS Archives.

"horse" and "little," from which we may get "little horse" or "pony" or possibly "colt." Therefore some of the above interpretations are questionable, especially since "Ka-wa," the Indian name for horse, most likely came from the Spanish word *cavallo*.[22]

Stranger Creek in Leavenworth County was already known by Lewis and Clark, who got the name from a French member of their crew. It was then called the Stranger's Wife River. Later, omitting the "wife" and changing the river to a creek, it became Stranger Creek. According to Isaac McCoy, the Kansas called it *Okeetsha*, which was said to mean "stranger" or "wandering aimlessly about." The Delawares had a different name with the same meaning; they called it *Mah-ha-hannake*. It would mean that a "stranger" was "wandering aimlessly about."[23] The name of the creek was the source for the name for Stranger post office. This name was later changed to Linwood, named for the trees in the vicinity. The place had been called Journey Cake, the name of a Delaware family, before it became the Stranger post office.[24]

One of the many Indian names for the Smoky Hill River, and a charming one, was *Chitolah* or *Chetolah*. If *che* meant a "house" or a "home," as it possibly does in Chetopa, and if *olah* meant "small," as it does in some names, then *Chetolah* could mean a "little house" or a "little home." The Osage word for house was *tzi* or *chee*, which Americans might modify to *chi*. However, neither the Sioux nor the Osage dictionary give sufficient proof to justify attributing any definite meaning to Chetolah. "Fort Riley," said Max Greene, "stands near the confluence of the Chetolah and Republican Fork of the Kanzas." Greene's opinion of the names for the Smoky Hill was that "it would be better taste to retain the musical Indian name, Chetolah, than the Smoky Hill Fork of the Kanzas, as it is now frequently called."[25]

Army officers and pioneers promoted a town near the mouth

[22] Andreas and Cutler, *History of Kansas*, 531; La Flesche, *A Dictionary of the Osage Language*, 83.

[23] "Survey of Kansas Indian Lands," *KHC*, IV, 305; "Journal of Isaac McCoy for the Exploring Expedition of 1830" (ed. by Lela Barnes), *KHQ*, V, 351n.

[24] *Atchison Daily Globe*, July 24, 1912; Howes, in *Kansas City Star*, Dec. 8, 1941.

[25] *The Kanzas Region*, 139–47.

of Lyon Creek and above Fort Riley in 1855, which they named Chetolah. The secretary of the town company was Captain Nathaniel Lyon for whom Lyon Creek was later named. The town of Chetolah failed, but the Chetolah name was too good to be lost. In 1888 a second Chetola was established near Fort Hays. It was at first to be a railway station at a crossing of the Smoky Hill, but the railway passed it on higher ground. It had a new boom after "gold" was discovered in its banks in 1893. When the gold shale mining declined, its second boom ended in a bust. A third boom based on oil did not materialize, and the town died, and with it, the "musical Indian Name" of Chetolah.[26]

When the Kansa Indians gave up their home on the lower Kaw in 1847, they were given a reservation on a creek near Council Grove. This creek bore the melodious Kansa name of Kahola or Cahola, also spelled Kawhola and Cawhola. In the Morris-Chase County area the name was spelled Kahola. When a post office was established on the Morris County side in what was later a part of Chase County, its name was spelled Cahola.[27]

Cahola may have been the name applied originally to the homes of the Kansa Indians. John Maloy said that the name was used for the Kansa village on the banks of the Cahola and that it meant "living by the river." It was probably from this that it was abbreviated to the less logical interpretation of "living water."[28] The Kansas were neither happy nor prosperous at Cahola, which was uncomfortably near their enemies, the Pawnees and the Cheyennes.

Cahola was popular enough to be used as a name for several townships. When Breckenridge County was under fire for being named for a Rebel, it was recommended that the name be changed to Cawhola, but the governor did not approve. Later it was renamed Lyon for General Nathaniel Lyon, a Kansan and a Civil War hero.[29]

[26] *Rush County News*, May 19, 1949; Martin, "The Territorial and Military Combine at Fort Riley," *KHC*, VII, 363n.; Kittie Dale, "Story of Chetolah," *Salina Journal*, April 12, 1964.

[27] Morehouse, *KHC*, X, 353; Patrick L. Gray, *Doniphan County History*, II, 146.

[28] *Council Grove Cosmos*, April 23, 1886.

[29] *Ibid.*; *Chase County Historical Sketches*, I, 21; Morehouse, *KHC*, X, 353; Andreas and Cutler, *History of Kansas*, 796; *KHC*, VI, 206.

In Saline County a post office named Poheta served seventeen years. After that Poheta was continued as the name of a school. The Bureau of American Ethnology suggested that this could be an Osage name which meant "in the direction of the fire, or camping place." This, then, could also mean "home," as the place of the fire or hearth.[30]

When Mill Creek in Wabaunsee County had an Indian name, it was called *Wa-nun-ja-hu*, and there, in a "most delightful" place, lived a Kansas chief named *E-ya-no-sa*, "Big both ways." *Wanunjahu* may have reference to a ceremony, or pointing the way.[31] *Wa-non-ce* means "point of attack," probably referring to direction, and *wa-non-ge* means a "stampede." It may, however, be a personal name, according to the Osage dictionary.

West of Fort Riley and between the Solomon Fork and the Republican flows a smaller stream now named Chapman's Creek. On a map of 1854, showing Indian reservations, this stream is named *Nishcoba*. Isaac McCoy was there in 1830, and his notes for November 12 read: "Travelled Southeastwardly down Niscoba, and encamped on its south bank." *Nishcoba* or *Niscoba* he interpreted to mean "deep water."[32] It has also been said to mean "crooked water." However, *Ni' shkube te*, the name of a branch of the Elkhorn in Nebraska, has been translated as "deep water." The Osage dictionary definition for deep or deep water is *shku-be*. George Root pointed out that after a cloudburst in 1869 the stream must have been fifty feet deep.[33]

The Red Vermillion, which flows into the Kaw east of the Big Blue, once had the Indian name of *Egoma Saba*. The *Saba* appears to be similar to *sapa*, *sappa*, or *sha-be* meaning "dark." The Sioux dictionary interprets *sab-ya* as "to blacken." If this interpretation were used, it might better have been the name for the Black Vermillion which flows into the Blue. But Meriwether Lewis called it "Black-paint" River in keeping with its Indian name.[34]

[30] Cora W. Reese, in *Gypsum Advocate*, Sept. 29, 1949.

[31] Barry, *KHQ*, XXIX, 345.

[32] "Journal of Isaac McCoy," *KHQ*, V, 374; Baughman, *Kansas in Maps*, 24.

[33] Root, *KHQ*, IV, 18; Theodore H. Scheffer, "Geographical Names in Ottawa

Mendota, located near the junction of the Little Labette and Labette Creek in Labette County, was named for "a thriving little city in northern Illinois." Since it was a Siouan name evolved from *mdote*, said to mean the mouth of a river or the junction, it could have been named for its Kansas location.[35]

A boom in Parsons ended "Little Mendota," said W. A. O'Connell. But this did not end the use of its name in Kansas. Three years after Mendota was closed as a post office in Labette County, it was revived as a post-office name in Decatur County, but there it lasted only through the summer of 1873. In 1882, Mendota replaced Halton as a place-name in Ellis County. There it survived as a post office until 1909. Three times the name has been on the map of Kansas only to disappear.

The town now named Natoma in Osborn County was first named Tapley by Boswell, the postmaster, who came from Tapley, Maine. It was proposed that the town be named Cresson, but that name had been pre-empted in Rooks County which had a town named for Cresson, Pennsylvania. Then Major Frieling Tufts, "a genuine Vermont Yankee," is believed to have proposed the name of Natoma. It is of Indian origin, and the local postmaster said that the accepted interpretation is "new birth" or "newly born."[36]

It was on Sappa Creek in Decatur County that the Cheyennes under Dull Knife, after escaping from their reservation, killed a number of white settlers. But the name of Sappa Creek seems most likely to be of Siouan origin. In the Sioux dictionary we find that *sápa* is a descriptive word meaning "dark." The accepted definition for Sappa Creek has been "dark waters," conforming to the Sioux translation.[37] One may compare it with *Paha Sapa* for Black Hills.

County," *KHQ*, III, 233; Fletcher and La Flesche, "The Omaha Tribe," *BAE Twenty-seventh Annual Report* (1905–1906), 89.

[34] Baughman, *Kansas in Maps*, 26; Aubrey Diller, "Origin of the Names of Tributaries of the Kansas River," *KHQ*, XXI, 405.

[35] W. A. O'Connell, in *Oswego Democrat*, Jan. 15, 1954; Vogel, *Indian Place Names in Illinois*, 68.

[36] *Natoma Independent*, Feb. 28, 1935, March 3, 1935, Feb. 2, 1939.

[37] Interview at Oberlin Museum; William Graves, *History of Neosho County*, I, 105.

In Decatur County there was once a place named Whitfield, but the name was changed to Sappa as a post office, then to Sappa City by the people. Finally it was changed to Oberlin, a German name from Ohio. The Sappa post office in Rawlins County lasted only a couple of years. After its closing the name was revived as Sappaton for another post office in Rawlins County. This name lasted four years, and then it, too, went into oblivion as the post office was renamed Chardon. Sappa now remains as the name of a creek and the name of a Decatur County township. Even a simple name like Sappa was misunderstood, and one letter writer, probably hungry, referred to it as Supper Creek.[38]

Tatonka was the name of a post office located northwest of Ellsworth from 1876 to 1885. *Ta-ton-ga* means a big deer or buck. In one Sioux glossary, *tam-do-ka* is given as the word for "buck." In Riggs's Sioux dictionary *ta-to-ka* is defined as "the big horned antelope." At any rate, it appears to be another name of Siouan origin, and was applied to a buck, be it deer or antelope.[39]

Most of the Siouan names in Kansas were of Kansa or Osage origin, but Oglala was a Siouan name which was taken from a tribe called the Oglala Sioux, also called the Ogallahah, a division of the Teton Sioux who lived on the Bad River in South Dakota. Oglala meant, according to Hodge, "to scatter one's own." W. J. McGee, an early authority on the Sioux, said it meant "she poured out her own."[40] The name was written O'Gallala in a treaty of 1866, which gives it an Irish look, but one need not take seriously the pioneer suggestion that the name came from "O Golly!"

As a place-name in South Dakota it is spelled Oglala, in Nebraska it is Ogallala, but in Kansas it is Ogallah, although on the Kansas Pacific map of 1858 it was listed as Ogallaha. It was once the name of a military camp and railroad camp, located a short

[38] Andreas and Cutler, *History of Kansas,* 1614; Miller, *Historic Sites,* 13; Louise Barry (ed.), "With the First U. S. Cavalry in Indian Country," KHQ, XXIV, 411.

[39] See Cram's map in Andreas and Cutler, *History of Kansas;* Fred M. Hans, *The Great Sioux Nation,* 316.

[40] "The Siouan Indians," *BAE Fifteenth Annual Report* (1893–94), 161.

distance west of Wakeeney, called Camp Ogallah. Now it is a railway station named Ogallah in Ogallah Township east of Wakeeney in Trego County.[41] From the Sioux came the name for Yankton in Harper County. Hodge defined it as "end village."

Geuda Springs is a town which has straddled the county lines of Sumner and Cowley. The name is of Dhegiha Sioux origin, attributed to the Poncas, and it is said to mean "healing water." It has been known as the mecca of health for the natives. Indians of various tribes assembled there peacefully to share in the benefits of its health-giving waters. Indian mothers came hundreds of miles to give birth to their babies at this health center.[42]

There was once a town near the seven springs named Remato which served as the post office for two years. In 1874 the name was changed to Salt City, which advertised the minerals of the springs. This name was changed to its Indian name Geuda in 1884, but later, as the post office inside the Sumner County line, it became Geuda Springs, with the "Springs" added to help its promotion and advertise its healing waters. White promoters thought it was "destined at no far distant day to render the name of Geuda as well known as that of Saratoga, or Arkansas Hot Springs."[43]

Nemaha is a Siouan name associated with the Omahas or possibly Otos. A simple translation would make it the river of the Mahas (Omahas) or, as John McCoy wrote to F. G. Adams in 1883, "stream of the Omahas."[44] In Thwaites's account of Long's expedition, *maha* was said to mean "cultivation," so Nemaha would make it the "river of cultivation." Riggs's dictionary gives *ma'ga* as meaning "a cultivated spot, garden, field." The pronunciation of Maha was probably not far from *ma'ga*, and the definition conforms. However, by moving the accent to the second syllable, *ma-ga'* meant "goose." Lewis H. Morgan referred to the Little

[41] Josiah Gregg, *Commerce of the Prairies* (ed. by Max L. Moorhead), 428; Garfield, "The Military Post as a Factor in the Frontier Defense of Kansas," *KHQ*, I, 58; Baughman, *Kansas in Maps*, 75.

[42] *South Haven New Era*, July 11, 1935; Frank W. Blackmar, *Kansas: A Cyclopedia of State History*, I, 748.

[43] Andreas and Cutler, *History of Kansas*, 1509.

[44] "Names," MS, KSHS Archives.

Nemaha as the *Ne-ma-la-ing* which he translated to mean "little muddy river." A branch of the Little Nemaha in Nebraska is still called Muddy Creek.[45] Somewhat similar is the assumption that Maha meant "miry" and that Nemaha meant "miry river."[46]

The South Fork of the Nemaha River, also called a creek, flows northward into Nebraska to join the North Fork in the making of the Grand Nemaha. It was the south fork, however, which was called the Grand Nemaha in distinction to the Petit Nemaha in Nebraska. In Perrin du Lac's map of 1802 these streams appear as two separate streams flowing into the Missouri, and the name is spelled Nimaka. The Nemaha crosses the Kansas border three times into Brown County before joining the Missouri on the Nebraska side.[47] One of its tributaries in Nemaha County was called Illinois Creek, and on Johnson's map of Kansas (1870), Illinois was mistakenly substituted for the Grand Nemaha.

Nemaha is also the name of a geological formation in eastern Kansas and Oklahoma. It is a submerged mountain chain which is sufficiently disturbed to have caused an earthquake in 1956. If it succeeds in its efforts to rise to the surface, it could produce a mountain chain in Kansas to replace the mountains which Kansas gave away to Colorado.

Nemaha is a simple name and yet its spelling baffled most of the pioneers. Members of the Lewis and Clark expedition showed a great deal of ingenuity and independence in the spelling of Nemaha, and the results would have been most entertaining at a spelling bee. Joseph Whitehouse spelled the name Grande-mo-haugh, indicating that he was at least referring to the Great Nemaha, or the *Grande*, as the French called it. Sergeants Floyd and Ordway were equally original. Floyd made it Gramma Mohug and Ordway made it Grow Mahhan. William Clark came a little closer when he spelled it Ne Ma How. One should, no doubt, make some allowance for error in transferring longhand manuscripts to type.[48]

[45] Root, *KHQ*, V, 378; *Morgan: The Indian Journals*, 68.

[46] Fitzpatrick, *Nebraska Place-Names*, 105.

[47] Root, *KHQ*, V, 378; Wheat, *Mapping the Trans-Mississippi West*, II, facing page 185.

[48] *The Journals of Lewis and Ordway*, 95.

Father De Smet gave a fair choice when he put the name on his 1884 map as *G. de Nemahas ou Nemawhaw R.*[49]

Even after Kansas became a state, the spelling of Nemaha continued to baffle the pioneers. George C. Duffield, who kept a diary on his travels in 1866, spelled it four ways in four days. On August 26 it was Nimehah, on the twenty-seventh, Nimekah, on the twenty-eighth, Nimahah, and finally on August 29 he made it Nemahah.[50]

Nemaha was a name which the early explorers knew well and it was used as a name in the first group of counties to be named by the territorial legislature in 1855. In addition to the river and a Kansas county being named Nemaha, there was a post office in Doniphan County named Nemaha Agency. It had been named Highland in 1855 for an Indiana town, then it became Nemaha Agency in 1856, but in 1857 the name was back to Highland.[51]

There appears to be a close relationship between the origin of Omaha and Nemaha. Kansas also had an Omaha. It was a short-lived town in Kearney County. The most common interpretation for Omaha is that it meant "those going against the wind or current." Those who continued upstream beyond the Kaw were naturally the "upstream people."[52]

South of the Kaw flows the little river with the big Indian name of Wakarusa. Its spelling has varied as much as its interpretation. It has been spelled Warreruza, Wahkarussi, Waukereusa, Wacharusa, and Warhusa. It is still occasionally pronounced "Wakarusee." This may be the result of a typical frontier pronunciation even for a name ending in "a." On the frontispiece map in E. E. Hale's 1854 book, *Kanzas and Nebraska*, the spelling conforms to this frontier dialect as Wakarusi.[53]

[49] Thwaites, *Early Western Travels*, XXVII, 227.

[50] Everett Dick, "The Long Drive," *KHC*, XVII, 92.

[51] C. W. Johnson, "Survey of the Northern Boundary Line of Kansas," *KHC*, VII, 321; *KHC*, VII, 443.

[52] *KHC*, XII, 484; Frederick W. Hodge (ed.), *Handbook of American Indians North of Mexico*, II, 119. (Hereafter referred to as *Handbook of American Indians.*)

[53] Root, *KHQ*, VI, 17; Thwaites, *Early Western Travels*, XIV, 183; Nathan H. Parker, *The Kansas and Nebraska Handbook*, 93.

According to Andreas, Wakarusa meant the "river of weeds" or the "river of big weeds," and "it was so named from a wild plant, partly covered with fine hairy fibre, that once grew along its banks."[54] A long-time resident on its banks, Dr. Jesse D. Wood, was of the opinion that in the Shawnee language the name meant "the river of big weeds." White Plume of the Kansa Indians told Colonel Holliday that Wakarusa was "the river upon whose banks grew the wild milkweeds."[55]

Some of the early immigrants were of the opinion that the name meant "to walk around" or "to surround."[56] This translation may have come from spelling it Walkarusha, which would be based on appearance or sound in a fallacious effort to make English words out of Indian words without translation. Also questionable is the translation of *wa-ka* for "snake" and *ni-chae* for "to eat" or "he eats," which was said to make Wakarusa the "snake-eater."[57] The Osage word for snake was *we'ts-a.*

The Indian story of how Wakarusa got its name is more popular but not necessarily more reliable. Albert D. Richardson, who visited Kansas in 1857, told the following story of how the river got its name:

> Many moons ago before white men ever saw these prairies, there was a great freshet. While the waters were rising, an Indian girl on horseback came to the stream and began fording it. Her steed went in deeper and deeper, until as she sat upon him she was half immersed. Surprised and affrighted she ejaculated "Wau-ka-ru-sa!" which meant hip-deep. She finally crossed in safety, but after the invariable custom of savages, they commemorated her adventure by re-naming both her and the stream, "Waukarusa."[58]

It was the practice of traveling Indians, according to legend, to check the depth and the possibility of crossing a stream by sending

[54] *History of Kansas,* 531 and 1529; Thwaites, *Early Western Travels,* XIV, 184n.

[55] Shawnee County Historical Society *Bulletin,* No. 13 (March, 1951), 19.

[56] Paden, *In the Wake of the Prairie Schooner,* 29.

[57] Dunbar to Cone, Oct. 6, 1877, "Names," MS, KSHS Archives.

[58] *Beyond the Mississippi,* 37.

a woman across the stream first. One need not conclude that this practice was due to the etiquette of "ladies first." According to one story, it was the Indian chief who shouted "Waukarusa" when he saw how deep the water rose on a woman crossing the river. We cannot be sure of what the chief said nor whether the water was just "hip deep" or "waist deep." It has also been said that it meant "deep water" or "bad bottom." The translation given in a Santa Fe bulletin becomes both a euphoneous and logical evasion and yet accurate enough. There it was called just "heap deep." This is safe and it still sounds like Indian talk.[59]

The naming and the placing of the town of Wakarusa was the result of several changes in name and location. When the first New England Emigrant Company came to the Mount Oread site, "they named the new settlement Wakarusa." But the name was not yet official. Another account said that they settled at "Wakarusa—or Lawrence, as it was by this time known."[60] Other names were competing with Wakarusa for this New England settlement. "The infant city," said Holloway, "wrapped in the swaddling of grass, thatch and canvass, was known by the name of Wakarusa, New Boston, and by the Missourians, Yankee Town."[61]

Then Wakarusa Station was established southeast of Lawrence. It was later moved into the next county to the west and became known as Wakarusa on the Wakarusa Crossing south of Topeka. It was also called Wakarusa City.[62] When a new townsite was chosen to be on the line of the anticipated Santa Fe Railway route, it was named Kingston for Zenos King of Topeka, one of the town promoters. The settlers preferred the name of Wakarusa to Kingston, and this preference had already been made official by the Post Office Department when the post office was moved a mile from Williamsport site to the Kingston-Wakarusa site. A short distance farther south a town in Osage County was also named Wakarusa,

[59] Beachy, in *Kansas City Times*, Jan. 17, 1950; William E. Webb, *Buffalo Land*, 35; Atchison, Topeka and Santa Fe Railway Company, *Along Your Way*, 12.

[60] Barry, "The Emigrant Aid Company Parties of 1854," *KHQ*, XII, 122 and 139.

[61] *History of Kansas*, 117.

[62] Andreas and Cutler, *History of Kansas*, 308.

but the name was saved from duplication when this Wakarusa was changed to Ridgeway.[63]

Any crossing of the Wakarusa was important, first as a source for a town and secondly as a source for a name. Blue Jacket's Crossing was well known for a time. Not far away was the land owned by a prominent Shawnee named Fish. S. C. Pomeroy, trying to get possession of a townsite, referred to the place as "Fish Crossing city." This was before it became a "city," but Pomeroy already knew what its name was to be, since he added that it was "hereafter to be called Wakarusa." It was also referred to as Wakarusa City. For a man who became senator from Kansas, he had a very modest ambition when he said, "I should like to be Post Master at Wakarusa." Then he added, "The name of every point and place in this city shall be Indian."[64]

What is commonly called the Divide, which separates the waters of the Osage from the Wakarusa, has also been known as Wakarusa Buttes.[65] A Wakarusa Township was named in 1857. Wakarusa is a name with distinction but it has not been important as a town-name; it is as the name of the Wakarusa River that it has distinction in Kansas.

[63] William W. Cone, "On the Wakarusa," Shawnee County Historical Society *Bulletin*, No. 31 (December, 1958), 41 and 69; Andreas and Cutler, *History of Kansas*, 596 and 1529.

[64] Cone, Shawnee County Historical Society *Bulletin*, No. 31, 41 and 45.

[65] Greene, *The Kanzas Region*, 106.

VI

Arkansas River: Tonga and Shunga

THE ARKANSAS RIVER has had native Indian names, Spanish names, religious names, French names, Americanized names, an Arabic name, and nicknames. If a river were big, the Indians named it the Big River, each tribe in its own language, and that is how we got such names as Chesapeake, Mississippi, and Yukon.[1] The term *Grande*, meaning big, has also been applied to the Arkansas.

Spain, too, had a big river. It was called the Guadalquivir, an Arabic name. *Guad* or *wuad* meant "water," and *quivir* meant "big." When Francisco de Coronado heard the Indians tell of a big river, he named it Guadalquiver for the big river in Spain. Like most people, the Spaniards were prone to abbreviate long and cumbersome names, so Guadalquivir became Quivir and this was later popularized into Quivira. Castañeda, a companion of Coronado, spoke of their dash to the "River of Quivira." Another said that "God was pleased that in thirty days we should come to the Quivira river." A note identified this as the Arkansas.[2]

The term which was started as the name of the river was also applied to the people and the land. *La Quivira*, as Coronado's followers called the land, could be centered in Kansas, but it was an elusive land and large, and occasionally it was called *Gran Quivira*. This may make a good appeal on a map, but it becomes a meaningless mixture of two languages when translated into English, since it meant "big big." Likewise, *Gran Guadalquivir* becomes ridicu-

[1] George R. Stewart, *Names on the Land*, 23, 87, and 398.
[2] Hammond and Rey, *Narrative of the Coronado Expedition*, II, 291.

lous when translated to "big river big." It is like appending "river" to Río Grande, making it the "river big river."[3]

Efforts have been made to find an Indian word as the origin for Quivira. According to Hodge, Quivira is possibly a Spanish corruption of *Kidikwiús* or *Kirikurus*, *Kirikiris* or *Kitikitish*, Pawnee names for one of their bands, also said to be the Wichita name for themselves. Similar in sound though they be, they may have no reliable relationship. The Arabic source seems to be well substantiated in its use by the Spaniards. Quivira soon became the name of the area where the natives lived, as well as the name of the natives. El Turko, the Indian who gave the Spaniards an exaggerated report on Kansas, also spoke of the river being two leagues wide, approximately six miles, which justified calling it the Guadalquivir or the Big River.[4]

The Spaniards had given the Arkansas River an Arabic name, but when Coronado reached the river, one of his companions, Jaramillo, gave it a religious name and a Spanish name. Not far from Ford, Kansas, Coronado crossed the river on the saint's day of Peter and Paul, June 28, and so Jaramillo named it *El Río de San Pedro y San Pablo*.[5] The name was not a lasting one, and other Spaniards gave the river new names equally transient.

In 1601, Juan de Oñate approached the Arkansas at a river junction which has been assumed to be that of the Big and Little Arkansas, but which was more likely that of the Walnut entering the Arkansas River near Arkansas City. He named the big river the *Robrodal* or *Rubredal*, meaning "oak tree" river or, more accurately, "oak grove" river.[6]

Juan de Uribarri, who led an expedition from Santa Fe to western Kansas in 1706, referred to the Arkansas River as the one which the Indians call "in their language the Napestle." It has been sug-

[3] David Sopher, "Arabic Place Names in Spain," *Names*, III, 8; *Pichardo's Treatise*, II, 376.

[4] Hodge, *Handbook of American Indians*, II, 346; Hyde, *Pawnee Indians*, 64; Arthur G. Day, *Coronado's Quest*, 358n.; Hammond and Rey, *Narrative of the Coronado Expedition*, II, 22 and 291.

[5] John B. Dunbar, "The White Man's Foot in Kansas," *KHC*, X, 75.

[6] Wheat, *Mapping the Trans-Mississippi West*, I, 29 and 32n.

gested that this could be a Ute name, although Uribarri was then in Apache country. Elliot Coues thought it was a Ute name. "We arrived," said Uribarri, "at the large river which all the tribes called the Napestle." After his expedition in 1720, San Miguel de Aguayo reported to his governor in Santa Fe, "I reached the *Río Napestle*," a large river, "its beauty rivalling that of the *Del Norte*."[7] Captain Juan de Anza also spelled it *Río Napestle* on his map of 1779, but Pedro Vial, traveling from Santa Fe to St. Louis in 1792, spoke of coming to the "Napeste River, which we call in French the Arkansas River."[8] Napeste is preserved today as the name of a small town on the Arkansas River in eastern Colorado.

The use of the name Napestle, occasionally together with Arkansas, continued well into the nineteenth century. Some used the Napestle name only for the upper part, possibly to the Purgatoire, called Picketwire by the Americans. Others called it the Napestle all the way to the mouth of the Arkansas or *Los Arcos*.[9] On a Lewis and Clark map it was spelled *Río Nanesi*; on Pike's map it was *Río de Napesi*.[10] Another called it *Le Río Napestle*, mixing three languages, French, Spanish, and Indian. Going downstream from the Spanish side it was the Napestle, but going upstream from the French side it was the Arkansas River.

Uribarri followed the Spanish custom of adding a religious name to a native name. "As an honorable memorial to his Christian zeal," he said of his governor, Don Francisco Cuerbo, he had given the river the "name of his saint, calling it the *Río Grande de San Francisco*." Occasionally he combined the Indian name with the descriptive, the religious, and the personal and political name by calling it the "Napestle or *Río Grande de San Francisco*."[11] The Pawnees were said to have hunted all the way to the "River of *San Francisco*

[7] Thomas, *After Coronado*, 30 and 65.

[8] *Pichardo's Treatise*, I, 192, and III, 337; Thomas, "An Eighteenth Century Comanche Document," *American Anthropologist* (n.s.), XXXI, 290; *Expedition of Pike*, II, 448n.; Archer B. Hulbert, *Southwest on the Turquoise Trail*, 51.

[9] Wheat, *Mapping the Trans-Mississippi West*, II, 126; *Pichardo's Treatise*, III, 337.

[10] *Expedition of Pike*, II, 448n.

[11] Thomas, *After Coronado*, 73; *Pichardo's Treatise*, II, 40.

de Arkansas." Here again, on its way to get a new name, the old and the new were used together.[12]

The Pawnees called the Arkansas River the *Kits-ka* and *Kits'ke-uts. Ti-ke'uts* was translated by Grinnell to mean "it is long"; the full name would then mean the "long river" or the "longest river." "This may be correct," said Hyde, "but most of the tribes, from at least as far back as the early 18th century, called the Arkansas . . . Flint or Flint-knife River." The Kiowas accepted the name given it by the Plains Indians and called it the *se'se-p'a*, "arrowhead river." The Pawnees had a club or organization called the *Kitsita* which means "knife lance." When the Arkansas was called the *Kitsita* it became known as the Flint River. The Pawnee name *Kitsita* resembles the word *kits-ka*, and the various forms of *kits*, such as *kitz*, *kitsa*, and *kizu*, mean "water" or "stream."[13]

The Osages named the Arkansas River for its color, calling it *Ni-Zhu-Dse* or *Ne Shutsa*, "water red," "river red," or the "red river." This descriptive name was particularly appropriate in Oklahoma where the Little Red Fork or Salt Fork carries the red soil of southern Kansas and Oklahoma into the *Ni-Zhu-Dse* or the Red Waters River. The spelling of the Osage name varied considerably, and in *Tixier's Travels* it was spelled *Nhi-Sudgeh.* On a map based on Auguste Cheauteau's information it was given as the Arkansas River or Nesutse. James R. Mead wrote *Ne Shutsa* and *Neshutsa.*[14]

The names given to the Arkansas River by the Utes, Pawnees, and Osages were no more permanent than those given by the Spaniards. The name by which the river is known today is an evolution of the names which the French gave to the Quapaws or a village of the Quapaws, the Akansa, located near the mouth of the Arkansas River. Akansa was likely an Algonquian name which they had

[12] Rydjord, "The Conquistadores Come to Kansas," in *Kansas: The First Century* (ed. by John D. Bright), I, 38.

[13] Hyde, *Pawnee Indians*, 282; Grinnell, *American Anthropologist*, XV, 331; James Mooney, "Calendar History of the Kiowa Indians," *BAE Seventeenth Annual Report* (1895–96), 431.

[14] *Tixier's Travels on the Osage Prairies* (ed. by John F. McDermott), 149; Baughman, *Kansas in Maps*, 25; James R. Mead, "The Little Arkansas," *KHC*, X, 8; Mathews, *The Osages*, 137.

learned from the Illinois. The French spelled it Akansea or Akamsea, which was later simplified to Akansa.

Marquette, who was the first to put Kansa on the map, was also the first to put Akansea on the map, creating no end of confusion by making Akansea look like Kansa and Arkansas look like Kansas. He expected to get information, he said, at a large village "called Akamsea." W. J. McGee, writing about the Sioux, suggested that the Akansa name could have been confused with the Kanza, explaining that the name was probably of Algonquian origin where the prefix "A" was quite common.[15] In long names we find that prefixes may come and go with careless abandon and with little thought to meaning, so one might conclude that Kansas was a name which had merely lost a syllable from Arkansas. When Arkansas was spelled Ah-Kan-Zau, it came very near the native pronunciation of "Kau-zau" for Kansas. However, putting an "Ah" before Kansas does not prove that the two names had the same origin. It was the evolution of their names that made them look alike, a coincidence which was probably not based on their origins.[16]

Hernando De Soto, while exploring the lower Mississippi, learned of Arkansas River tribes called Kappaws. LaSalle wrote about the "Kapahala village of the Akansea." Henri Tonty, a companion of LaSalle, called them Kappas and Cappas. One can make Quapaw out of Kappaws or Kappas or even out of such variations as *U-ka-gpa*, *Pacaha*, and *Kapaha*, but it is difficult to make Arkansas or even Akansea out of these. In Hodge's *Handbook*, however, we find a relationship in the reverse order: "Acansa, Acansea, Acansias-Quapaw." But Father Gravier spoke of the Akanseas as being "8 leagues from the village of the Kappa."[17]

Marquette distinguished between the Akanseas, which he placed opposite the mouth of the Arkansas on his map, and the Kapahalas, which he placed some distance up the same river. LaSalle also made

[15] "The Siouan Indians," *BAE Fifteenth Annual Report* (1893–94), 193.

[16] Thwaites, *Jesuit Relations and Allied Documents*, LIX, 152–53.

[17] There is a good discussion on the name by Louis Houck in *A History of Missouri*, I, 107–109; Hodge, *Handbook of American Indians*, II, 102; Thwaites, *Jesuit Relations and Allied Documents*, LXV, 125.

a distinction between these two as if there were two villages with different names. One might conclude that the name Quapaw grew out of one of these names, such as Kappaws, and Arkansas grew out of the other, Akansea. Yet both Quapaw and Arkansa have been used as the general name for the four villages of these related natives.[18] There is a distinction made between the two when referred to as the "Kapaha village of the Arkansas." The meaning of the name is as elusive as its origin.

In the westward migration of the Siouan tribes the Kansas and Osages went up the Missouri while the Quapaws, their kinfolk, went on down the Mississippi to the mouth of the Arkansas River. The Omahas who went on up beyond the Kansas were called the "upstream people," so it was natural to call the Quapaws "those-who-went-down-river" or the "downstream people." This descriptive name, especially if written Akansa, seems to have come from the Illinois, the natives who furnished so many names for the map of Marquette. Swanton said, however, that some form of the Quapaw name was used by the Omahas, Poncas, Kansas, Osages, and Creeks. Dorsey, Hodge, and Swanton have all assumed that Quapaw meant "downstream people." To be sure, the Quapaws lived downstream some distance, but that does not necessarily prove that Quapaw in any of its forms meant "downstream people."[19] The translation may be correct but it has been challenged.

According to Mathews, the Little Osages called the Quapaws the *U-Ga-Xpa*, "Pushed-off-the-hill-people," and he said that there is no part of this name which refers either to water or river. Then he added, "The name *U-Ga-Xpa* was Gallicized and Anglicized" and finally became both Quapaw and Arkansas. "Looked at closely," he continued, "one might find the original *U-Ga-Xpa* in both." Instead of using Arkansa and Quapaw as synonymous, these names have been used separately to make a tribal distinction, for example, the Arkansas and the Kappas.[20]

[18] For Marquette's map see *KHC*, X, 80; James Baskett, "Prehistoric Kansas," *KHC*, XII, 245; Houck, *A History of Missouri*, I, 107; Hay, *KHC*, IX, 522.

[19] Hodge, *Handbook of American Indians*, II, 119 and 336; John R. Swanton, *The Indian Tribes of North America*, 10 and 213.

[20] James Mooney, "The Siouan Tribes of the East," BAE *Bulletin 22*, 10;

The French had almost as great a variety of names for the Arkansas River as did the Spaniards before them. Joliet called it the *Bazire*, naming it for a French fur-trading friend of his in Montreal. As did the Pawnees and Spaniards before them, the French called the Arkansas the Big or Grand River, since it appeared on Antoine Soulard's map of 1795 as *R. Grande los Arkansas.*[21]

There were many forms of the name to choose from before the name of Arkansas became fixed and official. A good illustration of the variety of names for the Arkansas may be seen in the index to *Pichardo's Treatise on the Limits of Louisiana and Texas.* There the names are listed as follows: "Acansas, Akansas, Arcansas, Arcos, Ares, Chinali, La Zorca, Río Napeste or Napestle, Río Grande de San Francisco."[22]

This index introduced some new French names. Related to such names as *Los Arcos* and *La Zorca* (also written *Los Sarcos*) were such French names as *Rivière d'Osark* and *Rivière des Arks.* "Let us discuss a little further this word Arcos as signifying the Arcansas," said Father Pichardo. "Just as the Spaniards are accustomed to abbreviate various Mexican words," he said, "so likewise are the French."[23] Pedro Vial's map of 1787 shows a *Río de la Arga,* and it is difficult to decide whether he was changing the name of Arkansas or naming the Arkansas for the Arga River in northern Spain.[24]

From *Rivière des Arco* and *Aux Arcs,* it is also believed that the French invented the name River of Bows, unless it resulted only from a bad translation. In *Tixier's Travels,* the "River of the Bows *(rivière des arcs)*," the *aux arcs* was confused with the abbreviation for *aux Arkansas.* One could easily derive the name Ozark from *Aux Arc* and from *Los Arcos.* There is a case, however, for calling the Arkansas River the River of Bows. Swanton said that the Quapaws were called the Bow Indians because they used the Osage

Mathews, *The Osages,* 110; Alcée Fortier, *History of Louisiana,* I, 81; Hay, *KHC,* IX, 522.

[21] Baughman, *Kansas in Maps,* 16–17; *Pichardo's Treatise,* III, 184; Stewart, *Names on the Land,* 90.

[22] *Pichardo's Treatise,* III, 570.

[23] *Ibid.,* 316.

[24] Wheat, *Mapping the Trans-Mississippi West,* I, facing page 126; Henry Gannett, *American Names, A Guide,* 26.

orangewood for making their bows. That is, however, only one interpretation. "The Arkansaw Indians, an offshoot from the Kanzas," said Edward E. Hale, "struck the French as such fine men, that they called them 'Les Beaux Hommes,' supposing that to be the meaning of their name." The English phonetic spelling of the French *beaux* could also give us the source for "bow." It would not have taken much imagination to make the Arkansas the River of Bows because of the French having called the Quapaws *beaux hommes*.[25] It has been quite common to accept Swanton's interpretation that the Bow Indian name had its origin with the use of the Osage orangewood, the *bois d'arc*, for making the bows for their arrows.

It would probably be simpler to find a relationship between Kansas and Arkansas than between Quapaw and Arkansas, but it still remains a doubtful relationship. Yet Henry Schoolcraft assumed that Kansas and Arkansas had a common source. He made up the name of Arkansas from "Arc, Fr., and Kansaw, a tribe." To this he added that "a part of the Kanzas appear to have been so designated in the early days," and "not without probability, they were believed to have given its name to the river," the Arkansas.[26] This possibility may be questioned but not rejected. Both the pronunciation and the spelling of the two names have contributed to the confusion regarding their relationship.

Pioneers showed little consistency in spelling Arkansas. The French started the variation with Akansea and Akamsea, which La Salle simplified to Akansa. La Harpe wrote it Alkansas in 1720, inserting the "l" into the first syllable; and Du Tisné spelled it Atkansas, unless this is an error in printing. By 1753, Dumont substituted the "r" for the "l" but he also changed the "k" to a "c," so it became Arcansas. On D'Anville's map of 1756 it was still Akansis but in the next year Le Page du Pratz wrote it Arkansas, as we know it today. Thomas Jefferson spelled it Arkanzas, which was phonetically correct.[27] It took a long time before Arkansas be-

[25] Dolbee, *KHQ*, II, 166n.; *Tixier's Travels on the Osage Prairies*, 149n.

[26] Henry R. Schoolcraft, *Archives of Aboriginal Knowledge*, IV, 562.

[27] For additional forms see Hodge, *Handbook of American Indians*, II, 336–37; Chappell, *KHC*, IX, 253–54.

came standard usage, and variations continued far into the nineteenth century.

Much of the conflict over the spelling was caused by the difference between French and English pronunciation. The French added the "s" to Arkansas to make it plural but they did not pronounce it. Hearing no "s," many Americans wrote it Arkansa and pronounced it "Arkansaw," even in Kansas. Explorers such as Pike and Long generally referred to the Arkansa, which may be correct enough, but they also spelled it Arkansaw, as it was pronounced. John Bradbury in 1811 labeled the river Arkansa as it came out of the mountains, but spelled it Arkansas in the state of Arkansas. Schoolcraft spelled it Arkansaw in both poetry and prose.[28]

Unlike some rivers whose names change when they cross a state boundary, the Arkansas River changes only its pronunciation. In Kansas it has the accent on the second syllable and the "s" is not silent; but as soon as it crosses into Oklahoma, the accent moves up to the first syllable and the "s" becomes silent.[29] So Arkansas rhymes with Kansa in Kansas, which may be justified more by rhyme than reason. "I confess I prefer the sound of Arkansaw as being more musical than Arkansas," said Longfellow, who had an appreciation for the poetic line and who might modify a word for the sake of rhyme.[30] But Kansans would not listen to Longfellow; he did not make Arkansas rhyme with Kansas.

The controversy over the pronunciation of Arkansas spread from the "Hills of Arkansaw" to the "Halls of Congress." The suggestion that the Senate change the pronunciation of "Arkansaw" was countered by the cry of "Never!" by the senator from Arkansas, who dramatized the issue by an oratorical outburst to match his provincial pride. When a gazetteer boldly dared to determine the pronunciation by declaring it to be "Arkansas, formerly pronounced Arkansaw," the Arkansawers rose in righteous revolt and

[28] *Expedition of Pike*, II, 397; James, *Account of Long's Expedition* (vol. XIV in Thwaites' *Early Western Travels*), 96 and 144; Thwaites, *Early Western Travels*, XXVIII, 76; Paullin, *Atlas of the Historical Geography of the United States*, plate 29.

[29] *Kansas City Times*, Jan. 17, 1950.

[30] Stewart, *Names on the Land*, 336–37.

declared that the "Arkansas" pronunciation came from "Damn-Yankee books."[31] In a resort to reason and an effort to establish uniformity, the United States Board on Geographic Names decided in 1932 that the pronunciation of the river's name should be "Ark′en-saw." Government decree was as futile as Longfellow's poetic appeal; both were defeated by popular usage.[32]

The Arkansas River has had other names and nicknames. Sieur d'Iberville said that the French would trade with the Spaniards by going up the Marne, meaning the Arkansas. Émile Lauvrière said that the shortest road to the trade of New "Mexique" was "*par la rivière de Marne ou Arkansas et par le Missouri.*"[33] He identified the Marne by using it as a joint name with Arkansas. The mixture of names is well illustrated in one sentence by Mathews: "Iberville had some idea of exploring the Ni-Zhu-Dse, Red Waters, of the Little Ones, called by the French 'Marne'; later called 'Napestle' and by other names, and finally the Arkansas River." The Napestle was, of course, not a later name, but an earlier native name.[34] General Thomas J. Farnham, western explorer, called the Arkansas "that American Nile" and the "River of the Plains."[35]

What was once called the Little Red Arkansas River by the Osages was not the one we know now as the Little Arkansas. Both the Pawnees and the Osages knew the Red Fork or the Salt Fork of the Arkansas as the Little Red River and identified it as the Little Arkansas. Later the river lost its descriptive name of "Little" and became the Red Fork of the Arkansas and so released the "Little" to be used for the present Little Arkansas, which flows into the Big Arkansas from its left bank at Wichita.[36]

It has been suggested that the present Little River, which joins the Big Arkansas at Wichita, was named by the Mallet brothers, Pierre and Paul. These French explorers crossed Kansas too far

[31] *Ibid.*

[32] *Sixth Report*, 102.

[33] *Histoire de la Louisiane Française*, 300.

[34] Mathews, *The Osages*, 124 and 137.

[35] *Travels in the Great Western Prairies* (vol. XXVIII in Thwaites' *Early Western Travels*), 76–77.

[36] For a fuller account of the Little or Red Fork of the Arkansas, see Chapter VIII.

west to have seen the Little River, but they might have heard of it.[37]

In the *Wichita Evening Eagle*, Victor Murdock wrote the following headline for a story on Indian names: "When Little Arkansas Had Three Separate Names From Its Source to Mouth (Elcah, Hoh-cah-hah-shinker, and Ute-cha-og-ra)." Near its source the river was called *Elcah*, and this was interpreted to mean "white rock." It could have been spelled *El-cka*, since the *cka* was the Osage word for "white," which would have described the light-colored limestone in the area. The middle section was called *Ho-cah-hah-shinker*, which was understood to mean "fish creek," and *ho* does mean "fish." The *cah* may again refer to "white" and the *shinker*, as he wrote it, was the Osage *zhinga* or *shunga* for "small." At its confluence with the Arkansas, the Little River was called the *Ute-cha-og-ra*, which Murdock did not interpret. He was of the opinion that when early travelers called it the Little Arkansas, the Osages then began to call it the *Ne-shu-sha-shinker*, his way of writing *Ne Shutsa Shinka*. This would mean that the descriptive name of *Ne Shutsa Shinka* for the Red Fork of the Arkansas had been transferred to the Little River on the north or left side of the Arkansas.[38]

Murdock was correct in assuming that the early travelers had named the Little River of the Arkansas. James R. Mead said that the name was first used by Jacob Fowler who on October 9, 1821, wrote in his journal that the "Osage Indians say it is about two days' travel to the little Arkansas."[39] However, Edwin James not only knew the name a year earlier, but he also assumed that others knew it according to what he said: "This stream of water, we believe, is known to a few hunters, who have had the opportunity to visit it, by the name of *Little Arkansa*."[40] Joseph C. Brown put the Little Arkansas on his map of the Santa Fe Trail in 1827.[41] On Frémont's

[37] Isely, in *Wichita Beacon*, June 23, 1929; Henri Folmer, "Mallet Expedition of 1739 through Nebraska, Kansas and Colorado to Santa Fe," *The Colorado Magazine*, XVI, 164.

[38] *KHQ*, XII, 221; *Wichita Evening Eagle*, March 6, 1943.

[39] Mead, *KHC*, X, 8n.

[40] James, *Account of Long's Expedition* (vol XVI in Thwaites' *Early Western Travels*), 239.

[41] Baughman, *Kansas in Maps*, 30.

map of 1843 the Little Arkansas was penciled in. But the Red Fork did not immediately lose its claim to being the Little Arkansas. The Union Pacific map of 1866 still had "L. Arkansas" as the name for the Red and Salt Fork of the Arkansas.[42]

When James R. Mead talked about promoting the town of Wichita, he said that the plan was to locate it at the junction of the *Neshutsa* and the *Neshutsa Shinka* streams which "we now style the Little and Big Arkansas." In translation this would be the "red river" and the "little red river." The Osages had explained to him that *shinka* meant "little" in the sense of a "child" or "son" and that the Big and Little Arkansas would then be associated as "father" and "son." In this sense it could be applied to the present Little River except for the reference to "red" in *Ne Shutsa Tonga* referring to the "big red" river, as the Arkansas River was called.[43]

Another variation of the name is found in D. B. Emmert's "History of Sedgwick County" in Edwards' atlas. Emmert told of the Osages, under Chief Mintsho Shinka or Little Bear, coming to the Little Arkansas, which he referred to parenthetically as the *Tlo-Shusta-Shinka*, where they camped for their summer hunts. The *Tlo* was unusual and appears to be an error since the Osage used the prefix *ne* for water or river.[44] This is, of course, only another variation of *Ne Shutsa Shinka* which had earlier and correctly been applied to the Little Red Fork of the Arkansas.[45]

So the Little River should not have been called "little," nor was it correctly called the *Ne Shutsa Shinka*, since it was not the "red" river, and some would go so far as to say it should not have been called a river at all. Although "endowed with an imposing name" said Josiah Gregg, it was "only a small creek."[46] "Its bed was so miry, and its banks so steep," said Stanley Vestal (Walter S. Campbell), that "men were always sent ahead with axes, spades, and mat-

[42] Wheat, *Mapping the Trans-Mississippi West*, II, 128; Baughman, *Kansas in Maps*, 74.

[43] Mead, "The Wichita Indians in Kansas," *KHC*, VIII, 173; Mead, *KHC*, X, 8n.

[44] John P. Edwards, *Historical Atlas of Sedgwick County, Kansas*, 8.

[45] Victor Murdock, in *Wichita Evening Eagle*, March 6, 1943.

[46] *Commerce of the Prairies*, 39.

tocks to dig down its banks and cut willows to bridge the quagmire."[47] Max Greene said that its name was a misnomer; he thought it might better have been called Mud Creek.[48] Calling the Little Arkansas River by its full name relates it to the Big Arkansas, which is seldom referred to as the Big. Nor is the Little Arkansas generally spoken of as the Arkansas; it is popularly known as the Little River.

Near the river's source in Rice County is a town that took its name directly from the river; it was named Little River by promoters of a branch of the Santa Fe Railway.[49] In McPherson County a post office located in the valley of the Little River was given the name of Little Valley. The township which the Little River bisects is also called Little Valley.

As the town of Little River got its name from the Little Arkansas River, so Arkansas City derived its name from the Arkansas River. A station on the Santa Fe Trail was known for a time as Arkansas River, but it did not become a city. Arkansas City had four other names before it was renamed for the Arkansas. It had once had the Greek name of Adelphi, a name associated with "brother" as it is in Philadelphia, the "City of Brotherly Love." Adelphi was originally the name of a couple of small islands off the coast of Greece. Then the name was changed to Delphi, which may have been the name that was intended in the first place, since this was the name of the Greek town where the oracle of Apollo was located, familiar to those who knew Greek history. This was a standard form adopted by New York, Tennessee, Indiana, and Missouri, all of which had towns named Delphi.[50]

For a short time the town was named Cresswell. The most important contemporary person with that name was A. G. Cresswell, Postmaster General, who crossed Kansas on his way to Denver for the formal opening of the Kansas-Pacific Railroad in 1870, and

[47] *The Old Santa Fe Trail*, 69.

[48] *The Kanzas Region*, 119.

[49] *Little River Monitor*, Jan. 31 and May 23, 1945.

[50] Howes, in *Kansas City Star*, Dec. 8, 1941; "Dead Towns and Post Offices," KSHS Archives.

it is believed that the town was named for him. In the 1870's two towns, one in Labette County and then one in Marion County, were also named Cresswell.[51]

The present Arkansas City is located where the Walnut River joins the Arkansas, and for a time it was named Walnut City. There was another Walnut City in Rush County, but neither one became a post office before its name was changed. A slight variation of the name may be seen on the 1870 Johnson map of Kansas and Nebraska where it appears as Arkansas City or Little Walnut. This was the year when Arkansas City became the official name.[52] So the town had its name changed from Walnut City, for the name of the smaller river, to Arkansas City for the name of the larger river.

The Osages had their own name for Arkansas City; they called it *Ni-cho-cka ton-won*. It would seem that the first part referred to "salt water." The *ton won* was, of course, the Osage imitation of the English word for town. So the full name for Arkansas City was possibly "salt water town."[53]

Arkansas City is located near the Oklahoma border where the pronunciation of the river's name changes. The town, however, has kept its Kansas pronunciation. "In tribute to their own state, and in mild defiance of their neighbors," said one writer, "the people here call it 'ar-Kan'zas' City."[54] For the full name this is true, but it is a long name which the public has shortened to Ark City.

51 Mrs. Frank C. Montgomery, "Fort Wallace and its Relation to the Frontier," *KHC*, XVII, 246.

52 Howes, in *Kansas City Star*, Dec. 8, 1941; Missouri Pacific Railroad Company, *The Empire that the Missouri Pacific Built*, 91.

53 La Flesche, *A Dictionary of the Osage Language*, 106.

54 Alfred H. Holt, *American Place Names*, 20.

▲ VII

Nepaholla and Nemiskua: Solomon and Saline

THERE IS SALT IN THE SOIL of Kansas, salt in its streams and springs, and there is salt underneath its surface. The rock salt beneath the surface is from two hundred to four hundred feet in thickness. In round figures the amount has been estimated at five trillion tons, and that is a lot of round figures and a lot of salt.[1] Salt is a big industry in Kansas, and it is a commodity that has served as a source for a number of Kansas place-names. Seven Kansas post offices have contained the descriptive word "salt" in their names. Hutchinson, in the center of the salt industry, is nicknamed Salt City. The Indians were fully aware of the presence of salt in the Kansas streams long before the French discovered it. Their names tell us so.

John Bradbury, a contemporary of Captain Pike, realized the extent of the saline qualities of the Kansas streams. "It appears," he said, "that this salt deposit passes under the Arkansas to the northwest, and impregnates two branches of the Kanzas River of the Missouri."[2] "West of the Republican River," said Isaac McCoy, "are many running streams of salt water."[3] Zebulon M. Pike, the first of the Anglo-Americans to traverse central Kansas, said that he had camped on a stream which was "strongly impregnated with salt," a stream which was "distinctly called Great or Grand Saline."[4]

[1] Douglas, *KHC*, XI, 92 and 175; Kansas Industrial Development Commission, *Let's Look at Kansas*.

[2] *Travels in the Interior of America* (vol. V in Thwaites' *Early Western Travels*), 242.

[3] McCoy to Sec. of War, Jan. 31, 1831, 22 Cong., 1 sess., *Exec. Doc. No. 172*, 12.

[4] *Expedition of Pike*, II, 404–405n.

In the Pawnee language the word for salt was *kait*; in the Siouan language of the Kansas and Osages it was *skua* or *scua*. The meaning of *skua* was obscured by spelling it *skah* and pronouncing it "squaw." In most cases the French names for these streams were translations of the Indian names, but the Solomon River is an exception to this. The most distinctive feature of the Solomon is the presence of a remarkable spring which the natives believed had strong religious and spiritual powers. This spring was known as *Ne-Wakonda* or the "great spirit spring," a name closely linked with the native names for the Solomon River.

One of the Indian names for the Solomon was *Wisgapella*, which meant "salt water," said George Remsburg.[5] The Solomon is fed in part by Salt Creek which Zebulon M. Pike called the Little Saline.[6] It is also fed by *Ne-Wakonda*, "sacred springs," famous for their mineral content. Its name has been spelled *Wiskapella* and *Wus-cu-pa-lo*, but the meaning has not changed.[7] Perhaps it should have been spelled *Niscuapalla* or *Nescua-Pawhola*, which would have meant "salt water on a hill," the descriptive name for the sacred springs of Waconda.

The Pawnee name for the Solomon was *Kits-i-wits'uk*, which lends itself to some freedom in spelling. It may be *Kitz-a-witz-uk* or, possibly, *Kits'u-te-kit-uk*. The first part refers to water. George Grinnell, who associated the name with the sacred springs, said that *te-kit-uk* means "It is above." He also translated *Kitz-a-witz-uk* as "water on a bank" and "water over it." Hyde gave a similar name, *Kitsa-we-cha-ku*, translated as "fountain by a stream." "It is called *Pa'howa* sometimes," said Grinnell.[8] *Pa'howa* or *Pahola* means "hill." This could refer to the high bank built up by the mineral deposit of the spring.

Quite similar in meaning was the Indian name of *Nepaholla* for the Solomon River. This name was better known and much longer in use than was the Pawnee name of *Kitzawitzuk*. Isaac McCoy

[5] *Scrapbook*, I, 91.
[6] Scheffer, *KHQ*, III, 233.
[7] Root, *KHQ*, III, 339.
[8] Grinnell, *American Anthropologist* (n.s.), XV, 331; Grinnell, *Pawnee Hero Stories and Folk Tales*, 358.

said that *Nepaholla* was a "Kau-zau" or Kansas name for the Solomon, and he translated it to mean "water on a hill." When Captain L. H. North accompanied some Pawnees on their way to Fort Harker to return stolen horses, they crossed what the Pawnees called "salt creek," and from there they could see a hill in the distance. "That is *Pahowa*," said Fighting Chief of the Pawnees, pointing to the hill. There, he said, was the spring where the Pawnees in the past had offered their sacrifices.[9] It would not be unreasonable to assume that *Pahowa* had the same origin as *Ne Paholla*, meaning "water on a hill." The Siouan word for hill was *pa-ha*, and perhaps the Pawnee chief used a Siouan name when he said *Pahowa*.[10]

The source for the "water on a hill" description of the Solomon came evidently from the "great spirit spring" or *Wakonda*, which was also called *Nepaholla*. "Ne-pa-hol-la," wrote John McCoy to F. H. Adams, came from "the singular pool described in my father's book in your library."[11] "The name originated from the peculiar situation of the Great Spirit Spring, along the river's course near the present site of Cawker City," wrote another.[12] Both the river and the spring have been named the *Nepaholla*, but the description of "water on a hill" fits the spring better than the river. According to Isaac McCoy, the river was properly called *Nepaholla*. The Kansas called the sacred spring *Ne-Woh'kon-daga*. The Omahas also emphasized the sacred spirit in naming the Solomon River, which they called *Niwa'xube-ke*, translated as "holy river."[13]

Wakonda was the name of the great spirit or the supreme god not only of the Kansas and Osages but of all the related Siouan tribes. Among the spirits *Wakonda* was "the greatest and the best." He was the "creator," the "fountain of mystic medicine," and the "spirit of the sun." In a broader sense, "anything which exerted a

[9] *KHQ*, V, 373n.; McCoy to Adams, "Names," MS, KSHS Archives; Hyde, *Pawnee Indians*, 66–67; Grinnell, *Pawnee Hero Stories and Folk Tales*, 358.

[10] Hyde, *Pawnee Indians*, 66–67; Grinnell, *Pawnee Hero Stories and Folk Tales*, 358–59.

[11] "Names," MS, KSHS Archives.

[12] Scheffer, *KHQ*, III, 230.

[13] *KHQ*, V, 373n.; Fletcher and La Flesche, "The Omaha Tribe," *BAE Twenty-seventh Annual Report* (1905–1906), 94.

force which the Kansa did not understand was a Wakonda."[14] When the arrows of the *Nika-shu-Dse*, "the red man" (British soldiers), curved around George Washington and missed him, it was because he had been protected by *Wah' Kon*, the "mystery spirit," said the Indians.[15]

Ne Wakonda was not an exclusively Siouan center, since the Pawnees also held the place sacred, as did the Potawatomis, an Algonquian tribe from the East. Among the Algonquians, *Manitou* was the great spirit god comparable to *Wakonda*. The Potawatomis, immigrant tribes, also sacrificed to the great spirit of the springs, but they called the place *Meaton' beesh*.[16] The *Meaton* appears to be a variation of the French name *Manitou* or the English *Manito*.[17]

The Indians have a legend which adds romance to the story of the great spirit spring. The story tells about a beautiful Indian maid who was the pride and joy of her family. Her name was Waconda. One day she came across a wounded man who was crying for water. She hurried to the spring and brought back water in her deerskin bag to quench his thirst and she washed his wound. Then they discovered that they belonged to rival tribes. But the two met again, at first by chance and later secretly by plan. They fell in love. But Waconda's father could not permit their marriage contrary to the tribal laws. He called for a council with the enemy which ended in arguments and then war. During the battle, Takota, Waconda's lover, was struck by an arrow and fell into the blue-green waters of the pool. Waconda had been watching the battle and when she saw her lover fall, she dashed to the edge of the pool and with raised arms appealed to the gods and plunged in after him.

The battle ceased and the braves withdrew quietly. Then and forever after they called the pool where the spirit of the two lovers resided *Waconda*. And there the natives have assembled to offer their sacrifices and to worship.[18]

[14] Connelley, "Notes on the Early Indian Occupancy of the Great Plains," *KHC*, XIV, 458; James, *Account of Long's Expedition* (vol. XV in Thwaites' *Early Western Travels*), 51.

[15] Mathews, *The Osages*, 7 and 227.

[16] Root, *KHQ*, III, 339.

[17] Hodge, *Handbook of American Indians*, I, 800.

[18] Pamphlet advertising Waconda Springs; Blackmar, *Kansas: A Cyclopedia of*

Now the Indians are gone and *Ne Wakonda* is losing its popularity and prestige. It may not rise and fall with the tides, as suggested by Robert L. Ripley in *Believe It or Not*, but it may soon be submerged by a dam across the Solomon. *Ne Wakonda*, the great spirit spring, once a sacred Indian shrine and once known as "water on a hill," may soon be a shrine at the bottom of a lake. However, the lake will fortunately retain the name of the great Siouan spirit, *Wakonda*.

There were many ways to spell *Wakonda*. Lewis and Clark and Pike were quite perplexed by the name. Mathews spoke of the great spirit god of the Little Osages as *Wah' Kon-Tah*. This is also the way it was spelled in the story of the Black Dog band. But there was little reason to assume that this was much different from the French *Ouakondah*. Morehouse and Spencer spelled it *Waucondah* and *Wah-kun-dah*.[19] Other forms were *Waukantanka*, *Wahkundah*, *Waucondah*, *Wahkontah*, *Waconda Da*, and *Ne Woh'kon-daga*.

On the Johnson map of 1870 this historical site had the simple name of Salt Springs. In the following year the Mills and Smith map of Kansas retained the English name but restored its religious significance by giving it the double descriptive name of Great Spirit or Salt Spring. The Indian name for the springs was revived from time to time and finally survived. An early Mitchell County town was named Wauconda, but as a post office it was given the name of Waconda.

The endless search for health brought the white frontiersman to the health-giving waters of the Indian's great spirit springs. It was then commercialized as a health resort with a hotel and a brewery. There would surely be patients at the hotel who believed that if the spring water were good, beer made from good spring water would be better. The place was given the combination Indian and English name of Waconda Springs.[20]

State History, I, 787; G. E. Patrick, "The Great Spirit Spring," Kansas Academy of Science *Transactions*, VII, 23.

[19] Tillie Karns Newman, *Black Dog Trail*, 20; Morehouse, *KHC*, X, 358; Mathews, *The Osages*, 7, 32, 358, and 373.

[20] Andreas and Cutler, *History of Kansas*, 1028.

The *Wakonda* or *Wah' Kon Tah* name has been used in other areas. In Missouri it is spelled Wakenda and in South Dakota it is Wakonda. The name has also been used for a motel in Portland, Oregon, far from the great spirit springs, which indicates the migration of names; there it was spelled Wa-Kan-Da.

It took a long time for *Nepaholla* to be replaced by the name of Solomon. On a map in Hale's *Kanzas and Nebraska* the river was still listed as the "Nepahalla or Solomon's Fork." Catton's map of 1855 dropped the Indian name and called it just the Solomon. Yet in 1861 it was still "Solomon's F.'s or Nepaholla R." "Marched early," said Lieutenant Pike, "and passed a large fork of the Kans river, which I suppose to be the one generally called Solomon's." It is of interest to note that he used Kans instead of Smoky Hill and that the name Solomon's Fork had been "generally" known. The *Tescott News* mistakenly gave Pike credit for having named the Solomon.[21]

One Ottawa County resident came to the conclusion that Pike had derived the name Solomon from the French word *salement*, or, as he said, "sa-le-man," which meant "dirty." The words sound very much alike.[22] The Indians had called the Republican Fork the "dirty" or "filthy" river, but not the Solomon, as far as we know. The similarity in sound between *salement* and Solomon is, of course, poor proof of a common origin.

When Senator John J. Ingalls asked F. G. Adams of the state historical society for the origin of the name, Adams wrote to John C. McCoy to get the information. "My impression," wrote McCoy, "is that a man named 'Solomon' connected with a company of early Rocky Mountain trappers was either lost or robbed by the Indians on that stream." He realized that this was vague and added, "The first time I see Fred. Chouteau he can no doubt settle the fact." There is no evidence to show that he ever saw Chouteau "to settle the fact."[23]

"Our river has decidedly a Hebraic name," wrote W. L. Cham-

[21] Dec. 26, 1940.

[22] Scheffer, *KHQ*, III, 231.

[23] McCoy to Adams, July 5, 1883, "Names," MS, KSHS Archives; Scheffer, *KHQ*, III, 231; *Emporia Daily News*, July 23, 1883.

bers, and he concluded that it was "probably Solomonized from some early Jewish trader at Solomon City."[24] This is obviously an error, since the river had been "Solomonized" long before there was a Solomon City. Nor was it named for Everett Solomon, a half-breed on one of Frémont's expeditions, since that event was also too late. The town, of course, was named for the river. It was also said to have been called for a short time Wiskapella for the salt water of the Solomon. The source for the elusive Solomon name may be found in the name of a French trader or official.

Among the traders whose name may have been used was Solomon Petit, who was mentioned in Zinon Truteau's journal. He was a shrewd and sharp trader on the Missouri at the close of the eighteenth century. There is only a suggestion but no real evidence that the Solomon was named for Solomon Petit.[25]

In 1739 a French expedition under the Mallet brothers crossed Kansas in search of a route to the Spanish settlements at Santa Fe. They must have had trouble crossing the Solomon since they called it the *Rivière des Soucis*, the "river of worries." This was a name which deservedly disappeared. It would have been better, perhaps, to honor the French official who sent them.

The suggestion from William A. Phillips that the name came from Salmon was not a reference to fish but rather to a French official.[26] A possible source was found in a reference to a "*Lettre de MM. Bienville et Salmon.*"[27] In a report on the Mallet expedition, the two are identified as "Messr. de Bienville, Governor, and Salmon, Intendant of Louisiana." Both Bienville and Salmon wrote instructions regarding the Mallet brothers and the Fabry de la Bruyere expeditions to New Mexico. This makes Salmon important enough to have his name preserved as the name of a river. It was a relatively simple matter to change Salmon to Solomon. On a map based on the information of Isaac McCoy and his sons the river was called Nepaholla or "Salomon's Fork," as it was also on a War De-

[24] *Rooks County Record*, March 14, 1940.

[25] A. P. Nasatir, *Before Lewis and Clark*, I, 287–94; Diller, *KHQ*, XXI, 405.

[26] "Origin of City Names," *KHC*, VII, 484.

[27] Herbert E. Bolton, "French Intrusion into New Mexico," in *Pacific Ocean in History* (ed. by H. Morse Stephens and Herbert Bolton), 391n.

partment map for 1867.[28] There was seemingly a political reason for changing *Wisgapella* to Salmon or Solomon, and not, as was suggested, to make it "more euphonious."[29]

The best known of the salty streams was the Saline which, as Pike said, had been "distinctly called Great or Grand Saline." It may have been the Saline, however, that was called *Rivière de la Fleche*, or "river of the arrow," by the Mallet brothers. No doubt some incident was the source for this name, but it was neither official nor lasting. When the French named the river Saline, they could have named it for its saline content, but they seemingly knew the Siouan or Kansa language well enough to have translated its Indian name of *Ne-Miskua*, which meant "saline" or "salt river." The *ne* and *mi* referred to "water," as it does in Minnesota or Minnetonka, and *skua* meant "salt."[30]

The French gave the Saline a special distinction by calling it the *Grande Saline*. Since there were several Salines in Kansas, it was desirable to have a qualifying description. Yet for a time the French ignored the salt and deleted the "saline" part of the name and called it the *Grande*. This descriptive name was too common and confusing and it lacked distinction, so the *Grande* was dropped and again the river became known as the Saline, as it is today. Its full name now, however, is the Saline Fork of the Smoky Hill River.

The Saline River, which flows into the Smoky Hill at Salina, was the source for the name of Saline County. William A. Phillips, the founder of Salina, said that the name of the city originated as a "fancy" of his, and so it was; he named it Saliena. The fancy part of the name was soon deleted and it was simplified to Salina. This name was sufficiently common to have been a county name in five states and in Mexico. The Salina in Mexico or the Salinas in California brings out its Spanish character. The Indian origin of the

[28] Baughman, *Kansas in Maps*, 24; Library of Congress maps.

[29] Folmer, *The Colorado Magazine*, XVI, 164; Folmer, "Etienne Veniard de Bourgmont in the Missouri Country," *Missouri Historical Review*, XXXVI, 285; Nasatir, *Before Lewis and Clark*, I, 29; Remsburg, *Scrapbook*, I, 91.

[30] John C. McCoy, in *Emporia Democratic News*, July 23, 1883; Remsburg, *Scrapbook*, I, 73.

name was *Ne Miskua*, which the French changed to Saline. The name of the town was given a Spanish spelling as Salina, to which the Americans have now given an English pronunciation with little thought of its linguistic evolution.[31]

[31] *KHC*, VII, 484; Kane, *The American Counties*, 15; Federal Writers' Project, *A Guide to Salina*, 23.

VIII

Ninnescah to Nescatunga

All of the Kansas streams south of the Arkansas have enough salt to have earned, at some time or another, French variations of the name Saline. There was a *Grande Saline*, often confused with the Grande Saline Fork of the Smoky Hill, a *Forte Saline*, poorly translated as Fort Sal, a Saline Creek, and a Little Saline. Although the names were applied rather promiscuously to any and all of these southern streams, it was finally the Salt Fork (or Red Fork) of the Arkansas that preserved the name in English.

Stephen H. Long listed four Saline rivers in a row. He got the names from the French, no doubt, but he also retained a couple of the native names. He did not get them in proper order. He listed the first from the North as the Negracka or Red Fork, confusing it with the Ninnescah. His Strong Saline was likely the French *Forte Saline*, possibly for the Chikaskia. Then he had a Saline Creek, which might be the present Bluff Creek or possibly the Medicine Lodge River. Finally, he listed the "Nesuketonga or Grand Saline," which, in sequence, would be the present Red or Salt Fork.[1]

West of Wichita and following close to the Arkansas is a creek called the Big Slough. Farther west flows the Cowskin Creek. Both of the two creeks flowing into Cowskin Creek from the west are called Dry Creek, which might indicate that the Cowskin carries little water. However, it floods easily, as does Slough Creek, which explains the name of the latter. The name of the Cowskin is associated with the cattle trails into Kansas. Texas fever was a deadly disease, and, as the cattle died on the trail, only their hides had

[1] Wheat, *Mapping the Trans-Mississippi West*, II, 80–81.

value. When freighters saw numerous hides spread out above the creek bank for salting and drying, they named the creek Cowskin.[2]

The Indians, however, had named it the *Cah-hatshen-kah-itshisha*. This long name, according to Victor Murdock, meant "crooked creek," and the creek meanders enough to justify the name. Murdock liked the name so well, in spite of its cumbersome length, that he wrote articles in the *Wichita Eagle* to advocate changing the name of the Cowskin back to its Indian name. In this he failed—fortunately some would say. The translation may also be challenged, although the Anglicized spelling makes it difficult to identify the Indian name. It could possibly be translated to mean something about a "horse blanket." The difficulty with a name such as *Cah-hatsken-kah-itshisha* is its length, and it would surely have been abbreviated and easily shortened to Cah or Kah, which would have added confusion to the name of the Kansas river called the Kaw.[3]

The next south-side fork of the Arkansas is the lovely, tree-lined stream called the Ninnescah. Although variation in the spelling of Ninnescah may be confusing, it may also be a guide to a logical source. The name has been spelled Ninneskua, Neanesquaw, Ne-Ne-Squaw, and Nee-niskaw. A letter written from a post office named Lorette in Kingman County in 1879 identified its location and its name as follows: "We are 34 miles west and 6 south of Wichita—Smoot Creek and the South Ninnie Squaw."[4] Making the final syllable "squaw" was in keeping with the sound of *skua*, but the error in spelling was most misleading in regard to its meaning. Because of the "squaw" ending, there were those who said the Nenesquaw meant "beautiful squaw." School children took liberties with the name, and the Ninnescah neighborhood has accepted their interpretation that the name meant "Knee-deep-to-a-squaw."[5]

Ninnescah is an Osage-Siouan name. The first part of the name means "water," but what kind of water has become a matter of

[2] Isely quoting Russell Bigelow, in *Wichita Beacon*, June 30, 1929.

[3] *Wichita Evening Eagle*, March 6, 1943, and *Sumner County Press*, Jan. 29, 1874.

[4] Kingman County Diamond Jubilee *Souvenir Historical Program*.

[5] Root, *KHQ*, VI, 143.

choice. It has been defined as "salt," "good," "spring," "clear," "running white water," just "white water," and "white spring." James R. Mead said that its waters came out of "a group of springs flowing out of the Tertiary gravel," and he concluded that the name meant "good spring water."[6]

Some of the early maps combined the Indian name with the English name of "good." The Union Pacific map for 1868 had it listed as "Ne-ne-Sosh or Good R." Johnson's 1870 map of Kansas called it the "Ninne Scah or Good." On some maps this was simplified by dropping the Indian name and calling it the Good River. It was not the river that was "good," but the water that was supposed to be good. In fact, there was a post office on the Good River west of Clearwater in 1876 which was named Good Water.[7]

One descriptive name made it the "running white river." Then the "running" was left out and it became the "white river." Somewhat in keeping with this interpretation was the opinion of A. W. Stubbs who said that the name should be pronounced "Ne-thne-skah" and that *nethne* meant "spring" and *skah* meant "white." This would make it the "white spring" river. Murdock spelled it Nen-ne-scah and gave it the same meaning as Stubbs.[8] Nathan Boone used both the Indian name and its English translation, "Ne-ne-scah, or clear water river." The acceptance of "clear water" for the meaning of Ninnescah has been popularized by the naming of a town for the river and calling it Clear Water, now put into one word as Clearwater. This has become the most widely accepted translation for Ninnescah. It may be correct.

However, a more accurate translation may be found in one of the original forms of the word, Ninneskua. The ending of the name, whether spelled *escua* or *skua*, meant "salt" in the Osage language. The spelling of the final syllable as "squaw" tends to support the assumption that the original Indian word was Ninne-

[6] Baughman, *Kansas in Maps*, 74; Mead, "Origin of Names of Kansas Streams," Kansas Academy of Science *Transactions*, XVIII, 215.

[7] J. S. Bird (ed.), *Historical Plat Book of Jackson County*, 11; Baughman, *Kansas in Maps*, 74.

[8] Letter to Adams, May 23, 1896, "Names," MS, KSHS Archives; "Captain Nathan Boone's Journal" (ed. by W. Julian Fessler), *Chronicles of Oklahoma*, VII, 63; *Sumner County Press*, Jan. 29, 1874.

skua. So Ninnescah most likely meant "salt water" even though the water may run clear. This was also the opinion of John McCoy, and he appears to be correct.[9] The 1806 map of Lewis and Clark listed the first river south of the Arkansas as the Niscua, so this name, which means "salt water," was then applied to the Ninnescah, unless Lewis and Clark referred to the salty Rattlesnake Creek which flows into Salt Creek.[10]

By 1876, Rand McNally had adopted the present form for spelling Ninnescah, and this was the form used by the towns which were named for the river. The town named Ninnescah on the Arkansas River on the Sumner-Cowley county border seems to have been a post office name in both counties. The town company quarreled and split, and a New Ninnescah was founded. Neither one kept its name, and the place was renamed Bushnell and then disappeared.[11] When Charles N. Gould, Oklahoma geologist, came to Kingman County, Kansas, he said he settled at Ninnescah, "afterwards called Cunningham."[12] Ninnescah had been a post office on the Ninnescah River and was a stop for Colonel D. R. Green's "Cannonball" stage. The town blew away in a tornado in 1887, and with it went its name. When a new post office was established in the neighborhood the following year, it was promoted and established by James D. Cunningham on his land and named Cunningham.[13] Two Ninnescahs disappeared as post-office names, but three counties, Reno, Sedgwick, and Kingman, have townships named Ninnescah.

While surveying the southern boundary of Kansas, Colonel Joseph E. Johnston and his men crossed all the border streams. In most cases the colonel knew their Indian names, mostly Osage, and generally he knew the meaning of the names. While he was still on the east side of the Arkansas River, he crossed streams which had Osage names meaning "salt." There was, for example, the *Niskeo-*

[9] Letter to Adams, July 5, 1883, "Names," MS, KSHS Archives.

[10] Wheat, *Mapping the Trans-Mississippi West*, II, facing page 50.

[11] Andreas and Cutler, *History of Kansas*, 1495.

[12] *Covered Wagon Geologist*, 26 and 29.

[13] L. L. Michener to *Wichita Beacon*, June 9, 1929, MS, Kansas Collection, Wichita State University Library; Kingman County Diamond Jubilee *Souvenir Historical Program*.

kaka, as he wrote it, which he interpreted to mean "salt creek." It was probably Onion Creek. The name might better have been spelled *Neskuakaxa*. The *ne* for "water," *skua* for "salt," and *kaxa* or *gaxa* for "creek."[14] After crossing the Arkansas, Johnston was in an even more salty county. Early maps of eastern Sumner County refer to a Salt Springs Creek just west of Geuda Springs whose near neighbor and rival was Salt City. It had once been named Remato, which resembles the Spanish *remate*, meaning "end" or "border." Farther north is another Salt Springs.[15] In Sumner County, or just below, Johnston's company had first crossed the *Bay-Chay-ne-ata*, also written *Bache-e-ne-o-ta*, or "Whisky-drinking creek."[16] One might be sympathetic to those who found whisky preferable to the saline waters of southern Kansas.

The early travelers in the area must have tried the water, however, and found it unsatisfactory. The next branch of this creek, where the company camped, about fourteen miles west of the Arkansas, is now called Bitter Creek. This seems to be the one called *Ni-hi-pa* by the Osages and Good-for-nothing Creek by the Americans. The town which was once located on the creek took the English name of Bitter Creek rather than the Indian name.[17]

South of the Ninnescah flows the Chikaskia, another stream which has retained its distinctive Indian name. It joins Bluff Creek in Kansas and continues into Oklahoma to enter the Salt Fork of the Arkansas south of Blackwell. Chikaskia has been said to be of Caddoan origin, which would make it a Pawnee name. This may be open to question. Examination of the earlier forms of the name reveals hidden meanings and a possible source.[18]

Nathan Boone in 1843 camped on a ravine near the *Shaw-wa-cos-pay*. A note identified the location as on "the headwaters of Grove Creek, a tributary of the Chikaskia River, called by the Osages,

[14] Nyle H. Miller, "Surveying the Southern Boundary Line of Kansas," *KHQ*, I, 112.

[15] Andreas and Cutler, *History of Kansas*, 1494.

[16] Miller, *KHQ*, I, 116 and n.

[17] *Ibid.*; *KHQ*, IV, 402.

[18] Ingleman, "Indian Place Names in Kansas" (thesis, University of Kansas, 1929), 3.

Shaw-wa-cos-pa."[19] Josiah Gregg was probably more nearly correct when he spelled it *Shah-wa-cos-kah.*[20] According to A. W. Stubbs of Garden City, it should have been spelled *Shah-ya-skah* or *Shah-gas-skah.* Then he gave it a rather strange interpretation. He said that *shahga* meant "fingernails" and *skah* meant "white," so the name meant "white fingernails." An equally strange interpretation was given by Murdock, who spelled it *Shaw-wah-cas-pa* and suggested that it meant an "accident from a falling tree."[21] By deleting the second syllable from *Shaw-wa-cos-pa* or from Gregg's *Shaw-wa-cos-kah*, as was done by Stubbs, the evolution toward Chikaskia can be seen. Again, *skah* was probably a change from *skua* for "salt." Stubbs' statement that *skah* meant "white" may be justified, since the Osage *cka* meant "white." It may have been salt that made the banks of the saline river look white. There are several cases, including the Ninnescah, where the translation of the Indian word for salt has come out "white." It can be assumed that Chikaskia was an evolution of the earlier names, yet on the Rand McNally map of 1876 both names were used: "Shawacospah or Chikaskia."

In 1871 a post office in Sumner County was named Chikaskia. The town died and with it the name, except for its use as a township name in three counties, Sumner, Kingman, and Harper, and, of course, as the popular name of the Chikaskia River.

West of the Chikaskia flows Bluff Creek, which joins the Chikaskia just below the Kansas border. On its banks is Bluff City, a town that was once designated county seat of Harper County but was so elusive that it could not be found. While exploring the border, Colonel Boone said that he had camped on a "creek call'd Pa-ha-bee, a branch of the Red Fork."[22] Bluff Creek does become a branch of the Red Fork after it joins the Chikaskia. Before the Chikaskia name became fixed below the junction, there were those

[19] Boone, *Chronicles of Oklahoma*, VII, 60 and 72.

[20] Baughman, *Kansas in Maps*, 31; Wheat, *Mapping the Trans-Mississippi West*, II, 181.

[21] Letter to Adams, May 23, 1896, "Names," MS, KSHS Archives; *Sumner County Press*, Jan. 29, 1874.

[22] Boone, *Chronicles of Oklahoma*, VII, 60 and 72.

who used the Indian name for Bluff Creek all the way to the Red Fork. Watson's railroad and county map of 1875 put the *Pa-ha-bee* below the junction, calling it Pahakee Creek. Other forms of the name were *Pahobe* and *Pahabe*. It was even abbreviated to Pah. The Indians "call this Pa-ha-bee," said Boone, but he did not tell us which Indians. The *Pa-ha* of *Pa-ha-be* has a resemblance to the Siouan name for "hill," and this time the *Pa-ha* might have been a "bluff." The Indian artifacts found in the area, however, appear to be of Pawnee craftsmanship.

Colonel Johnston, the surveyor, said that his party had crossed "the red bluff seen already yesterday." This would imply that the red bluff was quite conspicuous. "The bank of the river," continued Johnston, "is perpendicular & 30 or 40 ft. high, of red clay."[23] Bluff Creek was also called *Ne-shu-che-sink*, obviously a Siouan name. Comparing this with other Osage or Siouan names, one may conclude that *shu-che*, like *sudgeh*, meant "red," and that *sink*, like *sinka* or *shinka*, meant "little." Then the name would mean "water, red, little," and that would make the name "little red river." The name fits well enough, but it does get confused with the Osage name for the Little Red Fork of the Arkansas which was called the *Ne-Shutsa Sinka*.[24]

Farther west, with its source in Comanche County, flows the Salt Fork of the Arkansas. It has had a troublesome time getting its identity established. It started with Indian names which few could spell. It has had French names which came from the Indians, and it has had, not one, but three English names—the Little Arkansas, the Red Fork, and the Salt Fork of the Arkansas, all translated from their native names. Calling it the Little Arkansas has confused it with the present Little River of the left bank of the Big Arkansas; calling it the Jefferson was a fleeting honor or an error; calling it the Cimarron gave it a Spanish name, which was a mistake in geography; calling it the *Grande Saline* gave it a French interpretation of its Indian name; calling it the Red Fork described it well and is still its name at its source; calling it the Salt Fork was also a trans-

[23] Miller, *KHQ*, I, 117.
[24] *Ibid.*; Mead, *KHC*, X, 8.

lation of its Indian name and a correct one for its downstream area.[25]

The Pawnees, who came all the way across Kansas to hunt, to steal horses, and to procure salt, had their own name for the Salt Fork of the Arkansas. They called it *Kiz pahuti hoddi*, which, like the Osage name, meant "little red river." Later the river became known as both the Little River and the Red River. The Pawnees are also said to have called it the *Kai it tu*, referring to its salty taste. So both the Red and the Salt names have Pawnee origins also.[26] Major George C. Sibley, traveling with an Osage hunting expedition in 1811, said that the streams on the southwest side of the Arkansas "are deeply tinged with red, and are slightly brackish."[27] Both of these characteristics of the river, "red" and "brackish," are found in the names of the Red or Salt Fork of the Arkansas.

The source for all the names may be found by taking the names step by step. The *Nescatunga* has been called "little" at one time and "big" at another; it has been called "red" at one time and "salt" at another. These apparent contradictions and differences can be explained by following the evolution of the name. Since the Big Arkansas was called by the Osages *Ne-Shutsa-Tonka*, the "big red river," then the Red Fork of the Arkansas was, by contrast, the *Ne-Shutsa-Shinka*, the "little red river." From this it became known as the Little Red Fork of the Arkansas.[28] Abbreviated as it was by deleting all but the first and last part of the name, it became the Little Arkansas. It could, however, easily lose its first name of Little and be shortened to Red Fork. And this, too, was done. In a report on the survey of the southern Kansas boundary in 1857 by Colonel Johnston, reference is made to what "Joe says the Osages call the Little Arkansas: the Red Fork as Col. Boone calls it." Each one used only a part of the full name.[29]

Mathews introduced a variation of the native names, *Ni-Ckiu-E-Tonkah*, said to mean "salt fork." With *tonkah* at the end, it really means the "Big" Salt Fork, or as the French named it, the

[25] *Expedition of Pike*, II, 552n.

[26] Hyde, *Pawnee Indians*, 282; Grinnell, *American Anthropologist* (n.s.), XV, 331.

[27] "Extracts from the Diary of Major Sibley," *Chronicles of Oklahoma*, V, 212.

[28] Mathews, *The Osages*, 137 and 187; *Expedition of Pike*, II, 552n.

[29] Miller, *KHQ*, I, 116.

Grande Saline. Victor Murdock understood the name to be *Ne-sne-e-cah-hah* which he translated as "big salt."[30] It has been suggested that the Kansas called the Nescatunga the *Che-tunga,* which meant "big lake." They may have seen it at high water when the flatlands were flooded, but it is more likely that the interpretation should have been "big salt." One may detect in *Che-tunga* an abbreviated form of *Ne-shu-che-tunga,* or *Ne-Shudse-Tonga,* which made it a "big" river or "lake," whether "red" or "salt."[31] Mathews added another interpretation or name when he called it the "Low-Forest-Water Salt Fork of the Arkansas." This must have been one of his Osage interpretations.[32]

There were many more varieties in the spelling of the name, but in some cases they were merely indicative of carelessness or lack of knowledge. The *Ne-scua-tunga,* also written *Neskuatonga,* meaning "water, salt, big," becomes the logical source for the French name of *Grande Saline,* from which the Salt Fork got its name.[33]

In the transition from the native names to the English or French, we find combination names. The French, for example, combined the names as *Nesuhutong R. ou Grande.* Even this name is abbreviated since the *Grande* should be describing something, in this case, *Saline.* William Clark's map of about 1809 included the Osage name for the Little Red River together with the French name. Stephen F. Long called it the "Nesuketonga or Red Fork," a dual name rather than an English translation. James Wilkinson, on Pike's expedition, spelled the name Neskalonska. Nathan Boone was not able to identify these saline rivers correctly until he met some Osage hunters; from then on he called the *Grand Saline* the Nescatunga. On Cram's map of 1883 it is the "Nestugunta River." By the twentieth century the acceptable names were Nescotonga and Nescatunga, neither of which is too far from its meaning if one were to spell it Nescuatunga.[34]

[30] Mathews, *The Osages,* 708; *Wichita Evening Eagle,* March 6, 1943.

[31] Sibley, *The Road to Santa Fe* (ed. by Kate L. Gregg), 62.

[32] *The Osages,* 305 and 708.

[33] A. A. Taylor, "Medicine Lodge Peace Council," *Chronicles of Oklahoma,* II, 117n.

[34] Andreas and Cutler, *History of Kansas,* frontispiece by Cram; *Expedition of*

Three of the names, Nescatunga, Red, and Salt, are still in use, but each is assigned to a separate part of the stream. Of the three converging sources of the river in Comanche County, the central one is called the Red Fork; the creek from the north is called the Nescotonga on the Gallup's 1930 Kansas wall map, but Nescatunga on more recent maps. From the south flows Mustang Creek, which joins the Red Fork very near its junction with the Nescatunga. Then, having acquired color and character from the red soil with its salty content, it becomes the Salt Fork of the Arkansas.

In 1884, Nescatunga became the name of a town in Comanche County. It was promoted by the Nescutunga Town and Immigration Company which changed one vowel for the name of the town. When Jeremiah E. Platt, a circuit rider, rode into "Nescotunga," he described it as "a bright little village." It lasted as a post office until 1894 and three years later the "bright little village" disappeared.[35]

The name that got lost was the Negracka. It had been used for the Ninnescah, but here it may have been out of order. It had also been used as one of the names for the Nescatunga or the Salt Fork.[36] The name was even given to the Cimarron, most likely in error. However, one may be tolerant of the error when one sees that the Cimarron and the Salt Fork were two names mistakenly used for the same river.[37]

Some of the early explorers of the Arkansas Valley and the Southwest did not realize that the Cimarron, after a couple of curves into Kansas, left for Oklahoma. In Comanche County it was within a few miles of connecting with the Salt Fork of the Arkansas, and it was a natural error to map it as a continuation. Even as late as 1839 one map, referring to it as the Cimarone, had it flowing into the Arkansas River near Dodge City. Another had it disappearing in the sands of the Southwest. This might explain

Pike, II, 552n. and 549n.; Boone, *Chronicles of Oklahoma*, VII, 68n.; cf. maps in Wheat, *Mapping the Trans-Mississippi West*, II.

[35] Platt, *KHQ*, XII, 381.

[36] *The Journal of Captain John R. Bell* (ed. by Harlin M. Fuller; vol. VI in Hafen's *The Far West and the Rockies*), 241n.

[37] Boone, *Chronicles of Oklahoma*, VII, 91n.

its being called the "Cimarron or Lost River."[38] Josiah Gregg in 1844 made the Salt Fork merely an extension of the Cimarron. The error was continued on Colton's map of Kansas in 1855, the Morse and Gaston map of 1856, and the J .G. Wells map of 1857.[39]

Like its neighbors, the Cimarron River was named by the Indians for its salt content, for it was there that they pounded and collected rock salt. The Little Osages gave it a big name; they called it the *Ni-Ckiu-Ega-Shki-Bi*, translated as "cut-rock-salt-water" or "cutting rock salt waters." By leaving out the "rock," it became the "cut-salt-river."[40] Before the High Plains Indians moved in, the Cimarron was also Pawnee hunting territory, and the Pawnees called the river *Kait* which meant "salt."[41]

The Sioux had called it the *Neatsi-ehi*, meaning "bull river." This was a common name for the river and was used by the Apaches, Kiowas, and Comanches, who adopted it from the Sioux. The Cheyenne name was *Hotu-do'he*, which also meant "bull river." It had earlier been used as a place for the ceremonial pipe dance and was then known as the "many pipe dance river."[42] The Cimarron was the only river in this area which retained its Spanish name. It meant "wild" or "unruly," probably referring to mountain sheep or, possibly, to the Texas longhorns.

From the Solomon on the northern border of Kansas to the Salt Fork and the Cimarron in southern Kansas all the streams had considerable salt content and most of them were accordingly given names by the Indians which included a reference to salt. There were distinctive variations in their names in most cases but the variations were difficult to detect. The French did reasonably well in recognizing the differences, if by nothing more than by size, as *grande*, *petite*, or just *saline*. Surveyors who had native interpreters also did reasonably well. However, the most significant factor was the preservation of such distinctive Indian names as Ninnescah, Chikaskia, and Nescatunga.

[38] Hafen, *The Overland Mail*, 17. [39] Baughman, *Kansas in Maps*, 31 and 34.
[40] Mathews, *The Osages*, 187 and 708.
[41] Hyde, *Pawnee Indians*, 282.
[42] Grinnell, "Cheyenne Stream Names," *American Anthropologist* (n.s.), VIII, 18.

▲ IX

Osage and Osage Chiefs

THE OSAGES formed one of the larger divisions of the western or Dakota Sioux. Washington Irving said that they were "stately fellows" and the "finest looking Indians" he had seen. There were many subdivisions among the Osages, each headed by its own chief. The two main divisions which came up the Osage River and entered Kansas were called the Big Osages and the Little Osages. Victor Tixier called them *Oussa Tanga*, Grand or Big Osages, and the *Oussa Chinga*, the Little Osages. The Big Osages were also known as the *Pa-he'tse*, meaning "campers on the mountain" although the "mountain" was only a big hill near St. Louis. The Little Osages were called *U-tseh-ta*, meaning "campers on the lowlands" or "those at the foot of the mountain."[1]

Father Marquette must have heard of the Osages from the Illinois Indians. It is possible that the Illinois had learned the name from the Little Osages who supposedly said, "We are the Deer People of the *Wah-Sha-She*." Mathews referred to the Osages in general as the "water people and name givers." But they were also the "land people" and the "sky people." According to their legends, "they came from the stars to the earth," and it was "Wa-zha-zhe" who represented the waters of the earth. But the "meaning of the name is obscure," said La Flesche in his Osage dictionary. The interpretation that they were the "name givers" has been simplified into the view that the Osage meant merely "their name." In their

[1] *Tixier's Travels on the Osage Prairies*, 126; J. W. Powell, "Indian Linguistic Families of America North of Mexico," *BAE Seventh Annual Report* (1885–86), 116; Morrison, *KHC*, XVIII, 695.

own mythology it was the waters of the river that gave them the name *Wah-Sha-She*, a spiritual name of great significance, meaning much more than its prosaic translation of "water people."[2]

When Marquette first heard of the Osages in 1673, he spelled their name the best he could in French. Because of his uncertainty, he spelled it two ways, *Ouchage* and *Outrechaha*. Even though *Ouchage* was very near the present Osage, the name went through a great variety of changes before it again took on its present form. After the turn of the century Penicaunt, another Frenchman, took liberties with the name and spelled it *Huzzau*, *Ous*, and *Waha*. Among the most popular early forms of the name were *Wa-sha-zhe* and *Wa-ca'ce*. These may not have been as far apart as they appeared to be. But *Washashe*, "suffering from phonetics," said Mathews, became *Ouazhaghi*, which still did not solve its phonetic difficulties. The English substituted "wa" and then "o" for the "oua" of the French and made it Ozazge. After that it was easily simplified to Osage.[3]

There continued to be considerable variation in the spelling of Osage in the first half of the nineteenth century. Captain Pike, who traveled with some Osage wards from Washington to the Osage villages, called them *Wabasha*, which resembles Wabash, the name of the stream where they had once lived with their related Siouan tribes. Major Long followed the French form by spelling it *Wah-sash-e*, as did Nathan Boone when he wrote *Wa-sha-shay*. To Maximilian of Wied it appeared to be *Wasaje*. The spelling seems to have varied more than the pronunciation. "Finally," said Mathews, "after many variations from tongues and pens of many, everyone, including the Little Ones, settled for 'Osage.' "[4]

When Charles Claude du Tisné led a French expedition from

[2] Mathews, *The Osage*, 12 and 107; La Flesche, *A Dictionary of the Osage Language*, 208; Stubbs to Adams, "Names," MS, KSHS Archives.

[3] McGee, "The Siouan Indians," *BAE Fifteenth Annual Report* (1893–94), 192; Donaldson, "The George Catlin Indian Gallery," *Annual Report* of the Board of Regents of the Smithsonian Institution to July 1885, Part II, 42 and 46; Mathews, *The Osages*, 108.

[4] James, *Account of Long's Expedition* (vol. XVI in Thwaites' *Early Western Travels*), 273; *Expedition of Pike*, II, 590; Boone, *Chronicles of Oklahoma*, VII, 72; McCoy, *KHQ*, V, 261; Mathews, *The Osages*, 108.

Missouri to Kansas in 1719, he came upon two rivers. One he named the *Rivière Bleue*; the other he named the *Rivière des Osage*, since he there came upon the Osage villages.[5] As the Osages moved upstream into Kansas, the Big Osages took the northern fork which then became the Grande Osage River, sometimes called the Grand, sometimes the Osage. The Little Osages moved up a southern tributary which became the Little Osage River, named for the "Little Ones," as Mathews called the Little Osages. The natives called it *Ni-cka*, "white river."

The Osages had a special name for the junction of the Grand and the Little Osage rivers; they called it *Mi'xa-ckau-tse*, which meant "where white swans are plentiful." *Mi-xa cka* was their name for the white swan. The French, who were remarkably adept at learning Indian languages, translated this name to *Marais des Cygnes*, which in turn has been translated to the "marsh of swans." What had been the Osage River now took on the name of Marais des Cygnes and for some time either or both names were used. Eventually it was the Kansas part of the Osage River that became the Marais des Cygnes, but after the river crossed the Missouri border it again became the Osage.

Seeking simplicity and a common name for the whole river, the United States Board of Geographical Names tried to make the Osage name official. Kansas refused to accept this verdict from Washington. Members of the state board of agriculture appealed to the state legislature to retain the French name. The Kansas legislature responded with provincial pride in 1918, and not only did it declare that Marais des Cygnes was to be the legal name, but it also forbade the official use of Osage. When the Rand McNally map came out in 1944 with the river named Osage, the Kansans were said to be "noisily perturbed and shocked."[6]

The French name retained only a translation of the Indian name but it retained its original meaning which was still appropriate when Kansas was opened to settlement. Ely Moore said that during

[5] Houck thought this was the Gasconade (see A *History of Missouri*, I, 256).
[6] Margaret Whittemore, *Historic Kansas*, 147; *Kansas City Star*, April 18, 1946; William B. Bracke, *Wheat County*, 268.

the 1850's he had frequently hunted along the banks of the Marais des Cygnes for "wild swan and turkey." Another said that he had hunted there for "swan and pelican."[7]

Marais des Cygnes is a distinctive name but difficult in both spelling and pronunciation. Isaac McCoy, who knew something about Indian languages, had trouble with his French. He called the river "Miry Desein" and translated it "miry swan river."[8] An easterner thought the river was the best he had seen in Kansas, but he was confused about the name and asked a Kansas pioneer, "How do you spell it?" "Well, there I cannot tell you," said the Kansan, but they agreed that it sounded as if it were "Merry Dezine."[9] Others wrote it Marie de Cine and Marais de Seine. Governor Geary made it Mary de Zene. Many must have thought that Marais was a typographical error and so they boldly changed it to "Marie" and "Marias," having, no doubt, a girl in mind. When two missionaries, whose minds should not have been on fair maids, arrived at the trading post site, they referred to the place as Marie des Cygne.[10]

There were others who avoided the use of the difficult French name by referring to the river as Swan Stream or Swan River.[11] Whittier, stirred by the Marais des Cygnes Massacre, wrote a poem to record the event. He used the term "Swan's Marsh" throughout except for the following lines:

> *How paled the May sunshine,*
> *Green Marais du Cygne,*
> *When the death-smoke blew over*
> *The lonely ravine.*

Back of the French interpretation and back of the original Osage description is a lovely legend. According to the legend, a warrior betrothed to a beautiful maiden was forced to go to war with a

[7] Moore, *KHC,* XII, 346.

[8] *Kansas City Star,* Aug. 27, 1938; McCoy, *KHQ,* V, 246.

[9] *The Kansas Weekly Tribune,* Jan. 13, 1870, quoted in *KHQ,* XV, 404.

[10] Whittemore, *Historic Kansas,* 147; Green, *Early Days in Kansas,* V, 14; A. H. Favour, *Old Bill Williams, Mountain Man,* 118; McCoy, *KHQ,* V, 248; Barry, XXIX, 433.

[11] Franklin County Historical Society, *Reflections of Franklin County and Chautauqua Days.*

neighboring tribe. The battle was won, but the rejoicing suddenly ceased for the Indian maid when she heard that her lover had been killed. Disconsolate and thinking life had no future without her lover, she ran to the river's steep bank, threw herself into the dark waters, and disappeared. But her lover was not dead. When he heard of his sweetheart's tragic plunge, he, too, threw himself into the river. When the tribe gathered at the river, they could at first see nothing; then out of the mist swam two white swans, gliding along the rippling waters. This, it was said, was how the river got its name.[12]

The Osage River in Kansas lost its Indian name to the French, but the name of the Osage tribe was widely used as a place-name in Kansas. What is now Osage County was first named Weller for John B. Weller, a roving politician who had represented both Ohio and California in the Senate. He had powerful political connections as well as political ability. His wife was the niece of Senator Benton of Missouri and a cousin of General Frémont's wife. By supporting the Kansas-Nebraska Bill, Weller had won favor with the first Kansas territorial legislature, the "Bogus" legislature. To the members of the Free-State legislature the association of the name Weller with the Bogus legislature was cause enough to have the name replaced, so in 1859 the name was changed to Osage. While this was an honor to the Osage Indians, Osage County was actually named for the Osage River whose headwaters are found in Osage County.[13] Four counties, Bourbon, Crawford, Labette, and Allen, have townships named Osage.

In order to compete for the county seat of Osage County, one town named itself Osage City, a typical political gesture. It lost the contest to Lyndon, a town which was more centrally located. But Lyndon had once been named Osage Centre. As a post office it dropped the Centre and became Osage. There a new town company was organized, and the name of the town was changed to Lyndon, honoring a local landowner, says one account, but for a

[12] Charles E. Cory, *Place Names in Bourbon County, Kansas*, 18; Andreas and Cutler, *History of Kansas*, 1095.

[13] *Peoples Herald*, March 11, 1948; Green, *Early Days in Kansas*, IV, 2 and 121.

town in Vermont, according to another.[14] According to the local press, a baby girl was born to the Smith family during the organizational meeting for the town, and the town company, "greatly excited" over the event, was accorded the privilege of naming the baby. They named her Lyndon and then decided that the town should also be named Lyndon to honor the first child born in the community.[15]

One of the prominent missions among the Indians was the Catholic mission in the Osage country of Kansas. The Osage town on Flat Rock Creek was called *Wei-chaka-Ougrin*, which was translated "cockle-bird," but probably should have been "cockleburs." Father Ponziglione called it Briar's Town. S. J. Gilmore laid out the town at the mission in 1856 and, as its first postmaster, named it Catholic Mission, but it was also known as Gilmore Town. The town was later renamed Osage Mission to identify the tribe rather than the church. When another town grew around the mission, some of the Osage Mission officials decided to change the name again, thinking that Mission had become a misnomer. The city council voted to rename the town Neona, said to be the name of the daughter of Chief Little Bear. This was approved by the house but the local protests were so strong that the bill failed to pass the senate.[16]

But the name was changed, this time to St. Paul, possibly in honor of Father Paul Ponziglione. Or the name may have been selected, as the local press suggested, "in honor of St. Paul of the Cross, founder of the Passionist order which had just then established a home in Osage Mission." The Osage name is gone, but the Mission name remains locally on a Neosho County township. The reason for requesting a change of name was that both freight and mail intended for Osage Mission were too often mistakenly sent to Osage City.[17]

In Neosho County railroads battled for rights of way, towns

[14] Andreas and Cutler, *History of Kansas*, 1546; Missouri Pacific Railroad Company, *The Empire that the Missouri Pacific Built*, 127; *KHC*, VII, 481.

[15] *Peoples Herald*, July 15, 1948 and March 26, 1953.

[16] Lew Wallace Duncan, *History of Neosho and Wilson Counties, Kansas*, 51–58; Barry, *KHQ*, XXXII, 80.

[17] *St. Paul Journal*, Dec. 15, 1949; Root, *KHQ*, IV, 279; Duncan, *History of Neosho and Wilson Counties, Kansas*, 58.

fought for terminals, and place-names were chosen for popular appeal, only to be replaced as towns were born but died in infancy. Such names as Osage City, Roger's Mills, New Chicago, Chicago, Tioga, and Alliance were all replaced by the neutral name of Chanute. A pioneer among the promoters was Darius Rogers who had a trading post among the Osages before the railway rivalry got under way. Rogers chose a townsite which he hoped could become both a railway center and county seat. He named the county seat Osage City. There were already too many post offices using the name of Osage. Since Rogers had established a mill at the site, the post office gave it the name of Roger's Mills. Then the rivalry started. New Chicago was born in 1870, "on the day before her twin sister, Tioga, had been ushered into the world." Rogers then moved into Tioga to become a merchant in the town which he hoped would win. But Tioga had to move to the tracks where New Chicago had the advantage. Because of all the rivalry, Rogers became one of the promoters of a united community which was then named Alliance to show that the townsite issue had been settled. The name was deceptive since the rivalry over names and places continued until the new name of Chanute replaced all of the old names.[18] Tioga was an Iroquoian name, Chicago was a Miami name, and Osage was a Siouan name, but all three Indian names were replaced by one French-American name.[19]

In Bourbon County the town of Carbondale, associated with the coal mines, changed its name to Osage. Neither Carbondale nor Osage are now found in Bourbon County, but both of these names are present in Osage County. In Miami County, the town named Osage for five years had its name changed to Fontania, a name with a little Latin touch, which was later simplified to Fontana.

In northern Bourbon County a town on the Little Osage was named Osaga. It was said to be named for the Osages, but Osaga had already been used as a name of a Miami village near Lake Michigan. The Post Office Department requested that the name be

[18] Bernice C. Shackleton, *Handbook on the Frontier Days of Southeast Kansas*, 136; *St. Paul Journal*, July 4, 1948.

[19] Amos S. Lapham, "Looking Backward," *KHC*, XVI, 505.

changed since it would be confused with Osage or Oswego. The name which replaced it was Fulton, the name of a popular doctor from Uniontown who later practiced in Kansas City.[20]

There were many subdivisions of the Osages and each had its chief and descriptive name. Their towns or villages were generally known by the name of the head chief. Among the well-known Osage village names were such names as White Hair's Town, Chetopa Town, Black Dog Town, Big Hill or Tanwashieshie Town, Talley's Town, and Clermont.

Chief White Hair got his name not from having white hair but from an incident in the War of 1812 when he grabbed for a scalp lock and found instead a white wig in his hand. This convertible scalp lock struck his fancy, and he put it on his head and wore it with proper dignity. From this event the chief was given the name of *Paw-Hiu-Skah*, or Pawhuska as it is written today, meaning "white hair."[21] One might compare this with Chief White Cloud's name of Mahushka.

The Osages had their own names for Chief White Hair's village. Among these were *Kee-I-Tone* or *Kleitone*, now listed among the extinct geographical locations of Kansas.[22] Together with these an Oswego writer lists *Mant-Zee-ake*, *Ton-Wa*. The name was written *Mo'n-Ce-Gaxe-To-Wo'n* by Mathews, who said it referred to the blacksmith shop of one John Mathews. The *Ton-Wa* or *To-Wo'n* was the Osage word for "town." The *Mo'n-Ce* meant "steel" or "metal." Altogether the name was said to mean "metal workers town."[23]

The white Americans found it easier to refer to the town by the name of the chief, so they called it Little White Hair's Town and Chief White Hair's Little Town. That was too long for ordinary conversation or even in writing, and the name was shortened and popularized as Little Town. When a group of settlers from Os-

[20] Cory, *Place Names in Bourbon County, Kansas*, 18; Andreas and Cutler, *History of Kansas*, 1095.

[21] Graves, *History of Neosho County*, I, 4; Hodge, *Handbook of American Indians*, I, 854.

[22] *KHC*, XII, 481; O'Connell, in *Oswego Democrat*, Jan. 15 and Jan. 22, 1954.

[23] *The Osages*, x.

wego, New York, came to Kansas, they chose Chief White Hair's Little Town in Labette County as a suitable site for their settlement. One historian said that the company which came to promote a town at Little Town was called the Little Town Town Company. It is best known, however, as the Oswego Town Company, and as New Yorkers from Oswego the settlers renamed the town Oswego, a name of Iroquoian origin.[24]

Several chiefs of White Hair's family were also called White Hair, and their names were also applied to their villages with an occasional identification such as George White Hair's Village to distinguish it from Old White Hair's Village. Father Ponziglione referred to George White Hair's Village near St. Paul as Pawhuska. An uncle of Chief White Hair was also called White Hair, and his village was called *Naniompa* by the Osages, meaning "the village of the pipe."[25] A crossing of the Verdigris River in Montgomery County was known as White Hair's Ford. After the Osages had been transferred to the Indian Territory, Oklahoma honored Chief White Hair by giving a town his Indian name of Pawhuska.

Chetopa in Labette County was named for a friendly Osage chief who was given a commission in the Union Army to command an Indian regiment during the Civil War. He was active in the white man's negotiations for Osage lands. His ability as a realtor could be questioned after he leased the Winfield townsite for six dollars, but he was smart enough to collect a poll tax from the white men who settled on Osage lands. The town of Chetopa was named by Dr. George Lisle who had served as a clerk for Andrew J. Dorn, the Osage Indian agent. Even the town company which had promoted the town of Chetopa had an Indian name; it was called the Powhattan Agricultural Association of Powhattan, Ohio.[26] There are two adjoining townships named Chetopa in Neosho and Wilson counties, and another Chetopa Township in Montgomery County.

[24] Nelson Chase, *History of Labette County, Kansas*, 141; Andreas and Cutler, *History of Kansas*, 1466; *Oswego Independent*, Dec. 19, 1958.

[25] Newman, *The Black Dog Trail*, 62; Graves, *History of Neosho County*, I, 102; Barry, *KHQ*, XXIX, 329, and XXXII, 80.

[26] Federal Writers' Project, *Kansas, A Guide*, 469; Duncan, *History of Neosho and Wilson Counties, Kansas*, 840; Mathews, *The Osages*, 634.

The creek in Montgomery County where Chetopa once lived is called Chetopa Creek.

Chetopa, which has been spelled Tzi-Topa and Citopa, means "four houses" or "four lodges" or better yet, "houses four." Chief Chetopa had four good reasons for having four lodges—he had four wives. The tale has been told of a missionary who instructed the chief to get rid of all his wives but one, the Christian quota. After a year's absence, the missionary returned to find that the chief had not obeyed. So once again he urged the chief to get rid of his surplus wives. The chief asked, "How?" The missionary simply said, "Tell them to get out." The chief hung his head and said, "You tell 'em."

The four wives' tale is folklore, whatever the facts may be to support it. There is, however, another account of how the Osage chief won the name of Chetopa. It was in war that an Indian had the best opportunity to earn a respected name, and a name won in battle was as good as a medal. Chetopa won his name by taking four lodges in an attack on a Pawnee village.[27]

It was from the Big Hill band of the Osages that Big Hill in Labette County got its name. There is also a Big Hill Creek flowing into the Verdigris above Coffeyville. The Osage name for the Big Hill was *Pa Solé*, "Top-of-the-tree-sitters" or "big hills." Their French name was *Gross Côte*. They were also called "Sitters-on-the-hilltops." When they fled from a devastating flood, they took refuge on high ground and some observed the tragedy from the treetops. This gave them the name from which we now have the Big Hill names in Kansas.[28] The "big hill town" near the site of Independence was also called *Pawnee-no-pah-tze* for an Osage chief. Since *non-pa-zhi* meant "not afraid," according to the Osage dictionary, the chief's name implied that he was not afraid of Pawnees.[29]

Black Dog was a big Osage chief who was said to be six feet,

[27] Duncan, *History of Neosho and Wilson Counties, Kansas*, 843; Mathews, *The Osages*, 634.

[28] Mathews, *The Osages*, 145 and 442.

[29] Barry, *KHQ*, XXXII, 80.

seven inches tall. His first Indian name had been *Zhin-ga-wa-ca.* The author of *The Black Dog Trail* said that "Zhin-ga-wa-ca is a very old Indian name which is not translatable since the last part is archaic and the meaning lost."[30] The difficulty with this name is that, like so many others, it has more than one meaning; and to add to the confusion, there were two chiefs with the same or a similar name, one an Osage and the other a Kansa. The spelling of *Zhin-ga-wa-ca* varied somewhat but in general it did conform to the pronunciation of *Shingawassa.*

Black Dog was, however, known by another name. Catlin called him *Tchong-Tas-Sab-Bee.* Nathan Boone met Black Dog and called him *To-ca-sab-be.*[31] Similar to this was *Shinka-Wa-Sa*, as Mathews wrote it, or "*Shonkah Sabe*, Black Dog (really Black Horse)." *Shonka*, like *shonge*, is supposed to mean "dog," but it could mean "horse." The confusion over whether it meant dog or horse was due to the fact that the Indians had no name for the Spanish horse and so they called it a "walking dog." A conspicuous characteristic of the horse, unlike their dogs which were generally running, was that the horse frequently walked. What seemed so conspicuous to the Indian may be illustrated by the story of a dog chasing a jackrabbit on a day when it was so hot that both of them were walking. Eventually the Indians did try to use the Spanish name, *cavallo*, for horse. When this was written phonetically, it came out *Ka-Wa.*[32]

But Mathews had other interpretations. "Shinka-wah-sa" was the "real name of Black Dog and has nothing to do with either black or dog," he said, adding that "Dark-Eagle or Sacred-Little-One" was the meaning of the name. Tixier changed the *Wah-Shinkah* into French and spelled it *Ouchinka-Lâgri*, which he translated to mean *bel oiseau* or "handsome bird." On treaties, however, the *Shingawassa* name had also been translated to mean "handsome

[30] Newman, *The Black Dog Trail*, 15; Mathews, *The Osages*, 598.

[31] Donaldson, "The George Catlin Indian Gallery," *Annual Report* of the Board of Regents of the Smithsonian Institution to July 1885, Part II, 42; *Chronicles of Oklahoma*, VII, 88n.

[32] Mathews, *The Osages*, 122, 552, 602, and 678.

bird," not that this giant of a one-eyed man was handsome. Mathews' reference to "Black Dog and Beautiful Bird" would indicate that these were two separate persons.[33]

There is an Indian legend which tells how Chief Black Dog earned his name. One dark night when the chief and some companions were silently crawling toward a Comanche camp, they were stopped by the barking of a little black dog. Irritated by this repeated interference, the chief shot an arrow in the direction of the dog, hit him in the head, and killed him. This lucky shot in the dark won him the name of Black Dog.[34]

Black Dog followed a trail from Oklahoma to Baxter Springs in southeastern Kansas. Then he extended the Black Dog Trail westward through Coffeyville to the Indian site called Napawalla on the Walnut where he established his hunting camp at the present site of Oxford. Farther west the ford of the Arkansas River was called Black Dog's Crossing. So there was once a Black Dog Town or Trading Post, a Black Dog Trail, and a Black Dog Crossing, all well-known names of a distinguished Osage chief.[35]

Northeast of Marion was the attractive little spa with the name of Shingawassa Springs, said to be named for a Kansa chief. "Ching-gah-was-see," said Morehouse, "was a good Indian . . . and had the honor of having a spring named for him." Since the Osage and Kansa languages were closely related, it was quite possible that chiefs from both tribes could have the same name. The Shingawassa Springs were considered important enough for a Wichita man to plan a railway to the place in order to tap the quarry and to carry picnickers and health-seekers to this spa which might compete with Waconda and Geuda Springs. The railway was called the Marion Belt and Chingawassa Springs Railroad. The promoter's dream of a profitable health resort failed to materialize. Even its attractive Indian name of Shingawassa has been changed to Quarry

[33] *The Osages*, 481, 671; *Tixier's Travels on the Osage Prairies*, 129 and 238; *KHC*, XVI, 749, 750, and 766.

[34] O'Connell, in *Oswego Democrat*, Jan. 15, 1954; Newman, *The Black Dog Trail*, 16–18 and 27 .

[35] Andreas and Cutler, *History of Kansas*, 1563–64; Newman, *The Black Dog Trail*, 23–28.

Springs and Rainbow Lake. It was called Rainbow Lake for "the many hues" of its stone quarry. As a resort it had somewhat of a shady reputation, but as Rainbow Spring it continued for a time to be a popular picnic place. It is now an abandoned spot and as nearly forgotten as Chief Shingawassa.[36]

The Osage Indians were generally tall and stately, and Chief Napawalla was no exception. Like Black Dog, he, too, is supposed to have weighed some 250 pounds. The most common variation in the spelling of his name was the choice of the first vowel, for every vowel was tried. So we find it spelled Napawalla, Nepawalla, Nipawalla, Nopawalla, and Numpawalla. Mathews started out differently by spelling the name *No-Pa-Watha* in the index but using *No-Pa-Wathe* in the text. When listed first, however, Nopawatha was followed by *No-Pa-Walla* with the explanation that it meant "thunder fear."[37]

Chief Napawalla was one of the signers of the Drum Creek Treaty which limited the lands of the Osages. Drum Creek was once called Nepawalla Creek, also spelled Nipawalla. When the Osages were moved out of their ceded lands, they established seven villages, and one of these on the north side of Elk Creek was named Napawalla.

At Oswego, Labette County, a company was organized which called itself the Napawalla Town Company. The town was established at the Cottonwood Crossing of the Walnut, not to be confused with the crossing of the Cottonwood River. The town was then named Napawalla. It was soon changed to Oxford, not because it was a ford, but to honor Oxford in England and in anticipation of making it a new center of learning.[38]

Among the rivals of White Hair was Clermont or Claremont, chief of the Little Osages. His Indian name was *Gra Mo'n* or *Gra Mon*, with variations such as *Grah Mon*, *Ghleh Mon*, and *Gle Mon*.

[36] Morehouse, *KHC*, X, 335; Marion Record-Review, Sept. 14, 1944; Mead, "The Saline River Valley," *KHC*, IX, 17.

[37] *The Osages*, 481, 537, and 671; Andreas and Cutler, *History of Kansas*, 1495; John R. Cook, *The Border and the Buffalo*, 28.

[38] Andreas and Cutler, *History of Kansas*, 1507; Whittemore, *Historic Kansas*, 192.

The change from the "r" to the "l" was not unusual, and *Ghleh* was simplified to *Gle* as if the "h" were superfluous. Mathews made a distinction, however, between the two Indian names. *Gra Mo'n* was said to mean "arrow going home," whereas *Ghleh Mon* was said to mean just "going."[39]

It has been suggested that the French made *Gra Mon* sound like "Cler-Mont," and from this it was an easy step to make it Claremont, Claremore, or any similar name. Chief Claremore has been referred to as "Clairmont (Clermont, Claymore), or Chief Cashesegra, the Builder of Towns." As a place-name in Kansas it was also spelled Clymore. Claremont and Cashesegra were not the same. "Though Cashesegra be the nominal leader," said one, "Clermont, or the Builder of Towns, is the greatest warrior and most influential man."[40]

Gra Mon's village in the Coffeyville area became known as Claymore, and there was established the Claymore Trading Post. Later the name was changed to Lushbaugh's Trading Post. Then there was in Labette County a Clymore post office which closed in 1872. There is a Claymore Creek which flows into the Verdigris north of Coffeyville. Like the name of Pawhuska, the name of Chief Claymore or Clermont became more important in Oklahoma than in Kansas. There the home town of Will Rogers, the great part-Indian humorist, is spelled Claremore.

Talley Springs, a competitor of Coffeyville, was located east of the Verdigris. It was also called Talley's Town. The town was located on an Osage village site and named for an Osage chief whose Indian name was *Ta-Eh-Ga-Xe* or *Ta-He-Gaxe*, according to Mathews. This meant the "antler-maker" or "buck-making-horns." He did not make horns; the name was supposed to describe the white-tailed buck scraping the velvet from his horns on a tree. Another writer refers to "Tal-lee" as a chief of Clermont's band by the name of *Kahatunka*, which Catlin said meant "crow." Mathews listed the same name but suggested that it should be *Ca-xe Tonkah*

39 *The Osages*, 236, 277, 299, and 417.

40 S. W. Brewster, "The Reverend Paul M. Ponziglione," *KHC*, IX, 26n.; Donaldson, "The George Catlin Indian Gallery," *Annual Report* of the Board of Regents of the Smithsonian Institution to July 1885, Part II, 42; *KHC*, XVI, 750.

and that it meant "raven."[41] There is little difference in the sound of *Kahatunka* and *Ca-xe Tonkah*, nor is there any great difference between a crow and a raven. In English, the name was Talley, Tal-lee, or Tallai.

The ambitions of Talley Springs had irritated the local railroad company and the town was ordered "cut." The name remained on the railroad for some time, and the town served as a post office until 1874. Now the name is preserved for the Calloch Cemetery. This name belongs more likely to the town of Kalloch just north of the Talley Springs location, a town which had been named for Rev. Isaac S. Kalloch, a gifted preacher, politician, and journalist.[42]

Identifying the tribe for which Osawatomie was named has surely baffled those who were not familiar with Indian names. The source for the name is the merging streams on which Osawatomie is located. These streams are the Osage (Marais des Cygnes) and the Pottawatomie, and the coined name of the town is a combination of the two river names, using the first three letters from Osage to replace the first two syllables of Pottawatomie, with the result, Osawatomie. Some of the Potawatomis had lived in this area before being removed to the Pottawatomie County area.[43]

When the town was organized, it had several names from which to choose. The town promoters were Orval C. Brown of Brooklyn and Baptiste Peoria for whom Paola and Baptiste Spring had been named. The meeting to name the town attracted a large crowd. Someone suggested that the town be named Brownville for Brown, the promoter, or Brooklyn for his home town. Baptiste Peoria objected to both Brownville and Brooklyn. Had it been named Brownville, the popular assumption could have been that it was so named for Old John Brown, the crusader. Baptiste Peoria wanted the place named the City of Kansas or Peoria, but neither of these won approval. Finally Colonel Ely Moore proposed the combination name of Osawatomie. This seems to have been accepted as a compromise between the two contestants. Efforts were

[41] Mathews, *The Osages*, 416, 432, and 558; Newman, *The Black Dog Trail*, 113.

[42] *Coffeyville Daily Journal*, Sept. 12, 1957; Anne Eloise Abel, "Indian Reservations in Kansas," VIII, 79n.

[43] August Bondi, "With John Brown in Kansas," *KHC*, VIII, 278.

made later to change the name, but the distinctive name of Osawatomie has survived.[44]

The fame of the name goes back to the struggle over slavery in "Bleeding Kansas" in which the Osawatomie Massacre was a significant event. Originally it was O. C. Brown, the founder of the town, who was known as "Osawatomie" Brown. But the public was led to believe that this title belonged to Old John Brown, the Kansas crusader. At Harper's Ferry when "Jeb" Stuart asked him, "You are Osawatomie Brown of Kansas, are you not?," Old John answered, "Well, they do call me that sometimes, Lieutenant." So O. C. Brown, the original Osawatomie Brown, lost his title to John Brown, who lived not in Osawatomie but on the Pottawatomie Creek.[45] John Brown's association with Osawatomie has been perpetuated even in verse:

> *. . . and Old Brown,*
> *Osawatomie Brown,*
> *Came homeward in the morning to*
> *find his house burned down.*[46]

The Osages left their names in eastern Kansas where they had long lived. Then they were given a wide stretch of land in southern Kansas, which was known as the Osage Strip. In the meantime they had extended their hunting area westward, frequently crossing the Arkansas. Every trail and every stream had its Osage name as did their villages and their camps.

44 Moore, *KHC*, XII, 339–40.

45 William H. Coffin, "Settlement of the Friends in Kansas," *KHC*, VII, 325; William Hutchinson, "Sketches of Kansas Pioneer Experience," *KHC*, VII, 397.

46 This poem by Edmund C. Stedman appears in *Emerson's Complete Works, Miscellanies*, XI–XII, 266.

X

Neosho to Neshutsatunga

THE NEOSHO RIVER was called *La Grande Rivière* or just *La Grande* by the French. The source for this name was most likely the name of the Grand Osages. Its origin lost, it was also used as a descriptive name when combined with the Indian name as Grand Neosho. The 1757 map of Le Page du Pratz names the Neosho the *R. Blanche*, the "white" river. He also located a "White Panis" village there. The La Paz map of 1783 listed the Neosho in Spanish as *R. Blanca*.[1] Zebulon Pike called it both the Grand and the White River. Elliot Coues explained that "This White or Grand r. of Pike is the Neosho," and he assumed that Pike called it the Grand because it was the site of the Grand Osage settlement. It is more likely that he called it the Grand because the French had named it *La Grande*. Calling the Neosho the White River persisted for some time, and a writer as late as 1841 spoke of Council Grove being "situated on the main White river."[2]

Later the dual descriptive name of Grand Neosho was divided, the upper part retaining the name of Neosho and the lower part flowing into Oklahoma as the Grand River. Grand Lake has there taken the name of the river, but it is also called the Grand Lake of the Cherokees.[3]

On February 3, 1823, the Rev. Benton Pixley from Harmony Mission wrote, "I am now at the trading establishment about ninety

[1] Wheat, *Mapping the Trans-Mississippi West*, I, 120.

[2] *Expedition of Pike*, II, 50, 394n., and 397n.; Duncan, *History of Neosho and Wilson Counties, Kansas*, 820; Root, *KHQ*, IV, 268; *KHQ*, VIII, 104; Le Page du Pratz, *History of Louisiana*, cf. map.

[3] Gould, *Oklahoma Place Names*, 28.

miles up the Grand river (Neosho) or the Six Bulls."[4] When Stephen H. Long referred to the Grand or Neosho, he said that it was "better known to the hunters by the singular name of Six Bulls."[5] In editing a reference to the "Notice, or Grand River," by John R. Bell, Harlin M. Fuller ignored the possible typographical error in the use of "Notice" for Neosho, but he identified the river as "The Grand, Neosho, or Six Bulls."[6]

One's first conclusion might be that naming the river Six Bulls made some reference to buffalo bulls. However, the name is just one bull short of being the name of *Oh-to-ah-ne-so-to-who*, or Seven Bulls, an Osage chief who signed the Little River Treaty in 1865.[7] One bull more or less does not rule out the suggestion that Six Bulls may have been named for Chief Seven Bulls.

Victor Tixier, a French medical student traveling through the Osage country in 1840, spoke of spending the night near the *Panie-Tanga*, the "big Pawnee." It was in reality only the little Pawnee Creek flowing into the Marmaton River and might have been better named *Panie-Shunga* rather than *Panie-Tanga*. Then "a beaten track led us to a ford of the Nion-Chou (Neosho) River," said Tixier. The name of *Nion-Chou* was also given to the Osage village across the river. In his words: "The Great Osage live in four villages located a few miles away from one another; Nion-Chou, otherwise called Manrinhabotso ('The Village Which Scrapes the Sky') is the commercial capital of the Osage." It was from Cortambert's *Voyage aux pays des Osages* that he got the name for the village "which touches the sky."[8]

At *Nion-Chou*, also written *Nioncho*, the French travelers were the guests of Pierre M. Papin, a French trader who had an Osage

[4] Graves, *History of Neosho County*, I, 30.

[5] Root, *KHQ*, IV, 268.

[6] *The Journal of Captain John R. Bell* (vol. VI in Hafen's *The Far West and the Rockies*), 261 n.

[7] Mead, "The Meaning of the Word 'Wichita,'" in *History of Sedgwick County* (ed. by O. H. Bentley), I, 127; Mead, "The Little Arkansas," *KHC*, X, 11.

[8] *Tixier's Travels on the Osage Prairies*, 115, 118, and 126; Barry, *KHQ*, XXVIII, 508, and XXIX, 329.

family. It was not long before the name of the French trader replaced that of the more difficult Indian name of *Manrinhabotso*, and for a time the place was called Papin's Town and Papin's Trading Post. Another Indian name for the place which could have been more popular than *Manrinhabotso* was *Nantze Waspe*. This name must have come from *No'n-Dse-Waspi*, which Mathews called the "Heart-Stays-People."[9]

Later a trading post was established there by A. B. Canville, a French Canadian who had married Cipriana, an Osage woman from Missouri who was one-quarter French. Canville's Trading Post became a post office with the name of Canville. The town of Shaw on the east side of the Neosho is near the site of these trading posts and White Hair's village, which was on the west side and about four miles down river.[10]

Before Tixier spelled the name *Nion-Chou*, Cortambert had given it the simple spelling of *Niocho*.[11] It would have been a short step to change *Niocho* to Neosho, but there was considerable variation in the spelling before it took shape. George C. Sibley, at the Council Grove negotiations of 1825, spelled it Neeozho and Nee-Ozho. Another wrote it Nee-o-jho. John McCoy said that the name was "properly" written *Ne-wo-sos-she*, with the accent on the penultimate. His father, Isaac McCoy, had written it Neozhoo. It would be easy to conclude from this, as did A. W. Stubbs, that the name should be pronounced "Ne-o-shu'," with the accent on the last syllable. Mathews wrote it *Ni-U-Sho*. Out of all of this came Neosho, not only acceptable to the public but popular. It still remains Indian in appearance even though one writer tried to Americanize it by calling it "No Show."[12]

The preservation of the Neosho name for the river has been

[9] *Tixier's Travels on the Osage Prairies*, 117ff.; Andreas and Cutler, *History of Kansas*, 826; *St. Paul Journal*, Sept. 1, 1949; Graves, *History of Neosho County*, I, 168.

[10] Graves, *History of Neosho County*, I, 30 and 125; Andreas and Cutler, *History of Kansas*, 826; Barry, *KHQ*, XXIX, 429; *St. Paul Journal*, Sept. 1, 1949.

[11] *Tixier's Travels on the Osage Prairies*, 139n.

[12] Brewster, *KHC*, IX, 26n.; McCoy to Adams, and Stubbs to Adams, "Names," MS, KSHS Archives; Mathews, *The Osages*, 181.

credited to William Sherley Williams, better known as "Old Bill" Williams, mountain man. He was married to an Osage woman and knew the language well enough to be the interpreter at the Council Grove Treaty conference in 1825.[13]

When the name was written *Ne-Was-She*, it has been assumed that *Was-She* was an abbreviation of *Wah-Sosh-She*, one of the many spellings for Osage. This would make it the "river of the Osages." However, this "river of the Osages" should not be confused with the Osage River, the earlier site of the Osages.[14]

Neosho is an Osage name with the Siouan or Dakota meaning of *ne* or *ni* for "water." Andreas said that the river had been named by the Kansa Indians who, when they found water after a long search, cried out "Ne-O-sho!" meaning "water-in-it" or "a stream with water." This was also the interpretation given by A. W. Stubbs, who was at one time interpreter for the Kansas. Others translated it simply to "wet bottoms."[15]

According to another story, when a scout rode into the river, his horse stumbled into a pothole and the horse and rider "went in all over." As the rider emerged, he muttered, "Wugh, Neosho!" for "pothole" or "water pocket." This gave rise to the belief that Neosho meant a river full of deep holes or "water bowls." The word *o-sho* could mean any kind of basin, bowl, or vessel.[16]

James R. Mead translated Neosho to mean "clear water" and so did Charles N. Gould of Oklahoma. Some said that it meant "bright water" and others, "clear, cold water." Adding the "cold" was probably superfluous. There may be a connection between its name as the White River and describing it as "clear." Calling the river "clear water" was undoubtedly correct, except when the

[13] O'Connell, in *Oswego Democrat*, Sept. 3, 1954.

[14] *Emporia Daily News*, July 23, 1883; McCoy to Adams, "Names," MS, KSHS Archives.

[15] Andreas and Cutler, *History of Kansas*, 796 and 826; Stubbs to Adams "Names," MS, KSHS Archives; John Maloy, "History of Morris County," *Kansas Cosmos*, April 23, 1886; Haucke, *KHQ*, XX, 49.

[16] Greene, *The Kanzas Region*, 112; Alice S. Smith, "Through the Eyes of my Father," *KHC*, XVII, 708n.; *Oswego Democrat*, Sept. 3, 1954; Graves, *History of Neosho County*, I, 255.

water was disturbed or roiled. Then the question arises, under what conditions did the Indians first see it? Victor Murdock said that Neosho, which he spelled Ne-o-lah-see, meant "dirty water," and he may be correct.[17]

There is support for the Murdock interpretation in a tale supposedly told by the Osage Indians. When the Osages moved westward to make room for the emigrant Indians after the Treaty of 1825, they went in search of an attractive river-front site. As the story is told:

> The scouts went southwestward and soon came to a long stretch of timber and a clear beautiful stream. The chief was pleased with the report of the scouts and the entire band set out for the river. Those who arrived first rode into the water to let their horses drink. When the chief arrived a few minutes later he found the river the opposite of "beautiful clear," and he reprimanded the scouts for their misrepresentation, and from this incident the river was given the name of "Neosho," which was said to mean "water made muddy."[18]

Only a few writers have accepted this interpretation, yet it may be the correct one. The Indian tale, which reads like folklore, may have solid support from the dictionary. The Osage word *o-sho'de* means the "smokelike appearance of water when the soft mud at the bottom is stirred." This definition should also be kept in mind for Neodesha, as we shall see below.

Mathews said that the name was *Ni-U-Sho*, and that it meant "Waters-(colored)-Like-Cows-Hide." He went on to say that the Little Osages had many camps, but that the one they favored became "a semipermanent village on the Gray-Green-Bark Waters, the modern Verdigris River and the Water-Like-a-Brown-Yellow Body, and the Neosho (Water-Like-the-Skin-of-a-Summer-Cow-Wapiti)." The Neosho name was complex; it took nine words to

[17] Mead, Kansas Academy of Science *Transactions*, XVIII, 216; *Wichita Evening Eagle*, March 6, 1943; Gould, *Oklahoma Place Names*, 103; Muriel Wright, "Some Geographical Names of French Origin," *Chronicles of Oklahoma*, VII, 190.

[18] Morrison, *KHC*, XVII, 695; Andreas and Cutler, *History of Kansas*, 826.

define it. The color of cowskin was not enough, and the summer color was not the same as the winter color, and the reference was not to an ordinary cow but to the Wapiti, the correct name for the elk, and not a bull elk but for a cow Wapiti.[19]

The name of Neosho has experienced a variety of spellings, several interpretations, and has persisted over other names in French and English or Americanese. Having survived, the name of the Neosho River became popular and has been used for towns, townships, and a county. The first to use it was the Protestant mission set up by the Rev. Benton Pixley which was known as Mission Neosho, a mission which had troubles with both the Indians and the Indian agent and lasted only from 1824 to 1829.[20]

The county now named Neosho had been named Dorn for Major Andrew Jackson Dorn, who had been appointed Indian agent to the Osages by President Buchanan. Dorn was a competent agent but he caused considerable trouble by urging the Osages to join the South in the Civil War. He himself left Kansas to become quartermaster of the Confederate Army. This was reason enough to replace the name of Dorn. "His name," said a county historian, "was a continual reminder of the aroma surrounding the Bogus legislature, so the legislature of 1861 did not lose any time wiping the name from the map." The county was then given the popular Indian name of Neosho, naming it for the river which follows a serpentine course across the county.[21]

One of the ambitious but ephemeral settlements on the Neosho River was that of the vegetarian colony, also known as the "hydropathic establishment." There were actually two colonies, one on the east side of the river which was called Neosho City and the other on the west side which was called Octagon City. Dr. John McLaren represented both of the vegetarian colonies and selected the townsites about six miles below Humboldt on the Neosho in Allen County. The vegetarians came poorly prepared to cope with

[19] *The Osages*, 181 and 298.

[20] Barry, *KHQ*, XXVIII, 50.

[21] Duncan, *History of Neosho and Wilson Counties, Kansas*, 23; Andreas and Cutler, *History of Kansas*, 1453.

the problems of a flesh-eating frontier. Neosho City had a brief boom and then died.[22]

Farther upstream on the Neosho in Coffey County there was for a few years a town composed of a sawmill and a gristmill, which had the post-office name of Neosho City. This was contemporary with the Neosho City of the vegetarians in Allen County and explains why the latter did not become a post office. Later there was a Neosho post office in Allen County, serving, however, for less than three months in 1871. The Coffey County post office of Neosho City did not last long, but the name is still there as Neosho Township. The Neosho River barely cuts the corner of Cherokee County where there is also a township named Neosho. For a few years in the 1870's there was a Neosho Station north of Chanute in Neosho County. Neosho City in Coffey County was located on Big Creek from 1856 to 1860. Two towns still retain the name of Neosho, Neosho Rapids in Lyon County and Neosho Falls in Woodson County, both properly on the Neosho River.[23]

Speaking of Neosho Rapids, John C. Van Gundy, a local pioneer, said that it had already had three names, and "it had lived them all out and is now trudging along with the fourth."[24] When Josiah Gregg started a store on the banks of the Neosho in 1856, his place was called Neosho City. But this name was given to a post office in Coffey County the following year, so Gregg's town had to change its name. Jefferson and Cobine, town promoters, named their town Florence. This place seems to have merged with one about two miles away called Neosho City. One writer suggests that only the name was changed.[25]

The next promoters were the Pigman brothers. When one of them was on his way to get a town charter, he is said to have

[22] Russell Hickman, "The Vegetarian and Octagon Settlement Companies," *KHQ*, II, 380–83; Duncan, *History of Neosho and Wilson Counties, Kansas*, 37.

[23] Kansas State Board of Agriculture *First Biennial Report* (1877–78), 336; *KHC*, XII, 484.

[24] *Reminiscences of Frontier Life on the Upper Neosho*, 32–34; *Emporia Times*, July 21, 1949.

[25] *Emporia Times*, July 21, 1949; Flora R. Godsey, "The Early Settlement and Raid on the 'Upper Neosho,' " *KHC*, XVI, 457–58.

turned to his companion and asked him to propose a name for the new town. As the story goes, "the man looking up at the clear blue sky said, 'Italia,' and it was so." The post office accepted this name, but the people did not. As one pioneer said, "Many a time I have walked to Florence to get mail addressed to Italia Post Office."[26]

In 1863 the name of the Neosho was again introduced as the town was renamed Neosho Rapids. It has been suggested that it was so named by Chris Carver for Neosho, Missouri, where two of his uncles lived. But since Neosho Rapids was located on the rapids of the Neosho, the name did not necessarily come from Missouri. The place which had been called Neosho City, Florence, and Italia finally became Neosho Rapids.

The falls for which Neosho Falls of Woodson County were named were in reality only rapids. Then after a dam was built, said Andreas, "the town became genuinely 'the falls.' "[27] Five townships were given the Neosho name, none of them far from the Neosho River. Naming them from the northwest, there were Neosho townships in Morris County and Coffey County, a Neosho Falls Township in Woodson County, and Neosho townships in Labette and Cherokee counties. So the Indian river name, modified to Neosho, is scattered well over the Osage country of Kansas.

Flowing into the Neosho along the eastern border of Morris County is Rock Creek. The Santa Fe travelers named it for the "rocky bluffs that confine the stream." But the Indians had earlier named it *Ne-co-its-ah-ba*, which meant "dead man's creek." There a bloody battle had been fought between the Indians in eastern Kansas and the Plains Indians.[28]

Westward from the Neosho to the Neshutsatunga, as the Big Arkansas was called, were many streams and towns with Osage names. Some of these names have remained, some have been modified, some have been translated into French or English, some have been replaced, and others have disappeared.

[26] Van Gundy, *Reminiscences*, 33; Godsey, *KHC*, XVI, 455.

[27] Van Gundy, *Reminiscences*, 33; Godsey, *KHC*, XVI, 363; Andreas and Cutler, *History of Kansas*, 1193.

[28] Maloy, in *Kansas Cosmos*, April 23, 1886.

A little stream by the French name of Labette flows into the Neosho in southeastern Kansas. It was called *En-gru-scah-opo* by the Osages. One may recognize the *scah* which has frequently been a corruption of the Osage *scua* or *skua* for "salt" or possibly "white." But *opo* or *opou* is the word for "elk," and it has been suggested that this may have been a reference to a tribal division.[29] Elk were, however, found in eastern Kansas.

The first big stream west of the Neosho is the one named Verdigris. It was on the Verdigris that the Little Osages had their favorite camping ground. They called it *Wa-Ce-Ton-Xo-E*, which has been translated to mean "gray-green-bark-waters." It was the bark of the sycamore tree to which they referred.[30] The French used only the first two words of the name, *vert y gris*, "green and gray," from which they made the name for the Verdigris. There were other forms for the Osage name, such as *Was-set-to-ho* and *Wasatuhoge*. Edwin James seems to have left out a couple of syllables when he called it the *Was-su-ja*.[31] The Osage dictionary spelled it the same as Mathews, *Wa-Ce-Ton-Xo-E*, and defined it as "green clay." Others said it meant "blue clay." The Osages were accustomed to use the "blue-colored mud" from the banks of the Verdigris to paint their apparel and themselves. To them the blue clay was a sacred color and they also used the clay to paint the faces of the dead. It is Indian in origin, French by translation, but it is generally English in pronunciation, which means that the final "i" is short and the supposedly silent "s" is pronounced.[32]

When Lieutenant Colonel Joseph E. Johnston surveyed the southern boundary of Kansas, the surveyors crossed several streams which still bore their Indian names. Near Chetopa in Labette County, they crossed a creek called *Su-ka-tuk*, which is now Turkey Creek. *Sukatunk* meant "turkey."[33] The Osage word for turkey

[29] O'Connell, in *Oswego Democrat*, July 2, 1954.

[30] Mathews, *The Osages*, 181.

[31] James, *Account of Long's Expedition* (vol. XVI of Thwaites' *Early Western Travels*), 281.

[32] John P. Edwards, *Atlas of Wilson County*, 7; *Expedition of Pike*, II, 555n. and 556; *Journal of Captain John R. Bell* (vol. VI in Hafen's *The Far West and the Rockies*), 268.

[33] Miller, *KHQ*, I, 112.

was *ciu'ka* and *ciu'ka ton-ga*. The latter looks as if it should be "big turkey," most likely the gobbler.

A creek which flows into the Verdigris from the east near Coffeyville had the Osage name of *Watunk-a-kashink*. This was Pumpkin Creek. The first part of the name may be from *wa-ton*, the Osage name for "pumpkin," but the rest is not easily translated, unless it is *shinka* for "little."[34]

When the Osages found the body of a strange Indian in a cave on a stream near Coffeyville, they named the creek *Pa'thin-wa-kon-da-gi ga-xa*. *Pa'thin* may mean a Pawnee or any foreign Indian; *wa-kon-da-gi* refers to the spirit or medicine man; *ga-xa* means creek. So the name became Pawnee Medicine Man Creek.[35]

Metsoshinco, Chief Little Bear of the Osages, chose an attractive site between the Verdigris and the Elk rivers for his village. The place was known as Little Bear's Mound. There between the rivers the white man also decided to locate a town. The "founding fathers," said Joseph Allen of Neodesha, asked a select committee to propose a name that would "hint at the river location of the town, its Indian connection, and at the same time be different from that of any other town in the nation."[36]

It was a big order, but the committee did well. They named the town Neodesha. This was a name with an Osage origin, there was then no such name in the nation, and it was descriptive. By re-arranging the Osage word *Ni-o-sho-de*, the committee had coined a new name, Neodesha, a melodious word which one editor described as "mellifluous" or "sweetly flowing." Mellifluous or not, it was misspelled and mispronounced, and its meaning remained in doubt. One county historian spelled it Neotisha, which reminds one of a native name for Missouri.[37]

The most common interpretation is still that Neodesha meant the "meeting place of the water" or, as another suggests, "the city between two rivers." In nearly all the Indian languages one may find that such a site was given a descriptive name to indicate its

[34] *Ibid.*
[35] La Flesche, *A Dictionary of the Osage Language*, 126.
[36] *Cho-O-Nee to High Iron*, 1–23.
[37] Graves, *History of Neosho County*, I, 171.

location between two streams, for example, Mendota or Tioga. It was Avoca in Celtic, Coblentz in German, Wedding of the Waters in Wyoming, and simply Junction City in Kansas.[38]

When Joseph Allen gave the title of his book on the Neodesha as *Cho-O-Nee*, he was probably basing it on the Osage word *zho-ni* which meant "wood water." Even though the word Neodesha had been rearranged, it was said to mean "meeting place of wooded waters." Another translated this as the "junction of timbers." The description was at least accurate. However, the original source of the name *Nioshode* must be considered in order to determine the correct meaning. Mr. Allen translated this as "the water is smoky with mud," and this he supported by pointing out that the Verdigris and Elk rivers are "slow-running mud-cutters."[39] In addition to being correct descriptively, this seems also to be correct in translation. *Nioshode* is, of course, one of the names for the Neosho; the names have the same origin. Assuming that Neodesha should retain its original meaning, in spite of the juggling of syllables, then its name would mean, according to the Osage dictionary, "the water is smoky with mud." This brings us back to the story of the Indian scouts riding their horses into the stream and the chief who followed them calling it *Neosho!* "Muddy water!"

Neodesha, which is pronounced with the accent on the last syllable, fulfilled the requirements of the city founders' desire to have an Indian name, a descriptive name, and an unusual name.[40] It was the only name of its kind in the nation until a man from Neodesha moved to Oklahoma and started a town which he named Neodesha for his home town in Kansas.

Beyond the Verdigris ford was a creek named *Nenetunk*, which was thought to be Big Spring Creek. The Osage name looks as if it should be "big spring" or "big creek." There is a small Spring Creek in Montgomery County which flows into Onion Creek from

[38] Andreas and Cutler, *History of Kansas*, 904; Missouri Pacific Railroad Company, *The Empire that the Missouri Pacific Built*, 132; *Topeka Capital*, May 4, 1956.
[39] *Cho-O-Nee to High Iron*, 1.
[40] When the first white child born in the town was named Neodesha Derry, the town company was so pleased that they gave a town lot to the child. (Allen, *Cho-O-Nee to High Iron*, 29).

the west, but this one does not quite fit the travel route of the Johnston surveyors; they should have come to Onion Creek first.

Onion Creek seems to be the one identified as *Niskeokaka* or "salt creek." Here the first syllable, meaning "water," is followed by a variation of *skua* to *skeo* for "salt," whatever the final *kaka* may mean. Another Osage name for Onion Creek, according to the dictionary, was *Ni-ckiu'e ga-xa*, which means the "salt branch." This would indicate that what had been written *ka-ka* comes from *ga-xa*, meaning "branch" or "creek."[41] There is now a Salt Creek, north of Onion Creek, flowing into the Elk River.

When Colonel Johnston and his men had traveled beyond the North Caney, they crossed a smaller creek with a deep channel where they camped. It was called the *Cow-a-wha*, which was translated to mean "horse head."[42] *Ka'wa* means horse, supposedly from *cavallo*, the Spanish name for horse. There was certainly no need for a name for horse until the horse was introduced by the Spaniards, and the name naturally came with the animal in Spanish. If *Cow-a-wha* did mean horse head, and it probably did, then it might better have been spelled *Ka-wa-pa*, since *ka'wa* means horse and *pa* means "head." *Cow-a-wha* or Kawa Creek, which is a branch of the Caney, may be the one which in Oklahoma was called *Ka'wa-in-gthon-ga-xthi-bi*, meaning the "creek where a horse was struck by lightning."[43]

When William Nicholson was inspecting Indian agencies in 1870, he mentioned a stop at a lone settler's place which he identified as being "near the Cana below Curleyhead Creek." That would be on the Oklahoma side.[44] The "Cana" was the Caney, which pioneers had also spelled Cainey. Calling it Cana was so well accepted that a branch of the Missouri Pacific Railroad was called the Cana Valley Branch.[45] It is believed that the abundance of cane and rushes in the valley was the inspiration for the name, similar to Cape Canaveral, now Cape Kennedy, in Florida. The name sup-

[41] Miller, *KHQ*, I, 112.

[42] *Ibid.*, 113.

[43] La Flesche, *A Dictionary of the Osage Language*, 82.

[44] "A Tour of Indian Agencies," *KHQ*, III, 318.

[45] C. S. Burch, *Handbook of Elk and Chautauqua Counties, Kansas*, 13.

posedly came from the Indians who are said to have had a name with the same meaning. Victor Murdock suggested that its Osage name was *Mur-sho*, which he interpreted to mean "stream with luxuriant cane growth." He referred to it, however, as the Little Verdigris.[46]

West of the Big Caney flows Grouse Creek, heading for the Arkansas in southern Cowley County. Murdock thought the Osage name was *Me-her* and that it meant "goose creek." The Walnut, which joins the Arkansas a short distance west of Grouse Creek, he called the *Ne-scahaes* or *Ne-saes-scah*. This, he said, was "a word that resisted all attempts at analysis."[47] It has such a close resemblance to the *Ninescua* that one would be tempted to assume that it has a similar meaning, "river salt."

As the Johnston surveyors approached the Arkansas River beyond the Caney, they camped on a small creek which was referred to as the "Ne-is-ka-bi-ka-kha or Spring creek." This has been identified by Nyle Miller as Beaver Creek, which flows into Oklahoma from Cowley County.[48] According to the Osage dictionary, the name by which Beaver Creek was identified was *Ni-ckon-cha ga-xe*, possibly meaning "middle creek" and having nothing to do with the name for beaver. If the *ka-bi* in *Ne-is-ka-bi-ka-kah* could be changed to *zha'be* or *xa'bi*, which means "beaver," this might be the source for the name of Beaver Creek.

In the Osage country of Chautauqua County there is a town with the strange but distinctive name of Niotaze. This place had had several names before it became Niotaze. The first name at this site was Jay Hawk, the name of the school. When the place became a post office, it was also named Jay Hawk. Then the place was renamed Matanzas, a Spanish name which is well known in Cuba and which is also the name of a bay in Florida near St. Augustine. It appears attractive but it means a "slaughter" or "massacre." However, the name lasted for sixteen years, and then, perhaps, the residents discovered what it meant.[49] The Missouri Pacific Railroad

[46] *Wichita Evening Eagle*, March 6, 1943; *Sumner County Press*, Jan. 29, 1874.
[47] *Sumner County Press*, Jan. 29, 1874.
[48] Miller, *KHQ*, I, 115.
[49] *Sedan Times-Star*, Aug. 14, 1941.

proposed that the place be renamed Niota. There was a Niota in Illinois on the site of an Iowa village across the river from Fort Madison. As an Iowa name it had a Siouan origin and could mean "much water" or "water's mouth."[50]

In Labette County there was a Neola, a name that was easily confused with Niota, especially by those who failed to dot their "i's" or cross their "t's." Niota was therefore changed to Newport. This did not end the confusion. There was also a Newport in Kentucky, and when Kansas and Kentucky were abbreviated to "Ka." or "Ks." for Kansas and to "Ky." for Kentucky, careless mail clerks would send the mail to the wrong state. This was like the mail intended for Reno, "Neb.," going to Reno, "Nev.," or vice versa. So the postmaster decided to restore the Indian name of Niota but he gave it distinction by adding an appendage. He named it Niotaze, a name which is found at no other place in the United States.[51] While this name is sufficiently distinctive, it is also meaningless.

The place called Neola in Labette County did not last long. Western settlements were free to use names which had disappeared from the map in eastern Kansas, and in Stafford County there is a new Neola. It is an attractive name of a little railway station on the Missouri Pacific. It appears to be an Indian name, but it is of uncertain origin.[52]

[50] Vogel, *Indian Place Names in Illinois,* 89.
[51] *Sedan Times-Star,* Aug. 14, 1941.
[52] Vogel, *Indian Place Names in Illinois,* 87.

▲ XI

Pawnee and Arikara

THE PAWNEES were southern Indians of the Caddoan linguistic group, as were also the Arikaràs, occasionally called Arikarees. They had moved northward from the Red River country and wedged their way up through Kansas and Nebraska and as far north as the Dakotas. Best known among the Pawnees were those living on the Platte and the Loup. Related tribes with different names lived in Kansas. They were the *Pitahauerats* and the *Kitkehahkis*. The *Pitahauerats*, called *Tapages* by the French, lived on the Kaw towards the Topeka area, and the *Kitkehahkis*, better known as the Republican Pawnees, lived on the Republican River.[1] In central Kansas and southward along the Arkansas lived the Wichitas whom the French called the *Panis piqués*. The greater part of Kansas was Pawnee hunting ground, restricted only by the ability of their rivals to hold them back.

The Pawnee name is scattered throughout the state. It became the name of a river, a creek, a county, a town, a trail, a territorial capital, several townships, and a famous rock. The name, according to John B. Dunbar's interpretation, may have come from the word that described their distinctive hair style. Their "topknot," it was said, was "daubed with bison fat and red ochre until stiff enough to stand erect, or curving slightly backward like a horn." The word for horn was *paríki*. A form of the name also applied to the Arikaras and to the Wichitas. The Dakota name for Pawnees was

[1] Hyde, *Pawnee Indians*, 13–15; Dunbar, "The Pawnee Indians," *Magazine of American History*, IV, 245. For maps of Caddoan tribes see Connelley, *KHC*, XIV, facing pages 438 and 448.

Padáni. This could be more easily slurred into *Pahni* or *Pani*, as the French wrote it, or *Panana*, as Antonio Valverde, the Spanish governor of New Mexico, wrote it. The Osage name for the Pawnees was *Pa-L'n* or *Pa-in*, meaning the "long-haired people." The Pawnees were also called "slaves" since the Apaches sold their Pawnee prisoners to other tribes, occasionally as far away as Illinois. One should not conclude that the word Pawnee meant "slave," even though this has been suggested. The Arapahos, Comanches, and Cheyennes called them "wolf people," and some of the Sioux called them "little wolf people." These names may have been derived from the Skidi Pawnees in Nebraska, whom the French called Loup, meaning "wolf."[2]

The Pawnees called themselves the *Chahiksichahiks* which was said to mean "civilized" people or "men of men." But this was not a name in common use. The Pawnees were great hunters and they were proud to refer to themselves as the *parisu*, meaning "hunters." It is as difficult to make Pawnee out of *parisu* as it is from *paríki.*[3] Twice a year the Pawnees made hunting expeditions into southwestern Kansas. This was buffalo country and the battleground for food. There they also stole horses. They started their expeditions on foot but they expected to ride back. Stealing horses was a sport and a business, and success brought to these horse thieves both the esteem of their people and a measure of prosperity. The rivalry over these happy hunting grounds was the chief cause for their wars with the Kiowas, Comanches, and Cheyennes.

The river which came out of the west in the heart of their hunting land and entered the Arkansas above its Great Bend the Indians named the "dark timber river," probably for the dark cedars in the area. This was the river the white man later named the Pawnee River or the Pawnee Fork of the Arkansas. Indians also called it Otter River.[4]

Since the Indians followed a fairly fixed route to this hunting

[2] Hyde, *Pawnee Indians*, 13–14; Wedel, *An Introduction to Pawnee Archaeology*, 2–3; Baskett, *KHC*, XII, 247.

[3] Hyde, *Pawnee Indians*, 13; Baskett, *KHC*, XII, 247.

[4] Vestal, *The Old Santa Fe Trail*, 121; Hyde, *Pawnee Indians*, 93; Barry, *KHQ*, XXX, 71.

territory, the route became known as the Pawnee Trail. It was also extended to the Salt Flats in Oklahoma. The Pawnee Trail was marked with Pawnee names. In Republic County the "big bend" of the Republican River was called Pawnee Bend, and a valley route through Ottawa County was called Pawnee Gap.[5]

No rock is better known in Kansas than Pawnee Rock, that famous landmark on the trail to the Southwest. It is located on the Arkansas River just above its Great Bend. It served long as a landmark and a guide and occasionally as a natural fort. In its early days it was also known as Painted Rock and Rock Point. Since the rock was composed of red Dakota sandstone, it had the appearance of a "painted rock." It was also called Inscription Rock.[6]

The face of Pawnee Rock served as a traveler's register for those who took time to carve their names on its soft sandstone surface. When James H. Birch came by there in 1848, "it was so full of names," he said, that he could find no room left for his own; nor could Max Greene, "even by stretching on tiptoe."[7] General St. George Cooke took a dim view of those who would leave their names to posterity in this manner. He described the rock as "a natural monument inscribed with the names of all the fools who passed that way."[8] So Inscription Rock was appropriate, but the name that stuck was Pawnee Rock.

There are various versions about how the rock got its name. According to one story, a large band of Comanches cornered a small band of Pawnee horse thieves on the top of this natural fortification. The Pawnees were not attacked merely because they were horse thieves, a profession as highly respected by the Comanches as by the Pawnees. They were also rivals for their hunting grounds. Far outnumbered, the Pawnees merely held their strategic position until they ran out of food and water. They had bled their horses for food, but they ran short of water. The Pawnees finally made a des-

[5] Hyde, *Pawnee Indians*, 93 and 200; Adolph Roenigh, *Pioneer History of Kansas*, 232.

[6] *Expedition of Pike*, II, 433.

[7] James H. Birch, "The Battle of Coon Creek," *KHC*, X, 410; Greene, *The Kanzas Region*, 128.

[8] Vestal, *The Old Santa Fe Trail*, 115; Andreas and Cutler, *History of Kansas*, 763.

perate attempt to escape, but the Comanches killed them to a man. So the rock, Painted Rock or Rock Point, became Pawnee Rock.[9]

Another bit of folklore attributed the name of Pawnee Rock to an incident in Kit Carson's adventures. Carson had taken refuge from an Indian attack on this natural fort, and there he killed his first Pawnee. From this incident, some would say, the rock got its name. A variation of this story suggests that what Carson killed was not a Pawnee but his own mule. In the darkness, Carson had mistaken the ears of his mule for the feathers on an Indian's head and he thought he had shot a skulking Indian. Stanley Vestal gives no credence to this story.[10] We do have another version of the story from James R. Mead who was a guest of Kit Carson at the Little River peace conference. Carson, generally reticent, entertained him with stories of his adventures. Mead gave Carson's account of the Pawnee Rock incident as follows:

> When I was a young man I was going out to Santa Fe with a pack-train of mules. We camped at Pawnee Rock and were all asleep in our blankets in the grass when a party of Indians rode over us in the dark, yelling to stampede our stock. I jumped up and fired my rifle in the direction they had gone, and shot one of my best mules through the heart.

Carson was not a fancy storyteller like Jim Bridger, and the Mead version may stand.[11]

Travelers recognized Pawnee Rock's strategic value for defense. Three mountain men led by Old Bill Williams were returning from a trapping trip in Wyoming when they were forced to take refuge on the Pawnee Rock to defend themselves from sixty Pawnees. This "Prairie Citadel" saved them from the Pawnees, and a "miraculous" change of wind saved them from a prairie fire which threatened their position and their lives.[12]

[9] Vestal, *The Old Santa Fe Trail*, 116; Andreas and Cutler, *History of Kansas*, 763.

[10] Paul Wellman, "Some Famous Frontier Scouts," *KHQ*, I, 358; Vestal, *Kit Carson*, 22.

[11] *KHC*, X, 12.

[12] Wellman, in *Wichita Beacon*, Dec. 16, 1928; Vestal, *The Old Santa Fe Trail*, 107–13; Mead, *KHC*, X, 12.

Alexander W. Doniphan and Frederic Remington, among others, have helped to publicize Pawnee Rock. General Doniphan paused for a rest when he reached Pawnee Rock with his Missouri troops on his way to Mexico, and there he raised the American flag.[13] Remington found Pawnee Rock a worthy subject for one of his popular western paintings.

Famous though it be, this natural monument has almost disappeared. Much of Pawnee Rock has been used for building material. The Women's Kansas Day Club has helped to preserve the name and the Rock, and in 1909 the state legislature took possession to make it a state memorial.[14]

In 1871, Pawnee Rock became a post office, but not for long. The Santa Fe Railway had, however, preserved the name on its station between Larned and Great Bend. Altogether there have been six post offices using the Pawnee name. The first post office to be given the name of Pawnee was the one that came near being the state capital. Its post office name was changed to Fort Riley in December, 1855. There was a Pawnee Fork post office, named for the river, in Pawnee County. Farther up the river in Hodgeman County there was a Pawnee Valley post office. In the Osage country of eastern Kansas, there was a Pawnee, later changed to Hyattville for James M. Hyatt, the owner of the townsite. Its post-office name was Hyatt. East of this town is Pawnee Station, which looks as if it were a railway station, but there the "Katy" named its station Anna. Bourbon County also has a Pawnee Creek and a Pawnee Township.[15]

Pawnee Creek was named by the Osages, who called it *No-Washie-Cow-Haw-Shing-gah*, which was said to mean "poor Pawnee creek."[16] However, the *shing-gah* at the end of the name would lead one to believe that its description was "little," as it is in so many names although spelled differently, such as *zinga*, *shinka*, and *shunga*. But in contradiction to this, it had also been called *Panie-*

13 Martin, "Memorial Monuments and Tablets in Kansas," *KHC*, XI, 267.

14 *Ibid.*

15 Andreas and Cutler, *History of Kansas*, 1092; Barry, *KHQ*, XXIX, 329; E. J. Dallas, "Early-Day Post-Offices in Kansas," *KHC*, VII, 443.

16 Newman, *The Black Dog Trail*, 27.

Tanga, which meant "big Pawnee."[17] The creek was not "big," nor was it called "big" by the Americans. Father Paul Ponziglione, said one writer, "preached on the creek called Little Pawnee."[18]

The town named Pawnee in what was Davis County, now Geary, was destined for a very short time to become the territorial capital of Kansas. It was located on a beautiful site near Fort Riley at a place where there was need for a town, and it was optimistically called Pawnee City. Andrew H. Reeder, territorial governor, risked his political reputation and his money in his dream of making it the capital. He called the legislature to meet there. There it met, but the legislature spent most of its time eliminating Free State delegates, after which it adjourned to Shawnee Mission, nearer its Missouri representatives and its pro-slavery supporters. Its excuse for abandoning Pawnee City was that Pawnee's facilities were inadequate, which was partly true, and that it was Governor Reeder's speculative investment, which was also partly true. When the governor visited his dream capital in 1856, it had only two buildings. A few settlers had drifted in, mostly Pennsylvanians from Reeder's home state. It was important enough, however, to have attracted the attention of President Pierce who said that it was "a proposed town-site only" and that Governor Reeder and his associates had attempted to locate it illegally within the military reservation.[19]

Several officers at Fort Riley were interested in promoting the town, including Colonel W. R. Montgomery, the commanding officer, and Captain Nathaniel Lyon, for whom Lyon County is named. Montgomery was accused of speculation, among other charges, court-martialed, and dismissed. Both of these officers were Free State men. The secretary of war, none other than Jefferson Davis, drew a new and arbitrary line for the extension of the military reservation which included the Pawnee townsite. He wiped out the town of Pawnee with the stroke of a pen. Pawnee, also called "Governor Reeder's Town," had lost its chance of becoming the capital of Kansas. It became known as Pawnee-on-the-

[17] *Tixier's Travels on the Osage Prairies*, 118; Barry, *KHQ*, XXIX, 329.

[18] Graves, *History of Neosho County*, I, 170.

[19] Isaac T. Goodnow, "Personal Reminiscences and Kansas Emigration," *KHC*, IV, 246; "Governor Shannon's Administration," *KHC*, V, 254.

Reserve. The capitol building has been restored and stands as a mute memorial to politicians and speculators and to Missouri influence over Kansas politics.[20]

In 1867 a large county southwest of the great bend of the Arkansas River was mapped and named Pawnee. Five years later it was cut down in size and organized. The county was named for the Pawnee Fork, which flows in from the west and enters the Arkansas River at Larned.[21] Pawnee Rock Township has now deleted the "Rock" from its name and remains Pawnee. Well within the Pawnee territory on the border of Kansas was Pawnee Township in Smith County.

Few names have been more popular in Kansas than the name of Pawnee. With Pawnee post offices, Pawnee County, Pawnee townships, Pawnee River, Pawnee Creek, Pawnee Rock, Pawnee Bend, Pawnee Gap, and Pawnee Trail, the name is sprinkled well over the map of Kansas.

Next to the Smoky Hill Fork of the Kaw, the most important tributary was the Republican Fork which joins the former at Junction City to make the Kaw. The Republican flows out of Colorado and follows the Nebraska side until it makes a big bend into Kansas through Jewell and Republic counties. It was possibly the Republican River that the Mallet brothers named *Costes Blanches*, "white hills."[22] One of the four large divisions or bands of Pawnees of the Platte settled near the big bend on the Kansas side. This Pawnee band was called the *Kitkehahkis*, which may mean "on a hill," or it may be *kitskakis*, *kits* or *kizu* for "water" and *kakis* for "rapid" or "swift."[23] Even the Osage name for the Republican Pawnees, *Ci-ci-ka a-ki-cin*, has a remote resemblance to the Pawnee name.

The river on which these Pawnees had settled on the Kansas border was a favorite grazing place and resting place for the buffalos. Thousands stood in the shade of the trees along its banks or

[20] Martin, *KHC*, VII, 367ff.

[21] *Larned Chronoscope*, Oct. 18, 1934; Andreas and Cutler, *History of Kansas*, 1350.

[22] Folmer, *The Colorado Magazine*, XVI, 165n.

[23] M. R. Gilmore, "Some Indian Place Names in Nebraska," Nebraska State Historical Society *Publications*, XIX, 134; Hyde, *Pawnee Indians*, 64.

in its cooling waters. The Pawnees or *Kitkehahkis* were annoyed by the pollution of the waters by these vast buffalo herds, and called the river the *Ki-rara-tu* or *Ki-ra-ru-tah*, meaning "turgid water," "filthy water," or, as Grinnell translated it, "manure river."[24] The Little Osages knew the Pawnee name for the river, since they too referred to it as the "buffalo-dung river." The Omahas found some squashes in an abandoned white-man's garden on the river, so they named it the *Watan-thata-i-ke*, "Where-they-ate-the-squashes-River."[25]

When the *Kitkehahkis* set up their tribal village on the Kansas border, independent of the Pawnees of the Platte, the French were so impressed that they called them the *Pahni Républicaine* and their organization the *Pahni République*, as written by J. C. McCoy. The French spoke of the river as the *Fourche de Républicaine*. Green combined the name to the Republican Pawnee Fork. Isaac McCoy had referred to the river as the "Republican, or Panee River." The settlement of the *Kitkehahki* Pawnees took place during the American Revolution, and it was this association that is supposed to have inspired the French to call them *Républicaine*.[26] The Spaniards, in nominal possession of this territory, knew these Pawnees by their French name as early as 1777 and referred to them as the *Nación de la República*. In 1785 they spoke of the *Aldea de la República*, the "Republican village."[27]

The site of the village of these Pawnees were made famous as the place where Pike first raised the American flag over Kansas. A Republican County historian speaks of it as "Pike's Pawnee Indian village."[28] Pike used the name Pawnee Republic on the letterhead in his letters to Generals Dearborn and Wilkinson. While the name of Republican is in this case of French origin, it is certainly much easier to remember and to use than the Indian name *Kitkehahkis*.

[24] Link *The Origin of the Place Names of Nebraska*, part II of Fitzpatrick's *Nebraska Place-Names*, 183; Hyde, *Pawnee Indians*, 281.

[25] Link, in Fitzpatrick's *Nebraska Place-Names*, 184; Mathews, *The Osages*, 139.

[26] McCoy to Sec. of War, Jan. 31, 1831, 22 Cong., 1 sess., *Exec. Doc. No. 172*, 13; "Names," MS, KSHS Archives; McCoy, *KHQ*, V, 368.

[27] Wedel, *An Introduction to Pawnee Archaeology*, 32; Diller, *KHQ*, XXI, 405; Hyde, *Pawnee Indians*, 74 and 78.

[28] I. O. Savage, *A History of Republic County, Kansas*, 19.

Closer to the modern Pawnee name was the name given to the river by the Kansa Indians who called it the *Pa-ne-ne-tah*, the "Pawnee River," as did McCoy. Isaac McCoy said he had proceeded from the "Nishcoba-or Deep Water," until he "fell in with Panie river." The next day he reached the "Panee" River and changed the spelling of the name.[29]

Republic County, through which flows the Republican River as it enters Kansas, was named in 1860 for the river. The first town to take its name from the Republican River was Republican City in Clay County. There it had been a post office with the interesting name of Five Creeks, named for the creeks flowing in from the west. The change of name took place in 1869, in time to change the name of the town with the same name in Republic County. Republican City promoters in Clay County hoped that "push and enterprise" would make it the county seat. Republican City had both a stage stop and a post office, but Clay Center won the coveted county-seat prize, after which Republican City had little to sustain its life. In Clay County the name Republic remains only as the name of a township.[30]

In Republic County the town of Republic City also had ambitions to become a county seat. It had been a post office with the name of Gomeria for a decade, 1870–80.[31] Changing its name to Republican City did not make it the county seat nor did it become a city. As a post office it had to drop the "City" part and became just Republic, now a name on a station on the Missouri Pacific. The Republic name may appear to most people to be a political party name, but it is, nevertheless, the name of an Indian tribe as it was applied by the French and modified by the English.

Prairie Dog Creek flows through five counties in northwestern Kansas before it enters the Republican River in Nebraska. Horace Greeley and other travelers were quite fascinated by the prairie-dog towns of western Kansas, and such keen observers as the Pawnees may have been equally fascinated. Prairie Dog Creek could

[29] *Expedition of Pike*, II, 582; Root, *KHQ*, III, 246; McCoy *KHC*, IV, 305; McCoy, *KHQ*, V, 374.

[30] W. P. Anthony, "Republican City, Clay County," *KHC*, XII, 440.

[31] Baughman, *Kansas Post Offices*, 51.

well have been a translation of *Uskuts*, meaning "prairie dog," which was the Pawnee name for the creek.[32]

The Arikaras or Arikarees, distant relatives of the Pawnees, extended the Caddoan domain into the Dakotas. This once-powerful branch of the Pawnees was under constant attack by the Sioux, and their population was decimated by the white man's smallpox. They seemed to have but a dismal and deadly choice: "If the Sioux don't get you, the small pox will."[33]

The Arikaras, who were found on the high plains of the West on a hunting expedition, had been pushed westward under pressure from the Sioux. In the northwestern corner of the state, the Arikaree, a fork of the Republican, barely cuts the corner of Kansas. It was the Battle of the Arikaree which gave its name to Beecher Island which was just outside the Kansas border. This was named in memory of the Lieutenant Beecher who gave his name to Camp Beecher which later became Wichita. In the neighborhood of the Arikaree River in Kansas, the Arikaree name was also given to the Arikaree Arroyos and to the Arikaree Hills.

To emphasize their pride and feeling of superiority, as did so many tribes, the Arikaras called themselves *Sa-Nish* or *Tanish*, meaning "the people." They were, however, generally referred to as Arikaras, with considerable freedom in spelling. Occasionally the first syllable was dropped to make the name Rikarees or even Ricarees. For brevity the next two syllables were dropped and the Arikarees became just Rees.[34]

Arikara meant "elk horn" or "antlered elk." In the Omaha language, Big Elk was called *Arre-catta-waho*, the *arre-catta* meaning "elk" and the *waho* meaning "big." We also have a reference to "horn" in the Skidi Pawnee word *iriki*, which Grinnell spelled *Paraki* and Hyde spelled *Pariki*. This had reference to the Pawnee hair style in which they wore two pieces of bone that looked like horns.[35] They were sometimes referred to as the *Ka'ta*, a name that

[32] Hyde, *Pawnee Indians*, 282.

[33] *Ibid.*, 6.

[34] Donaldson, "The George Catlin Indian Gallery," *Annual Report* of the Board of Regents of the Smithsonian Institution to July 1885, Part II, 79.

[35] Hyde, *Pawnee Indians*, 30; Baskett, *KHC*, XII, 246.

described their manner of eating corn and was interpreted to mean "biters."[36] *Iriki* or *paríki* could be better applied to the Arikaras than to the Pawnees. The name may be Arikara or Arikaree, Rickara or Ree, and together they sounded like a children's jingle or a college yell: "Arikara, Arikaree, Arrecatta, Waho!"

[36] Mooney, "Calendar History of the Kiowa Indians," *BAE Seventeenth Annual Report* (1895–96), 410 and 437.

XII ▲

Topeka

TOPEKA IS A NAME with distinction, and to many it personifies Kansas. What it means and from which language it came is still debatable. It may be a Siouan name, a Caddoan name, a Potawatomi name, or even a Cherokee or Choctaw name from the lower Mississippi. It may have a French origin. Finally, it may be based, but not too seriously, on an effort of the Indians to speak English.

The last should be disposed of first. According to W. A. Stubbs, the name came from a shout by the Indians when some travelers came to the ferry crossing of the Kaw at high water. The Indians, thinking the river was too high to cross, shouted to the travelers, "Too beega." This simple yet appealing source for the name Topeka fits better into folklore than fact.[1]

A rather remote source is that of a Cherokee or Choctaw name in Alabama which referred to the Indian defense against General Jackson at the Battle of the Horseshoe behind barricades and fortifications which they called *Tohipeka* or *Tohopeka.* From this it was assumed that *Tohipeka* meant "breastworks" and that *Tohipeka* became Topeka. These two names are only a short syllable apart in spelling, but they are far apart geographically.[2]

Two other interpretations may be mentioned. A missionary to the Otos was reported to have been told by a chief that Topeka meant "white breast" or "a missionary at home."[3] An official from the Department of the Interior said that Topeka was "a cor-

[1] Haucke, *KHQ*, XX, 49.

[2] Howes, "What About the Name, Topeka?" Shawnee County Historical Society *Bulletin*, I, 106; Giles, *Thirty Years in Topeka*, 54.

[3] Howes, Shawnee County Historical Society *Bulletin*, I, 106.

ruption of To-pen-ibe," the name of a prominent Potawatomi chief who had lived on the Topeka site. "I just drifted into this bit of Potawatomi history," he added.[4] Topenibe was truly a prominent Potawatomi chief, but the writer drifted too far when he gave his name to Topeka.

In some way or another the name of Topeka has been associated with a variety of names for potatoes—wild potatoes, little potatoes, *pommes de terre*, and tubers which were only reminders of potatoes. Ely Moore, hunting with the Miamis, wrote, "Our next camp was at 'To-pe-ka,' signifying, in the Kaw language, 'a place to find small or wild potatoes.' "[5]

When John D. Dunbar, professor of languages in Washburn University, came to the conclusion, as others had, that Topeka actually meant "a good place to pick potatoes," he was critically challenged by Connelley of the state historical society. According to Dunbar, *to* meant "potato," *pa* from *pekal* meant "good," and *okae*, "to dig." This, said Connelley, was "clothed in learned language acceptable to lexicographers." He added that by dropping parts of these words, Dunbar had Topeka left "as a sort of sediment." Resuming his ridicule, Connelley asked Dunbar whether Topeka meant "a good potato to dig at Topeka," "a good Topeka to dig at potato," or "Topeka potatoes to be dug good at that place."[6]

The potato interpretation had long been used, but Dunbar is supposed to have had it verified by a Kansa Indian known as Jo Jim, short for John James, whose Indian name was *Ge'he-ga-zhin-ga* or Little Chief. Connelley was somewhat intemperate in his ridicule and suggested that the "degraded Kaw would answer any question favorably if it were accompanied with a whiff of whiskey." He dismissed Jo Jim's interpretation as the "clap trap" of a drunken Kaw full of "bust head."[7]

In a letter from Brownsville, Texas, Lute P. Stover told Connelley that he had been too harsh on Dunbar and said that he agreed

[4] "Names," MS, KSHS Archives.
[5] "A Buffalo Hunt with the Miamis," *KHC*, X, 404.
[6] "Origin of the Name Topeka," *KHC*, XVII, 591ff.
[7] *Ibid.*; *Kansas City Star*, Nov. 25, 1944; Giles, *Thirty Years in Topeka*, 55.

with the views of the professor and the "drunken" Indian, supported by a sober squaw.[8] In fact, most of the writers on the subject seem to have agreed with Dunbar's interpretation. Lewis H. Morgan, an anthropologist visiting Kansas in the 1850's, also referred to "To-poo-ka" as a "good place to dig potatoes."[9]

One still has to discover the source for potatoes in a country which had no potatoes and among Indians who had no name for potatoes. There were, however, various plants which were carelessly called potatoes as a generic term for the edible tubers eaten by the Indians. One was called the Jerusalem artichoke, the *helianthus tuberosus* or sunflower tuber. This was not a potato, nor was it an artichoke, nor did it come from Jerusalem.[10] The name was *girasole articiocco*. The *girasole* referred to the flower's tendency to turn to the sun. Then the *girasole* was corrupted into Jerusalem and the *articiocco* into artichoke. And what is it? Just a sunflower.[11]

The *Kansas Free State* of Lawrence for April 14, 1855, made reference to the "strawberries" and "wild potatoe" to be found in the lowlands near Lawrence. Sergeant Ordway with Lewis and Clark wrote about the beautiful "bottom prairie" which was "covered with wild rye and wild potatoes."[12] The Canadian French spoke of a *pomme de terre* or "cowberry, ground nut, or wild bean," which was eaten by both the French and the Indians. The French *pomme de terre* again indicates potatoes. When Frémont came to Kansas, he found the women digging "prairie potatoes."[13] To add to the variety, William A. Phillips of the *New York Tribune* said that there was a Potawatomi word *tohopeka* or *topheika* which meant "mountain potato."[14] So, whether these tubers were "little" potatoes, "wild" potatoes, or "mountain" potatoes, the

[8] "Names," MS, KSHS Archives.

[9] *Morgan: The Indian Journals*, 68.

[10] *Kansas City Star*, Jan. 25, 1944.

[11] *Wichita Sunday Eagle and Beacon*, magazine section, July 5, 1964; McDermott, "Glossary of French," Washington University *Studies in Language and Literature*, No. 12 (1941), 125.

[12] *KHQ*, XIII, 148; *The Journals of Lewis and Ordway*, 95.

[13] McDermott, Washington University *Studies*, No. 12 (1941), 125; Hale, *Kansas*, 96.

[14] King, *History of Shawnee County, Kansas*, 133; Giles, *Thirty Years in Topeka*, 53.

potato interpretation had certainly become accepted and popular. Yet there are other interpretations equally worthy of consideration.

Since the name of Topeka was applied to the lower part of the Smoky Hill River, some have concluded that it meant Smoky Hill. Even Connelley, who had strong opinions on the subject, accepted this for a time. In a letter to William Gladstone Steel in 1930 he said, "I feel that Smoky Hill is the proper interpretation of this name and that it means smoky, dim, dimly seen."[15] But one need not assume that the two names mean the same even though they are applied to the same river.[16]

"Tä-pä′gĕ is the word from which the name 'Topeka' is derived," said Connelley. Ignoring the fact that *tapage* was a French word meaning "noisy," Connelley concluded: " 'Topeka,' then, is an old Caddoan Indian word, coming down to us from . . . the Tä-pä′gĕ Pawnee." Reluctant to give up his earlier interpretation, he added, "And if this old Indian word means 'Smoky Hill,' which I believe it does, it is not inappropriate for the name of the capital of Kansas."[17]

George E. Hyde, an authority on the Pawnees, said that there was no such word as *tapage* meaning "noisy" in Pawnee. He added that all Pawnees were noisy. This was, of course, irrelevant. Perhaps some were noisier than others, and the northern Pawnees spoke of the Pawnees on the Kaw as "noisy Pawnees." If the French knew this, then we have the explanation of why they called them *Tapage* meaning "noisy." The name was also written Tappago Pawnee and Pawnee Tappaye.[18]

The Pawnees living on the Kaw in the Topeka area were called *Pitahauerats*. When Hyde tried to analyze the meaning of *Pitahauerat*, he first gave Frank North's translation, "downstream" or "eastward." This was supposedly based on the fact that the *Pitahauerats* had lived on the lower Kaw which was downstream and eastward from the other Pawnees. The whole river had been called the Smoky Hill River, and so these *Pitahauerats* were also known

[15] *KHC*, XVII, 589; "Names," MS, KSHS Archives.
[16] Edward G. Nelson, *The Company and the Community*, 444n.
[17] *KHC*, XVII, 591–93.
[18] Foreman, *The Last Trek of the Indians*, 182.

as the Smoky Hill Pawnees.[19] In the appendix to his book on the Pawnees, Hyde reconsidered the meaning of *Pitahauerat*. "In the Pawnee Hako ceremony," he said "*rata* means *screaming*, *pita* means a *man*; and for all we know, some French trader with a smattering of Pawnee language may have guessed that these two words were the origin of the name Pitahauerat, which he built into 'Screamers or Tapages.' "[20] This conclusion seems to be logical, and it would not take much ingenuity to make Topeka out of Tapage.

The name in some form or another had long been in use by the natives in the area, especially by the Omahas, Otos, and the Kansas. Schoolcraft used the dual name of "Smoky Hill or Topeka" for the Kaw River. Following the Treaty of 1825, Major Angus L. Langham was sent from Jefferson Barracks to survey the Kansa lands in preparation for the great removal of the Indians from the East to this new Indian Territory. Langham's map and report refer to the Kansas River as the Topeka. Holliday, Giles, or any one of their associates could have adopted its use from either Schoolcraft or Langham. F. W. Giles may or may not have known French, but he has been given credit, among others, for changing Tapage to Topeka.[21]

Members of the association for the promotion of the town gave serious consideration to several names before deciding on Topeka. The scattered log houses which formed the beginning of the town had been called Kansasville before it was given an official name.[22] As a place where the Kaw was crossed, it was known as Papan's Ferry. The Papans, who came to Kansas from St. Louis, were French Canadians married to Indians. Their name has also been spelled both Pappan and Papin. Not only was the Papan name important in the early history of Kansas, but it also became a name of national significance when Charles Curtis, the grandson of Louis Papan, became the Vice President of the United States. The pro-

[19] *Pawnee Indians*, 63.

[20] *Ibid.*, 63–64 and 289.

[21] *Kansas City Star*, June 25, 1944; Root, *KHQ*, IV, 3; Howes, Shawnee County Historical Society *Bulletin*, No. 1, 106.

posal to name the town Papan's Ferry was, however, rejected, strangely enough as being "too provincial."[23]

As an appeal to the rest of the nation, the name of Midcontinent was proposed, and this was appropriate, since the geographical center of the nation was in Kansas, although farther west. But Midcontinent was rejected as being "too cumbersome."[24]

The most prominent of the men promoting Topeka was Cyrus K. Holliday. He has been given credit for selecting the townsite on Shunganunga Creek where he also planned a park for the public.[25] The town could have been appropriately named Holliday to do honor to its promoter, but Holliday proposed the name of Webster to honor Daniel Webster, the great statesman from Massachusetts. At least four men have been given credit for suggesting that the town be named Topeka—T. H. Webb, Holliday, S. Y. Lum, and Frye Giles. Holloway gave the credit to T. H. Webb, secretary of the New England Emigrant Aid Society. This was questioned by Giles, who attended the meetings for the selection of the name.[26]

On New Year's Eve, 1855, members of the town company spent the whole evening discussing names. On the next night the name of Topeka came up for discussion, introduced by F. W. Giles it is believed. The Rev. S. Y. Lum was not at the meeting, but he is given credit for having suggested the name of Topeka to Giles, and Giles presented the arguments. "You want a name," he is reported to have said, "that any man can pronounce if he sees it in print, and that any man can spell if he hears it spoken." Topeka had the distinction of being "a name not found in the list of post offices of the United States, nor in any lexicon of the English language." It was a novel name of Indian origin, euphonious of sound and simple. "Its Indian flavor could not be questioned and its equal division of vowels and consonants gave it a tripping and cadent

22 Paden, *In the Wake of the Prairie Schooner*, 83.
23 King, *History of Shawnee County, Kansas*, 133.
24 *Ibid.*
25 Wallace S. Boldinger, "The Amateur Plans a City," *KHQ*, XII, 7–8.
26 Holloway, *History of Kansas*, 118.

sound."[27] Few names in Kansas have been chosen with greater care. Names were rejected because they were "too provincial" or "too cumbersome," and then Topeka was selected because it was "novel," "euphonious," and "simple," and because it had an "Indian flavor." The men who chose this distinctive name were men of intelligent discrimination.

Cyrus K. Holliday had already used the Topeka name and he accepted it. He had written to his wife from "Topeka, K. T." on December 17, 1854, two weeks before the name was adopted by the town company. Holliday may therefore be given credit for introducing it by using it, and furthermore, he may have suggested the name to the Rev. Mr. Lum. Topeka was a better address than "Up the Stream," the address which Holliday had used a week earlier.[28]

The naming of the town might have called for some sort of celebration, but James King, the Shawnee County historian, said that "there was no formal ceremony of christening, no festal rites—Bacchus, Gambrinus and the goddess of hop tea had not yet penetrated the confines of the Missouri River." Without any reflection on the men who named Topeka, it may not have been any lack of liquor that stood in the way of any "formal ceremony of christening." Giles' simple comment was, "The name was received with favor and soon adopted with unanimity."[29]

To celebrate the anniversary of the founding of Topeka, someone wrote in 1871 what has been called "a poetical effusion." It may have had a political purpose and was written with some poetic license. This is the part that dealt with the naming of Topeka:

Then gathered in a circle,
Around their cabin fire,
They all agreed their city
To a name might now aspire.

[27] *Thirty Years in Topeka*, 51; Howes, "Ninety Years for the Santa Fe," *Kansas Teacher*, LVIII, 46.

[28] Holliday, *KHQ*, VI, 246–47.

[29] King, *History of Shawnee County, Kansas*, 133; Giles, *Thirty Years in Topeka*, 51; Howes, *Kansas Teacher*, LVIII, 46.

After many fruitless ballots,
The teller shouts "Eureka!"
Giles has won the right to sponsor—
The name shall be Topeka.

All honor to these noble men—
Chase, Giles, Horne, Holliday!
Their hopes have reached fruition—
True "city fathers" they. [30]

The Topeka name has been extended to North Topeka and to South Topeka. The name has been sufficiently popular to be adopted as a place name in Illinois, Indiana, and Minnesota, and there is a Topeka Junction in Georgia. The name is so unique that vaudeville performers could once get a sure laugh from such unusual combinations as "Kalamazoo, Topeka, and Timbuctu," not unlike Jack Benny's use of Azusa and Cucamonga.

The city of Topeka has also absorbed the surrounding suburbs of Arlington Heights, Auburndale, Potwin Place, Oakland, and Quinton Heights. The name of Arlington Heights commemorated a famous battle in Vermont during the American Revolution. The name for Auburndale seems to have come from New York. Oakland was a descriptive name. Quinter and Potwin were promoters and businessmen who helped build greater Topeka. Charles W. Potwin, who had a great love of trees, was responsible for the planting of a variety of trees along the Topeka streets, which were then named for the trees. This was most conspicuous in a suburb which for a time was called the City of Potwin Place and which was incorporated with Topeka in 1888. The area called Elm Grove also stressed the importance of trees. Another area that emphasized the beauty of the suburbs was Highland Park, promoted and named by Joseph Kennedy Hudson and his wife.[31] With its trees and parks and rolling hills, one can see why the attractive town of Topeka has deservedly been described as the "Isle of Beauty."

[30] Giles, *Thirty Years in Topeka*, 52–53.
[31] Howes, "Ghost Towns of Shawnee County," Shawnee County Historical Society *Bulletin*, I, 26–27.

XIII ▲

Wichita, Waco, and Kechai

THE WICHITA INDIANS, like the Pawnees, were Caddoan Indians who participated in a great migration northward from the Red River area in the south. It is possible that they had first gone to the Platte River country of Nebraska and then returned to settle in central Kansas. The tribes in the Wichita confederacy were the Tawehash, Tawakonis, Wacos, and Kichais. The Tawehash, also called Tayovayas, were eventually known as the Wichitas, and the Wichita name was frequently used for the Tawakonis fied as the Quivira country.

The Wichita Indians settled along the Arkansas River in central Kansas and southward into Oklahoma. At the time of the Coronado expedition they were living in the general area between Great Bend and Lindsborg, but most of their villages were concentrated in Rice County, the very center of Kansas. They left archaeological records on their campsites, where archaeologists, historians, journalists, pot hunters, and relic collectors have reaped a rich harvest of Indian artifacts.[2] This was the area which the Spaniards identified as the Quivira country.

It has been suggested that Quivira was most likely an abbreviation of Guadalquivir, the Arabic name for the "big river" in Spain. As the Delaware Indians got their name from the Delaware

[1] Elizabeth A. Harper, "The Taovayas Indians in the Frontier Trade and Diplomacy," *Chronicles of Oklahoma,* XXXI, 274n.; Hyde, *Pawnee Indians,* 138; Thomas, *After Coronado,* 26n.

[2] Wedel, *An Introduction to Pawnee Archaeology,* 305; Paul A. Jones, *Coronado and Quivira.*

River, so the Quivira Indians got their name from the "Quivira" River, where they lived, and indirectly from the Guadalquivir in Spain.[3]

The Wichita Indians have had many names, each tribe named according to its own description and each in its own language. Occasionally, however, the name was learned from other tribes, but the pronunciation varied sufficiently to change the spelling. Each of these names was given a Spanish, French, or English spelling, with great variations within each language. The result is that there has been considerable confusion over the origin, meaning, spelling, and pronunciation of Wichita.

Claude du Tisné, a Frenchman visiting the Osages in 1719, was the first European to meet the Wichitas in southern Kansas. Indian tribes were generally loath to let a friendly foreigner visit hostile neighbors. Irked by Osage threats to prevent his departure and fearing that they might scalp him, Du Tisné showed his ingenuity and audacity by taking off his wig and throwing it to the ground. He dared them to pick it up. Du Tisné's astounding demonstration with his convertible scalp left the Osages dumbfounded, and they dared not touch it. Du Tisné was then permitted to go on to the Wichitas, and he claimed that part of Kansas for the king of France. He did not call the natives Wichitas; he called them *Paniouassas*, a name which the French had already used on their maps.[4]

Paniouassa was a French form of the name as it was used by several Siouan tribes, from the Omahas to the Osages. It was also written *Pan-nye Wacène*, *Pácin Wasábe*, and *Pani Wasábe*. Riggs's Sioux dictionary defines *Was-sa-pe-dan* as "black bear." Because of the association with "black bear," the name was simplified to *Pani-wasaba* which Du Tisné and other Frenchmen wrote *Paniouassa*, *Paniassa*, and *Panioussa*. However, as a result of deleting the word "bear," the name was shortened to *Pani Noir* in French,

[3] See Chapter VI on the Arkansas River.

[4] Rydjord, "French Frontier and the Indian Trade," in Bright's *Kansas: The First Century*, I, 23.

meaning "black Pawnee." The Black Pawnee name was used broadly and included the Wichitas, although it was also applied to a band which was only associated with the Wichitas.[5]

A different association with "bear" came from *Kirikurus* or *Kirikurukstu*, which was said to mean "bear's eyes" because of the impression that the Wichitas had "eyes like bears." It has been assumed that this was due to their practice of painting circles around their eyes. This may also explain why a Wichita chief named Kiowa said that the Pawnees called them a name which meant "coon eyes." However, Dunbar said that *Kirikurukstu* meant "south." This interpretation, Dunbar explains, resulted from the Pawnees of the Platte using *Kirikurukstu* to mean "toward or with the Wichitas," and eventually that meant "south."[6]

Bernard de la Harpe, who came from New Orleans to explore the Texas-Oklahoma area in 1719, was evidently the first Frenchman to use the name which became Wichita. He referred to a tribe which he called the *Ositas*, also written *Ousitas* and *Wusitas*. His reference to the *Quiscasquiris* has also been identified with the Wichitas. This must have been the French way of writing such Pawnee names as *Kirikiris* or *Kirikurus*. Swanton identified *Quirasquiris* as simply "French form of native name." These are only a few of the many names for the Wichitas listed by Swanton and Hodge.[7]

The assumption that Wichita was a name of Creek origin was based on such Creek names as *We-chate* or *We-chata*. *We* was translated as "water" and *chata* as "red." The Wichitas were then said to be the "red river people," which they were, having come from the Red River in Texas. But this was based on the assumption that the name was first used in 1835 as Witchetaw by Lieutenant W. Seawell when he was accompanied by some Creek Indians.

[5] Hyde, *Pawnee Indians*, 6; Harper, *Chronicles of Oklahoma*, XXXI, 270; Swanton, *The Indian Tribes of North America*, 305.

[6] Grinnell, *Pawnee Hero Stories and Folk Tales*, 241; Hyde, *Pawnee Indians*, 78; Dunbar, *Magazine of American History*, IV, 251; Wedel, *An Introduction to Pawnee Archaeology*, 305.

[7] Mildred P. Mayhall, *The Kiowas*, 21; Arthur G. Day, *Coronado's Quest*, 358n.; Harper, *Chronicles of Oklahoma*, XXXI, 274n.

Since the name had already been used in various forms for over a century, the Creek interpretation has been challenged.[8]

It was not unusual to refer to Indian settlements by direction. But the name by direction depends on the direction from which one speaks. The Wichitas had been called the "people of the South," but the English are said to have derived the opposite meaning from the Caddoan name *Ahors–Widtsa-Tow*. According to Tawaconia Jim, a Wichita chief, *ahors* meant "people" and *widtsa-tow* meant "north," and this made the Wichitas the "people of the North." Since they had migrated originally from the Caddoan tribes in the South, they could well have been called the "men of the North," as they explained it to Colonel W. S. Nye.[9] In North Texas, said Herbert E. Bolton, the Wichitas and related tribes were called the *Norteños* or "natives of the North." This may be associated with the name meaning "north" or it may merely be a Spanish identification by direction.[10]

Wichita warriors were elaborately tattooed and they were lavish with their war paint. When Bliss Isely, a Wichita reporter, interviewed the Wichitas at Anadarko, one chief told him that "their tatooing was very distinctive. . . . No other tribe tatooed as they did."[11] The Wichita women, no less than the men, considered tattooing their chief ornament and made "a perfect calico of the whole underjaw, breasts, and arms." Tattooing was a decorative design which was an approved substitute for apparel on a topless dress. "When I first saw them," said James R. Mead, "many of the older women were artistically tattooed in pink and blue zigzag circles and lines." Ysopete, the Wichita Indian who guided Coronado to the Quivira country, was also described as "a painted Indian."[12] The practice of tattooing became the source for their name *Pani piqué*.

[8] Zoe A. Tilghman, "Origin of the Name Wichita," *American Anthropologist* (n.s.), XLIII, 488; Mary R. Haas, "Comments on the Name 'Wichita,' " *American Anthropologist* (n.s.), XLIV, 164–65.

[9] Hyde, *Pawnee Indians*, 20; *Wichita Eagle*, Nov. 10, 1934.

[10] *Texas in the Middle Eighteenth Century*, 4.

[11] Isely to Campbell, Clippings, Ablah Library, Wichita State University.

[12] Gregg, *Commerce of the Prairies*, 431; Mead, *KHC*, VIII, 174.

The Kiowas and Comanches called the Wichitas by names which meant "tattooed people." In Kiowa it was *Doguat* or *Do'gu'at*; in Comanche, *Do'kănă*. In French this became *Pahni piqué* or *Pani piqué*, occasionally written as one word. "They are called panipiques," because "all of them are painted," said a Spanish source. However, the Spaniards occasionally called them *Jumanos* or *Humanos*, which could also apply to other tribes, especially the Apaches, if they were tattooed.[13]

Early nineteenth-century American travelers gave the French name *Pani piqué* a phonetic English spelling and lost the meaning. Washington Irving wrote it Pawnee Pick; others wrote it Pawnee Picts. Some even called them just Picks. The Americans did much better when they translated the name into Freckled Pawnees and Speckled Pawnees, and possibly more accurately when they made it Prickled Pawnees. These translations could, at least, carry the implication that the Wichitas were the "tattooed Pawnees."[14] These *Panis piqués* or Pawnee Picts became better known as the Wichitas. Since these were names of the same people, it has been wrongly assumed that Wichita was a name which meant the same as *Pani piqué*, the "tattooed people" or "painted faces." The Wichita Indians accepted their descriptive name of *Pani piqué*, but the Americans made the mistake of assuming that this was the meaning of Wichita.

Bliss Isely, with two venerable plainsmen, Colonel S. S. Carter and William Peacock, went on an expedition from Wichita, Kansas, to Anadarko, Oklahoma, the present home of the Wichitas, to learn more about the name Wichita. There they interviewed the oldest chiefs of the tribe. Isely, with Peacock as interpreter, questioned Chief Yellowbird and Chief Kiowa, and the oldest of them all, Chief Chochofpy. By using the sign language, Chief Kiowa demonstrated the symbol for Wichita by drawing his fingers across his face as if he were painting it. The other Indians, also in the sign

13 Mayhall, *The Kiowas*, 5n.; Rydjord, in Bright's *Kansas: The First Century*, I, 23.

14 Swanton, *The Indian Tribes of North America*, 305.

Wichita Indian grass lodge, the most likely source for the name Wichita (Kansas State Historical Society)

language, concurred. This would indicate that the Wichita Indians were the "painted faces," but it does not prove that the name Wichita means "painted faces." Furthermore, Isely admitted later that the Indians got into a very hot argument over the name.[15]

Chief Kiowa made a distinction between Wichita and Washita. For Washita he not only made a motion to illustrate painting his face, but he "made a motion with his hand to indicate flowing water," said Isely. The Washita River joins the Red Fork, and both carry red silt from the soil of Oklahoma. Bliss Isely said, "Washita means water with a painted face." Of course, this is not the only interpretation. That Wichita was possibly the same as *Ouachita* has been both accepted and challenged. Charles N. Gould suggested that *Ouachita* meant "big hunt." Swanton listed the Ouachita Indians as a Caddoan member of the Natchitoches Confederacy.[16]

The large grass huts in which the Wichita lived were so conspicuous that they became a source for several of their names, including Wichita. The descriptive name was used by several tribes, each in its own language. For example, the Comanches called them *Sónik'ni* or *Sonikanink*, meaning "grass lodges," according to Swanton. In a somewhat similar manner, the Little Osages referred to the Pawnees of the Red River as the *Wi-tzi-ta*, surely the Wichitas, and this was translated as "lodges-far-away people." This leads to the conclusion that the name had a Siouan origin, especially considering the name *Mítsitá* used by the Kansas. Dorsey also believed that *Witsita* came from the Osages.[17] Chief Kiowa of the Wichitas said that the Osages, "whom we hate, called us a name which means scattered lodges, but they pronounced it Wee-chee-taw." Henry Roe Cloud, a Wichita resident and long the head of the Indian Institute in Wichita, said he could recall that the Osages referred to reeds as *Wee-chee-che*, and it was his opinion that *Wee-cheyo-chee* meant "dwellers in reed wigwams." Out of this the name was

[15] Isely, "Wichita," Clippings, Ablah Library, Wichita State University.

[16] Gould, *Oklahoma Place Names*, 28; Wright, *A Guide to the Indian Tribes of Oklahoma*, 255.

[17] Mathews, *The Osages*, 480; Hodge, *Handbook of American Indians*, II, 984.

changed to *Wee-chee-tah.*[18] Both James R. Mead and "Buffalo Bill" Mathewson accepted the interpretation that the name meant "scattered lodges."[19]

The Little Osages may have used the *Witzita* name, but it is more likely that Wichita has a Choctaw origin. When the French explorer La Harpe visited the Wichitas on the Arkansas River in Oklahoma, he called them "Wusitas and Ousitas (both identical with Wichita)," said Joseph B. Thoburn.[20] It seems logical that the "name was carried west by the French from contacts with the Choctaw-speaking peoples of the Lower Mississippi Valley."[21] Choctaw was the intertribal and commercial language in this region. Their name for Wichita as *Wia-chetoh.* Since *wia* means "arbor" and *chetoh* means "big," the Wichitas were the "people living in the big arbors." The name could also mean "a loft-like platform." Juan de Oñate, in his description of the Wichita lodges, said that "not a house lacked these platforms."[22]

David Leahy, distinguished journalist, challenged his associates who said that Wichita meant "scattered lodges." "In a spirit of fun," he said, he "needled them" by suggesting that it meant "painted faces." Leahy wrote to the Smithsonian Institution for information and found that there was some evidence to support his statement. Leahy's interpretation had a logical source in the French name *Panis piqués*, the "tatooed Pawnees," but probably not in the name Wichita.[23]

Quite a discussion was started when an Easterner came to town and found no one who was able to tell him the meaning of Wichita until he met James R. Mead, who had a ready answer and informed the visitor that it meant "scattered lodges." The argument between Mead and Leahy over the meaning of the name is best told in Mead's entertaining manner:

[18] *Wichita Eagle*, July 26, 1936; Isely, University of Wichita *Sunflower*, May 11, 1932.

[19] *Wichita Eagle*, Nov. 10, 1908; Isely, *Wichita Beacon*, April 14, 1929.

[20] Anna Lewis, "La Harpe's First Expedition in Oklahoma," *Chronicles of Oklahoma*, II, 334.

[21] Harper, *Chronicles of Oklahoma*, XXXI, 274n.

[22] Bolton (ed.), *Spanish Explorations in the Southwest*, 260.

[23] *Wichita Eagle*, June 31, 1935.

For fully two days this (Mead's) authority was accepted, until an Irishman came along and asserted to the "Eagle" that the word "Wichita" meant "Tattooed Faces." We hated to hear the decision of Mr. Mead disputed—especially by a foreigner—and we called upon William Mathewson, a man who was here before the Arkansas river was dug, and asked him about it. He dissented very strongly from the Irishman's opinion and stood loyally by his pioneer friend, J. R. Mead. He informed us also that the word "Wichita" is not a Wichita word at all, but an Osage word, and it was from the Osages themselves, many years ago, that he learned that the word meant "Scattered Villages," which means the same thing.

Now comes the Irishman, who cites as his authority no less a person than J. W. Powell, director of the Bureau of American Ethnology. We have examined Mr. Powell's references to the matter in the Seventeenth Annual Report of his bureau, and a casual reading of it would indicate that the Irishman was a little more than a match for the two famous Kansas pioneers. A more attentive reading, however, reveals the fact that "Tattooed Faces" comes from a Kiowa word which was applied to the Wichita, Waco, Tawakoni and Kichai Indians on account of their habit of tattooing their faces and mouths. The word in question is "Doguat," which evidently means "Wichita," for we find the Wichita mountains in Oklahoma called "Doguat kop" by the Kiowas even unto this day.

"The question now is whether the Osages knew more about the Wichitas than the Kiowas did," said Mead, and then he concluded that the government had accepted the Wichita name and "no one would be willing to give it up for such an ugly word as 'Doguat.' "[24] *Do'gu'at*, the Kiowa name for the Wichitas, did mean "tattooed people," but that is not the meaning of Wichita.

It is obvious that the Wichitas had several names. Hodge started his analysis of the name cautiously by saying that "Wichita . . . is of uncertain origin and etymology." Swanton simplified it all by saying that Wichita came from *wits*, meaning "man." This was, of course, the traditional way in which any tribe might answer a

[24] In Bentley's *History of Sedgwick County*, I, 111–12.

question about the meaning of its name. Hodge, who had a similar interpretation, suggested that, "like so many proper tribal names," it implied "preeminent men." The tribe might have no name for themselves except the "local people" or "men" or "people of the parent speech."[25]

Since it is uncertain which tribe originated the name Wichita, there can be no final interpretation. To the Kiowas and Comanches the Wichitas were the "tattooed Pawnees" or "painted people." To the Sioux they were the *Paniwasaba* or the "black bear Pawnees." According to the Osages, as well as the Choctaws, they were the ones who lived in "scattered lodges" or in "grass huts." Of all the interpretations, the one that refers to grass lodges in one form or another seems to be the most acceptable, and its Choctaw origin seems logical. Not until the Camp Holmes Treaty in 1835, when the Wichitas were living among the Choctaws in Oklahoma, did their name, even if spelled Wichitaw, become official.[26]

Wichita is well known as a place-name. The campground of the Little Osages at the Little River crossing already had a name before the white man settled in the area. As early as 1855, when the Kansas legislature provided for highways, one of the roads was to go from Iowa Point to Eujatah (Wichita). A report on Indian treaties stated, "Eujatah was the ending of a wagon road authorized to be surveyed from Iowa Point . . . to Eujatah on the Arkansas river." The site of Eujatah on the river is identified as "doubtless on the old Osage trail from Neosho river above present Wichita."[27]

It was at this terminal of the Osage Trail, later called the "O. T. Trail," that the Little River peace treaty was signed. It was also at this river crossing that two men by the names of Moxley and Mosely set up a trading post, but the place had a name before they settled there. Major Sibley's diary of 1811 refers to the hunting camp of the Little Osages on the Little River by a name which

[25] McGee, "The Siouan Indians," *BAE Fifteenth Annual Report* (1893–94), 194.

[26] Wright, *A Guide to the Indian Tribes of Oklahoma*, 225; Harper, *Chronicles of Oklahoma*, XXXI, 274n.; George H. Shirk, *Oklahoma Place Names*, 222.

[27] *KHC*, XVI, 746; Root, *KHQ*, II, 353.

resembles Eujatah. Sibley spelled it En-jet-tas, as well as Eu-jet-ta. The "n" may be a typographical error. Eujatah has also been listed as one of the extinct towns on the Arkansas River. It would not be difficult to make Wichita out of Eujatah, but Sibley said that Eu-jet-ta was the name for the Little Osages.[28] So the name of the Little Osages, if Eujatah was their name, was given to the terminal of their hunting trail on the Little Arkansas.

Pioneers were settling near the junction of the Big and Little Arkansas before the place had a name. At first it was an attractive site for trading posts and then it became a popular campground for the military. It was also the site for a village of the Wichita Indians. Any of these could have provided a name, but there were plenty of other names from which to choose. According to one account, it was first called Camp Butterfield, but that name was not long in use. It might have been named for David Butterfield, the most famous of several Butterfields in Kansas and the one who had recently promoted the Butterfield Overland Dispatch across Kansas.

In June, 1868, the place was known as Camp Davidson. During the Custer-Hancock expeditions against the Indians in 1867, General John W. Davidson was assigned to the expedition as inspector general. He was later the military instructor in Kansas State College at Manhattan.[29]

Camp Davidson had its name changed to Camp Beecher to honor Lieutenant Frederick Beecher, not because he was the nephew of Henry Ward Beecher, but because he was the "hero of the Battle of the Arickaree." There on an island just beyond the Kansas border Beecher and a few scouts under Colonel Forsyth held off a formidable attack of Cheyennes under Roman Nose. Both Beecher and Roman Nose were killed. When the rescue party arrived, Colonel Forsyth's comment was, "Welcome to Beecher's Island."[30] Then and there the island was named. To honor him further, Lieutenant Colonel J. Schuyler Crosby wrote the following order from Fort Hays on October 19, 1868: "The station of United

[28] *KHC*, XII, 477; Sibley, *Chronicles of Oklahoma*, V, 209 and 212.
[29] Campbell, "Down Among the Red Men," *KHC*, XVII, 647.
[30] Montgomery, *KHC*, XVII, 229.

States Troops at the mouth of the Little Arkansas river, Kansas, will hereafter be known as Camp Beecher, in commemoration of Frederick H. Beecher, 1st Lieutenant, 3d Infantry, who was killed in battle with Indians, on Arickaree Fork of the Republican river, September 17, 1868."[31] In spite of the term "hereafter," the name was soon changed.

A soldier in camp at the Wichita site gave his address on October 1, 1868, as "Camp Crawford, Wichita City." It was named Camp Crawford for Governor Crawford who gave up his governorship to participate in the defense of the frontier and to help General Sheridan remove the Indians to the Indian Territory.[32]

The names of the military camps at Wichita replaced one another so rapidly that none became fixed in the public mind. There were, however, plenty of suggestions for new names. The town promoters had a dozen names from which to choose—descriptive names, popular names, pioneer names, political names, and Indian names. Among the descriptive names suggested were Two Rivers, Grand Valley, Valley Center, Central City, Prairie City, Cottonwood Grove, Midway, Big Ford, and possibly Buffalo. These and other names deserve a brief consideration.

The junction of the Big and Little Arkansas would have justified naming the town Two Rivers. Grand Valley was a description with an appeal. When William C. Woodman first saw the valley from his covered wagon, he called it Happy Valley. He had tears in his eyes, but they were tears of joy.[33] Now there is a suburb of Wichita called Pleasant Valley. Advertising the town's central location was the significant factor in suggesting names such as Valley Center and Central City. Valley Center was a descriptive name adopted by a neighboring town a short distance up the Little River. But Wichita was still far from any significant center when it was started as a frontier town. Naming it Midway would have advertised the fact that it was about midway between the Atlantic and Pacific. Prairie City would have been an appropriate name

[31] Hortense B. Campbell, "Camp Beecher," *KHQ*, III, 174.
[32] *KHQ*, XX, 150.
[33] Rea Woodman, *Wichitana, 1877–1897*, 13.

almost anywhere in the state, but Wichita was too late; that name had already been given to a town in Douglas County. Big Ford was a name that would have been soon outdated by the building of a bridge across the Arkansas River, although some cattlemen preferred fording the river to paying toll. Calling the town Cottonwood Grove seemed fitting for a time, but the soldiers at Camp Beecher cut down most of the cottonwoods for fuel. Naming it Buffalo was logical, since Wichita was on the border of the buffalo country. But that name had been pre-empted for a post office and town in Wilson County.

Three famous Indian traders—Jesse Chisholm, James R. Mead, and William Greiffenstein—had trading posts at the Wichita site before the town was founded. The place could have been named for any one of them. Mead was an Indian trader and a good friend of the natives, Greiffenstein was married to an Indian woman, and Jesse Chisholm was part Cherokee and part Scotch. William Greiffenstein (pronounced "Griffensteen") was better known as Dutch Bill because of his difficult German name. Since his last name was considered too complicated to use as a street name, the street that honored him was named William Street.[34] Greiffenstein School and Greiffenstein Bridge across the Arkansas now bear his name to honor his service to the city. Mead, a Connecticut Yankee, was too busy considering other names to have his own adopted, but his name was given to Mead Island in the Little Arkansas, Mead Street, and Mead Junior High School.

It was Mead who named Chisholm Creek which flows through the city of Wichita. He named it for his old Cherokee Indian friend, Jesse Chisholm, who had a farm and trading post between the Little River and Chisholm Creek. Mead gave the place a name when he spoke of Chisholm's post as Willow Grove. It was the trading route of Chisholm, following an old Indian trail and military route from Kansas, through Oklahoma, to Texas, which became the famous cattle trail known in poetry, prose, and song as the Chisholm Trail. So it was recommended that the name Chisholmville be given to the new town of Wichita. It was also sug-

[34] Interview with Arch O'Bryant of the *Wichita Eagle and Beacon.*

gested that the town be named Carson to honor the distinguished frontiersman, Christopher "Kit" Carson, called Little Chief by the Cheyennes. Carson had visited Wichita at the time of the Little River peace conference in 1865 when James R. Mead was invited to share his camp. Mead later said that "General Harney and Kit Carson were the most noted persons present." Kit Carson's name has been widely used as a place-name in the West, from Kit Carson in Colorado to Carson City in Nevada, but it was not accepted for Wichita.

E. H. Durfee was another of the early settlers. Durfee bought land on the Wichita site and established a trading post. The place was known for a time as Durfee's Ranch or Ranche. The suggestion, however, that this be changed to Durfee's Post as a permanent name was not accepted. Durfee, by the way, was the first man to have Wichita's name printed on a circular.[35]

That the town be named Council Lodge was most likely proposed because of the important peace council held a few miles north of Wichita on the Little River. Colonel Leavenworth, one of the promoters of the council, hoped to undo some of the damage done by the Chivington Massacre. As Council Grove had been named for its treaty-making site forty years earlier, the Wichita site could have been named Council Lodge for the Little Arkansas peace treaty of 1865.

Out of all these proposed names for the new town, only one could be chosen, but more than one person has claimed the credit for selecting the name. John S. Barnum, a pioneer scout and trader in Kansas, said in a letter to the editor of the *Wichita Eagle* in March, 1900, that he had discussed the naming of the town with Munger, the postmaster, and with Vigus, the proprietor of the Buckhorn Hotel and a harness-maker. Vigus recommended the name of Sedgwick to honor General John Sedgwick for whom the local county was named. Barnum said he wanted an unusual name. His first choice was Opi Ela, the name of the daughter of a Wichita chief and the "handsomest squaw" he had ever seen. Opi Ela meant "elk tooth," but in the mind of the promoter it only meant a beau-

[35] *Wichita Evening Eagle*, Dec. 6, 1940.

tiful woman. Barnum then said that he proposed the name of Wichita, a name so unusual that one need not add Kansas to know where it is. "Yes, I am proud to say I did name Wichita," he concluded.[36]

Although Barnum may not have named the town, it was nevertheless named for the Wichita Indians. Some time after being visited by Coronado, the Wichitas and their related tribes were so hard pressed by their enemies that they migrated to the Red River, subsequently the Texas-Oklahoma border. They were again disturbed during the Civil War when they refused to co-operate with the Confederates. So they migrated back to Kansas, and after wandering toward the Neosho, they were guided to Wichita by Jesse Chisholm. It was residence in this area from 1863 to 1867 that brought them into contact with Chisholm, Mead, and Greiffenstein.

While the Wichitas lived there, the place had long been known "all over the plains," said Mead, as the "Wichita town."[37] Naming an Indian community by the name of the tribe and adding "town" was quite common in Kansas. Greiffenstein was in full accord with Mead and told his associates that "when they proposed to christen the infant, it had a name before it was born." "It was known," he said, "by Indians and traders far and near as Wichita." William Connelley is quoted as saying that "Wichita has been a town or city since time immemorial," and "was the capital of the Quivira for centuries." He was referring to the present site of Wichita, and he added, "there is compensation and recompense in the preservation and perpetuation of the proud name of the people of the kingdom of Quivira."[38]

There is also a fictional account of the naming of Wichita. The *Wichita Eagle* for May 19, 1910, which had been preserved in the cornerstone of the Forum Building and brought to light in 1965, contained a new version of the story of how Wichita got its name. Former governor W. E. Stanton of Wichita, in responding to a

[36] Letter to the editor, *Wichita Eagle*, March 25, 1900.

[37] *KHC*, VIII, 173.

[38] Edith Connelley Ross, "The Quivira Village," *KHC*, XVII, 524; D. B. Emmet, "Sedgwick County," in Edwards' *Historical Atlas of Sedgwick County, Kansas*, 100.

toast, had said: "Two little Indian boys were playing marbles one day up on what is now North Main Street. They played awhile and went away. The wind which was blowing hard that day obliterated part of the line the boys had chalked on the ground for the game. One of the lads could not find the chalk line effaced by the sand and said: 'Which is taw? Which is taw?' Greiffenstein and Munger, who happened to pass the boys at this juncture, heard them make this remark and said: 'That's a good idea; we'll call the town Wichita.' "[39] Be that as it may, there are more acceptable accounts.

Dave Leahy visited former governor Crawford who told him his story of the naming of Wichita. The governor had suggested naming the town Hamilton, but, he said, "James R. Mead held out for the name Wichita and finally won." Mead, supported by Dutch Bill, may therefore be given the chief credit for naming Wichita.[40]

It took a long time to learn how to spell Wichita because of its Indian source and the difficulty of putting the Indian word into French phonetics and Americanized spelling. The name had a long evolution from its Indian names as written by the French. Major Inman suggested that the French *Ouichita* should have been retained. The spelling had gone through many changes since it was first written *Osita*, *Ousita*, and *Wusita*. The Spaniards followed the pronunciation quite closely when they spelled it *Guitchita* and *Huitchita*, both equivalent to the French *Ouichita*. Dr. George Sibley in 1811 spelled it Wichata, corrected parenthetically to Witcheta.[41] The long list by Hodge shows the evolution in names like *Wasita*, *Wisita*, *Wishitah*, *Witchetaw*, *Wichitaw* until it became Wichita. A postal clerk told Dave Leahy that he had seen it spelled twenty-six ways, but there must have been more, considering the ingenuity of poor spellers.[42]

Pronunciation of Wichita varied but not as much as its spelling. Dave Leahy also had some definite ideas on how it should be pro-

[39] In addition to the *Wichita Eagle* report of May 19, 1910, see also Arch O'Bryant, "Punning 1910 Speech Suggests Marble Players Named Wichita," *Wichita Eagle*, Nov. 13, 1965.

[40] *Wichita Sunday Eagle*, Jan. 30, 1935.

[41] Bolton, *Texas in the Middle Eighteenth Century*, 398; Lewis, *Chronicles of Oklahoma*, II, 334n.; *Pichardo's Treatise*, II, 232.

[42] Leahy, in *Wichita Sunday Eagle*, June 30, 1935.

nounced. He objected to those who would pronounce Wichita as if it were "Oo-ish-it-taw" or "We-chee′ta."[43] The pronunciation came from the French spelling of *Ouichita*. Anyone who can say "yes" in French knows that it is as easy to change *Ouichita* to Wichita as it is to change *Ouisconsin* to Wisconsin, and in French or English, it is pronounced "Wich′ĭ-taw."

It was difficult to say which part of Wichita or which suburb would have the big name in the future. When Dan Cupp of Butler County was offered the Wichita townsite for a team of horses, he turned it down because Wichita was too low and swampy.[44] On the west side of the Arkansas a town company started the town of Elgin, but Elgin was already the name of a town in Kansas, so this Wichita suburb changed its name to Delano.

The town of Delano was named for Columbus Delano who had been appointed Secretary of Interior in President Grant's administration in 1870. In 1871 the Delano post office was named. This was the period when Othniel C. Marsh, one of the great pioneer paleontologists, led several "bone-picking" expeditions into the Indian country of the West. He was so disturbed by the venality of some of the Indian agents that he brought a report from Chief Red Cloud to Washington and exposed the practice of distributing not only rotten rations but short rations to the Indians. Delano tried to cover up for the corrupt "Indian ring," but in 1875 found it expedient to resign. In the following year the Delano post office name was temporarily dropped, but it served again from 1879 to 1880. When a free bridge replaced the toll bridge across the Arkansas, Douglas Avenue connected the two towns and made them one. Delano then became West Wichita, but the township has preserved the Delano name.[45]

As other suburbs grew up around Wichita, they, too, were known by direction. In addition to West Wichita, there were stations named North Wichita and South Wichita. Wichita Heights

[43] *Ibid.*

[44] Jesse P. Stratford, *Butler County's Eighty Years.*

[45] *Wichita Eagle*, Nov. 18, 1940; report on the name from Arch O'Bryant of the *Wichita Eagle;* Robert Plate, *The Dinosaur Hunters*, 148; Baughman, *Kansas Post Offices*, 34.

was in the Arkansas Valley lowlands north of Wichita, and only its new high school above the valley has justified its descriptive name.

Marsh M. Murdock, owner of the *Wichita Eagle* and a dauntless booster for Wichita, named his paper the *Wichita City Eagle*. As a state senator, Murdock proposed the name Wichita for a western county in Kansas. He liked the name and applied it even to a county far beyond the homes of the Wichita Indians.[46]

Wichita became a popular name not only in Kansas but also in Oklahoma and Texas. Fort Sill on the border of the Wichita Mountains in present Oklahoma was at first known as Camp Wichita, also called Fort Wichita.[47] Wichita Creek and Wichita Falls in Texas share the name. The Wichita Falls name in Texas has caused some confusion, because it is frequently shortened to just Wichita in conversation.

The Waco Indians were a Caddoan tribe closely associated with the Wichitas and Tawakonis. Waco was also written *Houechas* by the French and *Huecos* by the Spaniards, although the tribe, like the Wichitas, were occasionally called Tawakonis. Waco is said to mean "river bend in a sandy place."[48] According to one account, the name came from *Wehiko*, a corruption of the name Mexico. The name, no doubt, resulted from the Wacos frequent fighting with the Mexicans in Texas. A related tale gives another version of how the tribe was named. The Wacos in Texas were impressed by the remarkable cures performed by a Mexican *médico* or doctor. The Indians' imperfect pronunciation of *médico* sounded like "way-ako," which was simplified to Waco. The Waco Indians had a good reputation and took pride in being called the "gentlemen Indians."[49]

Another folklore account tells how Waco, a settlement south of Wichita, became Waco Wego. A Waco cafe owner, who special-

[46] *KHC*, XII, 442.

[47] Foreman, *The Last Trek of the Indians*, 298; Flora W. Seymour, *Indian Agents of the Old Frontier*, 85.

[48] Hodge, *Handbook of American Indians*, II, 887 and 947–48; *Pichardo's Treatise*, I, 393n.; Leland, *Names*, I, 272.

[49] Swanton, *The Indian Tribes of North America*, 304; Campbell, *KHC*, XVII, 642.

ized in chicken dinners, had to compete with Wichita for his trade. He put up advertising signs that ended with "To Waco We Go," and soon the name became Waco Wego. Waco was the station on the Midland Railroad, and Waco Wego was on the highway south of Wichita. The station has occasionally been distinguished as New Waco.

Kechi and Waco, suburbs of Wichita, were named for Caddoan relatives of the Wichita Indians. The term *Paniouassa* or "black bear Pawnee" was used in a broad sense to include all of them. The Wichitas called the Kichais *Kiétsash*, and the Spaniards called them *Quichais*. Swanton lists the name as "Kichai or (more phonetically) Kitsei." In Texas there is a town named Keechai. In Kansas the name lost a couple of vowels and became Kechi. Nonresidents have pronounced it "Ketchee," but in the correct pronunciation the sound of both vowels is long. The Kichais said that their name meant "going in wet sand," and their Pawnee relatives said that it meant "water turtle." These may not be too far apart; perhaps the turtle did go in wet sand.[50]

The Wichita Indians were quite pleased with the choice of their name for a white man's town. A quotation from Chief Kiowa, who was a Wichita chief, may serve as a good illustration of the interest the Indians had in the name. He said, "Wichita means the people, lodges, cities, mountains," and so it does. "We are proud," he concluded, "that there is a great city in Kansas which bears our name."[51]

[50] Swanton, *The Indian Tribes of North America*, 321; Lewis, *Chronicles of Oklahoma*, II, 334n.

[51] Isely, in *Wichita Eagle*, Nov. 10, 1908; *Wichita Beacon*, July 20, 1924.

XIV

Shawnee

THE ALGONQUIAN TRIBES occupied a wide area in the eastern part of the United States, from the Carolinas to Canada and westward along both sides of the Great Lakes, or, according to Hodge, "from the E. shore of Newfoundland to the Rocky Mtns. and from Churchill r. to Pamlico sd." In their midst in the East were the Iroquoians whose very name meant "adders" and who fought them on all sides. They would escape from these enemies only to run into the Nadouessioux whose Algonquian name also meant "adders" or "snakes." Tribe after tribe was forced to move out in search of a safe refuge from these frightful foes called snakes.

The Algonquian linguistic family was composed of many tribes. Among the first ones to break away from their Algonquian relatives were the Arapahos and the Cheyennes who had reached the northern High Plains near the Rockies before they came into Kansas. They came to Kansas from the West while the later arrivals entered Kansas from the East. Among the eastern Algonquians were the Shawnees, Delawares, Potawatomis, Ottawas, Peorias, Pequots, Powhattans, Sac and Foxes, Kickapoos, Weas, and Miamis. Representatives of all these tribes came to Kansas and each left their tribal names or personal names on the map.

The Shawnees were closely related to the Delawares, who called them their "grandsons," since the Shawnees, like children, had left the Delaware family in the East. The Ojibwas, Potawatomis, and Ottawas took the Shawnees into their "alliance," or, as Morgan said, "recognized an ancient connection still preserved by tradition, and acknowledged the Shawnee their uncles."[1]

[1] *Morgan: The Indian Journals*, 51.

The Shawnees had once lived in Georgia, Tennessee, and the Carolinas, but they were pushed into Pennsylvania and Ohio by the Cherokees, an Iroquoian tribe. After the American Revolution, when they resisted the advance of the white man into the Ohio Valley, they were defeated in 1794 by "Mad" Anthony Wayne at the Battle of Fallen Timbers. Wayne became a hero, and his name has been popular as a place-name in eastern United States. A township is named Wayne in Doniphan County, Kansas, in memory of the "mad" general who crushed the Indian resistance. After their defeat the Shawnees found new homes in Indiana, where under the strong leadership of Tecumseh they again tried to stem the tide of the advancing frontiersmen.

New treaties diminished their Indiana domains after the War of 1812. With the beginning of a new policy to give the Indians a permanent home in the West, the Shawnees accepted in 1825, after two years of negotiation, a fifty-square-mile reservation in Kansas just below the Kaw. In 1828, Captain Joseph Parks, a Shawnee chief, brought the Fish band and the Hog Creek band to Kansas. The Shawnees were settled in what are now Wyandotte and Johnson counties. Both counties have Shawnee townships across the county border from each other.[2]

The Shawnee name could have come from *shawun* or *suwan*, meaning "south," or from *shawunogi* or *shawanogi*, meaning "southerner." This Algonquian name was applied to the southernmost residents of these tribes when they were living in Georgia and the Carolinas. In a reference made to Shawan Cabin Branch and Shawan Run in Maryland, Shawan was interpreted to mean "south wind" or "blowing wind."[3] According to another interpretation, the Shawnee name came from *siutagan* or *sewan* which meant not only "sweet" or "pungent," but also "salt." These Algonquians were great salt eaters and salt traders and probably deserved a name associated with salt. However, the accepted meaning of Shawnee is still "southerner." The name is also associated

[2] Harrington, *Historic Spots in Wyandotte County*, 13; Lutz, *KHC*, IX, 166n.
[3] Hamill T. Kenny, *The Origin and Meaning of Indian Place Names of Maryland*, 127.

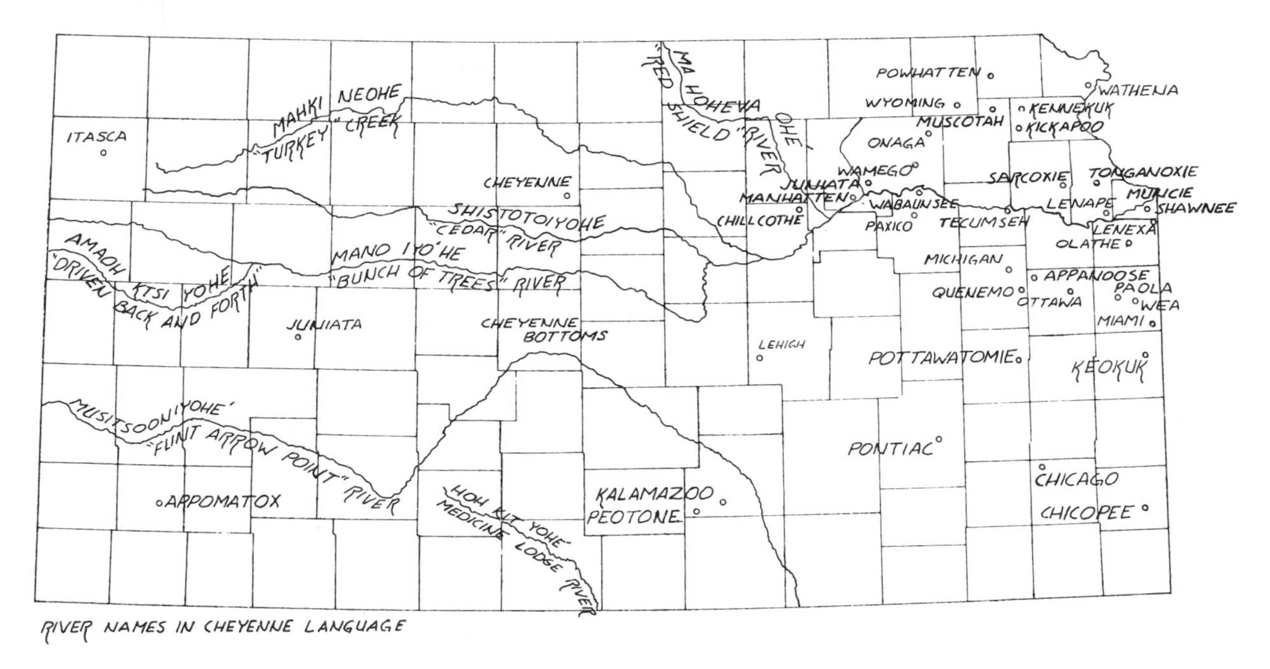

Algonquian Names in Kansas

with Savannah, the name of the river where they once had a village. This name, too, is supposed to refer to the South, but it may also mean marshy grasslands.[4] In Kansas there was once a little station on the Union Pacific named Savannah. It was located between Onaga and Havensville in Pottawatomie County.[5]

The Shawnee name went through many changes before it attained its present form. "The real name of the Shawnee," said one French authority, was *Chaouanon.* The French also wrote it *Chounois.*[6] Among the many forms of the Shawnee name is the one used by Jotham Meeker for the first newspaper in Kansas, the *Siwinowe Kesibwi,* meaning the "Shawnee sun."[7] Of all their names, Shawanoe, which resembles the French pronunciation of *Chaouanons,* was long accepted and popular. It continued in use until it finally lost a syllable and was corrupted to Shawnee.

That the Shawnees were a proud people is well illustrated in the story of their life as it was understood by the Rev. James B. Finley:

> The Master of Life, who was himself an Indian, made the Shawnees before any other of the human race, and they sprang from his brain. He gave all the knowledge he himself possessed, and placed them upon the great island, and all the other red people are descended from the Shawnees. After he made the Shawnees he made the French and English out of his breast, the Dutch out of his feet, and the Long Knives (Americans), out of his hands. All of these inferior races of men he made white, and placed them beyond the Stinking lake (the Atlantic ocean).

The Shawnees admitted that they had lost this superiority which the Master of Life had given temporarily to the white man. But soon, they said, "the Master of Life is about to restore to the Shawnee their knowledge and their rights, and he will trample the Long Knives under his feet."[8]

[4] Joab Spencer, "The Shawnee Indians," *KHC,* X, 388; Vogel, *Indian Place Names in Illinois,* 128.

[5] Blackmar, *Kansas: A Cyclopedia of State History,* II, 652.

[6] *Tixier's Travels on the Osage Prairies,* 105n.

[7] Douglas C. McMurtrie, "The Shawnee Sun," *KHQ,* II, 339; Mathews, *The Osages,* 110.

[8] Spencer, *KHC,* X, 384.

"Perhaps no Indians were superior to the Shawnees in courage and prowess," said William Connelley.[9] William Phillips, who visited Kansas before 1856, gave a journalistic description of the "semi-civilized Shawnee." He thought they were more industrious than most Indians, but described them as "half-educated, half-evangelized, half-laborized, half-whiskeyfied, half-white man, and half-Indian." The white man had given the Shawnees a part of his civilization, which on the frontier was not the best, and a part of his blood, which made them neither white nor red.[10]

The most important of all the Shawnee names in Kansas is the name of the county in which Kansas established its state capital. The Shawnee name was proposed for the county where Shawnee Mission was the temporary capital, but that county had been named Johnson for the Rev. Thomas Johnson. Yet Johnson was the one who had recommended that it be named Shawnee.[11] Shawnee County was at first south of the Kaw but later extended to the north side of the river.

Among the Shawnees in the Johnson County area lived Tecumseh's brother, The Prophet. His Indian name was *Ten-squa-ta-wa* or *Ten-squat-a-way*, a name so long that Chief Bluejacket first shortened it to Tensqua and then to Tens. The full name was said to mean "the open door." Tensqua, or The Prophet, was said to be "by far the most distinguished Shawnee Indian in Kansas," and his village was called Prophetstown. There he died in poverty, never reconciled to the white man's civilization, and there he lies buried.[12]

Not far from Prophetstown in Johnson County was the site of the new Methodist mission which had been moved from its location near what is now Turner in Wyandotte County. This became the famous Shawnee Mission and Indian Manual Labor School so ably

[9] *Ibid.*, 387.

[10] *The Conquest of Kansas*, 13–14.

[11] Inman, in *Topeka Daily Commonwealth*, Jan. 12, 1886.

[12] Donaldson, "The George Catlin Indian Gallery," *Annual Report* of the Board of Regents of the Smithsonian Institution to July 1885, Part V, 201; Harington, *Historic Spots in Wyandotte County*, 87; Ross, "The Old Shawnee Mission," *KHC*, XVII, 418; Lutz, *KHC*, IX, 164n.

directed by the Rev. Thomas Johnson.[13] It was twice the capital of territorial Kansas, *de facto* if not *de jure*.

The Baptists also had a Shawnee Mission, and there were several Shawnee names in the area which were either eliminated or changed. When Governor Walker referred to the "Shawanoe Baptist Mission," he added that it was commonly called Gum Springs, from the name given it by the natives. There was a Shawnee post office in 1857, several years before there was a Shawnee Mission post office. Shawnee Mission, which Isaac McCoy and Francis Parkman called the Shawanoe Mission, was the nucleus for a town which was for a time called Shawneetown. Later the "town" was deleted from the name and the place became logically known as Shawnee. It lasted as a post office until 1960, when the town became a part of Greater Kansas City.[14] The name Shawnee Mission was divided and given to two places, one called Shawnee and the other Mission. Added to this is Mission Hills, another suburb of Kansas City.

In Cherokee County, named for the former enemies of the Shawnees, there is a Shawnee Township; and Shawnee Creek, headed for Spring River near the Missouri border, flows through the township. The terminal of the Shawnee Trail was also in Cherokee County. The Chisholm name has been broadly used for several cattle trails from Texas into Kansas, but the Old Shawnee Trail was said to have "divided honors with the Chisholm Trail." The Shawnee Trail led from the Red River country to Baxter Springs. As the cattle trails moved westward the "Old" Shawnee Trail was replaced by the "Middle" or "West" Shawnee Trail which went up the Whitewater and along the Neosho to Junction City.[15]

Shawnee County is full of Indian names and names associated with the Indians. There is Topeka, Tecumseh, Soldier Creek, Indian Creek, Blacksmith Creek, Mission Creek, and Massasoit Creek. At the outskirts of Topeka is Shunganunga Creek and farther south

[13] Ross, *KHC*, XVII, 418.

[14] Blair, *History of Johnson County, Kansas*, 56, 92, and 160; Baughman, *Kansas Post Offices*, 117.

[15] Charles M. Harger, "Cattle Trails of the Prairies," *Scribner's Magazine*, XI, 734–35.

is the Wakarusa River. There is Half-Day Creek, named for a Potawatomi chief. There is Menoken, named for an old Kansa village. Of the Shawnee chiefs, Tecumseh has been given the greatest attention, and this name is a popular place-name. The Shawnee town named Tecumseh is in Shawnee Township.[16]

Colonel Thomas Nesbit Stinson, an Indian trader, knew the land along the Kaw before it was open to settlers in 1854. His chosen townsite was "as fertile and beautiful as the heart of man could desire." He acquired land by marriage to Betsy Rogers, a relative of Tecumseh. His place was first known as Stinson's Ferry or just Stinsons. Then Stinson named his town Tecumseh, a good choice for a relative of the renowned Shawnee chief and for a town in Shawnee County. Governor Reeder liked the place and suggested that it might well become the capital of Kansas, a political plum it lost to Topeka by one vote.[17]

Indian folklore tells the origin and meaning of the name Tecumseh. A meteor streaked through the sky on the night that the chief was born. When someone exclaimed "Tecumthe!" which meant "shooting star," the mother declared, "This is his name."[18]

The name has been written Tikamthi, Tecumtha, and Tecumseth, but the most common was Tecumthe. The name may mean a "shooting star," but it has been interpreted as "one who passed across intervening space from one point to another." This could still be associated with the shooting star or meteor since the Shawnees believed that "a meteor was a fiery panther flying across the sky." More briefly, it would be "one who springs," and it is only one step from this to "flying panther" and "crouching panther," as Tecumseh was called. And well he lived up to his name.[19]

Tecumseh has been called "the most extraordinary Indian character in United States history." Reviving the plans of Pontiac, he organized the Indians on both sides of the Ohio River into a federation to resist the advance of the white man. He was ably assisted

[16] Andreas and Cutler, *History of Kansas*, 531.

[17] Holliday, *KHC*, III, 397.

[18] C. B. Boynton and T. B. Mason, *A Journey through Kansas*, 157; Leland, *Names*, I, 272.

[19] Hodge, *Handbook of American Indians*, II, 714; Leland, *Names*, I, 272.

by his brother The Prophet. In 1811 a preliminary battle took place at Prophet's Town (Indiana Territory) on the Tippecanoe River, and General William H. Harrison burned the town. Although it was a questionable victory for Harrison, the battle became the basis for the political slogan, "Tippecanoe and Tyler too," which brought both Harrison and Tyler to the White House. Harrison also became known as "Old Indian Chaser."[20]

Tecumseh may have been only a "yaller devil" to the whites, but he was a great organizer, orator, and warrior, and to his own people, a heroic defender. Even though he lost in his resistance to the "Seventeen Fires," as the States were called, he was still the great hero of the Indians. The British made him a colonel. Tecumseh was killed in 1813 at the Battle of the Thames (Canada) by Colonel William Whitley of Kentucky, the grandfather of William Sublette who also gave his name to a Kansas town.[21]

The Tecumseh connection with place-names continued. Piqua, a little village west of Iola, Kansas, received its name from Piqua, Ohio, the birthplace of Tecumseh. (Piqua, Kansas, was the birthplace of Buster Keaton, the sad-faced comedian.) Originally it was the name of one of the five divisions of the Shawnees, the Piqua or "bear" clan. But the name was also said to mean "dust" or "ashes" or "a man formed from ashes."[22]

Another tribal division of the Shawnees was called *Chi-la-ka'tha* which became Chillicothe, a name well known in Ohio. The meaning of the name is in doubt, but Gannett suggests that it meant "man made perfect." Another has suggested that it meant a "place where people dwell." The Shawnees, who were not permitted to dwell in one place, were forced out of their first village named Chillicothe and established three new ones, one of which became Piqua. The name, which came to Kansas from Ohio, was used in Dickenson County, where a post office named New Chillicothe

[20] Ida M. Ferris, "Sauks and Foxes in Franklin and Osage Counties, Kansas," *KHC*, XI, 334.

[21] King, *History of Shawnee County, Kansas*, 59 and 557; Dorothy B. Goebel and Julius Goebel, Jr., *Generals in the White House*, 103; Connelley, "Characters and Incidents of the Plains," *KHC*, X, 112.

[22] Spencer, quoting Connelley in *KHC*, X, 386–87; W. M. Beauchamp, *Indian Names in New York*, 107.

lasted into the twentieth century. There was once a Chillicothe in Phillips County, but its name was changed first to Marvin and then to Glade in honor of a railroad engineer.[23]

The Rev. Charles Bluejacket, or Blue Jacket, was a descendant of the famous Chief Bluejacket who led the northwest Indian confederacy against General Wayne in 1794. Chief Bluejacket was a white man whose legal name was Marmaduke Van Swerangen, which was shortened to Duke. When he and his brother were captured by the Shawnees, he had agreed to become a member of the tribe if the Shawnees allowed his brother to return home to Virginia. The Indians named him Bluejacket because of the "blue linsey woolsey blouse" that he was wearing when he was captured. Bluejacket took an active part in tribal affairs, married a Shawnee woman, and was made a chief at the age of twenty-five. His grandson, Charles Bluejacket, was an Indian preacher who lived on the Wakarusa River at Bluejacket Crossing. The crossing was given official recognition by the Kansas legislature in an act which read: "Act to establish a road from the town of Olathe . . . to the crossing of the Wakarusa, at Blue Jacket." There he and others, including W. H. Sebastian, organized a town which they named Sebastian, but it did not even gain the prestige of becoming a post office. Charles Bluejacket later moved to Oklahoma and died in a town which still bears his name.[24]

Among the able Shawnee chiefs was Chief Black Bob who had settled his followers at Cape Girardeau in Missouri. This band was occasionally referred to as the Missouri Shawnees, but it was better known as the Black Bob band. After 1825, Black Bob and his followers lived on the Shawnee reservation in Kansas where they clashed over land rights, first with the Ohio Shawnees and later with white people who wanted to profit from the Shawnee removal from Kansas as they had profited from Black Bob's removal from Missouri. Black Bob's well-known name was given to the Black Bob post office in Johnson County in 1875. The life of the post

[23] Missouri Pacific Railroad Company, *The Empire that the Missouri Pacific Built*, 111; William D. Overman, *Ohio Town Names*, 27.

[24] Blair, *History of Johnson County, Kansas*, 39; *KHC*, IV, 722; *KHC*, IX, 182; Root, *KHQ*, VI, 17–19.

office was short, but the name continued to be known for the Black Bob band.[25]

Dr. John T. Barton, who surveyed the Olathe site for the county seat of Johnson County, was aided by a Shawnee Indian, Dave Daugherty, who served the double duty of chain carrier and interpreter. As Barton looked at the beautiful site from a hill, his eyes sparkled, and he was said to have remarked that "yonder were the quarter sections upon which the future county seat of Johnson county should be located." Daugherty "straightened himself up—took one good look—gave a few of his Indian grunts and thus exclaimed in Shawnee, 'Olathe! Beautiful!' " Barton liked the Indian's description so well that he gave the name of Olathe to the town which became, as he had hoped, the county seat.[26]

When the Shawnees came to Kansas, one of its important bands was called the Fish band, named for Chief Fish who was its leader. Isaac McCoy, traveling in the Shawnee reservation, wrote about "a white man by the name of Fish, who had lived with the Shawanoes from a small boy."[27] The Fish band included the families of Tecumseh and The Prophet. Chief Fish settled near Quenemo on a creek now named Fish Creek.[28] His son Paschal Fish, a preacher who kept a tavern on the side, was also a chief. When German colonists came to Kansas from Chicago, they bought land for a townsite from the Shawnees through Paschal Fish and named the town Eudora in honor of the chief's daughter. Eudora is located where the Wakarusa enters the Kaw River, near the place once called Fish House, which continued to be the name of the chief's hotel.[29]

Lenexa, another Shawnee name in Johnson County, was also the name of an Indian woman. Although it may not look like an Indian name, it came from *Len-ag-see*, which was the name of the wife of Chief Blackhoof. The name Lenexa is, as the county historian said,

[25] Foreman, *The Last Trek of the Indians*, 54, 169, and 177; Abel, *KHC*, VIII, 93.

[26] Blair, *History of Johnson County, Kansas*, 86.

[27] Lutz, *KHC*, IX, 166n.

[28] Spencer, *KHC*, X, 386; Green, *Early Days in Kansas*, I, 13.

[29] Andreas and Cutler, *History of Kansas*, 353; Root, *KHQ*, II, 276; *Topeka Capital*, June 30, 1956.

"the product of the name in the liquid pronunciation of the Shawnee language."[30]

Eudora and Lenexa have added a feminine touch to the Indian place-names in Kansas, although these names, as well as Black Bob, Bluejacket, and Fish, have lost their Indian characteristics. Black Bob was an English name given to an Indian, Bluejacket was a descriptive Indian name given to a white man, and Fish was the name of a white man who joined the Indians. The Prophet's name was descriptive, but it was not a translation of Tenskwatawa, his Indian name. Tecumseh, whatever the spelling, was only partially modified from the Indian name, and Shawnee was a simplified form for the Algonquian name of the Shawanoe tribe.

[30] Blair, *History of Johnson County, Kansas*, 53; Spencer, *KHC*, X, 389.

XV ▲

Ottawa, Potawatomi, and Chippewa

The Ottawas, Potawatomis, and Chippewas were closely related tribes of the Algonquian linguistic family from the Great Lakes area. The westward migration of the Ottawas was at first caused by the hostility of the Iroquois and later by the advancing English and American settlers. The Ottawas had moved into Michigan, Ohio, and Wisconsin, and then, like most of their neighbors, they reluctantly agreed to give up their homes for land in Kansas. When Chief Thunderbolt refused to sign the treaty for their removal from Ohio, the negotiators made him drunk and guided his hand for his sign. In 1836 the tribe came to Kansas, although a few had arrived earlier to settle on the Marais des Cygnes.[1]

Samuel de Champlain had found the Ottawas living along the Georgian Bay area of Lake Huron. He discovered that they were successful traders who served as middlemen between several Indian tribes. Then he learned that this trade had given them their name *Adawe* which was said to mean "trader" or "barterer." Ottawa could be a name from their own language or from a related language such as Chippewa, since the Chippewas called them *O-dah-wan*, which also meant "traders." Since the Chippewas found the Ottawas living among the bulrushes on the banks of the Ottawa River, they also called them *Watawawininiwok*, "men of the bulrushes."[2]

The Hurons called them *Ondatawawat*, which can be simplified

[1] Foreman, *The Last Trek of the Indians*, 191; Joseph B. King, "The Ottawa Indians in Kansas and Oklahoma," *KHC*, XIII, 373–74.

[2] William W. Warren, *History of the Ojibway Nation*, 31; Swanton, *The Indian Tribes of North America*, 244.

to *Atawa* by deleting the first three and last three letters. The French found it easy to change *Odahwan*, the Chippewa name, to *Outaouan* or *Outaois*, modified further to *Ottaois*, which Eloise Abel said was the correct pronunciation—in French, of course. The simplest of all was *Tawa*.[3]

American frontiersmen followed the spelling by Isaac McCoy and made Ottawa rhyme with "Ioway" by pronouncing it "Otto-way." Although Thomas J. Farnham, the explorer, had spelled it Ottowa earlier, Tomlinson in the 1850's said he had traveled "over the counties of Lykens, Lynn *(sic)*, and through the land of the Ottoways."[4]

The popular Ottawa name has been used as a place-name over a wide area from Canada to Kansas. The Ottawa reservation centered in Franklin County in Kansas. There a creek was named Ottawa Creek, and from this a post office was named Ottawa Creek. As the community grew, the name was shortened to Ottawa, which then became the county seat of Franklin County. North of the county seat is Ottawa Junction on the railroad in Ottawa Township. The original town of Ottawa, founded by C. C. Hutchinson, was near Ottawa Junction.[5]

Ottawa County in north central Kansas is far removed from the Ottawa reservation and the town of Ottawa. Ottawa was a second choice for the name of this county. The original proposal was to name it Wade for Benjamin F. Wade, a famous and fiery anti-slavery senator from Ohio, but the Ottawa name was substituted in the third reading of the bill. The Ottawa name might better have been given to Franklin County except for the popularity and great distinction of the name Franklin.[6]

The son of an English officer and a Chippewa woman was given the name of John Tecumseh Jones. But he was better known as John "Ottawa" Jones, and more briefly, John "Tauy" Jones. His

[3] *KHC*, VIII, 79; Swanton, *The Indian Tribes of North America*, 244.

[4] Farnham, *Travels in the Great Western Prairies* (vol. XXVIII in Thwaites' *Early Western Travels*), 135; William P. Tomlinson, *Kansas in Eighteen Fifty-Eight*, 47; Andreas and Cutler, *History of Kansas*, 602.

[5] McMurtrie, "Pioneer Printing in Kansas," *KHQ*, I, 3; Phillips, in *Kansas City Star*, April 21, 1954.

[6] Scheffer, *KHQ*, III, 229.

first name, no longer necessary for identification, was dropped and he became known as Tauy Jones. He lived with the Ottawas, which explains his middle name. It has been suggested that Tauy was an abbreviation of his middle name Tecumseh, but it was more likely an abbreviation of his nickname Ottawa. Ottawa Jones was the founder of Ottawa College. A creek in Franklin County was named Tauy Creek in his honor.[7]

Few Indian chiefs are better known than Pontiac, the Ottawa chief who, like Phillip before him and Tecumseh and Black Hawk after him, fought desperately to stem the westward tide of English settlers. By 1763 the French had given up the struggle, but not Pontiac who was still determined to capture Detroit. He might have been successful except for the defection of some of his own people, possibly including an old squaw so fond of liquor that she would squeal for a bottle of rum. In a sense Pontiac did not lose, since the British government tried for a time to keep its own restless settlers east of the watershed of the Alleghenies. Pontiac refused to recognize King George as his sovereign, but he was willing to compromise and call him an "uncle." The avuncular title, he assumed, would make the king a more remote relative with less paternalistic power. Pontiac was later assassinated at Cahokia by a Kaskaskia Indian who was supposedly bribed by an English trader. His story is well told by Francis Parkman in his dramatic account *The Conspiracy of Pontiac*. As a place-name, Pontiac is found in Butler County as the name of a Missouri Pacific station east of El Dorado.[8]

The Potawatomis, although closely related to the Ottawas, were occasionally their bitter rivals. The rivalry led to war. After a day's battle, according to legend, one of the chiefs went to sleep under an oak tree. Later a chief of the enemy fell asleep on the other side of the same tree. Then a third chief also chose this tree as a sheltered place where he would sleep. One slept on the north side, another

[7] *Morgan: The Indian Journals*, 38; *KHC*, IV, 617; Franklin County Historical Society, *Reflections of Franklin County and Chautauqua Days*, 5.

[8] Dale Van Every, *Forth to the Wilderness*, 173; Foreman, *The Last Trek of the Indians*, 20.

on the south side, and the third slept on the east side, each unaware of the others. There they were together when they awoke, and there under the influence of a beautiful dawn and of a fresh new day, they agreed that peace was preferable to war. Two of the chiefs were old and one was young. The old chiefs decided to let the young chief start the fire, and they named him *Potawatomi*, the "fire maker."[9] When the Potawatomis broke away from the Ottawas and Chippewas, it was said that "they had gone to build their own fire—a fire for themselves." In reference to the chief, Potawatomi meant "one who builds a fire for himself."

The Chippewa form of the name was *Patawatamink*, or *Potawagumink*, or *Powawandeeg*. One of the earliest French forms of the name is seen in a Jesuit report on a "mission to the Pouteouatamiouec." The Jesuits were, no doubt, good at spelling, but this was too much of a name and they soon shortened it to *Pouteouatami*. It was still a long name and many a pioneer found it convenient to abbreviate it to Poux. The Americans were not far from the French phonetics when they spelled the name as if it were Potawatomi. Even this attractive name, with its poetic rhythm, did not escape reduction to Pot. After all the effort at simplification, Potawatomi was enlarged to Pottawatomie when it was adopted as a place-name in Kansas.[10]

The Potawatomis were divided into two large bands, the Prairie band and the Potawatomis of the Woods. The Prairie band lived in Illinois and Indiana and had its own descriptive name which was in one way or another associated with the Algonquian name for prairie and which eventually became Muscotah. Father Marquette told about his approaching the *Machkoutens*. By the time he arrived at the village, he spelled the name differently and said, "Here we are at the Maskoutens." At their village he also found the Miamis and Kickapoos. Marquette assumed that Maskouten meant the "fire

[9] William E. Smith, "The Oregon Trail," *KHC*, XVII, 451.

[10] Connelley, "The Prairie Band of the Pottawatomie," *KHC*, XIV, 488; *Morgan: The Indian Journals*, 36n.; Russell Errett, "Indian Geographical Names," *Magazines of Western History*, II, 239; Kenton, *The Indians of North America*, II, 168.

nation." That was, "indeed," he said, "the name given to this tribe." "Fire nation" has been the suggested meaning for both Potawatomi and Maskouten.[11]

There were naturally many variations of the name in both spelling and interpretations. It has been written *Machkontench*, *Makskouteng*, and *Muscoteh*. Ingalls, the Atchison County historian, said that the name came from *Ma-shi O-shkoo-teh*, which was making it very difficult. He thought it was a descriptive name which referred to the great prairie fires on the plains. Another suggested that "prairie on fire" merely referred to the "ruddy sunsets." This may be only an interesting association but not necessarily an exact translation.

A popular definition, and one probably more correct, was given by Major Beckwith who said that the name *Mas-cou-tins* was the name of an Illinois band of Indians and that it meant "Indians of the prairies."[12] In Hodge's handbook the name is listed as of Fox or Chippewa origin and is interpreted as the "little prairie people," with the variation, "people of the small prairie." Muscotah seemed certainly to be associated with prairie of some kind, if not prairie fire, then more likely the Prairie band from Illinois. The connection with fire is more logically associated with the Potawatomi name. However, the name of Muscotah, Kansas, most likely came from the Kickapoos.

The name evolved from "fire makers" to "pipe lighters," until it became, as Marquette supposed, the "fire nation." Since there was also a Prairie band of these "fire makers," it was a short and simple step to combine these two into "prairie fire." This then is no longer a translation of one name but an interpretation of two names put together erroneously to make one name. The error was easily made since both descriptive names applied to the same people, one to the Mascoutens and the other to Potawatomis, each with its own meaning. One referred to prairie and the other referred to fire but that

[11] Kenton, *Black Gowns and Redskins*, 339–42; Andreas and Cutler, *History of Kansas*, 71.

[12] Sheffield Ingalls, *History of Atchison County, Kansas*, 29 and 107; Andreas and Cutler, *History of Kansas*, 410; Remsburg, in *Atchison Daily Globe*, Dec. 4, 1906.

does not say that either name could mean prairie fire. The reference to "Pattawatimas or Brave Men" is probably just another name rather than a translation.[13]

The Potawatomis of the Woods were the first to come to Kansas, and in 1837 were assigned a reservation near their relatives, the Ottawas, on the Osage River. Pottawatomie Creek flows into the Osage there and this junction gave rise to the combination of Osage and Pottawatomie to make Osawatomie. The creek crossed Pottawatomie Township in Franklin County. Jackson County also had a township named Pottawatomie as did Coffey County and Pottawatomie County. A town named Pottawatomie in Anderson County had its name changed first to Walker, then to Mount Gilead, but this in turn was changed to Greeley to honor the journalist. Pottawatomie in Coffey County disappeared after it ceased to be a post office in 1906.[14]

The Prairie Potawatomis or Mascoutens moved north of the Kaw and east of the Big Blue and settled near St. Mary's Mission in 1847. There it was later decided to create a county separate from Riley County along the Big Blue River. Dr. Luther R. Palmer, government physician for the Potawatomis, was one of the petitioners for the new county which was to be named Pottawatomie.[15] As Wyandot was changed to Wyandotte as a place-name, so Potawatomi was changed to Pottawatomie. In Iowa the name became Pottawattomie, going from two "t's" to four.

The names of individuals of the Potawatomi tribe were also used for place-names in Kansas. The most important of them was Wabaunsee, a Potawatomi chief. When J. M. Bisby of New York asked Dr. Johnston Lykens of the Baptist Mission to suggest a name for a new town settled largely by the Beecher Bible and Rifle Society, Lykens reportedly said, "Call it Waubaunsee, which means in the Indian tongue Dawn of Day." Lykens might have been as much interested in the meaning, "Dawn of Day," as he was in the chief who bore the name Waubaunsee. The name was accepted,

[13] Andreas and Cutler, *History of Kansas*, 71.
[14] *Ibid.*, 1324.
[15] *Wamego Reporter*, Jan. 2, 1947; Andreas and Cutler, *History of Kansas*, 974.

and it was so popular that the county below Pottawatomie County was also named Wabaunsee.[16]

Richard S. Elliot tells the story of how the Potawatomi chief got his name:

> This old fellow's name meant literally Dawn Of Day, and he gained it by an exploit in his youth. He went solo on an expedition against the Osages, to avenge the death of a friend; stole into their camp, tomahawked a dozen before the alarm was given, and then escaped just as the day was dawning. "Wah-bon-seh!" he exclaimed, "day a little!" and took that for his name.[17]

When Richardson, the journalist, told the accepted story, he concluded it cautiously in verse:

> *I cannot tell how the truth may be;*
> *I say the tale as 'twas told to me.*[18]

There are other interpretations of this interesting name. It could have come from *Wabonishi*, which meant "He lives through the winter." However, *Wapin'* is said to be the Potawatomi word for "daybreak," and this interpretation is supported by the title of a book, *Wau-Bun—Early Day*. Another interpreted it to mean just "daylight." Some have suggested that it means "foggy day," since such a day was appropriate for raids. Vogel told the story of how Waubansee had distinguished himself in 1811, "by leaping aboard one of Governor William Henry Harrison's supply boats on the Wabash near Terre Haute, and killing a man, following which he escaped without injury." This and a later raid were done on foggy mornings, and it was supposedly because of this that he earned his name of "foggy day." The association with "dawn" links the name with "aurora," which was done in Illinois.[19]

The county in which Wabaunsee was the county seat was first named Richardson to honor General William P. Richardson, who was a member of the Bogus legislature of 1855. By 1859 there was

[16] J. M. Bisby, "Pioneering in Wabaunsee County," *KHC*, XI, 594; Elizabeth N. Barr, *Wabaunsee County Directory and History*, 12.

[17] Bisby, *KHC*, XI, 595n.

[18] *Beyond the Mississippi*, 97.

[19] *Wharton, KHC*, XVI, 300; Vogel, *Indian Place Names in Illinois*, 160.

Wabaunsee, Potawatomi chief, the only chief for whom a county in Kansas is named (McKenney and Hall, *The Indian Tribes of North America*, II, 194)

sufficient opposition to the southern influence in naming counties to have the name changed to Wabaunsee. The chief had a great reputation and he had collected scalps like military medals, but he was not universally admired. When "hostile savages, mostly Pottawatomie," attacked Fort Dearborn in the War of 1812, the Indians were "inspired by the war whoops of the ferocious Wabaunsee."[20] One newspaper headline read, "Indian chief was a bloodthirsty scamp in his earlier days." But even the name of a "bloodthirsty scamp" was better than that of a pro-slavery politician for the name of a free county.[21] Wabaunsee County is the only county in Kansas named for an Indian chief. It is a good name but not simple. Early settlers wrote it Wauponsa, Wah-baun-sey, and even Wau-pon-eh-see. General Lane spelled it Wabonsa.[22]

In addition to Wabaunsee County the name has been used for Wabaunsee Township in that county, and in the township there is still a town named Wabaunsee. There is a Wabaunsee Creek which flows into the Kaw near St. George. Added to this list is Lake Wabaunsee.

The use of the word "half" as a part of an Indian name was not unusual and resulted in such names as Isaac Halftown. Sarah Half John, and Chief Half Day. The last was the worthy name of Aptakisic, a Potawatomi chief. Half Day was a famous orator and a prodigious worker; he accomplished in a half day what would require a full day by others. The name may have been associated with the "sun at meridian" or at the "center of the sky," meaning noon. Shawnee County commemorated Chief Half Day in the naming of Half Day Creek. The creek flows into Soldier Creek from the north. There was once a Halfday Township in Calhoun County, but the chief's name was replaced when Calhoun County became Jackson County.[23]

In Wabaunsee County, Paxico and Newberry were rival towns

[20] Foreman, *The Last Trek of the Indians*, 26.

[21] *St. Mary's Star*, April 23, 1942.

[22] Robert Taft, quoting the *Milwaukee Daily Sentinel*, March 15, 1855; *KHC*, V, 367.

[23] Andreas and Cutler, *History of Kansas*, 531; King, *History of Shawnee County, Kansas*, 29; Vogel, *Indian Place Names in Illinois*, 33; *KHC*, V, 453.

a mile apart. The railroad passed between them, and Old Paxico was the first to move to the railroad. What was left of Newberry joined it to survive, and the place retained the name of Paxico. The source for this name was Pashqua, the name of the chief who had owned the land where the town was built. He left for the Indian Territory in 1870.[24]

Onaga in Pottawatomie County is also a Potawatomi name. Paul E. Havens, president of Kansas Central Railroad, wanted an Indian name for a town and checked the Potawatomi "head rights book" in alphabetical order until he came to Onago. He asked if Onago were a chief. He was "just an Indian," said the agent, "peacefully inclined." Havens liked the name, and, chief or not, he said, "I'll take it." The final "o" was changed to an "a," supposedly to make it sound better.[25]

Indians with white blood generally took the names of their white or near-white fathers. Some of the names were English and others came from French. Abram Burnett was a Potawatomi chief who lived with his German wife on Shunganunga Creek at the base of the highest peak near Topeka, now named Burnett's Mound. His part-German daughter married William Greiffenstein, one of the founders of Wichita. It has been said that Burnett was "noted for his great size and his fondness of strong liquor." He was weighed in a Topeka grocery store and tipped the scales at 406 pounds. This was a lot of weight to get home when he had imbibed too freely.[26] Burnett lies buried at the base of Burnett's Mound. This peak or mound had been called Shunganunga Mound from Shunganunga Creek which flows between it and Topeka. The name of the mound was then changed to Webster's Peak, but big Burnett was so closely associated with the mound that it became better known as Burnett's Mound.[27]

[24] Barr, *Wabaunsee County Directory and History*, 90; *Topeka State Journal*, March 19, 1936.

[25] Isely, in *Wichita Beacon*, May 11, 1929; *St. Mary's Star*, Jan. 14, 1943; *KHC*, VII, 482.

[26] Murdock, in *Wichita Evening Eagle*, Aug. 12, 1943; *Topeka Capital*, Aug. 14, 1927; John Guthrie, "Primeval Heroes, Patriots and Priests," *The Agora*, III, 72.

[27] Andreas and Cutler, *History of Kansas*, 532; Federal Writers' Project, *Kansas, A Guide*, 343.

Bourbonnais Creek in Pottawatomie County was named for François or Frank Bourbonnais, a prominent Potawatomi Indian who lived there. He was enough of an Indian to be "buried on top of the ground, with a kettle of food placed at the foot of the grave to sustain him on his journey to the happy hunting ground." Americans had trouble with his French name and changed it to Bourbonny.[28]

Near Frank Bourbonnais' farm lived J. Nadeau. There was a post office by the name of Nadeau at the Indian agency in Jackson County which served until 1913. Among the Potawatomis listed for government allotment were several members of the Nadeau family—Eli, Mary T., John A., John C., and Ramona—and the town of Nadeau must have been named for one of them. John A. and Eli Nadeau were interpreters for the Potawatomis.[29]

Indian descriptive names were as pertinent and appealing as the French and English names. Netawaka is a Potawatomi word that refers to the view, but what kind of view has been left largely to the descriptive vocabulary of the translator. Among the various interpretations are "grand view," "fine view," and "fair view." Since the view is seen from an eminence, Netawaka has also been said to mean "divided ridge" or "high divide." This translation may be questioned although a high divide is the place from which to get a "grand view."[30] B. F. Baughn opened a tavern in a town that he named Netawaka, which was located in the northern part of Jackson County in Netawaka Township.[31] To keep in harmony with the town's Indian name, the local newspaper was named the *Netawaka Chief*.

In place-name folklore there is a story of a band of immigrants who were stranded on an island during a flood of the Kaw. They cried for help, but no one seemed to be brave enough to volunteer until one of the Indians cried out, "Wah, me go!" And that, says

[28] "Reminiscences of William Darnell" (ed. by George A. Root), *KHC*, XVII, 499.

[29] *KHC*, XVI, 739.

[30] Andreas and Cutler, *History of Kansas*, 1337; Bird, *Historical Plat Book of Jackson County*, 35; Remsburg, in *Atchison Daily Globe*, Jan. 27, 1900.

[31] Isely, in *Wichita Beacon*, Aug. 18, 1929.

Henry Malone, is the folklore of how Wamego in Pottawatomi County got its name. But a better explanation may be that the town was named for a Potawatomi chief whose name was Wamego. In the allotment list there was a George Wam-me-go as well as a Henry Wam-me-go. The name is said to mean "running water" or "clear of swamps" or possibly "many towns in one."[32]

The Chippewas formed one of the largest divisions of the Algonquian tribes. They were Great Lakes Indians, with territory extending from Lake Huron to Lake Superior and all the way to the Dakotas. In later years they have been associated with the Wisconsin-Minnesota territory and Canada where they are still to be found. They moved westward to escape from their enemies in the East only to encounter in the West the belligerent Sioux. In 1695, Pierre Sueur was sent out by the French at Montreal to make peace between the Chippewas and the Sioux; more than a hundred years later Henry Schoolcraft was sent as the United States Indian agent to the Chippewas for the same purpose.

These Algonquians were generally known by the name Ojibwa or Ojibway, which probably came from *Outchibouec*, which appears to be a French form. It could be written *Obidgewong* or, as Schoolcraft wrote it, *Ok-jib-wag* and *Ouchipawah*. According to James Mooney, the name came from *ojib*, "to pucker," and *ubway*, "to roast." This referred to the manner in which their moccasins puckered at the seams. Among the American versions of the name was Ojibaway, used by Lewis and Clark. Later the first syllable was dropped and Ojibaway became Americanized in the present popular form of Chippeway or Chippewa. There were several subdivisions of the tribes with localized names. Those who lived at Sault Sainte Marie were called *Saulteurs* or *Saulteaux*, which could have referred to the leaping of the falls or rapids. They were then called "leapers" and "jumpers." The English tried to imitate the French *Saulteurs* by calling them Sotoes.[33]

The Swan Creek and Black River bands of the Chippewas came

[32] *KHC*, VII, 485; *KHC*, XIV, 569; *St. Mary's Star*, Jan. 14, 1943.

[33] Hodge, *Handbook of American Indians*, I, 277; Swanton, *The Indian Tribes of North America*, 260. See also A. Irving Hollowell, *Culture and Experience*, 115; Schoolcraft, *Archives of Aboriginal Knowledge*, III, 565.

from Michigan to Kansas in 1839. They settled on the Marais des Cygnes and were assigned a little reservation in Franklin County near the Ottawa. Their neighbors were the Sac and Foxes who stole their hogs and cattle. There were only a few Chippewas there and they readily agreed to let the Munsees or Christian Indians join them. Their chief, Esh-ton-o-quot, whose name meant "clear sky," did his best to protect his wards, but as early as 1853, Mannypenny, the Indian commissioner, came to see if the Chippewas were willing to sell out, which they were reluctant to do. But by 1866 they were on their way into the Cherokee country of Oklahoma.[34]

The Chippewas lived in an attractive area and were, no doubt, fond of their home in Kansas. As one writer said, "The Hills, or Chippewa Hills, as the site of the old reservation is known, is a beautiful locality, and often visited by the people of Ottawa."[35] The place was evidently well enough known to be identified as "the Hills," without always referring to the full name of "the Chippewa Hills." There was also once a place named Chippewa in Dickenson County which served unofficially as a post office.[36]

There are too many elusive and contradictory sources for the name of Itasca to establish any one definite meaning. It is, of course, the name of the Minnesota lake which serves as the source of the Mississippi River. This lake was discovered and named by Henry Schoolcraft. The Chippewas already had a name for it; they called it *Omushkos*, which meant "elk lake." The French had a similar name, *Lac La Biche*, which referred to a "doe." Douglas Houghton, the geologist, combined the names in English and French and called it Elk Lake or "Lake la Beiche."[37] There have been other attempts to prove Itasca was an Indian name, even by Schoolcraft. One suggestion was that it meant a "woman's breast," from the Chippewa word *totosh*.

[34] Connelley, *KHC*, XIV, 488-91; Joseph Romig, "The Chippewa and Munsee Indians of Franklin County," *KHC*, XI, 316.

[35] Romig, *KHC*, XI, 323.

[36] See map in Andreas and Cutler, *History of Kansas*, 1563; *Abilene Reflector-Chronicle*, Jan. 30, 1959.

[37] Vogel, *Indian Place Names in Illinois*, 44-46; Gannett, *American Names*, 167.

However, that was only one of several of Schoolcraft's interpretations. He may even have made the name out of two Latin words, *veritas*, "truth," and *caput*, "head." This made it the true head or source of the river. But it took some juggling to make it Itasca from *veritas caput*. Dropping the first syllable of *veritas* and the last syllable of *caput* makes the combination "itasca." Perhaps a poet's mind would resort to such ingenuity, but Schoolcraft's poetic mind found a more fascinating source in the name of a maid. "Itasca was the name of an Indian maiden who was borne to the underworld by an evil spirit. Her tears for her lover formed the eternal springs which welled up to form Lake Itasca and the Mississippi River."[38]

Fitting or not, the name came to Kansas where it flourished briefly in a competitive county-seat conflict, a conflict in which towns and names had but an ephemeral existence. In Minnesota, Itasca, the source of the Mississippi River, has now reached the status of a popular park. In western Kansas it was the name of a small town in Sherman County. The town was one of several competitors of Goodland for the county seat. To be successful, a prospective county seat needed to be in the exact center, and Itasca boasted of being very near the center of the county. To add to its luster, Itasca called itself the "Queen City of the West," which it was not. For political strength Itasca joined a neighboring town but it gave up its name for that of Sherman Center which should have made it doubly attractive since it combined the name of a Civil War general and "Center." The attractive name Itasca was lost for the political popularity of a new name, then all was lost to the new town of Goodland which became the county seat.[39]

Peotone, the name of a post office in Sedgwick County, apparently came from a Potawatomi or Chippewa word, *petoan* or *petone*, meaning "bring to this place" or just "bring." The name could have come from Illinois where it had already been used as

[38] Philip P. Mason, *Schoolcraft's Expedition to Lake Itasca*, xix and 97n. For a good analysis and references see Vogel, *Indian Place Names in Illinois*, 44–46 and 46n.

[39] E. E. Blackman, "Sherman County and the H. U. A.," *KHC*, VIII, 50.

a place-name, since the Peotone-Viola area in Kansas was settled by people from Illinois.[40]

Long before Pasadena in California became famous for its Tournament of Roses and its Rose Bowl football game, Pasadena was used as a place-name in Kansas. Pasadena was the name of a town in Garfield County, which was made a part of Finney County in 1893. That year Pasadena disappeared, its demise described by the word "vacated."[41]

One might easily come to the conclusion that Pasadena is a Spanish name. It looks like a Spanish name, it sounds like a Spanish name, and it came from a state full of Spanish names. It is surprising, therefore, to discover that the name has a Chippewa origin. The California site of Pasadena, settled by Indiana people, was called the Indiana Colony. The settlers agreed, however, to choose a Spanish name for their town. When the Spanish owner of the land was asked why he had selected this site for his home, he answered, "*Porque es llave del rancho*," which means "because it is the key of the ranch." This gave little from which to choose a name, except *llave*, or "key." The president of the colony then wrote to a missionary among the Chippewas for an Indian name which meant "key to the valley." Four names were received: *Weoquan Pa-sa-de-na*, *Gish-ka-de-na Pa-sa-de-na*, *Tape Daegun Pa-sa-de-na*, and *Pa-qua-de-na Pa-sa-de-na*. These meant "crown of the valley," "peak of the valley," "key of the valley," and "hill of the valley." The names were too long and complex but they all had something in common; they all ended in *Pa sa de na*. So Pasadena, without its full meaning, was approved. The name was attractive, simple, and acceptable; and someone, probably not knowing that it had a Chippewa origin, brought it to Kansas.[42]

[40] Vogel, *Indian Place Names in Illinois*, 109; "Extinct Geographical Locations," *KHC*, XII, 485.

[41] "Extinct Geographical Locations," *KHC*, XII, 485.

[42] Erwin G. Gudde, *California Place Names*, 226.

▲ XVI

Sac, Fox, and Kickapoo

POPULATION PRESSURE WAS SO SEVERE in the Lake Huron and eastern Great Lakes when the French arrived that tribe after tribe was forced out. There was no way to go but westward. The Sac and Fox tribes, Algonquians, were caught in the same inter-tribal warfare as the Hurons, Eries, and other Iroquoian neighbors. Not only did they suffer from the attacks of their red neighbors, but the French took the side of their enemies. This forced the Sacs and Foxes into a closer union, but they found that it was better to retreat than to resist. First they crossed to the Detroit area and then they moved on into the Green Bay area of Wisconsin. From there they spread southward to Illinois.

In 1804 the two tribes were badly divided over a treaty which deprived them of much of their Illinois and Wisconsin lands. Many refused to sign, and, feeling that they had not been properly represented, the Foxes, angry at their allies, crossed the Mississippi into Iowa and Minnesota. Black Hawk led his Sac followers in a desperate effort to save their homes and their cornfields in Illinois. In the Black Hawk War of 1832, Black Hawk earned a great name in history, but he lost the war, partly because the Sacs and Foxes were no longer united. After the war the Sacs also crossed the Mississippi and joined their former friends and allies. It was a timely reunion since the two faced such serious enemies as the Omahas and other Siouan tribes. In 1843, only a decade after Black Hawk's defeat, they gave up their Iowa lands for a restricted reservation in Kansas.[1]

[1] Hodge, *Handbook of American Indians*, II, 471; Swanton, *The Indian Tribes of North America*, 256.

The name of the tribe has taken two forms, Sac and Sauk. In Kansas they were generally called Sacs, the name used by the French and Spaniards. The name has been preserved in both forms as Wisconsin place-names, Prairie du Sac and Sauk City. It was from the "Saukies" that Saginaw got its name. Ozawkie, the name of the first town in Jefferson County as well as the name of a township, appears to resemble this tribal name. But Ozawkie in Kansas was said to be named for a chief. Catlin, who painted his portrait, called him "On-sáw-kie," a Sauk chief. The name has been interpreted to mean "yellow leaf" or "golden falling leaves."[2] Perhaps it meant "yellow earth."

According to Swanton, the Sauk or Sac name came from *Osa'kiwug*, meaning "people of the outlet." Chippewas called them *O-saug-eeg*, which had a similar meaning, "those who live at the entry," which could mean outlet.[3] The Sacs were also called the "people of the yellow earth," which distinguishes them from the Foxes, "the red earth people." The Yankton and Santee Sioux called them *Za-ke* which is quite near the Americanized "Saukie." Schoolcraft gave *Saque* as the French name for the "Sawkee."

Originally the name Fox was applied only to one clan, the *Wagohug* or *Wagosh*. *Wagosh*, said Hodge, meant "red fox." When asked by some Frenchmen who they were, they answered that they were the Foxes, and since then the whole tribe has been known as Fox. The French naturally called them *Renard* or *Reynard*, their name for fox and a name that is well known from the story "Reynard the Fox." Both the Wyandots and the Potawatomis gave them Indian names which meant "fox." The Foxes called themselves *Muskwakiwuk* or *Meshkwa kihug* which described them as the "red earth people," since they were, according to tradition, created from red earth.[4] It was from this name that they were also known as the Musquakies.

[2] Donaldson, "The George Catlin Indian Gallery," *Annual Report* of the Board of Regents of the Smithsonian Institution to July 1885, Part II, 134; *Atchison Daily Globe*, Oct. 15, 1910; Richardson, *Beyond the Mississippi*, 97.

[3] *The Indian Tribes of North America*, 256; Warren, *History of the Ojibway Nation*, 32; Hodge, *Handbook of American Indians*, II, 471.

[4] Hodge, *Handbook of American Indians*, II, 472; Swanton, *The Indian Tribes of North America*, 250–52.

Another Chippewa name for the Foxes was *O-dug-am-eeg* which meant "those who live on the opposite side." This was an appropriate name when the Foxes lived in the Green Bay area of Wisconsin, where they gave their name to the Fox River. The name was written Outagomies and Ottagamies, with variations. The reference to "Outagamies, Renards, and Foxes" shows the name in Indian, French, and English.[5]

Most of the names which the Sac and Foxes left in Kansas have been names of their people, especially their chiefs. For a short time, however, there was a Sac Branch post office in Franklin County, and there is a Sac Creek in Anderson County. There was also a Fox Village, now Clifton, on the Washington-Clay county border which evidently was not an official post office although it did distribute the mail. Fox Town in Crawford County may have been named for the Indians, but the Fox Creek post office in Chase County was named for Edward Fox, a pioneer who lived near what was also called the Farm post office.[6]

There was a post office in Franklin County referred to as the Sac and Fox Agency, but its name was changed to Greenwood, probably for Alfred B. Greenwood, commissioner of Indian affairs. Another Sac and Fox Agency in Osage County had its post-office changed to Quenemo.[7]

Famous in the lore of the Sac and Foxes is the story of *Quenemo*, for whom Quenemo in Osage County was named. According to legend or "before time," seven Sac women had been captured by some Dakota tribesmen. They were released to return home in the winter, but their suffering was so great that six of them died. There was also a suggestion of cannibalism. The seventh gave birth to a child on the way, and in her desperation she cried out, "*Que-ne-mo! Que-ne-mo!*" meaning "Oh, my God! Oh, my God!" Charles R. Green admits that "there is no English equivalent" for the cry

[5] Warren, *History of the Ojibway Nation*, 32–33; Schoolcraft, *Archives of Aboriginal Knowledge*, III, 564.

[6] Savage, *A History of Republic County, Kansas*, 39; *Chase County Historical Sketches*, I, 27.

[7] Green, *Early Days in Kansas*, I, 97; Andreas and Cutler, *History of Kansas*, 1552.

of "*Que-ne-mo!*" It was, of course, a cry of despair, and the meaning may be, as Green suggested, "Oh, my God! Why hast thou deserted me!" The mother miraculously reached the village of her people who were then living near Milan in northern Ohio. There the tribe considered her survival so marvelous that the tribal council decided to make her son a chief. They named him Quenemo. From then on, said the council, each first-born child of the family should bear this name.[8]

Such legends could be preserved well in a stable Indian society where someone was in charge of the traditions of a people. But in the confusion of a mixed civilization the legitimate legends of a people could be partially forgotten and revised into quite a different tale. When one old pioneer heard the legend of Quenemo as the Indians told it, he gave his version, one that might also win the approval of the Indians. "I thought Quenemo was named from a woman," he said, "the wife of a Sac and Fox Indian interpreter John Goodell, the woman who in the Black Hawk war swam the Mississippi river with a child on her back to escape being shot by the soldiers."[9]

Back of this version is what appears to be a more reliable account, but it has no connection with Quenemo except in the similarity of the legends.

> During the Black Hawk War, when the Sauks and Foxes were hard pressed, the squaws packed hastily, and moved to safer ground. Mrs. Mitchell placed her few belongings on her pony, and swung her child upon her back. In the course of her flight it became necessary to swim the Wisconsin river near where it empties into the Mississippi, and where it is deep and swift and wide. Driving her pony before her, with her baby on her back, she plunged fearlessly into the stream. The pony drowned, but Mrs. Mitchell and little Mary gained the opposite shore in safety.[10]

Five generations of Quenemos left considerable confusion over which one was the source for the naming of the town of Quenemo.

[8] Ferris, *KHC*, XI, 333n. and 380; Green, *Early Days in Kansas*, V, 52–68; Howes, in *Kansas City Times*, May 13, 1947.

[9] Green, *Early Days in Kansas*, V, 3 and 11–12; *KHC*, XVI, 767.

[10] Ferris, *KHC*, XI, 355.

It has been supposed that the wife of John Goodell was named Quenemo, "after whom the town was named." This is an error. Goodell's wife was Mrs. Julia Mitchell, the one who swam across the Wisconsin River. The confusion came probably from associating this with the older legendary account of the woman who escaped with her baby son who was then named Quenemo. The confusion is understandable. Under the portrait of Mrs. Goodell in the Kansas historical publications is the statement: "Mrs. Goodell. Who swam the river with her child on her back." But her name was not Quenemo, nor was Quenemo the name of her child, who was not a son but a daughter whose name was Mary Mitchell.[11]

The most logical source for the name was an Indian by the name of Quenemo who was born at Milan, Ohio, possibly within a year or two of 1806. One who knew him well in Kansas said that he was the son of a "Sauk Warrior" and "an Ottawa and Seneca squaw." The Indians called him a brave but the white man called him a chief. Chief or brave, he willingly worked for the farmers and helped them to hoe and harvest their corn. He was a quiet and gentle man, but his second wife, "a sort of termagant," threatened to kill him with a butcher knife. He was one of the signers of the treaty of 1864, which permitted the sale of Sac and Fox lands. There his name was spelled Que-we-mo. George Throckmorton said that "Old Joe Quinemo" was a great friend of his father. As a child Throckmorton had been a playmate of a boy named Snowflake Kenemy. The name had been spelled Quinimo and Quinemo, but Kenemy adds an interesting phonetic form for Quenemo, which is now pronounced Kwen′e-moh. Among the ephemeral towns of Shawnee County was one named Kenemo or Kanemo, located within three miles of Tecumseh.[12]

Warner Craig, one of the promoters of a town, tells about attending a meeting to choose its name when "the door opened and in stepped Quenemo." Craig reacted quickly and said, "I name this town Quenemo after my old Indian friend here." Dr. E. B. Fenn

[11] *Ibid.*, 385.

[12] *Ibid.*, 333n.; Green, *Early Days in Kansas*, V, passim; George Throckmorton, *First Hand Historical Episodes of Early Coffey County*, 14; Howes, Shawnee County Historical Society *Bulletin*, I, 29.

suggested that the name could mean "longed for" or, more elaborately, "I am lonesome without you."[13]

The town named Quenemo was located at the Sac and Fox Indian Agency, and the township has retained the name of Agency. Although started as a town earlier, Quenemo became the post office name in 1870. The town has been described as "the pretty village that nestles at the foot of Agency hill." Whatever its source, it was proud to be "the only town in the world bearing the name," a name that would "perpetuate the legend of Quenemo."[14]

Tuquas and Appanoose, two of the Sac chiefs who signed the treaty of 1842 to give up their lands in Iowa in exchange for land in Kansas, left their names on the Kansas map in a small way. Tuquas Creek, just below the town named Quenemo, was named for one of the treaty signers whose name appeared as Tuk-quos on the treaty. It has also been spelled Tauqua and Tuck-quas. Chief Tuquos was a teetotaler and prohibited drinking of liquor among his people. He has therefore been considered to be the first real prohibitionist in Kansas, long before Carry Nation wielded her hatchet. The Indian agent said that he had the best regulated band in the area.[15]

Chief Appanoose signed several treaties and on each one his name is spelled differently. But this was not his fault; the Americans did the spelling. It was spelled Appenioce on one, Ap-pi-nuis on another, and, more elaborately. Appan-oze-o-kemar on a third. *Apenos* could mean "dear child" or "little child" or possibly just "child." The full name of Appan-oze-o-ke-mar has been translated to mean "He who was a chief when a child." A simpler translation made it "the hereditary chief."[16]

Appanoose was highly respected by both the Indians and the white man, and after visiting Washington in 1837, he gave a dramatic oration at Faneuil Hall in Boston. The chief lived for a time

[13] Green, *Early Days in Kansas*, V, passim, and I, 97; Andreas and Cutler, *History of Kansas*, 1552.

[14] Ferris, *KHC*, XI, 381; Andreas and Cutler, *History of Kansas*, 1552.

[15] Green, *Early Days in Kansas*, V, passim; Ferris, *KHC*, XI, 343 and 386.

[16] Vogel, *Indian Place Names in Illinois*, 11; McKenney and Hall, *Indian Tribes of North America*, II, 105; *KHC*, XVI, 759.

Appanoose, Sac chief, whose name was given to Appanoose Creek and Appanoose Township in Franklin County and Appanoose post office in Douglas County (McKenney and Hall, *The Indian Tribes of North America*, II, 106)

at Fort Madison and later at Ottumwa, Iowa. He lies buried on Appanoose Creek in Franklin County, Kansas. This county also has a township named Appanoose. A post office named Appanoose was established in Douglas County in 1857 but it lasted only a short time.[17]

Best known of the Sac chiefs were Black Hawk and Keokuk. Black Hawk had not been a chief at first, but he was an accepted and highly respected leader. He was tall and distinguished in appearance, hollow cheeked and hook nosed, and his bristly scalp lock rose over his head like a majestic crown. His superior chief and rival was Keokuk.[18] Black Hawk would stand up and fight the white man, whereas Keokuk, who was vain and easily flattered, would submit and accept the white man's domination. It was said that Keokuk could be won over by the gift of a colorful coat. Black Hawk had once fought with Tecumseh against the white man and he tried to unite the natives to resist them again. And again he lost.

That Black Hawk was highly respected and honored may be seen by the list of objects placed with his remains at the time of his burial. He was buried in Iowa in "a military uniform presented by General Jackson, accompanied by a sword also presented by Jackson, a cane given by Henry Clay, and medals from Jackson, John Quincy Adams, and the city of Boston." His remains were later robbed of these earthly honors.[19]

Black Hawk's Indian name was Ma-ka-tai-me-she-kia-kiak, which was a mouthful even when written Ma'katawimesheka'kaa. George Catlin, who painted his portrait, spelled his name Meek-A-Tah-Mish-O-Kah-Kaik. The name meant "black sparrow hawk," and although quite long, any omission in the name would distort the original meaning. The chief was occasionally called Black Sparrow, but by deleting the "Sparrow" and restoring the "Hawk," the name became Black Hawk. Neither is completely correct. He

17 Andreas and Cutler, *History of Kansas*, 529; Ferris, *KHC*, XI, 385; Green, *Early Days in Kansas*, I, 146.

18 Donald Jackson (ed.), *Black Hawk*, 1–2.

19 Hodge, *Handbook of American Indians*, I, 152; William T. Hagan, *The Sac and Fox Indians*, 89.

has also been referred to as "Black-big-chest."[20] It was, however, the feathered skin of a sparrow hawk which he wore on his side which was said to have earned him his name.

Black Hawk was more popular as a place-name than Keokuk. Both Black Hawk and Keokuk were used as county names in Iowa and as place-names in Kansas. Great as was the name of Black Hawk the chief, Black Hawk post office in Osborne County lasted but a few years, from 1873 to 1879.

Keokuk found it personally rewarding not to resist the white man. Unlike Black Hawk, he preferred to submit and survive to enjoy life. He loved the ladies and married seven of them; he loved liquor and imbibed too freely; and he loved horse racing, the sport of kings and the downfall of many a man. But he was a man with considerable ability.[21] Keokuk's name was a modernized version of Kiyo'kaga, meaning "one who moves about alert." This interpretation has also been given for the name Kickapoo. Keokuk has been called "the watchful Fox" and "the sly old Fox." He belonged to the Fox clan of the Sacs which could also explain his being called a Fox. Keokuk died and was buried in Kansas, but his body was later taken to Keokuk, Iowa, where it honors his namesake.[22] On the Johnson map of 1870 there was a place named Keokuk in Linn County, but, like Black Hawk, its life was brief.

The Kickapoos were relatives of the Sac and Fox tribes. The Hurons called them "the tribe living around the lakes." To escape from their Indian enemies and from the French and American frontiersmen, they migrated into the Illinois country and from there to Missouri. There were two bands of the Kickapoos. One, restless and belligerent, might be found anywhere from Kansas to Mexico, while the other, more peaceful, was the Illinois band or Northern Kickapoos under Chief Kennekuk. The Kickapoos arrived in Kan-

[20] Hodge, *Handbook of American Indians*, I, 150 and 673; Vogel, *Indian Place Names in Illinois*, 14; Donaldson, "The George Catlin Indian Gallery," *Annual Report* of the Board of Regents of the Smithsonian Institution to July 1885, Part V, 21; McKenney and Hall, *Indian Tribes of North America*, II, 92n.

[21] William W. Graves, *History of the Kickapoo Mission and Parish*, 98; Hagan, *The Sac and Fox Indians*, 89.

[22] Hodge, *Handbook of American Indians*, I, 673; Green, *Early Days in Kansas*, V, 7 and 12.

sas in 1832 and were given land in Atchison County. At last they had found a haven where they could remain unmolested "as long as the world stood." But the world seemed to be in a perpetual motion, much of it disturbing. The Kickapoos were soon to suffer from the white man's greed and aggression. The early trails to the West cut through the Kickapoo country and the travelers and migrants generally ignored the property rights of its occupants. One authority has concluded that "the activities of frontier railroad promoters, bankers, and businessmen in divesting the Kickapoos of their lands in Kansas during the 1860's comprise a sordid chronicle of man's inhumanity to man."[23]

The Kickapoo name is said to have come from *Kiwegawa* or *Kiwegapawa*. Various forms of the name resembling Kickapoo were accepted and used by several tribes. The Comanches called them *Sik-a-pu*, which resembled their Apache name of *Shigapo* or *Shikapu*. The Omahas called them *Higabu*. These names appear to have come from the French. Marquette's name for the Kickapoos was very similar to their present name; he called them *Kikabous*. Other French forms were *Quicapoo*, *Quicapu*, and *Quicapous*. The English changed the spelling to Kikapu which eventually became Kickapoo. The name is interpreted to mean "he moves about, standing now here, now there." Since "he" does not stand at any place, the better interpretation may be "he moves about." Quite different is Schoolcraft's suggestion that the name means "otter's ghost," which probably refers to a clan.[24]

A great variety of places were named for the Kickapoos. The town of Kickapoo in Leavenworth County is in Kickapoo Township. There is, or rather there was, a Kickapoo Island in the Missouri River north of Leavenworth. Owing to the meandering movements of the muddy Missouri, Kickapoo Island, a Kansas

[23] Root (ed.), "No-ko-aht's Talk," *KHQ*, I, 154; A. M. Gibson, *The Kickapoos*, 109 and 124.

[24] Bolton (ed.), *Athanase de Mézières and the Louisiana-Texas Frontier*, I, 74; Deatherage, *Greater Kansas City*, I, 48 and 69; Hodge, *Handbook of American Indians*, I, 684; Vogel, *Indian Place Names in Illinois*, 52; Graves, *History of the Kickapoo Mission and Parish*, 3.

possession, became a part of the Missouri mainland. In the Siouan language, Kickapoo Island was called *Wau-car-ba War-can-da*, meaning "bear medicine island." The first word may have been written *Wassaba* for bear, and *War-can-da*, referring to the Great Spirit, was generally written *Waconda*. North of Kickapoo Island, near Wathena, are the Kickapoo Bottoms. There is also a Kickapoo Creek. Near Winfield, at the west end of Nineteenth Street, is the Kickapoo Corral. This was formed by a horseshoe bend in the Walnut River which served as a natural moat on three sides and left only a narrow strip of land to be defended by the Kickapoos who had taken refuge there. There was a Kickapoo Mission near Fort Leavenworth and another in Atchison County and a Kickapoo Street in Leavenworth. The Kickapoo name was so popular that in the battles of Bleeding Kansas the Free State party christened its one piece of artillery Old Kickapoo. According to one account, it was placed on the esplanade at Leavenworth, loaded with the "bogus statutes," and fired across the river into Missouri.[25] The popularity of the Kickapoo name is illustrated by the name of the Kickapoo Rangers in Kansas as well as the names of "medicines" such as Kickapoo Joy Juice.

Those who promoted the town of Kickapoo City planned to make it the capital of Kansas. They assumed that the alliteration would give it popular appeal. C. K. Holliday, on his way to Kansas on the steamboat *F. X. Aubrey*, was told to settle at "the greatest city on the continent—and that city, sir, is Kickapoo."[26] In a contest for the county seat with Delaware City and Leavenworth, Kickapoo City won. But this was only the first round; in the third election it lost. Then it declined, and today it is no longer a "city" but just Kickapoo.

Kickapoo chiefs were not always well liked but they were well known. Most important was Chief Kennekuk, the "Kickapoo Prophet." Catlin spelled his name Kee-an-ne-kuk. J. C. Berrymore,

[25] Gibson, *The Kickapoos*, ix; Connelley, "Note on the Early Indian Occupancy of the Great Plains," *KHC*, XIV, 450; Remsburg, *Scrapbook*, IV, 107.

[26] *Wyandotte County and Kansas City, Kansas*, 95; Holliday, *KHC*, III, 397.

Kennekuk, Kickapoo chief, for whom Kennekuk in Atchison County was named (Gray, *Doniphan County History*, 12)

who knew the chief well and thoroughly disliked him, spelled his name Ke-en-e-kuk. His name was also spelled Keannakuk. Whatever its variations in spelling, Kennekuk's name came from the name for the Indian tobacco called kinnikinnick, kinikinik, or kinne kennick. Catlin spelled it K'nick K'nick. It was a mixture of some leaves and bark. In fact, the name is supposed to mean "a mixture." In Chippewa, *kinikinige* meant "he mixes by hand." A common mixture was sumac and the inner bark of the dogwood tree.[27]

A Jesuit priest referred to Chief Kennekuk as "*Kenekoek, ou Prophete des Kokopooks*." As a preacher and a prophet, Kennekuk was esteemed by some, but a missionary said that he had "two or three wives and is considered a great sinner." He was chief of the Illinois band which tried to adopt the white man's ways in Kansas.[28]

Kennekuk prophesied correctly that "a town would rise" on his camping ground. The town, in Atchison County, is named Kennekuk, often pronounced "Kinney Kirk." Some would attribute the origin of the name to John Kennekuk, the Prophet's son, who negotiated the treaty of 1854 with Mannypenny. Remsburg's assumption that it was named for the Kickapoo Prophet is more likely correct. One of the early stage stations on the Oregon Trail was first called Kickapoo Station and then Kennekuk Station.[29]

In 1853 a delegation of Kickapoo went to Washington to discuss their land holdings with George W. Mannypenny, the Indian commissioner. That was the year that Kennekuk the Prophet died, and so his son, John Kennekuk, or Pakahkah, headed the delegation. One of the subchiefs with the Kickapoo delegation was named Kapioma. He has also been called the Fox Carrier. The treaty reduced the Kickapoo land by 618,000 acres. The Kickapoos were, however, given compensation in money to be invested for income. The Kickapoos are among the few Indians who still have a home

[27] Ingalls, *History of Atchison County, Kansas*, 29; Root and Hickman, "Pike's Peak Express Companies," *KHQ*, XIII, 508n.; Vogel, *Indian Place Names in Illinois*, 53.

[28] Ingalls, *History of Atchison County, Kansas*, 29 and 191; Barry, *KHQ*, XXIX, 457; *Horton Headlight*, Nov. 29, 1936.

[29] Jerome C. Berryman, "A Circuit Rider's Frontier Experiences," *KHC*, XVI, 215; Gibson, *The Kickapoos*, 119; Remsburg, *Scrapbook*, I, 155 and 202; Paden, *In the Wake of the Prairie Schooner*, 59.

in Kansas. They live in Brown County and have made considerable progress along "the white man's road."[30]

Kapioma Township in Atchison County was named for Kapioma, subchief of the Kickapoos and one of the signers of the treaty of 1854. His name has been spelled both Kahpioma and Kapiomah as well as Capioma. The town named in the chief's honor in Nemaha County was called Capioma, as was also the township in which it was located.[31]

Chief Mashema, or Mashumah as it is spelled by Remsburg, was a Kickapoo chief who was at the Battle of Tippecanoe. His name was said to mean "elk horns." A town named Mashema was planned to compete with Kennekuk, but the town seems never to have gone beyond the paper stage. On paper, however, it had already been given street names, all of them named for trees. Chief Mashema was seemingly not an important man, nor was the town which was to honor his name.[32]

Where Chief Wathenah's wigwam once stood on Peter's Creek in Doniphan County, there now stands the town named Wathena. Wathenah, chief of the Kickapoos, won favor by permitting his wigwam to be used as a church. Later he sold his wigwam site to Milton E. Bryan, who became the first postmaster there and for whom the post office was then named Bryan. In 1856 the name was changed to Wathena to honor the chief. The place has been referred to phonetically as "Wa. Se. Na's." The form of Wathene was probably based on a simplified pronunciation that dropped a syllable.[33]

The town of Muscotah in Atchison County was founded by Dr. W. P. Badger and Major C. B. Keith. The townsite had been pur-

[30] Ingalls, *History of Atchison County, Kansas,* 29; Remsburg, in the *Atchison Daily Globe,* Dec. 4, 1906, and the *Sabetha Herald,* Jan. 28, 1909; Gibson, *The Kickapoos,* 110 and 119.

[31] Martha B. Caldwell, "Squatter Association of Doniphan County," *KHQ,* XIII, 26; Greene, *The Kanzas Region,* 143; *KHC,* I–II, 258; Gray, *Doniphan County History,* II, 22 and 86.

[32] *Atchison Daily Globe,* June 13, 1916; Ingalls, *History of Atchison County, Kansas,* 29 and 120.

[33] Ingalls, *History of Atchison County, Kansas,* 106; Remsburg, *Scrapbook,* I, 95 and 157.

chased from Chief Pe-At-e-quork or Pettiqunk, whose name meant "rolling thunder," and his two wives, Retobe and Ogetchahkah. Badger has been given credit for naming the town. Others have suggested, however, that the name was given by Paschal Pensoneau, also written Pascal Pensineau, an old Kickapoo trader and interpreter who was married to a Kickapoo woman. Mrs. Keith, the wife of one of the founders, wrote to George Remsburg and explained that Pensoneau had suggested the name and that William Badger, also an Indian trader, had named the town.[34]

The town with the attractive name of Muscotah is located in the Kickapoo area of northern Kansas. The name may be merely from a Kickapoo word meaning "prairie," or it may possibly have come from the name of the Prairie band of the Potawatomis which was known as the Mascoutens. The Kickapoos and Potawatomis had lived together, and their languages were quite similar. But Muscotah probably came from the Kickapoos, because it was in the Kickapoo country and the name was suggested by an interpreter for the Kickapoos whose wife was a Kickapoo woman.

Before the name became Muscotah, it had been spelled in a variety of ways such as Makskautang and Mascoutens. These were names of the Prairie band from Illinois and had been interpreted to mean "prairie" of some kind. The name has also been translated to mean "prairie fire," which has led to the conclusion that it referred to a "ruddy sunset." The "fire" part of the name probably came from a translation of Potawatomi.[35]

There were several translations that associated Muscotah with prairie. The Mascoutens were said to be the "prairie people" or the "little prairie people." The source for prairie was *muskodé*. Longfellow made the Indian name attractive as "Muskoday, the Meadow." Translators and commentators have added descriptions which may not have been in the original meaning of *muskodé* but which were pleasing, such as "pretty prairie."

If the interpretation that Muscotah meant "pretty prairie" is

[34] Ingalls, *History of Atchison County, Kansas*, 29 and 107; Andreas and Cutler, *History of Kansas*, 410; Remsburg, in *Atchison Daily Globe*, Dec. 4, 1906, and June 9, 1957.

[35] Remsburg, *Scrapbook*, I, 95 and 157.

accepted, then it can be said that three place-names in Kansas have the same meaning. The names are in three different languages, Indian, French, and English. In Indian it is Muscotah, in French, Belpré, and in English, Pretty Prairie. Muscotah is in northeastern Kansas, Pretty Prairie is near Hutchinson in central Kansas, and Belpré is farther west in Edwards County.

The Wisconsin influence in Kansas is seen in the town named New Milwaukee in Butler County, 1870–80, and the Milwaukee post office in Stafford County, 1878–87. Some of the prairie tribes of the Algonquian family in Wisconsin lived on a river which they called *Miloaki*, in which *milo* meant "good" and *aki* meant "land." This became Milwaukee. In the form Minewago it might mean "there is a point where huckleberries grow."[36]

[36] Stewart, *Names on the Land*, 86; Hodge, *Handbook of American Indians*, I, 863; *KHC*, XII, 484.

▲ XVII

Manhattans and Munsees

THE MANHATTANS, MUNSEES, DELAWARES, AND POWHATTANS were Algonquian tribes which occupied territory from Massachusetts Bay and the Hudson River in lower New York down to the James River in Virginia. These natives played a very important part in the early history of colonial settlements. They came into contact with the French, Dutch, Swedish, and English. Each of these tribes contributed place-names, directly or indirectly, to sites in Kansas.

Manhattan, said Washington Irving, should have been the name for New York City. He liked Indian names, and it would be difficult to guess what he would have said about giving the name of Manhattan to a town in Kansas which had already had three Indian names. Near the junction of the Big Blue and the Kaw a cluster of communities developed, each with a name that was here today and gone tomorrow. In rapid succession the new towns were given new names, and with all these worthy names from which to choose, the Kansas town ended by becoming Manhattan.

The attractiveness of the junction of the Big Blue and the Kaw as a site for settlements and cities was recognized even before Kansas was organized for white man's occupation. There were settlers on both sides of the Blue in 1853. On the left bank of the Blue was Samuel D. Dyer from Tennessee, and on the right bank was Samuel D. Houston from Illinois. Dyer was a preacher and a promoter, and his home, generally described as "one story high and three stories long," served as a "preaching house" for all denominations.

Dyer and his wife were kind, generous, and hospitable, and most people took advantage of them.[1]

Dyer settled about four or five miles up the Blue and located his homestead at the mouth of a little stream called the Junietta or Juniata Creek.[2] Since he was at the crossing of the military road to Fort Riley, he started a ferry system across the Blue. A bridge across the river put the ferry out of business, but within a year a flood put the bridge out of business. In the meantime a boom had started at the location of the bridge, and Dyer's place became known as Dyer's Town. It was made a post office in 1855 and given the delightful Indian name of Juniata. Noting the mention of Juniata in a letter, the *Philadelphia American* made the comment that such names "indicate that the Pennsylvanians are alive in Kansas."[3] It was, however, as well known by its earlier name of Dyer's Town as it was by its Pennsylvania Indian name of Juniata. It was sufficiently important for a time to be called "Gateway to Mid-Kansas."[4]

The source of the Juniata name was the Blue Juniata in Pennsylvania which had been named by the Delaware Indians who were said to have pronounced it "Juch-niada" or "Chuch-niada." Another form suggested was *Gunniade*, which was translated to mean "they stay long." But it was also said to mean "it is long since they were here." These are similar but not the same. According to Henry Gannett, it could also have meant "beyond the great bend."

Being named for the Blue Juniata in Pennsylvania, it was fitting that the Juniata in Kansas should also be located on a river named Blue. As early as January, 1855, six months before Juniata became a post office, one writer gave his address as "Juniata," and for additional identification he added in parenthesis, on the "Big Blue River." Neither the town nor the name survived on the east side of the river. The settlements moved downstream, then crossed the

1 "Juniata," *KHC*, XII, 426–27.

2 Smith, *KHC*, XVII, 461–64.

3 Martin, *KHC*, VII, 373n.

4 Goodnow, *KHC*, IV, 247; James C. Carey, "Juniata: Gateway to Mid-Kansas," *KHQ*, XXI, 87.

Blue to compete with the towns which eventually merged into Manhattan. The Juniata name did eventually cross the river and became the name of the Juniata Ranch owned by Dan D. Casement who has preserved the popular name from the Blue Juniata of Pennsylvania.[5]

The first Juniata on the Big Blue lost its name to Tauromee, the name of a highly respected Wyandot chief. As a Wyandot name it might better have been adopted for a name in Wyandotte County. It could have been a popular name, but there was considerable confusion over its spelling, discussed in the chapter on the Wyandots, and the name lasted only two years.[6]

Sam Houston's place on the right bank of the Blue was given the name of Canton, supposedly for Canton, Ohio. Actually, said one writer, it was only "a dugout at the base of Bluemont, and nothing else." But it did have something else; it had a location with a magnetic appeal and it had rivals. One of the rivals was Tauromee, but a new one was the town called Parksville for its founder, George S. Parks of Parksville, Missouri. Parks named his town Poliska, according to some records, but the name was also spelled Polistra, which appears to be a typographical error. This was only the beginning of the community competition in town building and name rivalry. Out of New England, New York, and Ohio came colonizing companies with strong backing from the East.[7]

There was rivalry and confusion at the mouth of the Blue, and it took more than a name, a claim, a cabin, or a dugout to make a town. The best organized of the town promoters in the Manhattan area were those who were supported by the New England Emigrant Aid Society. The leader of this group was Professor Isaac T. Goodnow of East Greenwich, Rhode Island. After listening to one of Ely Thayer's stimulating speeches he decided to join the Kansas crusade. Colonists for Kansas were leaving Boston daily, and help was needed to locate them in places which promised suc-

[5] Errett, *Magazine of Western History*, II, 245; Gannett, *American Names*, 171.
[6] *KHC*, IV, 713; *KHC*, XII, 426; *KHC*, XV, 112.
[7] Goodnow, *KHC*, IV, 247; "Poliska," *KHC*, index; *Manhattan Tribune-News*, Sept. 2, 1951.

cess. Selecting a site for a new Boston or what was to become another Manhattan was done by Professor Goodnow, assisted by the Rev. Charles E. Blood.

According to Goodnow, they "ascended from the north what is now called Bluemont Hill." To the beautiful but exaggerated name of Blue Mont or Bluemont someone honestly added "Hill" in order to lower the expectations of those who anticipated a more lofty land. However, from the highlands the lowlands looked beautiful. From the top of an Indian mound the professor and the preacher saw what Goodnow described as "the most beautiful townsite he had ever beheld." Goodnow is said to have quoted Brigham Young, "This is the place!" The professor, familiar with Greek, said that he felt like shouting "Eureka! Eureka! I have found it." He could then and there have named the place Eureka, as some townsite searchers under a similar experience did later in Greenwood County.[8]

As the two looked down into the valley, they saw smoke curling up from a campfire at Canton. The Boston agents also had to contend with the settlers at Tauromee and Poliska in order to take over the establishment of a town at this site. With the backing of Boston they did take over, and the choice of a name for the town was between Boston and New Boston. Promoters from New York and Ohio were attracted to the same site, and every group had its own proposal for a new name. The presence of these new promoters was owing to some of their own problems.

On the assumption that the Kaw River was navigable up to the junction of the Republican, Andrew J. Mead of New York had proposed to settle an Ohio company from Cincinnati on the site which is now Junction City. Some thought that the town was to be named New Cincinnati, but others said that their town charter required that "the town where they settled should be called Manhattan."[9] Mead, who had chosen the site, said that: "After the selection was made, surveyed and christened Manhattan (now Junction City), I . . . only waited the arrival of the steamer 'Hart-

[8] *KHC*, IV, 247.
[9] *Ibid.*, 250.

ford.' "[10] But the steamer was stranded downstream with its cargo, colony, and name.

Steamboat navigation of the Kaw was a promoter's dream but in reality quite precarious. The Cincinnati colony failed to reach the junction of the Republican. The *Hartford* got stuck on a sand bar near the junction of the Blue at the place with the many names. Later a prairie fire destroyed the stranded ship, and the Ohio settlers came to their journey's end at New Boston, better known as Boston. The Boston association then agreed to let the Ohio company share one half of their town. The Ohio settlers, who came from Cincinnati, wanted the name of the town changed from New Boston to New Cincinnati and started a conflict which could only have been settled by a compromise, for the town could not long remain half Boston and half Cincinnati. As a compromise both sides agreed to accept the name of Manhattan.[11]

Mead of New York, who had picked the site for his colony at the junction of the Republican and who had most likely put the name of Manhattan into the contract, was finally reconciled to the new downstream location for Manhattan at the junction of the Blue. To illustrate his accommodation, he quoted Burns: "The best laid schemes o' mice and men gang aft agley."[12]

So the name of Manhattan, which was to have been at Junction City, was moved downstream from the Republican junction to the Blue River junction. What might have been Dyer's Town, Juniata, Tauromee, Parksville, Poliska, Canton, Boston, New Boston, or New Cincinnati became Manhattan. The Manhattanese had many names from which to choose—personal names, Indian names, a Polish name, a classical Roman name, and eastern names. They settled for an Indian name whose Indian connection was generally ignored and whose meaning remains vague.[13]

The name of Manhattan may bring to mind a borough in New York, a cocktail, or a college in Kansas, but it is a name with an

[10] "Reminiscences of Kansas," *KHC,* VII, 469.

[11] *Ibid.,* 470; *St. Mary's Star,* Jan. 14, 1943.

[12] *KHC,* VII, 468.

[13] *Ibid.,* 469; *Manhattan Tribune-News,* Sept. 9, 1951; *Kansas City Times,* May 13, 1947.

Indian origin. The name also recalls one of America's biggest real estate deals when Manhattan Island was sold to Peter Minuit for beads and baubles worth approximately twenty-four dollars. According to one tale, the island was named *Manachaeteneid*, which supposedly meant "drunk" or a "place of drunkenness." Henry Hudson, the Dutch explorer of the Hudson River, invited some Indian chiefs into his cabin for a summit conference. Hudson was a generous host, and the Manhattan chiefs got drunk on his liquor. From this incident, so they tell, the island got its name.

The greater the uncertainty about the meaning of a name, the greater the opportunity to add new meanings from the folklore of the community. One of the Dutch governors of New Amsterdam is credited with a story which shows how a name may be developed. It was quite customary for Indian women to wear men's hats, and the sight of such a woman with a man's hat on gave the place the name "Man-hat-on." After telling this far-fetched story, Washington Irving admitted that it was "a stupid joke." Nevertheless he did publish it, and then he added another story with no greater merit. He suggested that he "preferred" the explanation that "Manna-hatta" came from "manna" and therefore meant "a land of milk and honey."[14]

The Manhattans belonged to an Algonquian confederacy that lived along the Hudson. They were closely related to their Delaware neighbors, and together they were given the name of *Wappingers* which meant "Easterners," according to Mooney.[15] *Wampanoag* and *Abnaki* were given the same interpretation. There is such a variety of interpretations for the Manhattan name that the correct one cannot be determined. As Vogel said, it is "bewildering." It may be that Manhattan was a modification of *Monahtanuk*, "the place of dangerous currents," which may have referred to Hellgate on the Hudson. Perhaps the name came from *Manahatin*, the "island hill." George Stewart suggested that the source of the name could have been *Mohican*, spelled "Manhecan or

[14] Beauchamp, *Indian Names in New York*, 46.
[15] Hodge, *Handbook of American Indians*, I, 800 and 903.

Manahegan," which mean "wolf." His own view, said Vogel, was "that the name simply meant 'island village' " and that its source was Delaware, as suggested by William Beauchamp.[16]

It was a long time before the name took shape as Manhattan, even though it was so printed on a Spanish map in Simancas as early as 1607. On the De Laet map of 1630 it appears to be *Manbattes* which probably should have been *Manhattes*. On Delisle's map of 1703 it was *Mahate*, and on his map of 1718 it was "*Manhate ou Nouv. le York*." It was occasionally written with an extra syllable as Manahatan. "Poets," said Washington Irving, "fondly clung to the euphoneous 'Manehata.' "[17]

Algonquian neighbors of the Delawares and Manhattans in the East were the Munsees who lived on the upper Delaware River in New York. After being converted by the Moravians, they were known as the "Christian Indians." When they lived in Ohio, their mission homes were given the German name of *Gnadenhuetten*, "tents of grace." Their Christianity did not, however, give them peace and security, and many of the Munsee Christians were massacred by other "Christians" during the American Revolution. The first Indian treaty to be signed by the United States was the treaty with the Munsees in 1778.[18]

The Munsees were occasionally called the "wolf tribe of the Delaware," which may be a reference to their totem. One of the names was *Ptuksit*, which meant "round foot," referring to the wolf. Among their names listed by Hodge is *Min-asin-ink*, meaning "the place where stones were gathered together." For a time they lived in the upper Delaware Valley and were called *Minsi*, "people of the stoney country." When they were called *Humenthi'*, they had a name which could have come from *menethi*, meaning "island." Their name varied at first from *Monthees*, *Monsees*, and *Munsays*

16 Van Engeln and Urquhart, *Story Key to Geographical Names*, 67; Stewart, *Names on the Land*, 68; Beauchamp, *Indian Names in New York*, 45; Vogel, *Indian Place Names in Illinois*, 60.

17 Louise Pound (ed.), "Miscellany," *American Speech*, IX, 154; Paullin, *Atlas of the Historical Geography of the United States*, plates 21, 23, and 24.

18 Romig, *KHC*, XI, 316; Connelley, *Kansas and Kansans*, I, 228.

until it became Munsee, the accepted name for the tribe. But it became Muncie as a place-name in Indiana.[19]

The Munsees' first home in Kansas was with the Delawares in Wyandotte County. They had purchased four square miles from the Delawares on the north side of the Kaw, between Bonner Springs and Kansas City. Located there today is the town of Muncie, spelled as it is in Indiana. The same spelling was then used in all of the states having towns named Muncie except for Muncy in Pennsylvania. Later the Munsee Indians in Kansas lived with the Chippewas on a small reservation in Franklin County where they eked out a meager living. They were still aided by Moravian missionaries.[20] In Kansas they had merged somewhat with their relatives, the Delawares, and when they were moved out of the state, they were only a small contingent associated with the Chippewas.

East of the Manhattans in the Rhode Island and Massachusetts Bay area lived the Wampanoags, one of several tribes called Abnakis or "eastern people." Geographically, they fit better in the story of the Manhattans and Munsees than they do with the Delawares. They were especially important historically since they were the hosts to the English Pilgrims. Chief Massasoit lived in the area which is now Rhode Island, and his tribe was frequently known as the Massasoits because of him. His name has been spelled many ways, some, such as Woosamequin, seemingly far from the present form. Woosamequin was interpreted to mean "great chief," and Massasoit was also said to mean "yellow feather."[21]

Chief Massasoit made a treaty of peace with the Pilgrims in 1623 and another treaty with Roger Williams in 1635. His friendship may have saved the English colony from extinction. Metacomet, known as King Phillip, his son, became disillusioned and fought a war to wipe out the white intruders. He came near succeeding.

Although no town in New England was named to honor the popular chief who was a friend of the Pilgrims, Massasoit became a place-name in Kansas. Massasoit Creek, which flows into Mission

[19] Hodge, *Handbook of American Indians*, I, 800; Connelley, *Kansas and Kansans*, I, 226.

[20] Andreas and Cutler, *History of Kansas*, 1254; Romig, *KHC*, XI, 317.

[21] Hodge, *Handbook of American Indians*, I, 817.

Creek in Shawnee County, preserves the name of the friendly chief. Searl's map of eastern Kansas in 1856 also shows a town or settlement named Massasoit on Mission Creek not far from Dover.[22] This Algonquian name illustrates another bit of New England influence in Kansas.

From Massachusetts also came the name of Chicopee, now the name of a town on the Missouri border in Crawford County, Kansas. In addition to the town of Chicopee, Massachusetts also has a Chicopee River and the Chicopee Falls. The name is said to have come from *chekee*, meaning "violent," and *sipe*, "river."[23] This is a good description for the rapids and falls above Springfield which have been the source for industrial power in Massachusetts. The *Encyclopedia Britannica*, however, interpreted Chicopee to mean "cedar tree" or "birchbark place." It is most likely an Abnaki name of Algonquian origin. People's reactions to a name may vary greatly, but Chicopee has an appealing sound like chickadee and has been characterized as "a cute name."

[22] Baughman, *Kansas in Maps*, 52–53.
[23] Stewart, *Names on the Land*, 276; Leland, *Names*, I, 267.

XVIII ▲

Delawares and Other Abnakis

The Delaware Indians were the most important of a group of related Algonquians living in eastern Pennsylvania and neighboring states. They were related not only to the Manhattans but also to the Munsees and the Powhattans, and all of these tribes contributed names to Kansas. Their Algonquian relatives who lived west of them naturally called them "Easterners." Among the names for Easterner were *Wapanachki* and *Wabanaki* which eventually became *Abanaki* or simply Abnaki. The Chippewas called them *Waub-un-uk-eeg*, which may have had the additional meaning of "eastern earth dweller" or "eastern land people." A more attractive name for the "people of the East" or the "Eastlanders" was "children of the dawn."[1]

The Delawares called themselves *Lenni Lenape* or just *Lenape*, meaning the "true men" or "standard men." The form *Renni Renape* shows an interesting exchange of letters. Like so many other tribes, the Delawares assumed that they were the "original people." They were not only the "fathers" of their Algonquian relatives but their "grandfathers." They naturally gave greater importance to some tribes than others, resulting in the use of common titles for relatives such as "children," "grandchildren," "nephews," "younger brothers," or "cousins." The Wyandots and Iroquois, who were not relatives but were considered superior, were called "uncles," and the Delawares were consequently called "nephews."

[1] Hodge, *Handbook of American Indians*, I, 385; Warren, *History of the Ojibway Nation*, 32; Natalie Curtis, *The Indian Book*, 3.

When the Iroquois dominated the Delawares, they deprived them of their weapons and called them "women."[2]

The Delawares called their river the *Lenapehittuck*, meaning "the Lenape river." They also referred to the river as the *Kit-haune*, the "great river." Early Americans called the tribe the "river Indians," but for identification they became known as the Delaware Indians, which was their name when they came to Kansas. On the Atlantic Seaboard the Delawares had been given the name of a river; in Kansas a river was named for the Delaware Indians. There is, however, a town upstream on the Kaw in Leavenworth County which was given their Indian name of Lenape.[3]

The source for the modern name of the Delaware Indians is a strange one. It came from the name of an Englishman who bore a Latinized or French name with a possible Viking origin. The Englishman's name was Thomas West, who, as governor of Virginia, had the title and name of Lord de la Warr. This was put together to make Delaware, which became the name of a bay, a river, a town, and a state, as well as a tribe of Indians. The Indians accepted the name as an honorable one since it was the name of a great English chief. It was, however, the name of the Delaware River which was given to the Delaware Indians.[4]

The Delawares were a highly respected tribe in the East, but they were pushed from eastern into western Pennsylvania and from there into Ohio, Indiana, and Illinois. Harassed by the thieving white man, as their Captain Pipe pointed out, they decided to seek asylum and freedom beyond the Mississippi. It was largely to find a place for the Delawares to live in the West that the Rev. Isaac McCoy came to investigate the environment in Kansas. Space was supposedly found in Kansas for the Delawares, but neither the Pawnees, Otos, nor Osages were willing to accept them as good

[2] Swanton, *The Indian Tribes of North America*, 48; Francis Parkman, *The Conspiracy of Pontiac*, 30n.

[3] Shankle, *State Names . . . and other Symbols*, 29–30; Remsburg, *Scrapbook*, I, 356.

[4] Shankle, *State Names . . . and other Symbols*, 29–30; Stewart, *Names on the Land*, 35.

neighbors. After the Pawnees had killed several defenseless Delawares, the Delawares destroyed the Pawnee village on the Republican River. Kansas was not to be a happy homeland for these eastern Indians. Many of the Delawares, including their chiefs, served as the white man's guide in the opening of the West.[5] They were good guides, even in the unknown West where a faint Indian trail was soon to become the white man's highway.

The Kansa Indians had given a Siouan name to the river which was later given a Delaware name before it became the Delaware River. The Kansas called it the *Nesh-cosh-cosh-che-ba*, which, by deleting one syllable, became *Nesh-cosh-che-ba.* This name, said Isaac McCoy, referred to the "swallows" or "martins," most likely cliff swallows nesting in its banks. So the *Nesh-cosh-cosh-che-ba* became known to the early pioneers as Martin's River. "Another mode of rendering the sounds of this Indian name of this river is Nach-uch-u-te-be," said McCoy, "and this is the orthography given on the map which we made of the Delaware reservation." Quite similar to the Kansa name was the Osage word for swallow, *ni-shku'shku.* On the McCoy map of 1830–36 the name was given not only in the Kansa Indian language, with a choice of spellings, but also in both English and French: "Martins or Nechuchutebe or Nesh-Cosh-Cosh-Che-Bah or Sauterelle River."[6] It is also worthy of note that the McCoys spelled *Sauterelle* correctly, but this spelling of the name will seldom be seen again, even from those who quoted the McCoys.[7]

One of the native names for the lower Delaware River was *Hingwi-men-o-ken*, translated to mean "big muddy." The town near the Kaw village of Fool Chief was also called Menoken with one of its translations being "muddy."[8]

The Delaware Indians called the river the *Chuck-kan-no*, meaning "they stopped here." This was said to refer to the place where the big grasshopper raid stopped in 1830.[9] Most of the Delawares

[5] Foreman, *The Last Trek of the Indians*, 42–45 and 237.
[6] *KHC*, IV, 305; Baughman, *Kansas in Maps*, 25.
[7] Remsburg, in *Atchison Daily Globe*, July 24, 1912.
[8] Remsburg, *Scrapbook*, I, 77, and II, 28; McCoy, *KHC*, IV, 305.
[9] Root, *KHQ*, V, 320; Remsburg, *Scrapbook*, II, 28.

did not settle in Kansas until 1835, and it is difficult to determine which of the grasshopper raids was responsible for the name. But the association of the name or river with grasshoppers was understood by the French, who named it the *Sauterelle*, the French word for "grasshopper." There were those who said that the river was named for a Frenchman by the name of Soutrelle who had drowned at the mouth of the river, but this would be too much of a coincidence. It is highly unlikely that a place the Indians had named for the grasshopper also happened to be named for a Frenchman whose name meant "grasshopper."[10]

When the Americans found out what the French name meant, they translated it into English and named the river the Grasshopper, which in Van Vranklin's advertising for his ferry was written Grass Hopper. Some maps carried both names, Soutrelle and Grasshopper, which gave a choice of languages. The French name began to lose favor when it was distorted by Americans. Sol Miller, salty editor from White Cloud, took delight in referring to the Sautrelle as Sowtail. Juveniles and jokers added insult to injury by changing Sowtail to Cowtail. Since this made the attractive French name of Sautrelle more obnoxious than the English name of Grasshopper, the French name was dropped.[11]

The result was that the pesky hopper was advertised in names such as Grasshopper River and Grasshopper Falls, and even the town located at the falls was named Grasshopper Falls. As a name Grasshopper had neither commercial appeal nor any pleasant association. There were those who thought that "there ought to be a law," and the Kansas legislature came to the rescue. In the laws of Kansas for 1875 there is an act to change the names of Grasshopper River, Grasshopper Falls Township, and Grasshopper Falls city to Delaware River, Delaware Township, and Valley Falls. This was the year after the grasshoppers had come in great clouds to destroy the crops of Kansas, after which the name Grasshopper was not tolerated. Yet Grasshopper is preserved as the name of a

[10] Thwaites, *Early Western Travels*, I, 210n.
[11] Remsburg, *Scrapbook*, IV, 40; Root, *KHQ*, II, 14.

township in Atchison County where a creek also named Grasshopper flows into the Delaware.[12]

In 1854 a ferry terminal in Leavenworth County, about six miles below Leavenworth, became the town of Delaware with the post-office name of Delaware City. Since there was another Delaware City later, this one was known for a time as Old Delaware. Its great ambition had been to become the county seat. It competed with Kickapoo and Leavenworth, and when Leavenworth won, Delaware City declined. The town disappeared but the township still carried the name of Delaware. There were Delaware townships in Jefferson and Wyandotte counties also.[13]

A second Delaware was established at what was called the Lower Delaware Crossing of the Kaw, located about seven miles above its junction with the Missouri. It was near the mouth of what is now Mill Creek which was then called Delaware Creek.[14] Even as a voting precinct it gained distinction. Delaware Crossing was a community with 35 legal voters, but when it voted on the Lecompton Constitution, someone placed a 5 in front of the number of legal ballots and turned in 535 votes. This called for an investigation, and the person in charge was none other than John Calhoun who was said to be "*particeps criminis* after the fact." This was the Calhoun for whom Calhoun (Jackson) County was named, a man who was as thoroughly southern in his sympathies as was his illustrious namesake of South Carolina.[15]

Delaware Crossing had a variety of names. The first ferry near this crossing was started by a Shawnee Indian named Tooley from the south side of the Kaw. He was a highly respected Indian and must have had considerable initiative since he also built a raft to be used at Bluejacket's Crossing of the Wakarusa. The Department of

[12] Root, *KHQ*, V, 320; *Topeka Capital*, June 23, 1938; Remsburg, in *Atchison Daily Globe*, July 24, 1912; *Laws of Kansas, 1875*, 178.

[13] Parker, *The Kansas and Nebraska Handbook for 1857–1858*, 106; Jesse A. Hall and Leroy T. Hand, *History of Leavenworth County, Kansas*, 142; Root, *KHQ*, II, 13.

[14] Miller, *KHQ*, I, 108n.

[15] Harrington, *Historic Spots in Wyandotte County*, 53; "First Free-State Territorial Legislature of 1857–58," *KHC*, X, 172n.; Alan W. Farley, *The Delaware Indians in Kansas*, 14.

Indian Affairs spelled his name Tooly, the Friends spelled it Tula, but John Speer spelled it Tooley. His ferry has also been referred to as Tola's Ferry. It was located about two miles above Grinter's Ferry which was also known as Delaware Crossing.

Moses Grinter, married to a Delaware woman who had a white father, ran a government ferry across the Kaw which was then known as Grinter's Ferry. Since it served as the ferry for the military, it was also called the Military Ferry. It was near enough to the Indian agency to be called the Delaware Agency Crossing. As its importance grew, it became popularly known as Delaware City. When it was made a post office in 1850, it was given the name of Delaware, and had the distinction of being the first post office in Kansas outside the military posts.[16]

With two other Delawares in Kansas a change of name was necessary. So the post office changed the name from Delaware to Secondine, in honor of James Secondine, a Delaware chief. This name was in keeping with the town's Delaware connection. Even after the official change of name in 1856, it was "most often known," said one writer, as "Delaware."[17] Secondine was a post office for three years and continued for a time to serve as a station of the Kansas Pacific Railroad, now the Union Pacific. It was located a short distance above the station which was called Lenape, the native name for the Delawares.[18]

James Secondine was one of several important Delaware chiefs who served the white man as guides, scouts, and soldiers. He had been a guide on General Frémont's expedition of 1843, and he carried a message back from Frémont in California to Senator Benton in Missouri. On his way he was pursued by hostile Comanches. When his horse stumbled into a hole in the ground and broke a leg, Secondine fought the pursuing Comanche chief, killed him, scalped him, stole his horse, and escaped. He was never paid for his services as a guide, but he proudly carried the Comanche scalp the rest of his life. His well-known name was spelled in a variety of

[16] Farley, *The Delaware Indians in Kansas*, 2; Albert R. Greene, "The Kansas River," *KHC*, IX, 331n.; Root, *KHQ*, II, 264–67.

[17] Farley, *The Delaware Indians in Kansas*, 2.

[18] Lutz, *KHC*, IX, 203n.

ways. Connelley spelled it Sagundai, and Alan W. Farley spelled it Sagundal. On the treaty of 1854, the name was "Qua-cor-now-ha, or James Segondyne." It was originally Sekendiathen, finally simplified to Secondine.[19]

A third site named Delaware, which also showed its ambition by calling itself Delaware City, was located north of the Kaw not far from Topeka. It failed to maintain its name because of the duplication, and it failed to become a "city" although the name was changed to Whitfield City. One of its chief promoters was J. Butler Chapman, and the town had been known as Chapman before it was named Delaware. Chapman, who boasted of the town's central location, said that "no other place had the claims for the seat of government that Whitfield had." Some people have suggested that it was named for the famous Methodist minister George Whitefield, but the suggestion that it was named for General John W. Whitfield, who was active in Kansas politics, may be more logical.[20]

To attract greater attention as a prospective capital of Kansas, the town discarded the name of Whitfield City and adopted the high-sounding, Indian-Greek name of Kansopolis, which meant "Kansas City." When Topeka became the capital, the Kansopolis boom was over. The name had not had the political appeal which its promoters had expected. So again the name was changed, this time to Rochester. Far from attaining the status of a capital with the name Rochester, the town did not even become a post office. None of its five names could keep it alive, and it declined and died.[21]

Two of the worthy Delaware chiefs whose names were used for Kansas place-names were Sarcoxie and Tonganoxie. It is tempting to add the name Hoxie because it is so similar, but the town of Hoxie in western Kansas was named for a railway official.

[19] Connelley, *Kansas and Kansans*, I, 230; Farley, *The Delaware Indians in Kansas*, 1–2; Andreas and Cutler, *History of Kansas*, 1226; Barry, *KHQ*, XXXI, 145; *KHC*, XVI, 763.

[20] Andreas and Cutler, *History of Kansas*, 534; Dolbee, *KHQ*, VIII, 244 and 254; Howes, Shawnee County Historical Society *Bulletin*, I, 28.

[21] Andreas and Cutler, *History of Kansas*, 534; Cole, *KHC*, XII, 354n.

Sarcoxie, also called *Kock-a-towha*, was chief of the Turtle band of the Delawares. He lived north of Lawrence on Mud Creek. His name was also written Sah-coc-sa.[22] In 1856 he had a monopoly on the ferry business at Lawrence. The treaty by which the Delawares sold most of their land in the Leavenworth-Jefferson county area was signed at Sarcoxieville in 1860. The place was also referred to occasionally as Sarcoxie with the "ville" left off. Sarcoxie is not even a "ville" anymore, but it is still the name of a township in Jefferson County.[23]

Tonganoxie gave his name to a town, a township, and a creek, all in Leavenworth County. Tonganoxie was also spelled Tonqua-Noxie and Tonganoxwha. The name, said to mean "little man" or "shorty," was given to the chief before he was fully grown. It does not accurately describe the big man that he was. In his later years he was known to his neighbors as Old Tonga or just Tonga. Tonganoxie was a descendant of Chief Tammanend who signed the treaty of friendship with William Penn and whose name was given to Tammany Hall. Tonganoxie, a Baptist, "neither smoked, drank whisky, or chewed tobacco," and consequently he was called "a good man."[24] The town of Tonganoxie was built where the chief had his home, a place which had served as a popular stopping place on the Lawrence-Leavenworth Road.[25]

Henry Tiblow has been described as "a club-footed Indian and official interpreter of the United States."[26] Another report said that he was "bow-legged" but not clubfooted. He was the interpreter for the Delawares at Sarcoxieville. Tiblow ran a ferry across the Kaw, where he built a cabin and established a post office named Tiblow. The name was later changed to Edwardsville and then to

[22] Barry, *KHQ*, XXXI, 145.

[23] Andreas and Cutler, *History of Kansas*, 69 and 1226; Lutz, *KHC*, IX, 233; Farley, *The Delaware Indians in Kansas*, 13.

[24] Remsburg, in *Leavenworth Post*, Jan. 11, 1907; *Topeka Capital*, May 11, 1954; George Griffith, "Chief Tonganoxie," in *Sunflower Petals* (ed. by Walt Neibarger).

[25] Hall and Hand, *History of Leavenworth County, Kansas*, 151.

[26] Root, *KHQ*, II, 272.

Bonner Springs. The site moved about a bit, but Tiblow's cabin was just west of Bonner Springs.[27]

Although James Connor was generally known by his Irish name, he was a Delaware chief whose Indian name was Ah-lah-a-chick, which Andreas spelled Ah-cah-chick. Connor had served as a guide for Joseph E. Johnston when he made the southern survey of the Kansas border, and he was used as an interpreter by Isaac McCoy. His Irish name of Connor, also spelled Conner, was adopted as the name of a railway station in the northern part of Wyandotte County called Conner's Station. The name of the station was changed to Walcott for H. W. Walcott, who was superintendent of the local line. Connor's name was also given to Connor's Creek which ran through the town of Connor in Wyandotte County.[28]

Another town in Leavenworth County which bore the name of a Delaware chief was Fall Leaf. The chief's Indian name was Po-na-kah-ko-wah, which was too long to use as a place-name. Evidently the local residents also thought that the name Fall Leaf was too long, because they shortened it to Fall, which obscured the original meaning of the name. However, maps continued to carry the full name of Fall Leaf for the town and just Fall for the post office. Half a name may be better than no name at all, but it is disconcerting to have the deletion destroy the meaning. Yet there may be justification for some abbreviation of Indian names, especially when such a simple word as "love" in the Delaware language is written *schelendamowitchewagan.*[29]

Major John Sedgwick, for whom Sedgwick County is named, employed a number of Delaware scouts in Kansas under the able leadership of Fall Leaf, this "Hercules of an Indian" who had also served as a guide for Frémont. When Fall Leaf was returning to Kansas after guiding Frémont to California, he found some gold in Colorado and tied it up in a rag. When he showed it to settlers in

[27] Harrington, *Historic Spots in Wyandotte County*, 12; Connelley to Martin, "Names," MS, KSHS Archives.

[28] *KHC*, XVI, 763; Andreas and Cutler, *History of Kansas*, 1226; Remsburg, *Scrapbook*, IV, 40; *Leavenworth Times*, Aug. 15, 1938.

[29] *Leavenworth Times*, Jan. 24, 1907, and Sept. 14, 1911; *KHQ*, XV, 405.

Kansas, he aroused a gold fever that started the Pike's Peak gold rush. Fall Leaf was the inspiration for the Lawrence expedition to Colorado in 1857. He was to be its guide, but he had suffered injuries in a drunken brawl and was unable to go.[30]

Charles Journey Cake, or Journeycake, a Delaware chief, earned his name when he escaped from captivity and on a long journey home ate nothing but a little loaf of cornbread. According to one newspaper account, his name had been Johnny Cake in Ohio, but he changed it to Journey Cake after he was appointed chief.[31] One writer referring to Journey Cake Road in Maryland was of the opinion that it came from Shawnee Cake.[32] Isaac Journeycake, the brother of Charles, was a Baptist minister and a scout. He lived in Leavenworth County at a place which became a station on the Union Pacific and which was then named Journey Cake. The name was hard to spell for those who "spelled by ear," said Cecil Howes, so the settlers changed it to Johnnycake. Some called it just Johnny. Then the town name was changed to Stranger because of its location on Stranger Creek. Later it was changed to the present name of Linwood by Senator W. A. Harris who named the town for its trees.[33]

In this neighborhood in Leavenworth County a stream named Big Woman Creek flows into Stranger Creek. It was not named for a big woman but for a Delaware chief.[34] In Wyandotte County a branch of Wolf Creek was named Neconhecon for another Delaware chief. Neconhecon, chief of the Wolf band, was one of the signers of the treaty of 1860 by which a railroad obtained much of the Delaware land.[35]

Wild Horse Creek in Atchison County was said to be named

[30] Hafen (ed.), *Pike's Peak Gold Rush Guidebooks of 1859* (vol. IX in *Southwest Historical Series*), 59–61; Andreas and Cutler, *History of Kansas*, 467; Robert M. Peck, "Recollections of Early Times in Kansas," *KHC*, VIII, 490; James Monaghan, *Civil War on the Frontier*, 197 and 204.

[31] *Leavenworth Times*, Sept. 14, 1911.

[32] Kenny, *Indian Place Names of Maryland*, 23 and 75; Andreas and Cutler, *History of Kansas*, 1226.

[33] Richardson, *Beyond the Mississippi*, 92; Howes, in *Kansas City Star*, Dec. 8, 1941; Harrington, *Historic Spots in Wyandotte County*, 34.

[34] *Leavenworth Times*, Sept. 14, 1911.

[35] Andreas and Cutler, *History of Kansas*, 1226; *KHC*, XVI, 765.

for an Indian. The search for an Indian with this name revealed one, but he was Pawnee. There was, however, an important connection between the Delawares and Chief Wild Horse of the Pawnees. Because the Pawnees had killed a few defenseless Delawares, the latter tribe took revenge on their enemies. In a powwow which ended peacefully, Sou-wah-nock, the Delaware chief, spoke his piece and magnanimously presented the Pawnee chief with a wampum belt. Chief Wild Horse was equally eloquent and promised to keep the peace. For assurance he said, "I cannot lie, for I am a Pawnee chief!"[36] It would be appropriate if Wild Horse Creek had been named for Chief Wild Horse of the Pawnees. The Delawares had another name for the creek in their own language; they called it *Ow-so-see-po*. However, this is very similar to *Ossen-see-poo*, which was the name they gave to the Kaw and which meant "rock river."[37]

Indians were occasionally named for some important event in their lives or for some conspicuous deed. Such was the case with Chief Four Mile of the Delawares who ran four miles to a creek and returned without stopping. Consequently he was named Four Mile although he might better have been named Eight Mile, and the creek to which he ran was also named Four Mile. There are at least seven other creeks named Four Mile in Kansas, but they are named for measures of distance rather than in honor of a chief.[38]

Another name with a Delaware association was White Church, a Methodist church built in 1832 and located among the Delawares in the central part of Wyandotte County. The church was constructed of walnut wood and painted white, which gave it the Indian name of White Church. It was located "near a spring, in a beautiful grove . . . on a high divide." White settlers established a town at the site of the church and named it White Church. The church was destroyed by a tornado in 1886, but the town of White Church has preserved its name.[39]

The Powhatans were an Algonquian tribe closely related to the

[36] Connelley, *Kansas and Kansans*, I, 230.
[37] Remsburg, *Scrapbook*, I, 315.
[38] Richardson, *Beyond the Mississippi*, 90.
[39] Lutz, *KHC*, IX, 204–206.

Delawares. They lived in the Chesapeake Bay area before Virginia had been named. On John Smith's map of 1612 this area was called Powhatan. According to one authority, the name was written *paw-e tan-wi* and translated to mean "it is a fall or a rapid in a stream" and, more elaborately, "a place where water has pierced the earth and rocks." Its simplest translation was "falls in a current," and the name referred to the falls on the James River. The British gave the tribal name Powhatan to a chief whose Indian name was Wahunsonacock.[40]

The Powhatan name became famous during the settlement of Jamestown when Pocahontas, the daughter of Powhatan, saved the life of Captain John Smith. Powhatan's name most likely came to Kansas from the history books, yet there was another Powhatan living in Kansas. Powhatan Phifer was an interpreter and an assistant smith for the Delawares, but he was scarcely important enough for his name to have been the source for the name Powhattan in Kansas.[41]

Powhattan in Brown County was first named Locknane for David M. Locknane or Lochnane. Locknane was such a strong pro-slavery advocate that the Free State settlers petitioned to have the name of the town changed to Powhattan.[42] It has been suggested that Locknane was located at the site called Log Chain, but an 1865 map of Kansas shows Log Chain farther west in Nemaha County.[43]

The town of Powhattan was first moved to avoid a big curve in the Overland Trail. What was called Old Powhattan was later moved several miles northeast to the railway tracks and located outside of Powhattan Township. The original Powhattan was on the site which became Wetmore, named for W. T. Wetmore, a Union Pacific official.[44]

A woman in Tennessee, hearing of a relative living in Powhattan,

[40] Kenny, *Indian Place Names of Maryland*, 116; William T. Tooker, "The Powhattan Name for Virginia," *American Anthropologist* (n.s.), VIII, 23; Hodge, *Handbook of American Indians*, II, 299.

[41] *KHC*, XVI, 728.

[42] James Grubb to Martin, Nov. 22, 1901, "Names," MS, KSHS Archives.

[43] Root and Hickman, *KHQ*, XIII, 508n.

[44] Andreas and Cutler, *History of Kansas*, 956; Remsburg, *Scrapbook*, I, 188.

Kansas, wrote to her: "Powhattan—why, that's an Indian name. I am grieved to believe my dear Martha is residing dangerously close to wild Indians. Be careful, my favorite, and don't let those accursed aborigines get your scalp!" It is interesting to note how emotions could be aroused over a name. People lived peacefully at Powhattan, mostly among friendly Kickapoos.[45]

Captain John Smith, in his association with the Indian natives of Virginia, tried to learn the names of animals and objects unknown in England. "There is a beast they call Aroughcun," he said, "much like the badger, but useth to live on trees as squirrels doe."[46] "Aroughcun" was an Algonquian, possibly Powhatan, name for the raccoon. It was a difficult name, and has been spelled *raugroughcum*, *rahaugcum*, and *rarowcun*.[47] By dropping a syllable and changing the spelling slightly the English name became raccoon. Simple though this was, as a place-name in Kansas the name lost another syllable and became merely Coon.

There were many raccoons in Kansas, but when the pioneers named a stream Coon Creek, they were likely unaware of the fact that the name had an Indian origin introduced by Captain John Smith. There is a Coon Creek flowing into the Delaware in Jefferson County. There is another Coon Creek flowing southward into Wolf Creek in Russell County. The creek was given this name because a large raccoon had been killed there, according to Captain John Fritts, the postmaster. Being out of meat, he explained, it was decided to eat it, which, he admitted, "resulted in a total failure." The raccoon proved to be "obnoxious in smell and taste."[48] Coon Creek in Chase County was named for "the numerous raccoons found there." A well-known Coon Creek is the one that flows through Ford, Edwards, and Pawnee counties to join the Arkansas River north of Kinsley. Major Sibley called it Clear Creek, but it has also been called "a puddlesome slough." It had earlier been named De Mun's or Dumun's Creek for Jules De Mun, a fur-trading companion of A. P. Chouteau. Today it is called Big

[45] John T. Bristow, *The Overland Trail*, 10 and 16.
[46] *Travels and Works*, I, 59.
[47] H. L. Mencken, *The American Language*, 104.
[48] *Luray Herald*, Aug. 28, 1952.

Coon Creek to distinguish it from Little Coon Creek. A mound on the California Trail near Lawrence was called Coon Point, and a camp site near Big Spring was called Coon Hollow Camp.[49]

The Appomattocs, whose name was the origin of Appomattox, were a tribe of the Powhattan confederation. The fame of the name goes back to the surrender of General Robert E. Lee at the Appomattox Court House in Virginia, and it was from this historical event that the town of Appomattox in Grant County got its name. The name was chosen for the purpose of winning votes in a county-seat election. The towns of Cincinnati, Surprise, and Tilden were all in the contest against Ulysses for the county seat of Grant County. Cincinnati had a name with a Roman background and a strong Ohio connection, Surprise had little in its favor except an unusual name, and Tilden was the name of an unsuccessful presidential candidate. But Ulysses, which had a classical Greek background, was the first name of President Grant, and it won popular appeal. Cincinnati and Surprise decided to unite into one town to gain strength, and they looked for a name which would have as much political appeal as Ulysses. Colonel Hutchinson, who had served under General Sheridan, suggested the name Appomattox because it symbolized Grant's final victory. Then both names were associated with General Grant, but Appomattox lost to Ulysses in the county-seat contest.[50]

In 1881 the *Marion Record* published a report of how the name Lehigh came to Kansas. According to this account, "some wealthy representatives of the celebrated Lehigh colony in Pennsylvania came out and selected a fine location for a town on the M & M (Marion-McPherson) Branch line which they went so far as to designate by the beautiful name of Lehigh."[51] Although Lehigh may not look like an Indian name, it has been accepted that it evolved from the Delaware name *Lechau* or *Lechau wekint*, mean-

[49] Moore, "The Story of Lecompton," *KHC*, XI, 465; *The Journal of Captain John R. Bell* (vol. VI in Hafen's *The Far West and the Rockies*), 218n.; Paden, *In the Wake of the Prairie Schooner*, 36.

[50] Hodge, *Handbook of American Indians*, I, 170; *KHC*, XII, 472; Robert R. Wilson and Ethel M. Sears, *History of Grant County, Kansas*, 68 and 87.

[51] David K. Wiebe, *They Seek a Country*, 120n.

ing "where there are forks." This was the name of a place where a stream joined the Delaware River, according to Hodge.

Nyack was once the name of a post office in Crawford County. According to Hodge's handbook, the name could have come from a village on the Hudson which was occupied by a band of Delawares. Nyack meant a "corner" or a "point."[52] This unusual name disappeared from Kansas when the post office was renamed Midway. Midway was so common that three post offices have been given this name, and two Kansas towns are still named Midway.

The name Wyoming was used twice in Kansas before it became the name of a state. The first was a town in Marshall County located near the present site of Lillis on the Union Pacific Railroad. Except for a brief interruption in 1886, Wyoming served as a post office until 1901. The Wyoming Valley post office in Clay County received its name from a town in Pennsylvania. It was located up the Republican River, northwest of Clay Center near the railway station now named Northern. On a Kansas map in 1865 the name of Wyoming Valley has a line drawn through it with Lima written just above. However, a war department map of 1867 shows the name as Wyoming Valley.

Wyoming is a corruption of the Delaware name *M'cheuwomink* or *Mecheweami-ing*, which was said to mean "upon the Great Plains" or "at the big plains." Another spelled the name *Maughwau-wama* and gave its meaning as "extensive plains." The native name, variously corrupted to *Chiwaumuc*, *Wiawamic*, and *Waiomink*, finally reached the euphonious form of Wyoming, which was supposed to signify "field of blood." The name has also been said to mean "large meadows." Another interpretation suggested that it meant "mountains with valleys alternating." This would be especially appropriate for the regular rows of ridges in Pennsylvania, and it may be an interpretation made to fit the contour of the country between Wilkes Barre and Scranton. There were several Delaware villages in the Wyoming Valley area of Pennsylvania,

[52] "Annals of Kansas," *KHQ*, XX, 288; Hodge, *Handbook of American Indians*, II, 100.

and eventually Wyoming Valley became the name of a town and the source of a Kansas place-name.[53]

The Iroquois massacre of the settlers in Wyoming, Pennsylvania, during the American Revolution gave the place wide publicity, and it could have been from this that some people thought the word meant the "field of blood," as mentioned by Hodge. The name became even more familiar after Thomas Campbell put the story into a dramatic and thrilling poem named "Gertrude of Wyoming."[54]

[53] Frederick W. Lawrence, "The Origin of American State Names," *National Geographic*, XXXVIII, 133; Shankle, *State Names . . . and other Symbols*, 94.
[54] Stewart, *Names on the Land*, 311.

XIX ▲

The Illinois, Miami, and Confederated Tribes

OUT OF ILLINOIS came more names for Kansas than from any state in the Union. Among these were several Indian names, some of Siouan and some of Iroquoian origins, but many were Algonquian, as was the name Illinois itself. The name Illinois came from *Iliniwek* or the simpler *Ilini*, meaning "man" or, as Swanton said, "people." This was, of course, their own idea of who they were, and is better illustrated by the phrase, "a perfect and accomplished man." The French spoke of them as *Aux Illinois.*

The names of several states have been used as post-office names in Kansas, but not the name of Illinois. In Montgomery County, however, there is an Illinois Creek which is a branch of the Caney watershed system. A small stream named Illinois Creek flows into the Nemaha River in the central part of Nemaha County.[1] Illinois Township in Sedgwick County illustrates a tie with the state of Illinois, as do the townships named Illinois in Nemaha, Sumner, and Rush counties.

Among the emigrant tribes of eastern Indians was a group known as the Confederated Tribes, which included the Miamis, Weas, Peorias, Kaskaskias, and Piankashaws. The first three tribes left their names on the Kansas map. These Indians belonged to the Algonquian linguistic group and were related to the confederacy of the Illinois Indians. Most important among the Confederated Tribes were the Miamis; the others have been considered their descendants.

The land of the Miamis was the Old Northwest which extended

[1] See county maps in Andreas and Cutler, *History of Kansas*, 940 and 1563.

from Lake Erie to Green Bay in Wisconsin. Although there is a tendency to think of them as having their homes in Ohio where they settled along the Maumee River upstream from Toledo, their land was limited in Ohio, and most of them moved on into Indiana, where they lived along the Wabash. In Ohio they left their name on four townships, a county, two towns, and a river. Their name spread far beyond their many homes. It is best known in Florida where it has become a symbol of sunshine, seashore, and sandy beaches.[2]

By a series of treaties starting in 1814, the Miamis gradually gave away millions of acres of land in the Old Northwest. There was neither peace nor security around the Great Lakes, and no treaty seemed to provide a solution. After 1839 a new series of treaties provided for their removal from the remnants of their lands east of the Mississippi for a new home in Kansas. They were loath to leave and postponed their departure until the government took action to force their removal. In Kansas they settled first on Sugar Creek and then on the Marais des Cygnes where their Miami Village became well known. But even this was only a temporary home, and by 1871 a remnant of the great Miami tribe was moved into the Indian Territory to be merged with the Peorias.[3]

The Miami name could have come from *Omaumeg*, a Chippewa word that Swanton said meant "people on the peninsula." They called themselves *Wa-ya-ta-no-ke* which was translated to mean "lovely or eddying water, out of which the nation sprang or were born." This is similar to the meaning of Wea. According to Lewis H. Morgan, the Miamis were also supposed to have called themselves *Me-a-me-a-ga*, which without the last two syllables is *Meame*. One interpretation is that Miami evolved from the Delaware name of *We-mi-a-mik* and that it meant "all beavers" or "all friends." The name as we know it today evolved from French forms such as *Oumamik*, *Oumamis*, and *Oumiamis*, in which the first syllable is considered an article. It was occasionally abbreviated to *Au Mi*

[2] Surrounding the main city of Miami, Florida, where the Miami River flows through Seminole country, are North Miami, West Miami, Miami Shores, Miami Springs, and Miami Beach, as well as two South Miami Stations.

[3] Abel, *KHC*, VIII, 85.

and *Omee*. A popular form of the name was Maumee which was given to the Maumee River in Ohio.[4]

Another name for the Miamis was *Twanh Twanh*, which was translated to mean the "cry of the crane." By evolution this name became *Tawatawas*, easily abbreviated to *Tawas*, which meant "naked." Francis Parkman called them "Twightwees," a form of the name which became quite popular. In the meantime the meaning of the name became obscure; some said it referred to a dove rather than to a crane. From *Tawas* the Miamis became known to the settlers as the Naked Indians. They were probably no more naked than other Indians, and Swanton has pointed out that one of their names meant "people dressing finely, or fantastically."[5]

Although it was not common for a town to cross a state boundary, names spread readily from one state to another, and names like Miami have spread far beyond the confines of the Miami Indians. Among the tall Texas tales is the story of the wife of a Texas millionaire who suggested to her husband that they go to Miami. With a snort, he said, "Why go to Miami? Send for it!" He must have been successful, since there is a Miami in Texas. Kansas did not send for Miami nor for the Miami Indians, but the Miamis did come to Kansas where they left their name.

The county now named Miami in Kansas had earlier been named Lykens, honoring David Lykens, a missionary and member of the first territorial council of Kansas. His good reputation as a missionary did not save him from his bad reputation for being a member of a legislature dominated by slave-holders and southern sympathizers. In 1861 the name of Lykens was replaced by the name of Miami. The county was named Miami for the Miami Indian reservation which overlapped into Linn County. A post office in Linn County which had been called Waytown had its name changed to Miami, a name which lasted for twelve years before it was changed to Linton. But there is now a Miami on a branch of the Missouri in Linn County. In Miami County there was in the early days a post

[4] In addition to references by Hodge and Swanton, see Vogel, *Indian Place Names in Illinois*, 72.

[5] Warren, *History of the Ojibway Nation*, 33; Wright, *A Guide to the Indian Tribes of Oklahoma*, 182; Swanton, *The Indian Tribes of North America*, 237,

office named Miami Village, but it was popularly called just Miami.[6] Reno County, where there were no Miamis, has a township named Miami.

Isaac Taylor refers to Chicago as being located on the Chicago River, "which rises in a boggy district of 'evil savour,' either because frequented by 'skunks' (cikak, plural cikakong), or because overgrown with garlic." Of the many interpretations of Chicago, Taylor has given the two most popular.[7] Hodge said that Chicago was a Sac, Fox, and Kickapoo name. He, too, gave it the skunk interpretation: *shekagua*, meaning "skunk," and *shekakahegi*, "place of the skunk." Another source could have been the name of a "Mitchigamia" chief, Chicagou, who had the distinction of traveling to Paris and Versailles with Father Beaubois.[8] The suggestion that the name came from "skunkweed" may explain the source for the opinion that Chicago meant skunk. However, the source for the name was seemingly the weed and not the skunk.

Virgil Vogel expressed the view that "carelessness" was the cause for the "proliferation of nonsense" regarding the meaning of Chicago. According to him, the name was in the Algonquian language of the Illinois, and it was Henri Joutel, a companion of La Salle, who first wrote it Chicagou and translated it to mean "garlic." In drawing a boundary line for the Illinois Confederacy, a reference was made to a line from the Illinois River to "Chicagou or Garlick creek." This does not prove that Chicagou meant garlic. According to Vogel, it could mean "garlic, leek, or onion." This removes the skunk from the name, with the possible exception of the skunkweed. The odor might still remain from "the river of the wild onion smell," as Carl Sandburg called the Chicago River. Vogel's conclusion that the name came not from the animal but from the plant kingdom seems to be the most acceptable.[9]

Town promoters in Kansas who wanted to give their town the

[6] Andreas and Cutler, *History of Kansas*, 875, 891, and 1101; Edwards and Edwards, *An Illustrated Historical Atlas of Miami County*, 9.

[7] *Names and their Histories*, 92.

[8] Kenton, *Black Gowns and Redskins*, 426.

[9] "The Mystery of Chicago's Name," *Mid-America*, XL, 163–74; Vogel, *Indian Place Names in Illinois*, 24; Foreman, *The Last Trek of the Indians*, 21.

reputation of a boom town could do no better than to give it the name Chicago. Kansas tried several times to get the name Chicago on the map but with no lasting success. Three of the five towns which merged to make Chanute were named for Chicago; they were identified as Chicago, Chicago Junction, and New Chicago. New Chicago in Kansas actually grew more rapidly than did Chicago, Illinois, in its first three years. All of these names disappeared when they were replaced by the neutral name of Chanute, in honor of Octave Chanute, a bridge-builder and engineer. When the Osages lived there, they called it *Ugckzecto* or *Huzegta*. With the second spelling such a name might have survived.[10]

There was another New Chicago on Coal Creek east of Emporia, but it had only a brief existence. The name of the town was associated with an eminence called Chicago Mound, and the name was then transferred to the local school as the Chicago Mound School.[11] In the lonely, north-eastern part of Sheridan County a post office named Chicago lasted about seven years. One of the suburbs of Topeka was called Chicago Heights, but it is now absorbed by greater Topeka. So all of the Chicagos of Kansas have disappeared.[12]

Kokomo is a well known name in Indiana. Since the Miamis had established one of their villages there, the place was named for Kokomo, a Miami chief. Hodge has interpreted Kokomo to mean "young grandmother." In what was for a few years Garfield County, Kansas, 1887 to 1893, there was a town named Kokomo, but it did not attain the distinction of becoming a post office. The source of the name in Kansas could have been Kokomo, the chief; Kokomo, the town in Indiana; or Kokomo, a Kansas scout. During the wars of 1878 in Kansas, Colonel Lewis had among his scouts, said George Brown, "a man we called 'Kokomo'—we never knew his real name."[13]

[10] Lapham, *KHC*, XVI, 505 and 511; Barry, *KHQ*, XXXII, 80.

[11] Van Gundy, *Reminiscences*, 40.

[12] Andreas and Cutler, *History of Kansas*, 836 and 1520.

[13] George W. Brown, "Kansas Indian Wars," (ed. by Connelley), *KHC*, XVII, 135.

Out of Iowa and Illinois came the Peorias who settled where the town of Peoria in Illinois has preserved their name. They formed one of several bands of the Illinois Indians and were listed as a member of the Confederated Tribes. They have also been identified with the Mascoutens, the Prairie band. Marquette called these Illinois Indians the *Peouarea*, which others spelled *Pewarea*. By deleting a couple of French vowels from *Peouarea*, the name was Anglicized to Peoria.[14]

The name was supposed to mean, according to Hodge, "he comes carrying a pack on his back." When the Peorias left their Illinois relatives, they must have wandered off with packs on their backs. The interpretation has been abbreviated to "runaways" and "seceders," as well as "packers." But this interpretation is challeged by Vogel who gave *Pireouah* as an Illinois name meaning "turkey."[15]

The Peorias had been decimated by their belligerent neighbors on the Mississippi, and by 1832 they were ready to join others in the great trek into Kansas to get away from their enemies, red or white. They were given a little reservation next to the Weas and Piankashaws in Franklin County, Kansas. In Peoria Township in that county there is a little town named Peoria. Earlier there had been a town named Peoria Village in Miami County, but the name was changed or "corrupted" into Paola. Horace Greeley called the Kansas town "Paoli."[16] Pennsylvania, Indiana, and Oklahoma have towns named Paoli, but the Kansas town of Paola is said to have come from the inability of the natives to pronounce the "r" in Peoria. The practice of substituting an "l" for an "r" by children, natives, and some Orientals is called lallation. It was pronouncing the name of Baptiste Peoria that brought about the change from Peoria to Paola, since this chief was called "Peolia" by his own people. This interpretation could be questioned, but even more questionable is the interesting suggestion by Father Kinsella that

[14] Edward Taube, "Tribal Names Related to Algonkin," *Names*, III, 77.

[15] Leland, *Names*, I, 270; Gregg, *Commerce of the Prairies*, 396n.; Vogel, *Indian Place Names in Illinois*, 108.

[16] *The Overland Journey from New York to San Francisco*, 30.

the origin of the name was *Citta de Paul*, the "city of Paul," which may have been a reference to Paoli in Italy.[17]

Before Baptiste Peoria had given his last name to Peoria Village which became Paola, the townsite had been known as Baptiste Spring. Lewis H. Morgan, who knew Peoria, called him "Battisse," which should be an acceptable English spelling of a French name. Peoria was one-quarter French. He could not read or write, but he was a brilliant linguist. He knew all of the languages of the Five Confederated Tribes. These were, of course, related languages with variations in dialect. But he also knew the languages of the Shawnees, Delawares, and Potawatomis, as well as both English and French. He became the trusted spokesman of his people and a most useful interpreter in their negotiations with the white man. Morgan said that he was invariably spoken of in terms of highest praise and that natives looked to him "as children to an affectionate father."[18]

Not far from Paola is a place called Wea, named for a subtribe of the Miamis. Like so many other tribes, the Weas had been reduced in numbers by smallpox and whisky, two of the most devastating consequences of contact with the white man. The Weas were given a small reservation together with the Piankashaws in the Miami County area between the Shawnees and the Miamis. They began to give up their Indiana lands in the treaty of 1817, signed by a chief with the interesting name of Christmas Dagnet. With others they had for a time been crowded into a reservation near St. Geneviève in Missouri. They came to Kansas in the thirties and were moved out in the sixties.[19]

Wea or Weah, also spelled Wee-ah, is a convenient abbreviation for such a cumbersome name as *Wawiaqtenang*. Schoolcraft suggested that it meant a "place of the curved channel." That was where the water would form an eddy, so the Weas were also called

17 Bernice Wallace, "History of Paola," 2; Andreas and Cutler, *History of Kansas*, 876 and 881.

18 *Morgan: The Indian Journals*, 41 and 205n.; Moore, *KHC*, XI, 464; Moore, *KHC*, XII, 339n.; Murdock, in *Wichita Evening Eagle*, Aug. 4, 1943.

19 Foreman, *The Last Trek of the Indians*, 33; Abel, *KHC*, VIII, 81 and 92.

the "eddy people." Another form of the name was *Wayah-tonuki* which has also been interpreted to mean "eddy people." According to Hodge, the French spelled their tribal name *Ouiatinons*, which became *Wyatenons*, which was then shortened to Wea.[20]

Not far from Paola is a town named Wea in Miami County, a county which has townships named Miami, Osage, and Osawatomie, as well as Wea. There is a fairly good sized creek named Wea Creek which flows into Bull Creek shortly before it reaches the Marais des Cygnes. Several oil and tar pits have been found in Miami County, among them the Wea Tar Pits.[21]

The Michigamea tribe was one of the several Algonquian tribes of the Illinois Confederacy. These Indians were squeezed out of their lake country by pressure from the Sioux and Foxes in the North, and they moved into southern Illinois and Missouri only to encounter new pressures from the Quapaws and Chickasaws in the South. They sought safety by joining the Kaskaskians in Illinois where their identity appears to have been lost.

Among the early forms for the name of the Michigamea were *Mitchigama* and *Mishigamaw*. The accepted meaning has been *michi*, "great," and *guma* or *gamaw* for "water," making the name mean "great water." It could also be translated as "big water" or "big lake." This was appropriate for the people living on Lake Michigan. Thomas Jefferson has been given credit for suggesting the name of Michigania for the upper part of Louisiana, a name which later became the name for the northern territory of the Old Northwest. Finally the state of Michigan was given the name without the classical ending.[22]

A town south of Topeka in Osage County was named Michigan Valley by its Michigan settlers who wanted to keep alive the memory of their former home in a name. The Missouri Pacific Railroad dropped the "Valley" part of the name. The post office seems to have moved to the railway station on higher ground, but it con-

[20] Wright, *A Guide to the Indian Tribes of Oklahoma*, 254.

[21] Andreas and Cutler, *History of Kansas*, 875, cf. map.

[22] Lawrence, *National Geographic*, XXXVIII, 129; Stewart, *Names on the Land*, 227.

tinued to use the double name, and some maps list the two together as Michigan and Michigan Valley.[23] In western Kansas, Scott County has a township named Michigan.

Kalamazoo was the Indian name given to the springs on what is now the Kalamazoo River in Michigan. Gannett has given several interpretations for the name, and among them is "otter tail," a translation of *negikanamazo*. Also related to "otter" was the translation which made it mean "stones like otters." Other translations would make it mean "beautiful water," "boiling water," or "bright sparkling water." A logical interpretation is "boiling pot," a description of the bubbling springs where the rising gas bubbles look like boiling water.[24]

There was once a Kalamazoo post office in Kingman County which lasted only a year. Then there was a Kalamazoo in Sedgwick County, but the name lasted only about four years and then was changed to Annes. The new name was an unusual combination of the name of Anne S. Wilson who was the wife of a New Yorker who owned the townsite. In 1886 there was a Kalamazoo in Decatur County. Three times this name was put on the Kansas map only to fade away.[25]

Kalamazoo is a fascinating name. It has been said that "Kalamazoo has been made a symbol of Midwesternism by authors who cannot resist the sound of its name." Carl Sandburg's comment on the name was:

> *Kalamazoo, you ain't in a class by yourself;*
> *I seen you before in a lot of places.*[26]

The name is well known in Michigan where it has been widely used, but the name has not been popular elsewhere except in Kansas where it did not survive.

[23] Andreas and Cutler, *History of Kansas*, 1529; Missouri Pacific, *The Empire that the Missouri Pacific Built*, 129.

[24] Kane, *The American Counties*, 153; Gannett, *American Names*, 171.

[25] "Annals of Kansas," *KHQ*, XX, 288.

[26] Federal Writers' Project, *Michigan, A Guide*, 322.

▲ XX

Five Iroquoian Nations

EXCEPT FOR THE TUSCARORAS AND CHEROKEES, who lived in the area around the western part of the Carolinas, the Iroquoian tribes lived in the upper St. Lawrence Valley, the lower Great Lakes area, and in an area which centered in New York state. Hiawatha, lost in legend and revived in literature, has been given credit for uniting five of the many Iroquoian tribes into a confederation known as the Five Nations. Naming them from the east to the west, they were the Mohawks, Oneidas, Onondagas, Cayugas, and Senecas. The league of the Five Nations became powerful and belligerent, and they fought their neighbors, including those who spoke the Iroquoian language, such at the Wyandot, Huron, and Erie tribes. Their neighbors were enemies to be defeated and then destroyed, absorbed, or driven away. The confederation of the Five Nations had an organization which has been given credit for contributing ideas to and serving as an example for the unification of the thirteen British colonies.

During the period of colonial rivalry the Iroquois were strategically located between the British and the French. Because of an early battle with the French, the Iroquois generally took the side of the British. Even in the American Revolution they were on the side of the British, fighting to stop the advance of the American frontier. In this they failed, and like many other tribes, they were soon sent in search of new homes in the West. The attempt to resettle them in Wisconsin was a failure because of fraud. They continued to suffer from exploitation by people who have been characterized as "unscrupulous speculators . . . political demagogues and a few traitorous chiefs."[1]

The Treaty of Buffalo Creek in 1838 provided for the removal of the Iroquois to Kansas. All of the Five Nations and a few other tribes commonly referred to as the "New York Indians" were to be settled on lands adjoining the Osages and Cherokees. Few came, and a clause in the treaty gave the government an excuse to rescind the treaty, causing a legal controversy which lasted until 1898.[2] Meanwhile the Iroquois had come and gone from Kansas.

As they migrated westward, the Iroquois tribes left their names on the land, especially in the Old Northwest. In the westward movement of the white man, these Indian names took on a new meaning. They were reminders not so much of the Iroquois as of towns in the East with Iroquoian names. Such names as Oneida, Seneca, and Geneseo had an Iroquoian or a New York origin, but they came to Kansas from Ohio and Illinois. Others, such as Cayuga and Onondaga, came from New York. The difficult and complex Iroquoian names had been trimmed and simplified or "corrupted" before they became place-names in Kansas.

When the Five Nations prepared for war, they sent sachems or chiefs as delegates to meet in a council hut known as the long house, from which they took their name. "The five nations in their symbolical language formed a cabin," said one authority, "the Mohawks holding the door and the Onondagas the fire. They called themselves as a nation Hotinonsiooni (French notation) or Hodenosausee (English notation), meaning 'they form a cabin.' "[3] According to Swanton, the Iroquois called themselves *Ongwanonsionni*, but Francis Parkman and Lewis H. Morgan wrote it *Hodenosaunee*. The name was said to mean "we of the extended lodge," which was popularized into "people of the long house."[4]

The Algonkins, who had good reasons for not liking the Iroquois, called them *Irinakhoiw*, meaning "snakes" or "adders," which was a popular way of referring to enemies. The French changed this

[1] Abel, *KHC*, VIII, 83.

[2] *Ibid.*, 83–84.

[3] Kenton, *The Indians of North America*, II, 351n.

[4] Morgan, *League of the Ho-de-no-sau-nee or Iroquois.*

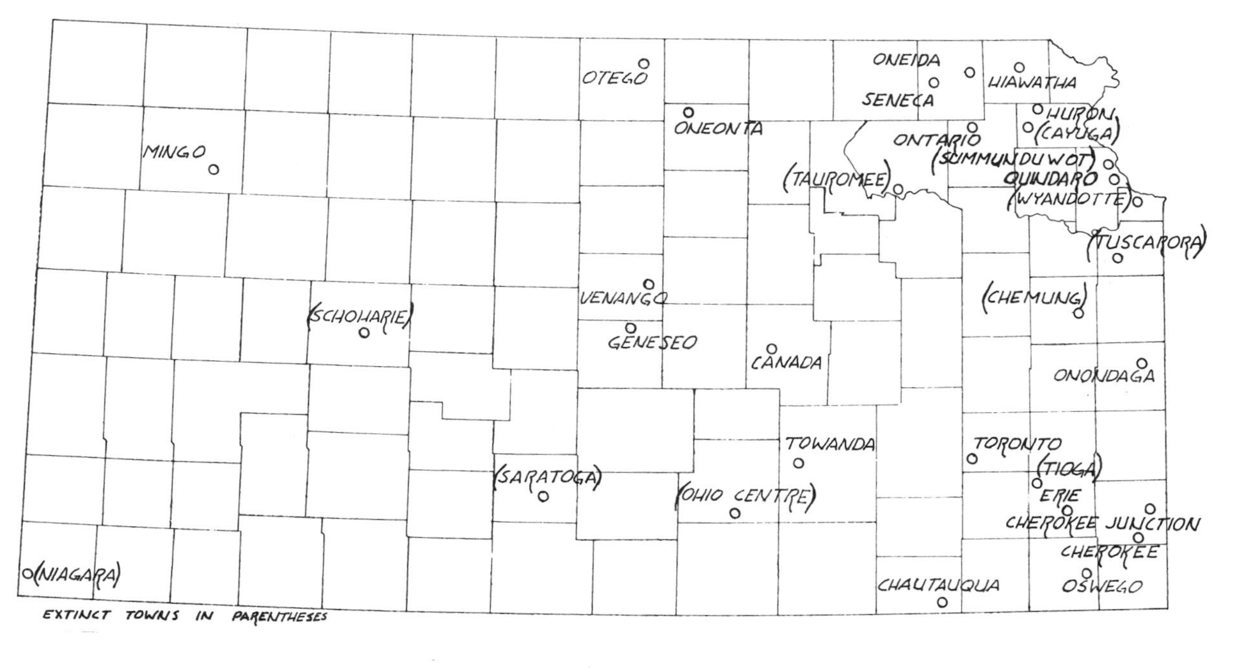

Iroquoian Names in Kansas

name to *Hiroquois* and then to *Iroquois*. With arrogant pride not unlike some twentieth-century nationalists the Iroquois spoke of themselves as "the men surpassing all men."[5]

Mingo was a name which was used rather loosely by the Delawares and the Dutch for the Iroquois in general and the Senecas in particular. Travelers applied the name to any detached band of Iroquois. Those of the Iroquois who had moved into the Ohio Valley were also called Mingos. The name came from *Mingwe* or *Menqua* and was a term of "peculiar reproach" meaning "treacherous" or "stealthy," said Cooper. The site of Pittsburgh was once a Mingo town, known then as Queen Aliquipa's Town and referred to as "a beautiful town, at the Forks of the Ohio." Zane's Trace, the well-known highway across Ohio, was near the old Mingo Trail.[6]

Eventually the name of Mingo came to Kansas where it replaced the name of Hurford in Thomas County. Mingo is not a common name, and at the time of the settlement of Kansas the only other place that used the name was Mingo Flat in Virginia. Its source might well have been the popular *Leatherstocking Tales* of James Fenimore Cooper.

New York colonists who came to Kansas in 1856 settled in Grasshopper Township in Atchison County, where they built a town and named it Cayuga for Cayuga, New York. The original name, said J. B. N. Hewitt, was *Kwenio'gwen* which meant the place "where the locusts were taken out." It was a strange coincidence that a name referring to locusts appeared in a township named Grasshopper. The locusts had not yet been "taken out" of Kansas, but the town disappeared before the big grasshopper invasion of 1874.[7]

The Cayugas had other names which may have come from

[5] Hodge, *Handbook of American Indians*, I, 617; Parkman, *The Conspiracy of Pontiac*, 7 and 21.

[6] James F. Cooper, *The Last of the Mohicans*, 72n.; Stewart, *U.S. 40*, 18; Hodge, *Handbook of American Indians*, I, 867; Van Every, *Forth to the Wilderness*, 66–67.

[7] Ingalls, *History of Atchison County, Kansas*, 118; Hodge, *Handbook of American Indians*, I, 223.

their lake or their villages. *Go-yo-goh* was said to mean "mountain rising from the water." *Kwe-u-kwe* meant "where they drew their boats ashore," whereas *Gwe-u-gweh* was translated to mean "at the mucky land." The last two have enough similarity to have been given one meaning, but the interpretations vary.[8]

When a group of settlers from Oswego, New York, came to Kansas, they chose White Hair's Little Town in Labette County as a suitable townsite. To commemorate its New York source, the Little Town Town Company changed its name to the Oswego Town Company. Then Little Town was renamed Oswego. The wooded hills and valleys of eastern Kansas were attractive enough to remind the settlers of their homeland in northern New York.[9]

Oswego is an Iroquoian name which was used in New York for a river, a county, and a town. The Oswego River flows out of Onondaga County through Oswego County into Lake Ontario. At the inlet of the lake there is a town named Oswego. Oswego was also the name which the Onondagas and Oneidas gave to Lake Ontario. The name is said to mean "flowing out" or "where the river widens." The town could appropriately have been named Oswegatchie which means "at the very outlet," but it is not on the Oswegatchie River.[10] The name of Oswego spread westward into Indiana and Illinois and eventually into Kansas where it replaced the name of White Hair's Little Town.

Oneida was also used in New York where it was the name of a creek, a county, a township, a lake, and four post offices: Oneida Castle, Oneida Depot, Oneida Mills, and Oneida Valley. However, the name came to Kansas from Illinois rather than New York. The town with the appealing name of Oneida in Nemaha County was first called Shinntown in honor of its founder, Colonel Cyrus Shinn. The name of Oneida was associated with the hometown of several of the settlers, including Cyrus Shinn, who came from

[8] Kenton, *The Indians of North America*, I, 227n.

[9] Nelson Case, *History of Labette County, Kansas*, 141; Andreas and Cutler, *History of Kansas*, 1466; *Oswego Independent*, Dec. 19, 1958.

[10] Van Engeln and Urquhart, *Story Key to Geographical Names*, 68; Gannett, *American Names*, 234.

Oneida in Knox County, Illinois. The colonel agreed with the rest of the settlers to change the name of Shinntown to Oneida.[11] Oneida and Seneca, two Iroquoian names from the Five Nations, are both in Nemaha County.

Dr. Broomhill, a pioneer of Anderson County, promoted a town that his daughters decided to name Oneida. When informed by the Post Office Department that the name was already used in Kansas, the doctor named his town Mont Ida for one of the daughters who had given it the name of Oneida.[12]

The Oneida name evolved from *Tiioneniote* or *O-na-yote'ka-o-no* into *Onayoteka*, *Oneniote*, and *Oneiout*, which the English modified until it became Oneida, a name they could spell and pronounce. The Iroquoian word *tiioneniote* was said to mean "there it it-rock has-set-up." The antecedent of "it" is unknown, but the translation must mean that something had set up a rock which is still standing. The name refers to a large syenite boulder, the Oneida Stone, which stood near the Oneida village. So the Oneidas were identified as the "standing stone people," the "people of the stone," and the "granite people."[13]

Somewhat elusive are such names as Otego, the name of a town in Jewell County, and Oneonta, a post office in Cloud County. Both of these names seem to stem from the Iroquois in New York. There was an Otego in central New York in a county with the strikingly similar name of Otsego. The New York town of Otego, which may have lost an "s" from Otsego, was likely the source for the name of the Kansas town. Lake Otsego was the site on which the father of James Fenimore Cooper built Cooperstown. Cooper's novels were so well known and so popular that the town names from his neighborhood could have been quite familiar. The first Otego in Kansas was a post office in Harper County; later another Otego replaced the name of Elium in Jewell County.

[11] "Names," MS, KSHS Archives; *Seneca Courier-Tribune*, Dec. 15, 1938.

[12] "Names," MS, KSHS Archives; Remsburg, *Scrapbook*, I, 270; Johnson, *The History of Anderson County, Kansas*, 348.

[13] Hodge, *Handbook of American Indians*, II, 123; Von Engeln and Urquhart, *Story Key to Geographical Names*, 65; Kenton, *The Indians of North America*, I, 557.

A second name in the same New York area was Oneonta, a town in Oneonta Township, which is in Otsego County where Cooper lived. A similar name is Oneota, which may have a different origin since it has been used as the name of an upper Mississippi Indian culture as well as one in the eastern Kansas-Nebraska area. Schoolcraft used Oneota as a name for a totem. It is quite possible that Oneniote, Hodge's name for Oneida, could have become Oneonta and then Oneota. In Kansas there was an Oneonta in Cloud County. Whether the name came from the Oneida Indians, a college town in New York, or a Siouan culture in the Mississippi region still remains a secret. In the Mohawk language *oneote* meant "maize."[14]

The Onondagas lived in central New York, and the long house where the Iroquois league met was located in their village. Their name was Anglicized from *Onontage* or *Onnondague* or a similar form, which meant "on, or top of, the hill or mountain." Although many of the Onondagas lived in the lowland near the lake, their most important village seems to have been on a hill. Therefore they were called the "hill people." Since their village, Onondaga or Onnontague, was the capital of the confederation, it was not strange that they should be called the *Hadisennageta* which meant "they (are) the name bearers."[15] They evidently bore the name of the whole confederation. Furthermore, they gave their name Onondaga to the New York area before it was known as New Netherlands or was named for the Duke of York.[16]

Settlers from Onondaga County in New York came to western Kansas in 1873. As farmers they were failures. One commentator said that "they did not even know how to skin a buffalo." Many of the discouraged New Yorkers left Kansas, but before they left, they changed the name of Hollydaysburg to Syracuse, the classical

[14] Wedel, "Some Problems and Prospects in Kansas Prehistory," *KHQ*, VII, 125; Parkman, *The Conspiracy of Pontiac*, 5n.; James G. Wilson, "Arent Van Curler and his Journal of 1634–35," American Historical Association *Annual Report* (1895), 100.

[15] Leland, *Names*, I, 270; Hodge, *Handbook of American Indians*, II, 129.

[16] W. George Beers, "The Canadian Mecca," *The Century Magazine*, XXIV, 1.

name of the county seat of Onondaga County in New York. Hollydaysburg had been named for Cyrus K. Holliday, the promoter of the Santa Fe Railway. The New Yorkers also wished to change the name of Hamilton County to Onondaga but failed to do so. After all, Hamilton County was named for the great New Yorker, Alexander Hamilton.[17] However, there was an Onondaga in Kansas—a railway station on the Missouri Pacific in Linn County. It was located a short distance north of the reservation for the New York Indians, and its name may have commemorated the tribe's brief residence in Kansas.

The Senecas, like the Oneidas, have also been called the "standing stone people." One analysis gave their name a Mohican origin with *assini* meaning "stone" and *ka* meaning "people." Thus Seneca was translated as "people of the stone."[18] The combination of *sinni* plus *ika* was translated as the "place of the projecting stone." Another translation, thought to be Algonquian, was "there are plenty of stones." Morgan called them *Nun-da'wa-o-no* or "great hill people." A bizarre interpretation was made by W. M. Beauchamp who analyzed part of *Sin-ne-ke* or *Sou-e-ka* as *sinne*, "to eat." He concluded that this could make the name mean "man-eaters." The Senecas called themselves *Hodonnis'hen*, which implied that "they were clansmen of their fathers." This name may have referred to the time they called on the Mohawks for men to marry their women after a war in which they lost most of their own men.[19]

The Dutch used the name Sennekins to include all of the Five Nations except the Mohawks, whom they called Maquas. The English called them Sinnegar or Sennicky. Sennicky appears to be typical of the frontiersman's pronunciation. The name was finally simplified to Seneca, which led some people to believe that it came

[17] H. N. Lester, "Colonization of the Upper Arkansas Valley in Kansas," *KHC*, IV, 263; "Some of the Lost Towns of Kansas," *KHC*, XII, 459; *KHQ*, XVII, 87.

[18] Leland, *Names*, I, 271; Von Engeln and Urquhart, *Story Key to Geographical Names*, 64; *Seneca Courier-Tribune*, Dec. 15, 1938.

[19] Kenny, *Indian Place Names of Maryland*, 125; Morgan, *League of the Ho-de-no-sau-nee*, I, 6; Beauchamp, *Indian Names in New York*, 77.

from Seneca, the name of the Roman philosopher. This sort of substitution of a personal name for a name in the native Indian language is most misleading.[20]

The Kansas town that was named Seneca was first known as Castle Rock or Rock Castle. It had been named Rock Castle by J. B. Ingersoll who had staked out the town. According to the Seneca *Centennial History*, "there is no rock in this vicinity resembling a castle." Finly Lappin from Ohio, who was part owner of the townsite, was the person who named it Seneca, but he named it for Seneca County in Ohio, not Seneca, New York.[21] It is only a coincidence, evidently, that the name of Seneca, meaning "standing stone people," replaced the similar name of Castle Rock in Kansas.

A sidelight on the evolution of the name Seneca may be seen in the story of the origin of the name in Oklahoma, where it supposedly evolved from the name *Cieneguilla de Burro*, "donkey lake." Since the homesteaders could not "twist their tongues" around the words *Cieneguilla de Burro*, they simplified it to Seneca. This tendency to simplify spelling was illustrated by a sign in a Seneca store which advertised "Flower and Mell, Chese, Egse, Lagar Bear, Liker 5 cents a glass."[22]

Another town associated with the Senecas is Geneseo on the Genesee River in New York. A New York county also bears the name spelled Genesee. It has been written Gennisheyo, which was a descriptive name meaning the "shining valley" and the "beautiful valley." William Cullen Bryant said that the name "aptly termed the paradise of the red man." It has been praised in verse:

> *Go, tourist, where the Genesee,*
> *In falling shakes the solid land,*

[20] Wilson, "Arent Van Curler," American Historical Association *Annual Report* (1895), 86n.; Stewart, *Names on the Land*, 184.

[21] *Seneca Courier-Tribune*, Dec. 15, 1938; Andreas and Cutler, *History of Kansas*, 944.

[22] Gould, *Oklahoma Place Names*, 25; "Albert D. Richardson's Letters" (ed. by Louise Barry), *KHQ*, XII, 18; *Sabetha Herald*, Jan. 28, 1909; *St. Mary's Star*, Jan. 14, 1943.

Cam, Avon, Tevoit, and Dee,
Roll not through scenes more truly grand.[23]

The name Genesee, in one form or another, spread from New York to Pennsylvania, Michigan, Wisconsin, and Illinois. It was brought from Illinois to Kansas by Major E. C. Moderwill of Geneseo, Illinois. In Kansas the town of Geneseo is located at a railway crossing which had two railway stations known as Old Ben and Old Tom. The town had formerly been named Bluffville, but today it is Geneseo.[24]

Near the north end of Kanopolis Dam in Kansas is a little place called Venango. The name had earlier been given to a post office farther down the Smoky Hill River in Ellsworth County. Venango had been the name of a Seneca village site in Pennsylvania at the mouth of French Creek, and it has been spelled Omingo, Veneango, Weningo, and Wenango. One writer on Indian names suggested that the name came from an obscene picture which had been painted on a tree near the stream.[25]

Venango in Pennsylvania was located above the forks of the Ohio where the French and British had fought for control of a strategic site. The French called it Fort Michault; the English called it "the French fort at Venango." A county in Pennsylvania was also named Venango, but the town of Venango was renamed Franklin. In Kansas, as in Pennsylvania, Venango was located near a fort, Fort Harker on the Indian frontier. The *Venango Spectator*, a journal published in Pennsylvania, seems to have been well known in Kansas and might have contributed to the popularity of the name.[26]

[23] Von Engeln and Urquhart, *Story Key to Geographical Names*, 65; Vogel, *Indian Place Names in Illinois*, 31; Frederick G. Mather, "The River of Gennis-he-yo," *Magazine of Western History*, III, 101; Donaldson, "The George Catlin Indian Gallery," *Annual Report* of the Board of Regents of the Smithsonian Institution to July 1885, Part V, 175.

[24] Bill Billieu, in *Wichita Evening Eagle*, Oct. 23, 1953; Missouri Pacific, *The Empire that the Missouri Pacific Built*, 110; Hodge, *Handbook of American Indians*, I, 489.

[25] Beauchamp, *Indian Names in New York*, 105.

[26] Hodge, *Handbook of American Indians*, II, 880; Paul H. Giddens, "Eastern Kansas in 1869–70," *KHQ*, IX, 371ff.

A voting precinct south of Ottawa in Franklin County was named Chemung, which was originally the name of an "Iroquois village, probably of Seneca origin," according to Hodge. Morgan interpreted the Chemung River name as "a log in the water." It has also been said to mean a "big horn," and the source for this meaning was possibly a large fossil tusk. Closer to the idea of "a log in the water" was the definition of *cheemaun*, "a birch canoe," according to Longfellow. Chemung remains as the name of a river, a town, and a county in New York, any of which may have been the source for the name of the Kansas location, which is now listed only as one of the many "extinct geographical locations."[27]

Tioga was the name of an Iroquois village in Pennsylvania, and it is still the name of a town and a county in the state. It is also the name of a river and a county in New York. Like Lehigh, it means "at the forks" or "where it forks." It has also been used to describe a "junction" or a "crossroad."[28] Tioga was at the junction of the Chemung and the Susquehana rivers on the border of New York and Pennsylvania. The name of Tioga crossed the continent to California where the name was given to Tioga Pass in Yosemite Park.

Several New Yorkers who came from the Tioga River Valley of New York settled on the Neosho near Chanute. Among them was Israel Stoddard who has been given credit for naming Tioga Township. Then the town of Tioga, founded by T. C. Jones, was named for the township.[29] Tioga, Kansas, was located at the crossroads of two railroads, the Santa Fe and the Katy, so this attractive name was appropriate for the site. In addition to rival railroads, there were also rival town companies with rival names, Chicago, New Chicago, and Alliance. New Chicago won the battle for the site but lost the battle over the name. The town of Tioga merged with the others, and the name is preserved only as the name of the township where Chanute is now located.[30]

[27] *KHC*, V, 367; *KHC*, XII, 475; Morgan, *League of the Ho-de-no-sau-nee*, II, 133; Gannett, *American Names*, 78.

[28] Hodge, *Handbook of American Indians*, II, 755; Shackleton, *Handbook on the Frontier Days of Southeast Kansas*, 133.

[29] Shackleton, *Handbook on Frontier Days*, 134–36; *South Kansas Tribune*, Sept. 10, 1902.

[30] Blackmar, *Kansas*, I, 309; Shackleton, *Handbook on Frontier Days*, 136; Lapham, *KHC*, XVI, 509.

The town of Towanda in Butler County, Kansas, has an Indian name whose origin is probably Iroquoian. It is located on an old Indian campsite where James R. Mead had a trading post later bought by the Rev. Isaac Mooney.[31] There is also a Towanda Township in Phillips County. The name may have the same origin as Tonawanda. It is apparently a Seneca name derived from the Seneca word *gowanda*, which may mean "almost surrounded by hills or cliffs." In New York the name was Tonawanda; in Pennsylvania it was Towanda. If it came from the Delaware name of *Tawundunk*, the meaning would be "where we bury the dead." Tonawanda, according to Hodge, meant "a confluent stream." It was also the name of a Seneca village on Tonawanda Creek in New York. The name has been interpreted to mean "swift water," "at the rapids," and "rough water."[32]

Mrs. Roy Culp, the first postmistress at Towanda, Kansas, said that the name meant "much water," but she assumed that it was an Osage name. Nathan Boone told a story about meeting an Osage hunting party led by a chief named Towanga, which was spelled *To-wand-ga-hee* on the Drum Creek Treaty. Towanga resembles the present name of Towanda, but the similarity of sound may be misleading.[33]

Although the argument that the town was named for the Osage chief cannot be disproved, there is sound evidence that supports the Iroquoian origin of the name. Transportation promoters came to Kansas from both the Pennsylvania town of Towanda and the New York town of Tonawanda. Chester Thomas, Jr., came from Towanda, Pennsylvania, and Colonel Robert S. Stevens came from New York where his parents had lived in the Towanda Valley. Evidently Towanda, Pennsylvania, gave its name to a town in Illinois, and the name probably came to Kansas from there, since many Kansas settlers came from McLane County, Illinois, where Towanda is located. Since the Rev. Isaac Mooney, founder of

31 Stratford, *Butler County's Eighty Years*, 12.

32 Beauchamp, *Indian Names in New York*, 20 and 28; Vogel, *Indian Place Names in Illinois*, 15–21.

33 Stratford, *Butler County's Eighty Years*, 12; Boone, *Chronicles of Oklahoma*, VII, 60; Isely, "Chisholm Trail," *Wichita Beacon*, July 7, 1929.

Towanda in Kansas, was a Pennsylvanian, he could also have brought the name from his home state. Some of the Senecas who gave up their Kansas lands in 1857 were known as the Towanda band. So the name was well known in Kansas.[34]

When Edward Jaquins of New York proposed to the Kansas legislature to settle the county-seat war of Howard County by splitting the county in two, he recommended that the southern county be named Chautauqua for his home county in New York. To the New Yorkers the timbered valleys of the Caney River and the abundance of springs in the area were reminiscent of New York's Chautauqua County.[35]

The Kansas settlers were quite shocked when they first saw the strange name of Chautauqua. They could neither spell it nor pronounce it and said that Jaquins could not have if he had not come from New York.[36] Later the Chautauqua lecture series made the name a household word. Chautauqua was originally a Seneca name for a lake which they called *Tken chiata kwen.* The Jesuits had spelled it *Yjadakoin* and *Chadakoin,* and Celeron de Bienville spelled it *Chatakouin.* William Johnson, the Indian agent, must have tried to imitate the French when he wrote it Jadaghque. The Senecas pronounced it as if it were "Chaud-dauk-wa." "Chadakoin," said one writer, was "one of a dozen spellings devised by the French for phonetic equivalence to the Indian name which, much later, the Americans spelled Chautauqua." For a time the English spelled it Chatakwa, but it eventually reverted back to a French form as Chautauqua.[37]

Although there is a wide variation in the interpretations of Chautauqua, there is considerable agreement that it pertains to some phase of fishing. The most popular interpretation is that it meant "one has taken fish here" or "where the fish was taken out."

[34] V. V. Masterson, *The Katy Railroad and the Last Frontier*, 46; Vogel, *Indian Place Names in Illinois*, 152; Root and Connelley, *The Overland Stage to California*, 83 and 470; *KHC*, XVI, 765.

[35] Isely, in *Wichita Beacon*, May 19, 1929; H. B. Kelly, "Building the Sedan Court House," *KHC*, IX, 89.

[36] Thomas E. Thompson, "Early Days in 'Old Boston,'" *KHC*, XVI, 485.

[37] L. F. Hawley, "The Chadakoin River," *Names*, III, 32; Beauchamp; *Indian Names in New York*, 13; Kenton, *The Indians of North America*, II, 473n.

The story behind this tells of a strange fish that had been caught in the lake. When the fishermen reached Lake Erie, the fish was still alive, and they threw it into the lake, where the new species became abundant. The lake was then called *Ja-dah-gwah*, which the French first spelled *Chadakoin* and eventually Chautauqua. Some other interpretations of the name are "place where child was washed away," "place where one was lost," "place of easy death," "foggy place," and, rather strangely, "bag tied in the middle." The "bag" or "sack tied in the middle" was merely a description of the shape or contour of the lake.[38]

Among the ambitious towns in Chautauqua County, Kansas, was Chautauqua Springs, appropriately named for the many springs in the vicinity which were advertised as having potent healing powers. The town was located on the site of an old Indian trading post. Since it did not become famous as a health center, the "Springs" was dropped from the name. There is still a little station named Chautauqua in Chautauqua County.[39]

There were few Mohawk names in Kansas. The name Hiawatha might be included as a Mohawk name, but it will be considered in the final chapter on the literary names. The Mohawk name of Schoharie was for a short time a place-name in Ness County. It had been a Mohawk village name and became the name of a New York county, town, and creek. L. H. Morgan assumed that its correct spelling was "Sko-har'le." It meant "the driftwood" or "the floating," according to Hewitt.[40] In Kansas, Schoharie was one of three towns competing for a post office and county seat in Ness County. Nelson Spencer, postmaster and storekeeper, named the office Schoharie, "after his native town in New York."[41]

The name of Saratoga came from New York where it was the name of a county, a lake, the famous springs, and the town where

[38] Hodge, *Handbook of American Indians*, I, 239; Vogel, *Indian Place Names in Illinois*, 20; Beachy, in *Kansas City Times*, Dec. 6, 1951; Beauchamp, *Indian Names in New York*, 13.

[39] *Sedan Times-Star*, Chautauqua County Scrapbook, KSHS Library.

[40] Hodge, *Handbook of American Indians*, II, 488; Beauchamp, *Indian Names in New York*, 76.

[41] "Extinct Geographical Locations," *KHC*, XII, 487; Millbrook, *Ness: Western County, Kansas*, 85.

General Burgoyne surrendered in 1777 after the famous Battle of Saratoga. It was Saratoga Springs, however, which made the name well known. The resort became popular not only because of its healing waters, but also because of its casinos, horse racing, and other activities that attracted the moneyed aristocracy of New York.

Saratoga was believed to be a Mohawk name. According to Beauchamp, its meaning is "purely conjectural, and the conjectures are wild enough." One of these conjectures was that it meant "where the tracks of hills may be seen." Hewitt said that it could mean "the place where ashes or alkaline substances float." Another suggested that it meant "a place of people." The form Saraghoga was said to mean "swift water." Saratoga may have come from such Mohawk names as *Ochseratongue* or *Ochsechrage*, but if it has, it has come a long way. The Mohegan name *Amissohaendiek*, which appears to have a Dutch spelling, was said to mean "beaver place," which could also be the meaning of the Mohawk name. The interpretation that seems to be the most fitting today, both in New York and in Kansas, was the simple one of "hillside springs."[42]

The Saratoga name was first used in Kansas by the Saratoga Springs Town Company which promoted a town near Bonner Springs. The name it left in the area was Saratoga Park.[43] Later the name of Saratoga was given to an ambitious town on the Ninnescah in Pratt County. Both Saratoga and Iuka lost in the county-seat contest with Pratt. Saratoga served as a post office from 1878 until 1895 and eventually disappeared, but the name remains on a narrow township east of Pratt.

On a river between Lake Erie and Lake Ontario lived an Iroquoian tribe known as the "people of Ongniarahronon." The *ronon* at the end of the name merely referred to the "people" of the place. *Ongniaahra* or *Onguiaahra*, as the French spelled it, could mean "a point of land cut in two," which describes the Niagara River between the lakes. The area has also been called a

[42] Hodge, *Handbook of American Indians*, II, 466; Cram's map in Andreas and Cutler, *History of Kansas*, 126; Beauchamp, *Indian Names in New York*, 74; Vogel, *Indian Place Names in Illinois*, 125.

[43] *Wyandotte County and Kansas City, Kansas*, 348.

"neck." Hodge said that the Onondagas and Senecas called it *Ohniaga* which probably meant "bisected bottomland." It was the river that was described in the name and not the falls. When Samuel de Champlain first saw the falls, he had no name for them. Later the falls were listed as Ongiara Sault on Sanson's map of 1656. Out of these Iroquoian names with French and English variations came the rather unusual name of Niagara, a name which has become world renowned because of its association with Niagara Falls.[44]

Lippincott listed no such name in any place but New York in 1853, yet the name came half way across the continent to become a place-name in Kansas. Niagara was the name of a post office in Stevens County from 1887 until 1894 and from 1905 until 1926. It was located near the sand hills southwest of Hugoton.

The Ohio River was known to Europeans first by the names of two of its tributaries. The upper part was called the Allegheny all the way to the Wabash, and below that junction to the Mississippi it was called the Wabash. The French picked up the name of the Ohio from an Iroquoian tribe, possibly the Senecas, although some have claimed it was an Algonquian name. The English adopted the French name of Ohio for the river below Pittsburg all the way to the Mississippi, making the Allegheny and the Wabash only tributaries. When the French first called it the "beautiful river," they possibly may have been looking at the Allegheny. Beauchamp referred to the "O-hee-yo" as if it were the Allegheny, and he also interpreted the name to mean "beautiful river."[45]

The name may have come from a descriptive word used as a prefix. Some thought it was *oyo*, others *ohi*. One form of the name was *Ohiopeek*, *ohi* meaning "very" and *peek* meaning "white," which makes it the "very white" river. More elaborately the river was called *Ohiopeekhanne*, meaning "the river of many whitecaps." It was turbulent and foamy upstream, and downstream whitecaps were easily formed on a windy day. From these names it became known also as the "white" river and the "sparkling" river. Some

[44] Hodge, *Handbook of American Indians*, II, 68; Stewart, *Names on the Land*, 3; Kenton, *The Indians of North America*, I, 420 n.

[45] Stewart, *Names on the Land*, 148; Archer B. Hulbert, *The Ohio River*, 4; Beauchamp, *Indian Names in New York*, 10.

of the Sioux once resided on the Ohio, and the Omahas called it the *Uhaike*, meaning "river down which they came." Others have called it the "big river." The French called it *La Belle Rivière*, "the beautiful river," which some have thought was a translation of an Indian name. John Heckewelder, an eighteenth-century Moravian missionary, said the name could not be translated as "beautiful," but this should not detract from the beauty of the river.[46]

At least nine places have used the Ohio name in Kansas. Four were post offices, none of which survived. There has been an Ohio in Smith County, Ohio Grove in Ottawa County, an Ohio Centre in Sedgwick County, and an Ohio City in Franklin County.[47] Ohio Grove in Ottawa County was called just an "embryo town." The Ohio City in Franklin County had earlier been named Bowling Green, a name which could have come from Ohio, Kentucky, or any one of the other eight Bowling Greens in the East. The town promoters were from Lawrence, Kansas, and their interest in Ohio was shown in their naming all the streets in Ohio City for Ohio towns. When the railroad from Lawrence headed southward, it called the crossing of the Marais des Cygnes at Ottawa its Ohio City Crossing. Ohio City became the county seat and had promise of growth if it could have become a railway station, but the railroad bypassed the town and the people moved to the tracks where the new station was named Princeton.[48]

As the first towns named Ohio disappeared, new ones adopted the name. One was Ohio City in Marshall County, planned and plotted by an Ohio colony, but it came to naught. In Edwards County another town given the same name was the result of a "wildcat promotion scheme" which originated in Ohio. The "town" was sold for two hundred dollars at a sheriff's sale.[49]

[46] Hulbert, *The Ohio River*, 2–4; R. E. Banta, *The Ohio*, 8; Fletcher and La Flesche, "The Omaha Tribe," *BAE Twenty-seventh Annual Report* (1905–1906), 94.

[47] *KHC*, XII, 484.

[48] Andreas and Cutler, *History of Kansas*, 827; Franklin County Historical Society, *Reflections of Franklin County and Chautauqua Days*.

[49] James C. Malin, "The Kinsley Boom of the late Eighties," *KHQ*, IV, 177 and 185n.

Such names generally identified the origin of the settlers or promoters and referred to the state of Ohio rather than the famous river although it was an important route to the West. In some places where the towns have disappeared townships in the area have preserved the name. Referring to the one in Sedgwick County, Andreas said, "Ohio township was named in honor of the modern father of heroes, statesmen and presidents."[50] Many of the settlers in the townships named Ohio were from Ohio. Townships named Ohio may also be found in Saline, Ness, and Franklin counties.

The Iroquoian names of the East were greatly changed from their original Indian forms by the French, Dutch, and English. According to Schoolcraft, the Americanization of the names resulted in further changes such as Sinikers for Senecas, Cayuckers for Cayugas, and Oneiders for Oneidas.[51] These forms must have been based on popular and provincial pronunciations. The names took shape as place-names in the East before they were adopted in Kansas and then moved westward with but few changes. In addition to the names from the Five Nations, Kansas has also adopted names from other Iroquoian tribes, such as the Cherokees, Wyandots, and Eries, as well as the Tuscaroras who joined the Five Nations, making them the Six Nations.

[50] *History of Kansas*, 1387.
[51] *Archives of Aboriginal Knowledge*, IV, 605.

XXI

Wyandot, Huron, and Erie

The Iroquoian linguistic family included many tribes which were not members of the Iroquois Confederation. Among them were the Cherokees, Eries, Hurons, and Wyandots. The unattached Iroquoian tribes were frequently attacked, defeated, and driven out by the more powerful united Iroquois. Except for those absorbed locally, they became a part of the great westward movement, migrating at first from their eastern Indian enemies only to encounter new ones in the West. They were finally pushed relentlessly into little reservations by the advancing wave of land-hungry, white pioneers.

When the French first saw the Wyandots, they called them Hurons. This Iroquoian tribe had the same bristly hair style as the Hurons and were described as "shockheads." For a time they had lived on the upper St. Lawrence River and then on the peninsula between Lake Erie and Lake Huron which was too close to the Five Nations for security. As they were decimated and driven from the area by the stronger Iroquois, the Hurons and Wyandots merged into one tribal organization under the Wyandot name. The Wyandots had been known as Hurons, then the Hurons became known as Wyandots. Hodge, however, tells the Wyandot story under the name of Huron, a name which has become popular as a place-name in America.

Huron sounds like a pleasing name, but according to its source it has a most unpleasant meaning. Father Bressani, a Jesuit missionary, explained that the name described the manner in which the Hurons wore their hair. Some let it grow "in the middle," he said, "or on the forehead, straight as bristles. From this the first Frenchmen gave our Barbarians the name of Hurons, because of the *hure*, —that is to say, because of the straight locks, like bristles of a wild boar."[1] The French word *hure* was used in a derogatory sense for an uncouth ruffian, "base" or "villainous." The name was even used in England where the peasants who had dared to rebel in 1358 were called Hurons, as well as Jacques. But the Huron Indians won their name because they wore their hair in a high ridge like the bristles of a boar's head. They lived east of the Great Lake that bears their name and formed a confederation which was, however, unable to cope with the combined forces of the Five Iroquois Nations. They were defeated and driven westward where they were absorbed by the Wyandots.[2]

Kansas has a town named Huron in Atchison County. Since it is not on the exact site of the first Huron in that area, there was a distinction made between the two by calling the first one Old Huron and the later one New Huron. After Old Huron disappeared, the later one dropped "New" from its name and became Huron.

D. R. Anthony, commenting on the name, wrote to George Martin at the state historical society in 1901: "I named the present Huron. It had been named 'Anthony' but two Anthonys in Kansas was not fair." The town of Anthony, named for Governor George T. Anthony, was not established until several years after Huron. Dr. Amarziah Moore, who came from Huron County in Ohio, was responsible for getting a post office near his home, and he is given credit for naming it Huron for his home county.[3]

When the French first met the Wyandots, they found these Indians at war with the Senecas, supposedly over a woman. A Wyandot man, in order to prove himself worthy of this woman, had tried to enhance his reputation by being overzealous in his collec-

[1] Kenton, *The Indians of North America*, II, 31.

[2] Hodge, *Handbook of American Indians*, I, 584; Connelley, "Religious Conceptions of the Modern Hurons," *KHC*, XV, 92.

[3] Andreas and Cutler, *History of Kansas*, 410; Stabler to Remsburg, May 14, 1909, and Anthony to Martin, Nov. 7, 1901, "Names," MS, KSHS Archives; *KHC*, VII, 480.

tion of Seneca scalps. Whatever the cause, it was a long and bloody conflict. The remnants of the Huron-Wyandot confederation were driven westward along the Great Lakes. As they found new homes near Lake Superior, the Hurons were absorbed by the Wyandots and lost their identity. It has been assumed that the Hurons changed their name to Wyandot because they disliked the connotation of Huron.[4] It is more likely that the name became lost from lack of use as the Hurons became an integral part of the Wyandot nation.

Having escaped from enemies in the East, the Wyandots met new enemies in the West, the *Nadouessioux*, whose very name meant "snakes" or "enemies." Even the Huron-Wyandot tribes had been called *Nadowek* and *Nadowa* by their Algonquian enemies, according to Hodge and Swanton. *Nadowa* also meant "snake," having the same origin as the first part of *Nadouessioux*. Yet Nadowa, its derogatory meaning probably unknown, has become a popular place-name. Nadowa is the name of a stream flowing into the Missouri River from the east in the area which was once a part of Kansas and was sold to Missouri in the Platte Purchase. Even the river boat on which the Wyandots started their trek to Kansas was named *Nadowa*.[5]

The Wyandots have been known by many names, and the names have been given many meanings. According to Lewis H. Morgan, Wyandot meant "calf of the leg." He said it was an Iroquoian name and explained that it was based on their "manner of stringing jerked buffalo meat."[6] Those who were friendly with the Huron-Wyandot tribes called them *Les bon Iroquois*.[7] Since Iroquois meant "snakes" with the implication of bad snakes, then *Les bon Iroquois* would paradoxically mean "the good, bad snakes."

When the French Jesuits first met the Wyandots or Hurons, they learned their language. The Jesuits assumed that the Wyandot name was something like *Tionontatis*, *Diondaddies*, or *Etionontates*.

[4] Merwin, *KHC*, IX, 77; Deatherage, *Greater Kansas City*, I, 688; Overman, *Ohio Town Names*, 63.

[5] Andreas and Cutler, *History of Kansas*, 1227.

[6] *The Indian Journals*, 58.

[7] Hodge, *Handbook of American Indians*, I, 584.

The central part of the name, *ionontat* or *iondad*, might be the origin of Wyandot. This name has been associated with their occupation as tobacco growers. The French referred to them as the *Nation du Petun*, "tobacco nation," also written *Petuneaux*. Hodge lists them as the "Tionontati, or Tobacco tribe."[8]

Other forms of the Wyandot name were *Gahwendo*, *Gah-wen-dut*, and *Guyandotte*. The name lost a syllable when it became Wen'doot. Schoolcraft and Parkman used the simple form of Yendat. The English spelling of Wendat adopted the phonetics of the French name of *Ouendat*. The name has been interpreted to mean "people dwelling in the vicinity of bays and inlets of a large body of water."[9] This is, of course, a correct description of the land in the Georgian Bay and Lake Huron area, but it is somewhat long. More briefly the name was said to mean "dwellers on a peninsula" or "islanders."[10]

Long Indian names have generally been abbreviated and simplified. But the simple name of Wendat became Wyandot. The name has also been given an extra terminal "t" and a silent "e." This gave it a French touch, and it was as Wyandotte that the name was used as a Kansas place-name. This is, however, slightly simpler than the French *Guyandotte* and a lot simpler than *Khionontaterrhonons*, an early effort to spell the Iroquoian name.[11]

The Wyandots had been on the losing side in the War of 1812, but the British made sure that the peace treaty provided for the restoration of their lands and protection from the United States. They were then settled along the Sandusky River in Ohio. After their lands had been diminished, the Wyandots, like many other tribes, were encouraged to move on. They agreed in 1842 to sell their lands, and then they began a search for a new home in the West. They were the last tribe to sell out in Ohio.

The Wyandots might have settled on the Neosho, but since they had accepted the white man's civilization, they preferred being

[8] Deatherage, *Greater Kansas City*, I, 687; Merwin, *KHC*, IX, 74; Kenton, *The Indians of North America*, 257n.

[9] Connelley, *KHC*, XV, 92.

[10] Errett, *Magazine of Western History*, II, 240.

[11] Merwin, *KHC*, 74–76; Connelley, *Kansas and Kansans*, I, 235.

nearer the white settlements. There were no longer any pure-blooded Indians among them. According to Connelley, "There was not so much as a quarter-blood Indian in the entire nation." So they were more white than red. They had hoped to acquire a strip of Kansas land along the Missouri border from their friends, the Shawnees. When that failed, they decided to buy thirty-nine sections of land on the north side of the Kaw from the Delawares.[12] They chose well.

When the Wyandots came to Kansas in 1843, they settled in the strategic triangle between the Kaw and the Missouri which furnished sites for Kansas City and several suburbs. The leaders of the Wyandots were economically sharp and politically shrewd; they were organizers, promoters, and builders. Most of the leaders had English names which they had acquired from their Anglo-American fathers on the frontier; nevertheless, they were members of the Wyandot tribe.

Among the most important of the Wyandot leaders were the Armstrongs, John M. Armstrong, his wife Lucy Bigelow Armstrong, and Silas Armstrong. The father of the Armstrongs was Robert Armstrong who had been stolen by the Indians when he was but a boy in Pennsylvania. He was later adopted into the Wyandot tribe, and his children became chiefs. His first Indian wife was evidently the daughter of a chief—and a vixen. He later married Sarah, or Sallie, Zane whose father was English and whose mother was French and Wyandot.[13]

By December, 1843, John M. Armstrong, United States interpreter, had built the first log cabin on the site which became Wyandotte City. He also built the first Wyandot council house and the first free schoolhouse. He was a lawyer, but there was little business for a lawyer even though modern civilization was moving in; so John became the first schoolmaster in the schoolhouse which he had built.[14] However, it was Silas Armstrong who was the most active in town promotion. With his fine, white man's beard and

[12] Connelley (ed.), *The Provisional Government of Nebraska Territory*, 2n.

[13] Lutz, *KHC*, IX, 225; Andreas and Cutler, *History of Kansas*, 1227.

[14] Harrington, *Historic Spots in Wyandotte County*, 110 and 134; Andreas and Cutler, *History of Kansas*, 1229.

his penetrating, brown Indian eyes, Silas was an impressive figure. An earlier portrait shows him, however, as clean shaven and nattily dressed like a white man.[15]

In 1855 a treaty was signed which permitted individual ownership of land by the Wyandots. They could henceforth buy and sell land just as any other citizen could. White promoters and speculators, backed by eastern money, moved in quickly to purchase choice townsites from the Wyandots. Within a year they had organized a town company of seven members, but three of its members were Wyandots. Silas Armstrong was chosen president.[16]

The new town was named for the Wyandot Indians, but it was spelled Wyandott as a post office in 1855 and the following year when it was incorporated. Later it was changed to Wyandotte, with the final "e" added. The builders and boosters of these new towns saw them all as "Chicagos in embryo," said one commentator.[17] Like so many other towns, Wyandott showed its confidence in its future growth by adding "City" to its name. So it became Wyandotte City before it was changed to Kansas City.

When the town of Wyandott was established, it was still within Atchison County which extended to the junction of the Kaw and the Missouri. In 1859 this precious corner was cut off from Atchison County and organized into a new county which was then named Wyandotte for the Wyandot Indians.[18] A township was also added from the south side of the Kaw and named for the Shawnee Indians who had resided there. Within Wyandotte County four of its five townships were given Indian names. Three of these were tribal names: Delaware, Shawnee, and Wyandotte. The fourth was named Quindaro for a distinguished woman of mixed blood who was a member of the Wyandot tribe.

Silas Armstrong was a member of the Kansas City Town Company which was organized in 1868. It was on the "Armstrong float"

15 *KHC*, IX, 216; *KHC*, XV, 105.

16 Frank H. Betton, "The Genesis of a State's Metropolis," *KHC*, VII, 115; Harrington, *Historic Spots in Wyandotte County*, 243; Andreas and Cutler, *History of Kansas*, 1231.

17 Robert Morrow, "Emigration to Kansas in 1856," *KHC*, VIII, 307.

18 Gill, *KHC*, VIII, 452.

that the town was founded. Much of it was washed away in the periodic floods of the Kaw and the Big Muddy, but not because it was on a "float." Wyandot lands were called floats because the Indians were free to choose the location of the section of land which had been allowed them and which they could sell. Several of the leading towns in eastern Kansas were built on these floats.[19]

Either one of the two cities which Armstrong promoted could justifiably have been named Armstrong, but both were given tribal names of distinction. Armstrong died before Kansas City was established, but his son, Silas Armstrong, Jr., participated in the founding of the town. Kansas City was not incorporated until 1873.[20]

The elder Armstrong was honored by a place-name in the area. One of the several new towns was built on the bluffs south of Kansas City. The town was not established until two years after the death of Silas Armstrong, yet it was named Armstrong in his honor. It was known as Armstrong a few years after its post office was discontinued but it eventually lost its identity to Kansas City. As it expanded downhill towards Kansas City, the upper part became known as Old Armstrong.[21] A street named Armstrong in Kansas City is still a reminder of Silas Armstrong, the distinguished Wyandot town builder.

One of the towns competing with Wyandott was the town with the distinctive and attractive name of Quindaro. This was the name of a prominent woman who was part Delaware and part Wyandot, with considerable white blood from both sides of the family. She has been called a Delaware as well as a Wyandot, but she lived with the Wyandots and was a member of the Wyandot tribe. Her Wyandot name was Seh Quindaro. In the Big Turtle clan of the Wyandots the word for woman was *quindaro*. Originally the name meant much more; it was interpreted to mean "the female turtle covering up her eggs in the sand." It also included a reference to

[19] *Wyandotte County and Kansas City, Kansas*, 327ff.; Merwin, *KHC*, IX, 82n.; Andreas and Cutler, *History of Kansas*, 1240.

[20] Betton, *KHC*, VII, 116; Harrington, *Historic Spots in Wyandotte County*, 243.

[21] Harrington, *Historic Spots in Wyandotte County*, 134 and 136; Andreas and Cutler, *History of Kansas*, 1240.

the eggs being hatched in the sun. Then the meaning became "the daughter of the sun," which made good sense. A quite different suggestion was that Quindaro meant "a bundle of sticks," suggesting "strength in union" and resembling the Latin *fascia*, popularized by Mussolini.[22]

Quindaro was the descendant of Adam Brown of Virginia who had been captured by the Wyandots in Dunmore's War. Like so many white captives, Brown had been adopted by the tribe. Abelard Guthrie, according to Connelley, "came down from Dayton, Ohio, to marry the beautiful Quindaro Brown." After her marriage she was known as Nancy Guthrie, but her husband made sure that her Indian name was not forgotten. It was she who negotiated successfully with the Wyandots for a new townsite, and in appreciation Guthrie named the town Quindaro.[23]

Abelard Guthrie, a popular politician among the Wyandots, in 1852 was their representative in Washington to promote territorial organization for what was then the Platte country or Nebraska which included Kansas. Although he was not officially received in Washington, he had planted a seed. He was supported by Governor Robinson and others in the founding of the hilltop town of Quindaro as a Free State center. It was high, dry, and isolated, but its promoters published a map to show that all roads led to Quindaro —a map which included railroads which had not yet been built and which crossed the rivers on nonexistent bridges. A critic said that "Governor Robinson and a few other lunatics" had founded "a town called Quindaro among the rocks and hills," three miles above Wyandotte, on an "utterly impractical site." One contemporary, very self-assured, said that "Qwindare" never would be much of a town. It did decline, especially during the Civil War.[24] Quindaro was unable to compete successfully with its neighbors,

[22] George W. Veale, "Coming in and Going out," *KHC*, XI, 6n.; Harrington, *Historic Spots in Wyandotte County*, 183–92; Andreas and Cutler, *History of Kansas*, 1229.

[23] Connelley, "Kansas City, Kansas," *KHC*, XV, 185.

[24] Richardson, *Beyond the Mississippi*, 30–32; "Diary of George H. Hildt" (ed. by Martha B. Caldwell), *KHQ*, X, 261; Harrington, *Historic Spots in Wyandotte County*, 183 and 191.

and, "in the classical language of the jayhawker," it was said to be "too dead to skin."[25]

Quindaro was made a post office in 1857 and served until 1909; it was revived as a post office in 1921 and served until 1954. In its early optimistic days it had a newspaper which was called the *Quindaro Chindowan*, the Chindowan meaning "leader." Its name was also used for a proposed railroad, the Quindaro, Parkville, and Burlington.[26] Quindaro's dream to become a second St. Louis was not realized except as it became a part of metropolitan Kansas City. It is no longer the name of an independent town, but Quindaro's name may still be seen on a railway station, on a township, and on a boulevard in Kansas City, as well as on a park and a cemetery.

Mathias Splitlog was said to be of Cayuga-Seneca descent, but he was more white than Indian. He married a Wyandot woman, Eliza Carloe, or Charloe, and joined the Wyandot Nation. The Seneca and Wyandot languages were quite similar, and Splitlog became an interpreter.[27] He was a somewhat eccentric individualist and a most ingenious mechanic. He built a sawmill at a time when Wyandotte City was in desperate need of lumber. Later in life, while living in the Ozarks, he became known as the "millionaire Indian."

A local legend explains how Splitlog got his name. The Indians came to see the opening of his sawmill. When they saw the logs going through, sawed into beautiful boards, they picked up the owner on their shoulders, marched him around as if he were a winning coach, and yelled, "Heap split log!" This incident, according to the story, gave him his name and the name stuck. Not only was Splitlog henceforth known by that name, but the mill became the Splitlog Mill, the stream on which the mill was built became Splitlog's Run, the hill south of Jersey Creek where Split-

[25] J. H. Beadle, *The Undeveloped West*, 214.

[26] Andreas and Cutler, *History of Kansas*, 1230; Hildt; *KHQ*, X, 282; Harrington, *Historic Spots in Wyandotte County*, 183.

[27] Lutz, *KHC*, IX, 187; Connelley, "First Provisional Constitution of Kansas," *KHC*, VI, 113n.

log lived became known as Splitlog Hill, and Kansas City has a Splitlog Street. There was also some interest in promoting a Splitlog Railroad.[28]

Distances were important for the Kansas pioneer, and many a place was named by the mile. When a post office was established six miles northwest of Wyandotte City in 1874, it was simply called Six Mile. Then for a few years it was called Braman Hill. Next it was named Summunduwot for a Wyandot family, Mary and Eliza Monocue Summonduwot, with a slight change in spelling. In 1891 this interesting name was changed to Fairdale.[29]

Tauromee has been mentioned in connection with the towns which preceded Manhattan at the mouth of the Blue. Tauromee was a Wyandot chief, characterized as "wise and just," whose main interest was to defend the rights of his people. He was one of the reluctant signers of the treaty which changed the status of the Wyandots to citizens in 1855.[30]

Tauromee, seemingly a simple name, was nevertheless troublesome and was spelled in various ways. In the act incorporating the town of Tauromee the company was called the Tarromee Town Company. The name was also written Tauroma, Tauroomee, and Tauroru. Allowances for typographical errors should be made, especially when the name was spelled Gau-roome. It has been suggested that the town might better have been named Do-Re-Me. Most Americans called Chief Tauromee simply Hat John. Among the many Hat Johns, there was also a John Hat John, Jr. There was a John Hat listed as a Wyandot chief below the name of Tauromee on a treaty of 1867.[31] This seems to have been merely an identification of Tauromee, since in most cases Tauromee and Hat John are used together. Although the name lasted less than two years as a post office, Tauromee has remained the name of a Kansas City avenue.

28 Connelley, *KHC*, VI, 113n.; Andreas and Cutler, *History of Kansas*, 1226; Roenigh, *Pioneer History of Kansas*, 20.

29 *KHC*, XV, 116 and 145; Baughman, *Kansas Post Offices*, 124.

30 *KHC*, XVI, 764; Merwin, *KHC*, IX, 87n.

31 *KHC*, XV, 126 and 128; Andreas and Cutler, *History of Kansas*, 1229; Carey, *KHQ*, XXI, 92.

The Wyandots recognized their common background with the Hurons and named their final resting place the Huron cemetery, where Tauromee and many another Wyandot chief were buried. The "good" Indians who lie buried there occupy peacefully a very precious piece of land. The cemetery has been protected by the treaty of 1855, but there are some speculators who are of the opinion that this land is too valuable to be dedicated to the dead. Bordering on the Huron cemetery is Huron Park. Originally both were known as Huron Place.[32]

The Erie Indians, like the Wyandots, were also members of the Iroquoian linguistic family. Lake Erie separated the two tribes, the Wyandots living on the north side and the Eries on the south side. The Seneca tribe of the Five Nations and their neighbors and relatives carried on the most persistent hostility against the Wyandots and the Eries. The Eries were unable to defend themselves, and some of them were absorbed by their conquerors. Others drifted off to join neighboring tribes. They may have disappeared as an identifiable tribe, but their name is still prominent in their homeland. Erie, Pennsylvania, the Erie Canal, and Lake Erie preserve the name of these Iroquoian natives. The name traveled westward and was used in Ohio, Indiana, Illinois, Michigan, and Missouri before it came to Kansas.

The French Jesuits and other French frontiersmen were the first to refer to these Iroquoians with their long and complicated native names, such as *Rhiierrhonons*, which had variations such as *Riguehronons*, *Eriechronons*, *Errieronons*, and *Erigas*. Others spelled the name *Hirri-ronon* and *Irri-ronon*. As in other Iroquoian languages with similar words, *ronon* referred to "people" or "tribe." *Irri* or *Errie* was translated to mean "cat," so these people were called by the French, *Le Nation du Chat* or the Cat Nation. Without *rhonon* or *ronon*, the "people" part, the name becomes a form of Erie.[33]

Although cat seems to be a simple name, the number of interpre-

[32] Harrington, *Historic Spots in Wyandotte County*, 113; Federal Writers' Project, *Kansas, A Guide*, 215.

[33] Kenton, *The Indians of North America*, I, 227n.; Errett, *Magazine of Western History*, II, 238.

tations for the identification of the cat is confusing. One of the earliest French accounts explained that the Eries were called cats "because in their country are a prodigious number of wild cats," *chat sauvage*. Most authorities seem to think that the cat was a puma or panther. Some support for this may be found in the name *Yenresh*, which the Eries called themselves and which was said to mean "it is long tailed" or just "long tail." This would refer to a panther, not to the wildcat which was a lynx or a bobtailed cat. There are those who have assumed that the Eries were also called *Kah-Kwah*, which was interpreted to mean "an eye swelled like a cat's." This would mean that they had prominent eyes, which may also explain why they have been called "raccoons" since the rings around the eyes of raccoons make them appear prominent. However, calling the Eries the Cat Nation, whatever the cat might be, is commonly accepted, and perhaps they were called the "panther people" even though they were whipped by their Iroquoian neighbors. Lake Erie was also occasionally known by the name "Lake of the Cat."[34]

A trading post was established near the center of Neosho County to deal with an Osage band under Chief Hard Rope. It had been known as Jereau Town, named for Michael Giraud whose last name was also spelled Gireau. Giraud was a well-known fur-trader among the Osages.[35] The post was located on the shores of a little lake which was facetiously called Lake Erie, and in consequence the trading post was known as Erie, which became its official name as a post office in 1866.[36]

J. L. Denison of Westmoreland, Pennsylvania, promoted a town within a mile and a half of Erie. He named his town New Erie, and for identification the trading past became popularly known as Old Erie. All of the little towns in the area battled for the position of county seat, and the town named Geographical Center won, more for its name and location than for its facilities, since even the county records had to be stored in Old Erie. Three successive

[34] Kenton, *The Indians of North America*, I, 559; Hodge, *Handbook of American Indians*, I, 430; Stewart, *Names on the Land*, 83.

[35] Shackleton, *Handbook on Frontier Days*, 13.

[36] *St. Paul Journal*, July 7, 1949.

events demolished Old Erie: first it lost the county-seat election; then in 1872 it was destroyed by fire; and finally it was blown away in a tornado. New Erie survived to become the county seat, and the "New" was dropped from its name as the "Old" blew away.[37]

A town named Fayette in Sedgwick County had its name changed to Erie. Both of these names could have had a Pennsylvania source. Erie could not be a post office name in Sedgwick County since there was already an Erie post office in Neosho County. But Erie remains on the Sedgwick County map as the name of a township.

Toronto is the provincial capital of Ontario, Canada's most populous province. Both of these names, Toronto and Ontario, have an Iroquoian origin. Toronto was most likely named by the Hurons or Wyandots who lived on the Bay of Toronto. The Wyandot name of *Toh-roohn-toh* was said to mean "plenty" or "abundance." It has also been interpreted to mean "a place of meeting" or simply "meeting place." The town of Toronto had been a French trading post and fort which the French called first Fort Rouillé and then Fort Toronto. The British renamed it York but then changed it back to Toronto.[38]

What became Toronto in Woodson County, Kansas, was at first a post office named Pleasant Grove. In 1875, according to the laws of Kansas, the town was renamed Rivere, but this did not become its post-office name. The Post Office Department, influenced by the Canadian settlers at Pleasant Grove, renamed the place Toronto. According to the local press, "thrifty and intelligent Canadians" settled in the "Greenwood Hills" of the beautiful valley of the Verdigris in 1869, and in the following year they were successful in changing the name of the town to Toronto. Now both the town and the township are named Toronto.[39]

The name of Ontario in Canada was applied to the Great Lake

[37] *Ibid.*; Shackleton, *Handbook on Frontier Days*, 115; Andreas and Cutler, *History of Kansas*, 828.

[38] Leland, *Names*, I, 272; Marjorie W. Campbell, "Canada's Dynamic Heartland, Ontario," *National Geographic*, CXXIV, 64; Merwin, *KHC*, IX, 76n.

[39] *Toronto Republican*, Oct. 12, 1933; *Topeka Daily Commonwealth*, Feb. 27, 1875.

before it was made the name of a province. In the language of the Hurons the lake was called *ontara* or *ontar*, to which was added *io* meaning "good," "large," or "beautiful," which, according to Stewart, made the name mean a "fine lake." So Ontario meant "the beautiful lake," "the good lake," or "the large lake." A longer Iroquoian name was *Skanodario* which was translated to mean a "very pretty lake." The French called it for a time Lake Frontenac, then *Lac Frontenac ou Ontario*, marking the transition. The Indian name was preserved to pass all the way to Kansas, where Ontario, the name of a small place near Holton in Jackson County, serves as an interesting example of the migration of Iroquoian names from the East.[40]

The name of Canada also appears in Kansas. It is the name of a community located between Marion and Hillsboro in the Mennonite country. There has long been a close connection between the Mennonites of Kansas and Canada. Since some of the Mennonites came to Kansas from Canada, it was logical for them to name one of their communities for their Canadian background. Canada was also used as the name of a township in Labette County, a county which is named for a French-Canadian family.

The French used the term *Kanada* for the Iroquoian tribes living on the upper St. Lawrence Valley. They seem to have learned the name from the Hurons. The name was also used for all the Indians in the area, including the Algonquian tribes. The New England writers applied the name to some of the Abnakis who had moved there from Maine. *Kanada* was said to mean "village" or, as Beauchamp suggested, "where they live." The first village to which the name was evidently applied was the one at the site of Quebec which was under the rule of Chief Stadacone.[41] Some have tried to find a Portuguese or Spanish source for the name. The Spaniards, disappointed in what they found there, are supposed to have said, "*Il capa di nada*," meaning "cape nothing." The Portuguese, who wanted to use the St. Lawrence as a passageway to

[40] Stewart, *Names on the Land*, 82; Beauchamp, *Indian Names in New York*, 12 and 60.

[41] Hodge, *Handbook of American Indians*, I, 198; Beauchamp, *Indian Names in New York*, 104.

India, were disappointed and supposedly said, "*Canada*," or "nothing here." Another tried to make Canada out of *kan*, "a mouth," and *ada*, "a country," resulting in "the mouth of the country." Joseph Brant, a well-educated Mohawk chief, supported the French interpretation that Canada meant "village."[42] So what was probably the name of a village or town became the name of the country.

[42] Gannett, *American Names*, 67.

XXII ▲

The Five Civilized Tribes

The Five Civilized Tribes were the Cherokees, Choctaws, Chickasaws, Seminoles, and Creeks, all southern Indians. Since they were not all equally well civilized, some people refer to them as the "so-called" civilized tribes. They had to a great extent accepted the white man's way of life, which was said to be the civilized way. The Indians were occasionally helped in this direction, but they were also frequently hindered and then condemned for their lack of success in achieving civilization.

Four of the Five Civilized Tribes were members of the Muskogean linguistic family; the Cherokees were Iroquoian. All contributed place-names to Kansas. The Cherokees lived in the western part of the Carolinas and in the neighboring states with their headquarters for a time in eastern Tennessee. South and west of the Cherokees lived the others, with the Creeks and Seminoles in the southern part and the Choctaws and Chickasaws farther west. Since these Indians lived in the same general area, they had much in common. For the most part the Cherokees got along better with their Muskogean neighbors than they did with their Iroquoian relatives, the Tuscaroras. It was partly due to the hostility of the Cherokees that the Tuscaroras were driven out of the South and sought union with the Five Nations of the Iroquois in New York. The Creeks and Seminoles may have dominated the Muskogean tribes for a time, but it was the Choctaw language which became the intertribal language of the area.

There are not many Muskogean names in Kansas; a far greater number are found in Oklahoma. Even the name of Oklahoma has

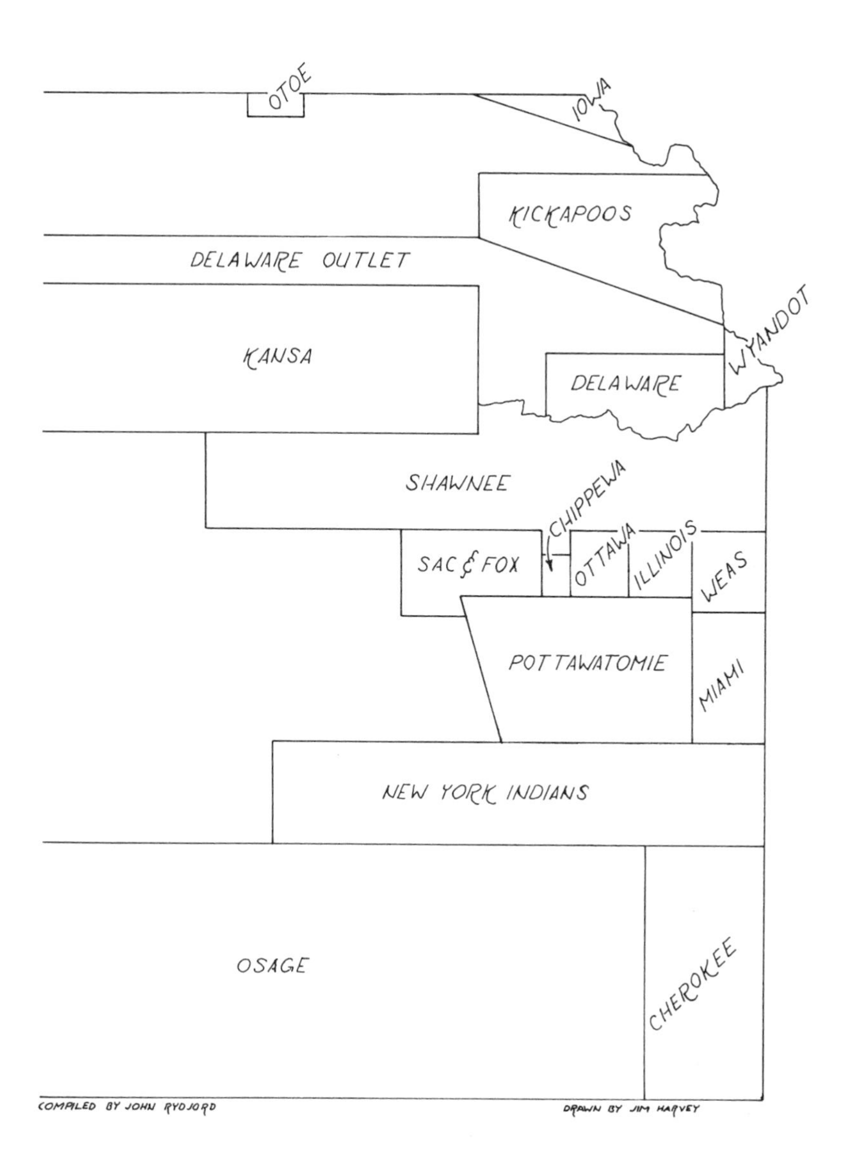

Indian Reservations in Kansas Before 1854

a Choctaw source. When the Rev. Allen Wright, chief of the Choctaws, signed the treaty for the settlement of the Five Civilized Tribes in Indian Territory, he was asked what he would name the territory. His answer was Oklahoma. In Choctaw, *Okla-homma* meant "red people"; *okla* meant "people" and *homma* or *humma* meant "red."[1] So Oklahoma got its name from the treaty of 1866.

In the 1880's there was an Oklahoma in Kingman County, Kansas, which was spelled Oklohoma on the Union Pacific Railroad map. After it was no longer useful as a post office, it disappeared.

The Chickasaws lived in Mississippi and neighboring states near their relatives and rivals, the Choctaws. Their best-known center was at Chickasaw Bluffs, now Memphis. Hernando de Soto, who was the first European to meet them, called them *Chicaza*. The French called them *Tchikacha*. The Creeks called them *Tchikasa*, and the Kansas, using the name as they had heard it, called them *Tcikasa*. According to Swanton, the meaning of the name is unknown. The name may refer to the departure of the Chickasaws from the Choctaws. In the Choctaw language, *chikkih* meant "not a very great while ago" and *ashachi*, "to leave." Such a source for a name is not uncommon. It could also mean "rebellion."[2] Perhaps those who left were "deserters."

An effort was made to use Chickasaw as a place-name in Kansas when Kentucky town promoters in Coffey County planned a town in 1857 to compete with the town of Hampden. The town named Chickasaw was never built and it remained "purely a paper town."[3]

The name Wewoka is an example of the Creek influence. There was a Wewoka listed as one of the extinct towns of Kansas as early as 1857. It had been promoted by Alexander Majors of the famous Russell-Majors freighters. Later there was a Wewoka post office established in Kiowa County, but it won no fame and disappeared

[1] Gould, *Oklahoma Place Names*, 21; Wright, *A Guide to the Indian Tribes of Oklahoma*, 4.

[2] Swanton, *The Indian Tribes of North America*, 177; Wright, *A Guide to the Indian Tribes of Oklahoma*, 84; Kenton, *The Indians of North America*, II, 445.

[3] Andreas and Cutler, *History of Kansas*, 663; *KHC*, XII, 475.

within a year. The name is better known in Oklahoma. Its meaning has been given as "roaring water" and even "barking water."[4]

Iuka is an Indian name from Iuka in Tishomingo County, Mississippi. The chief who lies buried in the town's public square was named Iuka, and he was a friend of the chief for whom Tishomingo County was named. He may have been a Chickasaw or a Choctaw. His name could have come from the Choctaw word *i-yuk-hana*, meaning "where two roads cross." Another has interpreted it to mean "place by the water." The name is also said to be a contraction of *Ish-ta-ki-yu-ka-tubb*. By deleting the first two and the last syllables, the remainder is *kiyuka*, easily shortened to Iuka.[5]

During the Civil War, General Sterling Price, who had been the greatest Confederate threat to Kansas, was stationed at Iuka, Mississippi, when General Grant was organizing his army in Tennessee. General Price, fearing reinforcements that General Rosecrans would get from General Ord, retreated to avoid a major battle near Iuka. However, Iuka, in the northeastern corner of Mississippi, was near Shiloh, where one of the great battles of the war took place.

Although Iuka is an unusual name, it has become popular and may be found in five states. It has been used twice in Kansas; the second time it survived. Shortly after the Civil War the name of Iuka was given to a post office in Labette County. It was discontinued after a few years, revived in 1869, and again discontinued. Then the name was given to a town in north-central Pratt County where there is also an Iuka Township. There was once an Iuka in Iowa, but its name was changed to Tama. The Iowa character of the Kansas town was so strong that Andreas said that "Iuka is an Iowa town, out and out, only located in Kansas." It was settled, he said, by "Iowa exclusively." It seems logical, therefore, that the Kansas town got its name from Iowa. The town may have been

[4] *KHC*, IV, 723; *KHC*, XII, 490; Shirk, *Oklahoma Place Names*, 220; Raymond W. Settle and Mary L. Settle, *Empire on Wheels*, 16; Tilghman, *American Anthropologist* (n.s.), XLIII, 488.

[5] Vogel, *Indian Place Names in Illinois*, 46; Thomas P. Field, "The Indian Place Names of Kentucky," *Names*, VII, 163.

named by Mrs. Sam Dunn, presumably from Iowa, who was said to be the first white woman to spend a night in Iuka.

There is, however, a more popular version of how the town got its name. The choice was supposedly made by placing all the proposed names in a hat and drawing out one for the name of the town. The Rev. A. Axline, who was reported to have been in the Battle of Iuka, proposed the name of Iuka, and it was his ballot which was drawn from the hat. The Rev. Mr. Axline, who was one of the town promoters, was both preacher and postmaster.[6]

The Cherokee language is remotely related to the Iroquoian language. Although the Iroquois were generally associated with the New York area, the Cherokees were at home in Tennessee, Kentucky, the Carolinas, and Georgia, where they were neighbors of the Tuscaroras. Hodge called the Cherokees "a powerful detached tribe of the Iroquois." It is difficult to determine the source of the name, since, as James Mooney said, the "name occurs in fully fifty different spellings." But Mooney thought that the name had a Choctaw origin.[7]

DeSoto, the first Spaniard to meet the Cherokees, called them *Chalaque*. Hodge gave the origin of their name as *Tsalagi* or *Tsaragi*, which was the name they called themselves. Their name may have come from *Chiluk-ki*, the name given them by the Choctaws, which was said to mean "cave people." Mooney interpreted the Choctaw word *choluk*, as meaning "a hole" or a "pit" or "chasm," which could easily have been changed to "cave." He showed that the word could also mean a "hollow" by translating *iti chiluk* as a "hollow tree." The Wyandots called the Cherokees "mountain people." Since the Cherokees lived in the cave country of the mountains, one name was as good as the other.[8]

Swanton hesitated to give a definite source and translation of the name except for suggesting the possibility that it came from the Creek word *tciloki*, meaning "people of different language."

[6] *Pratt Daily Tribune*, March 1, 1937, and Aug. 30, 1951; Andreas and Cutler, *History of Kansas*, 1267 and 1269.

[7] "Myths of the Cherokee," *BAE Nineteenth Annual Report* (1897–98), Part I, 187.

[8] *Ibid.*, 183; Wright, *A Guide to the Indian Tribes of Oklahoma*, 58.

Chiluk-ki and *tciloki*, whether Choctaw or Creek, are sufficiently alike to risk the assumption that they have the same meaning. One interpretation of *Tsalagi* was that it was made up from words meaning "tobacco," and since tobacco was important in their religious ceremonies, the Cherokees were also called the "ancient tobacco people." The Cherokee name took shape quite early. By 1674 the English referred to the "Cherakae Indians." Their present name is not unlike *Chiraquis*, the name given them by the French.[9]

Under pressure from white settlers and the government of the state of Georgia, the Cherokees began a search for a new home in the West. A few came first to Arkansas, and by 1825 some came to Kansas. In Kansas they were in Osage territory, and land had to be bought in the Osage Neutral Lands to make room for more Cherokees. A second group was then brought in under the military guidance of General Winfield Scott. They became known as the Western Cherokees or Cherokee West, and their land was called the Cherokee Neutral Lands, but it was popularly known as the "buffer state." The Cherokee Nation split over the issue of removal, but by 1838 nearly all were forced from their homes in the East.[10]

The removal of the Cherokees from their homes in Georgia and rich hunting grounds of the Carolinas and Kentucky to the unknown lands of Kansas and Oklahoma was a traumatic experience and a tragic migration, best characterized as the "Trail of Tears."

Cherokee County is the corner county in southeastern Kansas. The Bogus legislature had named it McGee for Mabillon McGee, a member of the Kansas legislature. McGee's residence was at Westport, Missouri. The legislature seemed to have few scruples about being represented by Missouri residents, but McGee tried to rectify the legality of his representation not by moving into Kansas but by adding this bit of the Missouri border to Kansas.[11]

In 1860 the name of McGee smacked too much of Missouri and the Rebellion, and the name was changed to the more neutral name

[9] Swanton, *The Indian Tribes of North America*, 215; Lauvrière, *Histoire de la Louisiane Française*, 276; Wright, *A Guide to the Indian Tribes of Oklahoma*, 56–59.

[10] Abel, *KHC*, VIII, 77.

[11] Andreas and Cutler, *History of Kansas*, 1150; *KHC*, XI, xvii–xviii.

of Cherokee for the Indians who had lived there on their temporary reservation. Overlapping into the southeastern corner of Kansas is also the geological formation known as the Cherokee Sea. Of the three towns named Cherokee in Kansas, one still survives. In Cherokee County there was a Cherokee City, known also as Old Cherokee. It was destroyed by federal troops because it was located in Indian territory and not yet open to settlement. Not far from Baxter Springs was the post office known as Cherokee Mound which lasted less than a year. The residents of the town now named Cherokee thought it was located within Cherokee County, but it is just across the border in Crawford County. In the northern tier of townships in Cherokee County there is also a Cherokee Township. The name is musical and popular, and eight states have counties named Cherokee.[12]

Elias Boudinot, a Cherokee chief with a French name, was one of the distinguished leaders of the Cherokees in Georgia. His Indian name was *Ga-la-ge-noh* which meant a "male deer." From his Indian name he became known as Buck, and from his father's name, O. O. Watie, he was known as Watie. He was the brother of General Stand Watie. For a time he was known as Buck Watie, but he gave up his Indian name and family name for the name of a French benefactor named Boudinot.

Elias Boudinot was the editor of the *Cherokee Phoenix*, a paper which was later denied the freedom of the press by the governor of Georgia. The Cherokee Nation split over the issue of removal. As one who accepted the removal of the Cherokees as inevitable, Boudinot became the rival of John Ross, a well-educated and powerful chief of the Cherokees. The rivalry continued after the Cherokees had settled in Indian Territory, and as a result of the bitter feeling Boudinot was assassinated.[13]

Boudinot Creek and Boudinot Mission were both named for Elias Boudinot. The mission was a Presbyterian mission among the Osages not far from the Osage mission which became St. Paul. It

[12] Andreas and Cutler, *History of Kansas*, 1149; Federal Writers' Project, *Kansas, A Guide*, 413; *KHQ*, XIX, 317; Kane, *The American Counties*, 73.

[13] Grace Steele Woodward, *The Cherokees*, 114, 181, and 225; Edward E. Dale, "Letters of the Two Boudinots," *Chronicles of Oklahoma*, VI, 328.

has been referred to as the "Mission at Boudinot on the Neosho" and was located at the mouth of Four Mile Creek in Neosho County. The place was also identified in a letter of March 12, 1832, with the address of "Boudinot, Osage Nation."[14] On the 1870 Johnson map of Kansas it is listed as just Boudinot.

Most distinguished of the Cherokees was Sequoyah, whose name was also spelled Sequoya and Sequoia. His father was possibly Nathaniel Gist, an itinerant peddler or trader. When Sequoyah used his father's name, he generally wrote it George Guess. His mother was Wut-teh, the daughter of a Cherokee chief in Tennessee. Because of an accident from which he did not fully recover, Sequoyah was frequently called just "The Lame One." Impressed by the white man's writing, which he called "talking leaves," he decided to invent such a system for his people. It has been said that he became interested in writing when he wished to put his name on his silverwork. His greatest achievement was the creation of a Cherokee alphabet, laboriously pictured on pieces of bark. His wife could see no sense in this "foolishness," and one day she burned the pieces of bark with the strange, possibly dangerous, symbols. Sad but determined, Sequoyah went into the woods and built a new cabin for his study, married a more sympathetic wife, and finally achieved fame by his remarkable alphabet of eighty-six symbols based largely on the sound of syllables.[15] This made possible the foundation of the *Cherokee Phoenix*, for which Boudinot helped to raise the money.

Since he worked alone, Sequoyah aroused the suspicion and ridicule of his Cherokee tribesmen, who were of the opinion that he was up to no good. His neighbors would yell at him as they passed his cabin: "Ha-ya! Maker of spells, you of the Red Paint Clan! Sequoyah! Sequoyah!" The Cherokees had given the name of *sequoyah* to the oppossum and then applied the name to the white man's pig. To ridicule the lone worker as they passed his isolated hut, they yelled: "Sequoyah! Possum in a pen! Pig in a poke!" And

[14] Duncan, *History of Neosho and Wilson Counties, Kansas*, 17 and 19; Howes, "Indian Missions," *The Kansas Teacher*, LVIII, 46–48.

[15] Foreman, *Sequoyah*, 39–43; Catherine C. Coblentz, *Sequoyah*, 109.

Sequoyah, also spelled Sik-wa-yi, became the accepted name for the "Lonely Lame One."[16]

After he won fame, Sequoyah began to be recognized even by his white relatives, including members of the Blair family, the founders of Blair House, which has been used as a President's residence in Washington. His tribesmen honored him by making him president of the Western Cherokees. Kansas honored him by naming one of its counties Sequoyah. According to Joseph B. Thoburn, the name was probably suggested by Colonel William A. Phillips who had been a lawyer for the Cherokees.[17]

Sequoyah County was located among Scott, Kearny, and Haskell counties in western Kansas. When these counties had sufficient population to be administered by their own county governments, the boundaries were changed. Some of the county names were also changed, and two interesting Indian names, Arapahoe and Sequoyah, were deleted.[18] What had been Sequoyah was largely taken over by Finney County which was named for David Wesley Finney, lieutenant governor of Kansas. There was once a township named Sequoyah in Ford County, but after a short time it was also renamed. Oklahoma preserved the name of Sequoyah for one of its counties, and the name, spelled Sequoia, was further honored as the name of one of the famous species of redwood trees in California. Even some of the trees in the Petrified Forest of Arizona belong to the Sequoia family.

All it took to put the name of Kentucky on the map of Kansas was for a Kentucky trapper to settle on a creek east of Lindsborg in McPherson County, for the creek was then dubbed Kentuck Creek. There also must have been Kentucky settlers in Jefferson County where there is a Kentucky Township. The name is considered to be of Iroquoian origin, most likely Cherokee. Two translations, "head of a river" and "river of blood," have associated the name with a river, but other translations have associated the name with prairies. As *Kentahkee* or *Kentake* it was said to mean "big

[16] Coblentz, *Sequoyah*, 110; Gould, *Oklahoma Place Names*, 56.

[17] Leola H. Blanchard, *Conquest of Southwest Kansas*, 98.

[18] Gill, *KHC*, VIII, 451, 461, and 463; *Garden City Evening Telegraph*, March 1, 1907.

swamp" or "meadowland" or "among the meadows." The meaning has also been given as just "prairie." The name could have come from *Eskippakithiki*, which was said to mean a "place where it is green all over."[19] As the Bluegrass State, Kentucky has kept its connection with the original Indian name.

Like the Cherokees, the Tuscaroras were southern members of the Iroquoian linguistic family. They were neighbors of the Cherokees in the Carolinas—but not good neighbors. Not only were they defeated by the British, but they were also attacked and defeated by their red brethren, the Cherokees. Under the pressure of hostile neighbors they migrated northward and eventually joined the Five Nations of the Iroquois to make it the Six Nations, but their story may preferably be told with that of their neighbors and relatives, the Cherokees.

Each tribe had its own name for the Tuscaroras, and the one used by the Mohawks, *A-ko-tas-ka-ro-ren*, is not far from the modernized version. When they were called *Ska-ru-ren* in the Carolinas, they were known as the "hemp gatherers." Beauchamp listed *Tus-ca-ro-ra* as the "shirt-weavers." Aside from their original Indian names, they have also been called the "white Indians," and an effort has been made by those with good imaginations to link them with the lost Welsh colony of King Modoc in the twelfth century.[20]

George H. Hildt, a settler in Johnson County, Kansas, liked the sound of the name Tuscarora and said: "We have named the lake on my claim Tuscarora lake and the town which our shanties will make when completed the same name 'Tuscarora' . . . We did think of naming it Dover for some time," he added, "but finally agreed that Tuscarora would sound more romantic." Dover was the name of his home town in Ohio. "Shanties" did not make a lasting town, and so Kansas lost another "romantic" name. Tuscarora has been a very popular name, and, according to Lippincott, there were nine places with the name before a tenth was attempted in Kansas. The name finally moved as far west as Nevada.[21]

[19] Beauchamp, *Indian Names in New York*, 97; Field, *Names*, VII, 159 and 163.

[20] Beauchamp, *Indian Names in New York*, 37; Hodge, *Handbook of American Indians*, II, 842; Parkman, *The Conspiracy of Pontiac*, 27; Dan Cushman, *The Great North Trail*, 32.

[21] Hildt, *KHQ*, X, 271.

When Iowa settlers from Mahaska County, Iowa, settled at Newell's Mills in Jefferson County, Kansas, they renamed the place Oskaloosa for the county seat of their Iowa home in Mahaska County. But who was Oskaloosa? According to Gannett, Oskaloosa was the wife of Mahaska, Chief White Cloud of the Iowas.[22] Others have said that she was the wife of Osceola, chief of the Seminoles.

There is more than one Mahaska, and Mahaska the Elder had seven wives. The youngest and favorite wife of Old White Cloud or Mahaska was the beautiful woman called Rant-che-wai-me, "Female Flying Pigeon." She was also known by the more elaborate name of "The Beautiful Eagle that Flies in the Air." Making an "eagle" out of a dove may have been flattering but was probably incorrect.[23]

Old White Cloud's son, also called White Cloud, was the one for whom White Cloud in Kansas was named. He visited Europe with his wife in 1845. His wife's name, Ru-tan-ye-wee-ma, "Strutting Pigeon," was very similar to the name of his mother. George Catlin referred to the couple as Mew-hew-she-kaw and Ru-ton-wee-me.[24] White Cloud II also had several wives, but that any one of them was named Oskaloosa remains doubtful.

Oskaloosa has been translated as meaning the "Last of the Beautiful." This is a questionable translation and does not seem to stand on any reasonable source. Although it is seemingly a romantic suggestion, it has been rather widely accepted.[25]

Most authorities assume that Oskaloosa was the wife of Osceola, the Creek-Seminole leader. The name of one of his wives was Che-cho-ter, "Morning Dawn." Since she had "a trace of Negro blood," as so many Seminoles did, she was taken into slavery. The

[22] *American Names*, 233.

[23] For interesting accounts of both Mahaska and Rantchewaime, with portraits, see McKenney and Hall, *The Indian Tribes of North America*, I, 283–311. See also Henry Sabin and Edwin Sabin, *The Making of Iowa*, 60.

[24] Donaldson, "The George Catlin Indian Gallery," *Annual Report* of the Board of Regents of the Smithsonian Institution to July 1885, Part V, 598,

[25] Henry G. Alsberg (ed.), *The American Guide*, 647; Federal Writers' Project, *Iowa, A Guide*, 515; *Oskaloosa Independent*, June 6, 1935.

enslavement of his wife, who was the mother of his four children, made Osceola an irreconcilable enemy of the white man. This was not the only cause for the Seminole War, but it was a likely cause for the intractability of Osceola in all efforts to remove the Seminoles from their homes in the Southeast.[26] Osceola was imprisoned in Fort Moultrie where he died, most likely of natural causes, but it has been said that he died of a broken heart. His two devoted wives accompanied him to Fort Moultrie, but which one was named Oskaloosa is in doubt.[27] One was said to be very beautiful but perhaps not the "Last of the Beautiful."

In the Southeastern part of the United States there are Creek and Seminole names such as Okaloosa in Florida and Tuscaloosa in Alabama. Although Oskaloosa and Okaloosa may not have the same meaning, a relationship is possible. Okaloosa came from *oka*, meaning "water," and *lusa*, "black." Tuscaloosa came from *tascalusa: tasca*, meaning "warrior," and *lusa*, "black." This was the name of a chief whom the Spaniards knew as Black Warrior. Vogel suggested that Oskaloosa could be from *ishki*, "mother," and *lusa*, "black." That would make Oskaloosa the "Black Mother."[28] This suggests Che-cho-ter, "Morning Dove," the first-mentioned wife of Osceola, who was enslaved for having black blood in her veins. Whatever the meaning, the least logical suggestion was made by a New York journalist who said that Oskaloosa came from *Oska*, the name of a chief, and *Loosa*, his squaw.[29]

One more Creek Indian name may be added to the Kansas list of names from the Five Civilized Tribes. On a high bluff overlooking Elm Creek and within two miles of Iola was the Kansas town with the intriguing name of Cofachiqui. The town of Cofachiqui, incorporated in 1855, was the first settlement in Allen County, and the legislature made it the "permanent" county seat.

[26] Federal Writers' Project, *Florida, A Guide*, 42.

[27] McKenney and Hall, *The Indian Tribes of North America*, II, 389 and 391n.

[28] Clarence Simpson, *Florida Place-Names of Indian Origin*, 80 and 87; see "Tascalusa" in Hodge, *Handbook of American Indians*, II, 694; Vogel, *Indian Place Names in Illinois*, 100.

[29] Richardson, *Beyond the Mississippi*, 97.

It was popular for a year but not permanent. It lost politically first to Humboldt and then to Iola. Most of its residents moved to Iola, which was named for the wife of one of the townsite owners, J. F. Colburn. In spite of its "most mellifluous" name, as Victor Murdock described it, Cofachiqui declined and disappeared. Cofachiqui was also the name of the local township, but that, too, was replaced by the name of Iola.[30]

Cofachiqui was the name of a Creek Indian town on the Savannah River. It may be found on the map showing De Soto's explorations and the Sanson map of 1656.[31] In Hodge's handbook it is spelled Cofitachequi, and it is said to mean "dogwood town." It was not unusual to ascribe the origin of an unknown Indian name to an Indian chief. Cofachiqui was believed by some to be the name of an Osage chief. It was not the name of a chief but the name of a princess and a place, far removed from Kansas and the Osages. It is as the name of an Indian princess that it introduces a romance of the Spanish conquistadors.

Cofachique, said one writer, was "named after an Indian Princess Cofachique, who, Cleopatra-like, met Hernando de Soto on the Savannah river."[32] She enchanted De Soto and gave him a string of pearls which she was wearing, and he gave her a ruby-set ring. She informed the Spaniards that there were plenty of pearls, as well as gold and silver, but what the natives called gold was copper and what they called silver turned out to be mica. But pearls were plentiful, and De Soto's men were reported to have collected 350 pounds of pearls. While his men carried away the pearls, De Soto carried away the princess. Cofachique, however, managed to escape with one of De Soto's slaves.[33]

As a Creek Indian place-name and as the name of a charming Indian princess, it is to be lamented that this unique name could not be preserved as a place-name in Kansas. The spelling of the

[30] Isaac Moffatt, "The Kansas Prairie," *KHQ*, VI, 163; Andreas and Cutler, *History of Kansas*, 668; Murdock, in *Wichita Evening Eagle*, Aug. 14, 1943.

[31] Woodbury Lowery, *The Spanish Settlements within the Present Limits of the United States*, 228; Paullin, *Atlas of the Historical Geography of the United States*, plate 20B.

[32] Charles E. Cory, "Slavery in Kansas," *KHC*, VII, 238.

[33] Theodore Maynard, *DeSoto and the Conquistadores*, 176.

name could have caused some confusion. It has been spelled Cutifachique, Cofitachequi, Cofachiqui, and Cofachique. It appears to be a difficult name, but in conversation Kansas residents found a solution by simply calling it "Coffeechee."[34]

[34] Shackleton, *Handbook on Frontier Days*, 74; *St. Paul Journal*, May 13, 1937.

XXIII ▲

Cheyenne and Arapaho

THE CHEYENNE INDIANS seem to have been among the earliest of the Algonquians to have left their relatives in the East and to have started a westward migration which eventually brought them to western Kansas. They lived for a time in the Sioux country of Minnesota and North Dakota, and in North Dakota they left their name on the Sheyenne River where they had once lived. For a time they were peaceful neutrals between the Sioux and the Chippewas. When war broke out, the Cheyennes were almost annihilated by the Chippewas, and they fled across the Missouri River for security. For a time the Cheyennes made their home between the Missouri and the Black Hills. Like so many of the other plains tribes, they gradually moved southward, and eventually they came to the western borders of Kansas.[1]

The Cheyennes were of the same Algonquian linguistic family as the Arapahos, and with common enemies on all sides the two tribes became, by necessity, friends and allies. Among their enemies on the plains were the Kiowas whom they fought all the way to Oklahoma. Yet the time came when they were forced to join in a common cause against a greater enemy, the white man. But even the Cheyennes were divided. By the Treaty of Laramie in 1851, they were separated into the Northern and Southern Cheyennes. By this treaty the Cheyennes and Arapahos were granted the land in Kansas which lay west of the Osage, Kansa, and Pawnee lands and north of the Arkansas River. Since 1832 the Southern Cheyennes

[1] Blackmar, *Kansas*, I, 929; Grinnell, *The Cheyenne Indians*, I, 5ff. and 22; D. J. Berthrong, *The Southern Cheyennes*, 7.

had been settled on the Arkansas River near Bent's Fort. They had been befriended by William Bent, who had married Owl Woman, daughter of Chief White Thunder.[2]

The Southern Cheyennes roamed all over the western part of Kansas and even cut through the Pawnee territory to threaten the Kansa Indians at their Cahola settlement near Council Grove. The Kansas were terrified by the Cheyennes, who were fearless fighters, but they later found satisfaction in selling Cheyenne scalps for ten cents apiece, a strange business before the tourists made souvenir selling profitable.

Indian wars broke out along the border at the close of the Civil War. The Cheyennes raided in eastern Colorado, yet they agreed to peace and surrendered Chief Black Kettle and Chief White Antelope as hostages. They accepted their assignment to a reservation in the desolate Sand Creek area. Their name for Sand Creek was *Pun oiohe*, which meant "dry creek." Meanwhile there was a change of command at Fort Lyon and the organization of a volunteer regiment in Colorado to fight Indians. Colonel John M. Chivington, a preacher who a decade earlier had been a missionary to the Wyandots, was put in command. The Colorado troops found the Cheyennes peacefully assembled in camp where the soldiers killed some five hundred men, women, and children. They burned their camp and captured their horses. This dark day in Cheyenne history was November 27, 1864. The Chivington Massacre has been described as "the foulest and most unjustifiable crime in the annals of America." The little town of Chivington near the Big Sandy Creek has preserved the colonel's name in Colorado.[3]

The Little Arkansas Peace Council of 1865 was called partly to make amends for the Chivington Massacre, but also to restrict the Indians to an area south of the Arkansas River. Black Kettle was one of the most eloquent speakers for the Cheyennes at this conference, but Indian eloquence was no match for the white man's "diplomacy." The Cheyennes were denied a reservation in Kansas

[2] *KHQ*, XI, 206.

[3] Edward E. Wynkoop, "Edward Wanshear Wynkoop," *KHC*, XIII, 76–78; *KHC*, IX, 192 and 230; Wright, *A Guide to the Indian Tribes of Oklahoma*, 80.

by a congressional amendment to the Little Arkansas Treaty. Nothing is said about any approval by the Cheyennes nor about any amendment the Cheyennes might have proposed. Congress also deleted any reference to Colonel Chivington.[4]

In 1867 the natives were assembled at Medicine Lodge for another peace talk and again for further restrictions on their freedom. Black Kettle, head chief of the Cheyennes, was then an advocate of peace, but his Cheyenne subjects had lost their confidence in the white man after their experience at Sand Creek, and they were the last to assemble. By the Medicine Lodge Treaty of 1867 they were assigned a reservation in the Indian Territory. To the Cheyennes a reservation was a restricted concentration camp where they suffered from hunger and homesickness. In 1868 warfare was resumed on the Plains. In that year Black Kettle led a small band of raiders who attacked the white settlers in the Spillman Creek area of the Solomon valley. About a decade earlier Jeb Stuart had been wounded in a battle with the Cheyennes in the same area.[5] Black Kettle later settled his people on the Washita in a village that Colonel Custer and his men destroyed. It was "a terrible slaughter" in which Black Kettle was killed.[6]

Chief Moketavito, as Black Kettle was known to his people, has only a little creek to honor his name in Kansas. Black Kettle Creek flows into the Little Arkansas at Halstead in Harvey County. In this small way the name of one of the great Cheyenne chiefs has been preserved.

One last effort was made by the Cheyennes to escape from their unhappy confinement in the Indian Territory. The Northern Cheyennes believed that they had a legal right to escape from this humiliation and return to their homelands in the North. Chief Dull Knife led their tragic flight. They were pursued by the relentless soldiers as they fought their way across the prairies of western Kansas, taking advantage of every little shelter which the high plains might provide, and they left their names along their bloody

[4] Marvin H. Garfield, "Defense of the Kansas Frontier," *KHQ*, I, 151.

[5] *KHQ*, XXIII, 172; Thomas F. Doran, "Kansas Sixty Years Ago," *KHC*, XV, 492n.

[6] Hill P. Wilson, "Black Kettle's Last Raid," *KHC*, VIII, 115.

trail. Their pathetic story is ably and sympathetically told in *Cheyenne Autumn* by Mari Sandoz.

The place where the Cheyenne women and children hid in the cave of a canyon in Scott County State Park is known as Squaw Den. It was in this canyon that the Cheyennes made a temporary stand, and the canyon is still called Battle Canyon. When the Cheyennes reached Sappa Creek, they found shelter in a natural hollow which became known as Cheyenne Hole.[7] It was on the Middle Fork of the Sappa in Rawlins County that a band of Cheyenne had been massacred by soldiers only three years earlier, and again they met defeat on Sappa Creek.[8]

The Cheyennes were proud people and competent. It must have been before they acquired the horse that the Little Osages called them "walking-on-prairie people." They have been described as "good shots, good riders, and the best fighters the sun ever shone upon." Yet they had been diplomatic enough to make peace with the Mandans and the Arapahos and eventually with their bitter enemies, the Kiowas. Waldo Wedel called them the "flower of the Plains chivalry."[9] The roaming life of these hardy horsemen earned them the popular title of "bedouins of the plains."[10]

When the Cheyennes spoke of themselves, they used the name *Dzitzistas* or *Tsistsistas*, which was supposed to mean "people alike" or "our people." The name is associated with *ehista*, translated to mean "he is from, or of, the same kind."[11] The name could have other meanings, but to themselves the Cheyennes were people who were alike.

The name of the Cheyennes has seemingly evolved from the names given them by the Sioux, such as *Sha-hiyena* and *Shaiena*, which have been translated as "those who speak a strange language"

[7] *Scott City News Chronicle*, Feb. 25, 1937; *KHQ*, XXIII, 168; William D. Street, "Cheyenne Indian Massacre on the Middle Fork of the Sappa," *KHC*, X, 369.

[8] Street, *KHC*, X, 369.

[9] Mathews, *The Osages*, 172; Wedel, "Prehistory and Environment in Central Great Plains," Kansas Academy of Science *Transactions*, L, 8.

[10] Morehouse, *KHC*, X, 361.

[11] Grinnell, *The Cheyenne Indians*, I, 3; Hodge, *Handbook of American Indians*, I, 250.

or, as Swanton said, "people of alien speech." This was equivalent to calling them "barbarians," as the Greeks had used the term for strangers whom they did not understand. The Cheyennes adorned their brown bodies with plenty of red paint, and they spoke a strange language. When the Sioux first saw them, they are supposed to have said, "*Shah-shah ee-a loo hah*," or "you have painted yourself red." Words were extracted from this statement and assembled as *Shy-ale-ah*, and out of this, it was said, came the name "Sheyenne." In telling of this evolution, one writer also said that the name should be pronounced "Shy Anne." Then his mind wandered off to thoughts of women, and he added, "Who would ever suspect that timid female to be descended from those bold and indelicate 'red legs'?" This reference to the "red legs" suggests another Sioux name for the Cheyennes, "red talkers." This was a reference to the red-painted Indians who talked a language which the Sioux could not understand. Indians who talked a language which they understood were called "white talkers." The word *sha-sha* for "red" is only a slight variation of the Osage *shutsa* or *zhu-dse* for "red," used for the name of the Arkansas which they called the "red river."[12]

To some tribes the Cheyennes were known as the "striped arrows" or the "striped feathers." They were so named because they winged their arrows with turkey feathers. But the meaning of this name became distorted from a poorly understood sign language and the name was interpreted to mean "scarred people," "spotted people," or "cut arms."[13]

There are two explanations why the Cheyennes were called "dog Indians." First, they had a fighting band among them known as the Dog Soldiers. Also, people assumed that their name, Cheyenne, came from *chien*, the French word for "dog." There is no relationship between the French *chien* and Cheyenne, except that they have occasionally been spelled the same. Lewis and Clark wrote the name first as Chien and later as Chyannes. Washington Irving's

[12] Swanton, *Indian Tribes of North America*, 278; Grinnell, *The Cheyenne Indians*, I, 2 and n.; "The Contributor's Club," *Atlantic Monthly*, XLVII, 733.

[13] Grinnell, *The Cheyenne Indians*, I, 2–4; Hodge, *Handbook of American Indians*, I, 250.

son simplified it to Shian without changing its pronunciation. The spelling has been stabilized as Cheyenne, except in North Dakota where a river is named Sheyenne.[14]

The Cheyennes had their own names for the rivers in Kansas. The Republican River was called the *Ma-hoheva-ohé*, translated to mean "Red Shield river." Young men had gathered there for a meeting of the Red Shield fighting band, and from this the river was named.[15]

The Arikaree River, which cut the northwest corner of Kansas, was called the *O-nonió-he*, the "Ree river." The Cheyennes called the Arikaras the *Ononi*. *Ohé* meant "water" or "river."

The Solomon River was called *Mahki-neohe* which meant "turkey creek." Cedar trees were once plentiful along the upper part of the Saline, and the Cheyennes, seemingly more impressed by its cedars than its salt, named it the "cedar river." In their language it was *shistotoiyohe* or *shistote* for "cedar" and *ohe* for "river."[16]

The Smoky Hill, which had such a wide variety of names, was called *Mano-iyó-he*, "bunch of trees river." The source of this name was a large grove of cottonwood trees on the upper part of the river where Cheyenne survivors took refuge after the Chivington Massacre. The Pawnees also used this cottonwood grove as a favorite camping ground and they called the river the *Rohota-katit-hiburu* which meant "big black forest." Both the Cheyennes and the Pawnees used this cottonwood grove for identifying the Smoky Hill River.[17]

Because of conflicting accounts, it has been difficult to identify Punished Woman's Fork from White Woman Creek. They are not the same. According to one legend, told by a couple of bone pickers, a white woman was captured by Indians, and the chief forced her to become "one of his wives." When a baby boy was born, the chief rejoiced, but when the child died, the chief accused the mother of having caused his death. He then punished her so

[14] Hodge, *Handbook of American Indians*, I, 251 and 256; Connelley, *Kansas and Kansans*, I, 220; Mari Sandoz, *Cheyenne Autumn*, passim.

[15] Grinnell, *American Anthropologist* (n.s.), VIII, 17.

[16] *Ibid.*, 15 and 21.

[17] *Ibid.*, 18; Hyde, *Pawnee Indians*, 63 and 282.

severely that she died. So the place became known as Punished Woman's Fork. Hunters are supposed to have confused this with White Woman Creek.[18]

Punished Woman's Fork became a battleground in 1878 when the Southern Cheyennes tried to escape from their reservation in Indian Territory to return to their old home in the north. One sentence may be quoted to illustrate the confusion over its name. The Cheyennes "posted themselves on the tops of conical hills which bordered a canyon on Punished Woman's fork or Famished Woman's fork, later known as Ladder or Beaver creek." This gives four names from which to choose without adding White Woman Creek which is farther south and which flows into a sandy sink.[19]

The Cheyennes had their own name for Punished Woman's Fork long before Dull Knife led his followers in their fatal retreat. They had earlier fought the Pawnees there, probably in 1835. They had battled up and down the stream as the advantage changed from side to side. So they named the river *Amaoh-ktsi-yohe*, "driven (back and forth) river." *Ná-Maov* meant "I drive" and *yohe* or *ohé*, "river." So here is another one of the many names of Punished Woman's Fork.[20]

The Cheyennes and the Pawnees, who had similar names for the Smoky Hill, also had similar names for the Arkansas River. The Pawnees called it the "flint" or "flint-knife" river.[21] Its Cheyenne name was *Musitsooniyohé*. *Mutsi-soon* meant "flint arrow point," and *ohé* meant "river." It was said that the Cheyennes found many flint arrow points there and so they named it the "flint arrow point river." Before the Cimarron was given its Spanish name, it had been called the *Neatsi-ohé*, "bull river," by the Cheyennes who got this name from the Sioux.[22]

The Cheyennes also accepted the descriptive name of the Medicine Lodge River. In their language it was *Hoh-kit-yohé*. *Hohke-*

[18] Montgomery, *KHC*, XVII, 275.

[19] *Ibid.*, 272; Oliver S. Lawson, "History of Scott County, Kansas," (thesis, Colorado State College, 1936), quoting *Scott City News Chronicle*, Dec. 8, 1932; John A. Boyer to author, Aug. 25, 1961.

[20] Grinnell, *American Anthropologist* (n.s.), VIII, 18.

[21] Hyde, *Pawnee Indians*, 282.

[22] Grinnell, *American Anthropologist* (n.s.), VIII, 18.

ayum was said to mean "medicine lodge." On a branch of the Medicine Lodge Creek they saw a thick stand of willows, so they named this stream the *min'oshé*, meaning "where willows stand thick."[23]

In spite of the frequent and recent battles and the bitterness between the Indian and white civilizations, Kansas honored the Cheyennes by giving their name to a county in the northwestern corner of the state near the scene of the battle on the Arikara in which Lieutenant Beecher and the famous Cheyenne warrior, Roman Nose, were killed. The county was named in 1873, a few years before the final defeat of the Cheyennes under Chief Dull Knife.

Cheyenne Bottoms in Barton County was a marshy lowland which has been turned into a lake and a game refuge. In 1849 the Cheyennes and Pawnees are said to have fought for possession of this popular hunting area. Since the Cheyennes won, the place became known as Cheyenne Bottoms.[24] A post office was also named Cheyenne Bottom.

Flowing into Cheyenne Bottoms from the west is Blood Creek which also is associated with the Cheyenne-Pawnee battle. It was said that the battle was so bloody that the creek and its banks were covered with blood, and that is why it was named Blood Creek.[25]

In 1865 a Cheyenne raid into Jewell and Cloud counties ended in the killing of five or six white hunters. The attack took place on a little creek flowing into Beaver Creek, and from this incident the stream was named Little Cheyenne Creek.[26] In the same neighborhood in Osborne County there was a post office named Cheyenne until 1907. In the Osage country of southeastern Kansas, far from Cheyenne County and the Cheyenne country, there was a Cheyenne Creek near Caney in Montgomery County.[27]

The Arapahos, relatives of the Cheyennes, were members of the Algonquian family who had migrated to the High Plains in the

[23] *Ibid.*, 18–20.

[24] Howes, "Largest Lake in Kansas," *The Kansas Teacher*, LVIII, 39.

[25] *Hoisington Dispatch*, Aug. 13, 1936.

[26] Andreas and Cutler, *History of Kansas*, 1015, 1313, and map on 1014; *KHC*, XVII, 391.

[27] Andreas and Cutler, *History of Kansas*, map on 1563.

West. While the Cheyennes were east of the Black Hills living on the Moreau River, the Arapahos had been their neighbors living on the Cheyenne River. Later the Arapaho homeland was west of the Black Hills in Wyoming.[28] Like the Cheyennes, the Arapahos were also divided into the northern and southern tribes. The Southern Arapahos extended their buffalo hunts into the Arkansas River Valley.

The Cheyennes called them *Num-o-sin-ha-nhia*, which meant those who "build their fires to the south." The Northern Arapahos gave the southern band a similar name; they called them *Nawathineha*, meaning "southerner." Hodge said that they were also called "Gros Ventres of the Prairies." Adding "prairie" should distinguish them from the other "big bellies," the Hidatsa Indians on the Missouri River. Less flattering were such names as "beggars" and "spongers." The Kiowas called them "men of the worn leggings." They called themselves *Inunaina*, "our people." Their present name seems to have come from the Pawnee word *larapihu* or *tirapihu*, said to mean "traders," according to Swanton. The name went through many variations of spelling until it was finally simplified to Arapaho.[29]

While half of Colorado was still a part of Kansas, the territorial legislature organized it all as one big county named Arapahoe.[30] The rush to the "Kansas gold fields" by the "Peakers" made it necessary to organize the county. Because Pikes Peak was the best known of the Rocky Mountain landmarks, the "fifty-niners" were known as "Peakers" even though they were heading for Cherry Creek near Denver. "The County of Arapahoe," said Governor Medary of Kansas, "already established and organized by my predecessor, Governor Denver . . . includes within its boundary nearly, if not the whole, of the gold-field."[31] Then it was reorganized and five new counties were carved out of a part of Arapahoe County, leaving Arapahoe as a long county bordering on Kansas. Arapahoe, as a name, was so popular that it was seriously considered as the

[28] Grinnell, *The Cheyenne Indians*, I, 9.
[29] Connelley, *Kansas and Kansans*, I, 219.
[30] *Statutes of Kansas Territory, 1855*, 217.
[31] *KHC*, V, 572.

name for the whole state of Colorado.[32] In 1857, "all the county west of the 6th principal meridian was unorganized territory, known as the Arrapahoe district."[33]

After Kansas had lost much of Colorado, including its rich and scenic mountains, it was free to revive the name of Arapahoe for one of its new counties. In the reorganization of the turbulent western counties of Kansas, Arapahoe got lost in the shuffle, and for a time it was a part of Finney County. The county was revived in 1886 but not its name. What had been named Arapahoe County was renamed Haskell for Dudley C. Haskell who served several terms as a Kansas representative in Congress.

There was also a town named Arapahoe in Arapahoe County on the Colorado side. Two Kansas towns were named Arapahoe. Finney County had a post office named Arapahoe in 1885, but it lasted less than a year. In Dickinson County there was an Arapahoe in the neighborhood of Detroit.[34] The name has been popular and widely used in other states.

The High Plains Indians fought a losing battle for the rich buffalo-hunting lands in Kansas. The Arapahos, like so many others, could have been named the "bison path Indians" as they were by the Hidatsa Sioux, but the buffalo, this great resource for the "affluent society" of the Indians, was ruthlessly destroyed by the invading white man.[35] The bison path Indians were relegated to reservations and a restricted life in a competitive economy about which they had little understanding. Yet these Indians have left their names on the land as reminders of a civilization which was once adjusted to its Kansas environment but which was destroyed by a more aggressive and more materialistic civilization.

[32] See map in Gill, *KHC*, VIII, 450.

[33] Andreas and Cutler, *History of Kansas*, 698; Baughman, *Kansas Post Offices*, 241 and 249.

[34] *Abilene Reflector-Chronicle*, June 8, 1948.

[35] Swanton, *The Indian Tribes of North America*, 384.

XXIV ▲

Kiowa and Comanche

An old Indian woman named Ziracuny, "Water Monster," told the story of the migrations of the Kiowas as follows: "We first lived north of the Great rock that rose out of the plain, pushing up the boys." This great rock was the Devil's Tower in eastern Wyoming. Then, she said, they lived "in the country where hot water shot up out of the ground, high in the air. . . . We grew up in that hot-water country." This was, of course, "Colter's Hell" or Yellowstone. From there the Kiowas went eastward "to the land of the Crows" where they learned about the Cheyennes and Arapahos, the two western Algonquian tribes.[1] The Kiowas were different from most of the tribes in the area, since they came from Shoshoni country and were probably of Shoshonean stock. But this may be questioned.

The Shoshonis were mountain Indians who lived in the Rockies from Canada to Colorado and Utah. They were appropriately named the "sentinels of the Rockies." Two of the Shoshonean tribes, the Kiowas and the Comanches, drifted out on the western plains. Caught between the Shoshonean tribes of the West and the advancing Sioux in the East, other Plains tribes were forced southward. Among these advancing tribes were the Apaches, Kiowas, and Comanches, as well as the Cheyennes, Arapahos, and Arikaras. The Kiowas came from the upper Missouri and Yellowstone country of Montana, and they fought their way southward between enemies on all sides during the eighteenth century. The Kiowa-Comanche conflict continued all the way to the Colorado-Kansas

[1] Wilbur S. Nye, *Bad Medicine and Good*, vii.

border, where both tribes discovered a new menace, the white man.

The palefaces were gradually and ruthlessly taking possession of the red man's hunting ground and destroying his livelihood. If this advancing wave were not stopped, the natives would be driven from the land they loved. The Indians who had fought one another as traditional enemies recognized the greater danger from this new and deadly menace. Tribe after tribe made peace with old rivals and formed alliances to resist the common enemy. Had they known the history of Pontiac, Tecumseh, and Black Hawk, they might have realized the futility of fighting the white man. But they were proud and loyal to their own people, and they would not give up their homes without a struggle.

The Kiowas and Comanches had a long history of bitter rivalry and warfare. The Comanches called the Kiowas "scoundrels," and the Kiowas called the Comanches "snakes." During one of their wars the Comanches captured a Kiowa by the name of Pago-to-goodle, and they treated him well. In the eighteenth century peace between the two tribes became possible. Through the influence of a Mexican mediator in 1790, the Kiowa chief, Wolf-Lying-Down, and the Comanche chief, Afraid-of-Water, agreed to end their wars.[2] In the nineteenth century they became allies and fought together, first against the Eastern Indians moving into Kansas and then against the white man.

The Kiowas were said to be the most feared and hated of the Plains Indians. Stephen H. Long called them "bad hearts." They have been called "tigers of the Plains." Others, more tolerant, called them simply "prairie men." By the Osages they were called "Bor-rows-from-other-People"—horses, perchance.[3] They have been described as "great horsemen, horse thieves, horse breeders, and horse traders."[4] They were dangerous raiders along the white man's frontier and they were fit competitors or companions of the hard-

[2] *Ibid.*, ix and 303–309; Mooney, "Calendar History of the Kiowa Indians," *BAE Seventeenth Annual Report* (1895–96), 162 and 437; Mayhall, *The Kiowas*, 5ff.

[3] J. Emmor Harston, *Comanche Land*, 25; Donaldson, "The George Catlin Indian Gallery," *Annual Report* of the Board of Regents of the Smithsonian Institution to July 1885, Part II, 52; Mathews, *The Osages*, 480.

[4] Mayhall, *The Kiowas*, 3ff.

riding Comanches. The activities of the Kiowas are recorded in Kansas history, and their names have a place on the Kansas map.

According to legend, the Kiowas came originally from a hollow log, and from this they called themselves *Kwuda*, "going out," or *Tepda*, "coming out." With personal pride they also called themselves *Kiowagan* or *Kaigwu*, meaning "prominent people" or "principal people." *Caygua* was interpreted to mean "two halves of the body or of the face painted in different colors." The Dakotas name *Wi'tapahatu*, "people of the island butte," may refer to their place of residence in the Devil's Tower area of Wyoming.[5] The Comanches, in addition to calling the Kiowas "scoundrels," also called them *Wea-Paphs*, a descriptive name which meant "rope heads." The Kiowas had the custom of braiding horsetail hair into their own until "it dragged behind them as they walked." Catlin, the artist, mistakenly thought this was their real hair.[6]

Kiowa is a simple and attractive Indian name, yet it took some time to learn how to spell it. The Kiowas may have called themselves *Kaigwu*, quite similar to their Wichita name of *Gahewa*. The Spaniards called them *Caygua* or *Caigua*, which is not far from Kiowa since the "g" was scarcely audible. Farnham spelled the name Keaways, and Pike spelled it Kyaways.[7] It was quite common on the frontier to pronounce the name "Kioway" to rhyme with "Ioway." The pronunciation should have changed when the spelling was changed to Kiowah, and eventually it did change, even after the deletion of the final "h" which had served its purpose.

The Kansas county named Kiowa is in the central area south of the Arkansas River where the Kiowas lived for some time before being removed into the Indian Territory. The town of Kiowa on the Oklahoma border is not in Kiowa County but in Barber County. Since the railroad bypassed the first town named Kiowa, it became known as Old Kiowa, and the one that moved to the tracks

[5] Mooney, "Calendar History of the Kiowa Indians," *BAE Seventeenth Annual Report* (1895–96), 49 and 150–52; Connelley, *Kansas and Kansans*, I, 220; Mayhall, *The Kiowas*, 17.

[6] Harston, *Comanche Land*, xi.

[7] Thwaites, *Early Western Travels*, XXVIII, 138; *Expedition of Pike*, II, 535 and 537.

became New Kiowa and later Kiowa. It was on William Campbell's ranch that the town of Kiowa was established. Even as a ranch it was identified by attractive names: first a Spanish name, *Palo Alto*, meaning "tall trees" or "tall stakes," and then Rosewood for the roses which Campbell had planted. It was also called Bovine Park, a euphemism for a cattle ranch, but none of these names could compete with Kiowa.[8]

Southwestern Kansas, which was Kiowa country, has many Kiowa names for creeks, trails, and towns. Henry H. Raymond, a buffalo hunter in the Dodge City area in 1872, told in his diary of going to "Chiwa Camp." He was undoubtedly spelling Kiowa as he had heard the name spoken. Later, however, he learned its accepted spelling, since he wrote about hunting on Kiowa Creek. This creek flows from the south and joins the Mulberry just before it flows into the Arkansas River east of Dodge City. Raymond also spoke of the East Kiowa Trail.[9]

Bear Creek in the southwestern corner of Kansas flows into the sand hills in Kearny County. The Kiowas called it *Ta-zo-to-pa* which was translated to mean "antelope corral creek." Although *t'a* or *ta* meant "antelope," the *pa* at the end of the name meant "bear," which may have associated the name with Bear Creek. However, the *pa* is very similar to *p'a* which meant "creek."[10]

The Salt Fork of the Arkansas already had its descriptive name of Nescatunga or "big salt river" used by the Osages before the Kiowas came to this area. The Kiowas must have known of the meaning of its name, since they, too, called it by a name meaning "salt" in their own language. Their name for the river was *Da-matá'n-a-p'a* or *A-tantai-p'a*, *A-tantai* for "salt" and *p'a* for "creek" or "river."[11]

In Barber County of south-central Kansas flows the Medicine Lodge River, also called just the Medicine River. An early govern-

[8] C. W. Campbell, "W. E. Campbell, Pioneer Kansas Livestockman," *KHQ*, XVI, 249 and 265.

[9] Joseph W. Snell (ed.), "Diary of a Dodge City Buffalo Hunter," *KHQ*, XXXI, 349n. and 384.

[10] Mooney, "Calendar History of the Kiowa Indians," *BAE Seventeenth Annual Report* (1895–96), 424, 430, and 432.

[11] *Ibid.*, 396 and 437.

ment survey put it on the map as Medicine Creek. In springtime, the Kiowas came to the mouth of Elm Creek to make "big medicine." The medicine man practiced his mysterious medical art by incantation and torture, using his lodge for the sweat-bath treatment. It was torture in the sense that it was a test of endurance.

The medicine lodge was "an arbor-like shelter of tree trunks and leafy branches," said Alfred A. Taylor who was present during the Medicine Lodge negotiations. He said that there were "many circles of these trees and bushes." The Indians left valuable gifts and trophies on the trunks and branches of the trees as offerings to the great spirit and, unknowingly, as temptation to the filching whites who were collectors of Indian relics and who stole the gifts to the gods. The Indian ceremony lasted "five sleeps," followed by a big feast. The Medicine Lodge River got its name from these medicine lodges where the ceremonials were performed. Before the white man had named the river for these lodges, the Kiowas had called it the *A-ya-dalda P'a*, which meant "timber-hill river."[12]

Making big medicine was important among other Indians too, and Big Medicine Creek in Rooks County and Little Medicine Creek in Osborne County were named for these ceremonies. The Indians, no doubt, made "big medicine" on Little Medicine Creek.[13] There was also a Medicine Man Creek in Osage County near Coffeyville, and within a day's travel, a Fire Medicine Creek, where the Indians had seen smoke rising from the stream. Mist rising from a stream like smoke is not unusual, but it is a phenomenon which the Indians may have attributed to the spirits.[14]

It was the Medicine Lodge Council of 1867 that gave the place its historical fame. The Indians chose the site, far from the whites and where the great spirit would protect them.[15] There, under orders of the government, Jesse Chisholm and "Buffalo Bill" Mathewson helped to assemble the Kiowas, Comanches, Prairie Apaches, Arapahos, and Cheyennes in order to make a treaty

[12] Taylor, *Chronicles of Oklahoma*, II, 118n.; Grinnell, *American Anthropologist* (n.s.), VIII, 19.

[13] Isely, in *Wichita Beacon*, Sept. 8, 1929.

[14] Mathews, *The Osages*, 452.

[15] Federal Writers' Project, *Kansas, A Guide*, 256.

which would remove the Indians from the white man's path across Kansas and bring permanent peace to the frontier. The government was generous in granting gifts to soften the resistance of the signers of the treaty, but gifts did not solve the economic and social problems of the Indians. Henceforth the Indians saw themselves as prisoners of the military on restricted reservations. General Sherman, for whom a Kansas county is also named, wanted all Indians found outside of the reservations declared outlaws.[16]

Six years after the signing of the peace treaty John Hutchinson laid out the town of Medicine Lodge and named it for the river. The name of Medicine Lodge brings to mind the great Indian peace treaty (honored every five years by the Medicine Lodge Pageant) or perhaps such prominent persons as "Sockless" Jerry Simpson, Poly Tincher, Chester I. Long, Tom McNeal, and the crusading Carry Nation.

This was Kiowa country. One of the most brilliant and belligerent of the Kiowa chiefs was Satanta. He was, however, second in command to Chief Satank, whose name was also written Sitankki and Satang. Unfortunately his name was so similar to Satanta that it caused some confusion. When Satanta was a boy, he was called Gu'aton-bian, "Big Ribs." As a chief he was named Sept'ain-te or Set'tainte. Since *set* meant "bear" and *tainte* meant "white," the meaning of Satanta's name was "White Bear." Setangya or Satank meant "Sitting Bear."

James R. Mead said that Satanta was "the most dreaded warrior of the plains." Another spoke of him as being as "sharp as a brier." It may be that the bad reputation of Satanta was responsible for the suggestion his name was the feminine form for "Satan." This is, of course, a questionable interpretation.[17] It was Satanta who was the chief spokesman of the Indians assembled at the Medicine Lodge Council. There he dramatically told how the Indian had lost his freedom and his food, how the Indian had been deceived by the white man, and how his people loved the open prairies.

[16] Mooney, "Calendar History of the Kiowa Indians," *BAE Seventeenth Annual Report* (1895–96), 187.

[17] *Ibid.*, 185, 190, and 422; *Wichita Beacon,* July 14, 1929.

Yet he promised to work for peace. He deservedly won the title of "orator of the plains."[18]

Satanta had had his troubles, and once he threatened to kill Bill Mathewson at his post near Great Bend. Mathewson gave him a thorough beating and threw him out. It is not strange that the Kiowas called this bearded white man Simper Sel-bee, a name which meant "Dangerous Beard." Mooney wrote it Sénpo-zédalbe and translated it as "Terrible Beard."[19]

The similarity of the names of the two Kiowa chiefs, Satanta and Satank, has caused confusion, particularly in one story in which both names have been used. The Kiowa chief, whoever he was, had asked his good friend George Peacock, Indian trader and dealer in whisky, for a letter of recommendation so that he could deal with Santa Fe freighters. He wanted Peacock to say that he was the best chief of the Kiowas. Peacock agreed and wrote the letter, but this is what he is reported to have written: "This is Satank, the biggest liar, begger and thief on the plains. What he can't beg of you he will steal. Kick him out of your camp, as he is a lazy, good-for-nothing Indian." There is another version of this letter, but it used Satanta's name although the general content of the letter expressed the same view in different words. This one, reported by James R. Mead, quoted Peacock as writing: "The bearer of this, Satanta, is the dirtiest, laziest, lousyest vagabond on the plains; if he comes to your camp kick him out." Ridiculed and abused by those who read the letter, the chief asked Mathewson to explain its contents. Peacock's practical joke was not funny to Satank (or Satanta), and the Kiowa chief called Peacock out of his trading post one day and shot him.[20] This was most likely the experience of Satank rather than Satanta.

[18] Mooney, "Calendar History of the Kiowa Indians," *BAE Seventeenth Annual Report,* (1895–96), 206–209; Henry Schmidt, "Naming Southwestern Cities," *Dodge City Journal,* Jan. 8, 1948; R. M. Wright, "Personal Reminiscences of Frontier Life in Southwest Kansas," *KHC,* VII, 48.

[19] Jones, *The Story of Early Rice County,* 70; *Lyons Daily News,* April 2, 1961; Campbell, *KHC,* XVII, 640; Mooney, "Calendar History of the Kiowa Indians," *BAE Seventeenth Annual Report* (1895–96), 172.

[20] James R. Mead to George W. Martin, July 11, 1908, in "Addenda," *KHC,* X, 665; Wright, *KHC,* VII, 48.

Satanta or White Bear, Kiowa chief, for whom Satanta in Haskell County was named

Satanta should be remembered for the part he played in the early history of western Kansas. He signed the Medicine Lodge Treaty, though he was one of its most sullen signers. Later he was seized by Custer as a hostage to enforce the peace treaty, and soon thereafter he committed suicide by jumping from an upper-story window of a Texas prison. Satanta was described by one who had seen him in prison as "a tall, finely formed man, princely in carriage, on whom even the prison garb seemed elegant."[21] He had once been given a major general's coat by General Hancock.

In Haskell County, once named Arapahoe, the town named Satanta honors the memory of one of the most eloquent, sincere, and persistent spokesmen for the Kiowas and other displaced Indians. Comanche County at one time also had a post office named Satanta. Satanta's Fork or Kiowa Creek was the name of a little stream running into Bluff Creek in Clark County. This creek once had a much longer name and a special distinction. It was called *Set-t'ai-nte Ta ka-imai mo-e paga ni-de p'a.* Satanta had captured some white women in Texas, and he brought them to this creek in Comanche County. The long and complicated name meant the "river where Set-tai-nte brought the white women." The story was lost when it was simply called "Satanta creek, alias North or Kiowa creek." It is now Kiowa Creek, Middle Kiowa, and East Kiowa flowing into Sand Creek.[22]

Sand Creek flows into the Cimarron, which the Kiowas called *A-patdo-p'a.* Since the first part of the name meant "low spreading branches" and *p'a* meant "stream," the Kiowa name for the Cimarron was "a river of trees with low spreading branches."[23]

The southward push of the roaming Plains Indians brought the Comanches out of Wyoming into western Kansas. In the early eighteenth century they stood as a barrier between the French in the East and the Spaniards in the West. They made peace with the Kiowas, but they continued to fight the Pawnees over the buffalo country of western Kansas. The Wichitas called them *Na'taa* or

[21] Blackmar, *Kansas,* II, 651.

[22] Mooney, "Calendar History of the Kiowa Indians," *BAE Seventeenth Annual Report* (1895–96), 422 and 434.

[23] *Ibid.,* 417 and 432.

Na'tan, meaning "snakes." This enmity kept Du Tisné from leaving the Wichitas to visit the Comanches.

Peace among the Kansa, Pawnee, and Comanche Indians was essential for the French to cross Kansas on their way to the rich and romantic land of the Spaniards. In order to make peace between these hostile Indians in 1724, Sieur de Bourgmont led a French and Indian expedition up the Smoky Hill to the Comanche country. His diplomacy, tact, and a generous distribution of gifts brought about a promise of peace, the first great peace treaty to be made in Kansas. It opened the Santa Fe trade for the French a century before the Anglo-Americans promoted the Santa Fe Trail.[24]

But Bourgmont did not call these Plains Indians Comanches; he called them *Padoucas*. The Smoky Hill River was called the Padouca River for the people found living on its banks. Bourgmont was not the first to use this name; it had appeared on the Sinex map of 1719 as "River of the Padoucah." Beauvillier's map of 1720 has a reference to the "*village du padouka blanc, Ennemies des Espagnols*." South of these were the *Padouka Noirs*, or Black Padoucas.[25]

The Padouca name, as used by the French, was possibly of Siouan origin. The Little Osages and the Omahas called the Comanches *Pa-Do'n-Ka*, the "wet nose people," because they had met them when their noses were wet from sweat. Dorsey gave *Paduka* as the name used by the Kansa Indians which also supports the Siouan origin of the name. *Padonka* was said to have been "Hispaniolized or Gallicized" into Padoucah and Padouca. Swanton suggested that the name came from *Penateka*, the name of the band that headed the Comanche migration southward into Texas. Herman Moll's map of 1701 showed a "Panetoka vil" on one of the north forks of the Smoky Hill. But for a time the name was used for all of the Comanches.[26] Lewis and Clark picked up the abbreviated

[24] Rydjord, in Bright's *Kansas: The First Century*, I, 23–29.

[25] Montgomery, *KHC*, XVII, 198; Mathews, *The Osages*, 126; *Tixier's Travels on the Osage Prairies*, 125 and 150; Wheat, *Mapping the Trans-Mississippi West*, I, 68 and map on 101.

[26] For a variety of interpretations for Paducah, Kentucky, see Field, *Names*, VII, 162.

French name of *Padoų* and called them "La Paddo" and "Padoo." This could have a Pawnee origin, according to George E. Hyde, who also thought there was some evidence to support the opinion that the Padoucas were Apaches.[27]

J. Emmor Harston's sympathetic account of the Comanches must be used cautiously, and his suggestion that Cabeza de Vaca knew the Comanches and named them in the 1530's may be questioned. Harston also assumed that they were the same as the *Teichas* or *Tejas* and that the Shoshonis had named them *Coum-onses*, meaning "bald heads or shaved heads." *Coum-onses* was then "corrupted to Comanches." Harston described how they shaved their heads, leaving "only a scalplock—with an eagle feather securely fastened to it." The last syllable in Comanche meant "horrible," he said, or the superlative of "bad." So the full name meant the "bald heads horrible" or the "bad bald heads."[28]

This does introduce a name which the French used, since they, too, called them *Tête Pelée* or "bald heads." This name was sufficiently well known to be used by Major Long who spoke of the Comanches in English as "bald heads." Of course, the Comanches were not bald, but their shaved heads with the challenging scalp lock could well have been the reason for calling the Comanches "bald heads." Stephen H. Long most likely learned this name from the French, but it could have a Shoshoni source. The Comanche chief who signed the Fort Atkinson Treaty of 1853 was Wuleaboo, whose name meant "shaved head."[29]

These "bald heads" became known as Comanches rather than Padoucas. In early Spanish records they are spoken of as the Cumanches. La Harpe, the Frenchman exploring the Red River in 1719, called them Caumuches. Pike, coming to Kansas soon after Lewis and Clark, adopted the new name and called them Camanche. Even Stephen H. Long, who knew them as "bald heads," called them Cumancias; Schoolcraft called them Comances; and Gregg called them both Cumantz and Comanchero. Comanchero, which

[27] Hodge, *Handbook of American Indians,* I, 328; Hyde, *Pawnee Indians,* 279.
[28] *Comanche Land*, 38.
[29] Grinnell, "Bent's Old Fort and its Builders," *KHC*, XV, 42.

has a Spanish ring to it, could have referred to traders with the Comanches. There is a rather questionable interpretation of the name from Camanche, which was said to be a corruption of the Spanish *Camino Ancho*, meaning "broad road," which supposedly referred to "the great trail over which the Comanches raided from the Great Plains into the country south of the Río Grande."[30]

The Cheyennes, Wichitas, and Kiowas spoke of the Comanches as "snakes" or "reptile people," each in their own language but with a common meaning which was "enemies." Comanches were belligerent, and one interpretation of the name Comanche was that it meant "Anyone-Who-Wants-to-Fight-Me-All-the-Time." This is putting a lot of meaning into one word. It also appears to be a name given by those who were quite irritated by the warlike spirit of these enemies.[31]

It is difficult to identify the meaning of Comanche, and Swanton cautiously starts his summary by the heading: "Comanche. Significance unknown." Harston, who had lived among the Comanches for many years, referred to them as the "eater" tribes, but what they ate could vary from the yampa root, which gave them the name of *Yamparikas* or "yampa eaters," to buffalo, which gave them the name *Kotsotekas* or "buffalo-eaters." The band named *Penateka*, a probable source for Padouca, were known as the "honey eaters." But these names varied with each subtribe, and none of them is necessarily the translation for Comanche.[32]

To the Siouan name of Padouca, which the French used, and the name of Comanche from the Spanish, may be added variations of *Ietan*, a name which Swanton has associated with the Utes, another Shoshonean group. Pike spoke of the Comanches as being Tetaus or Tetans, which Elliot Coues, his editor, expanded to "Ietans, Jetans, Hietans, Aiatans, etc."[33] Dr. George Sibley referred to the "Hietans' or Cumanches" as if they were the same, but Father Pichardo said that the two were "very different."[34]

[30] *Chronicles of Oklahoma*, II, 77.

[31] Mathews, *The Osages*, 138.

[32] R. N. Richardson, *The Comanche Barrier*, 18; Harston, *Comanche Land*, 3; Campbell, *KHC*, XVII, 634.

[33] *Expedition of Pike*, II, 412n.

[34] *Pichardo's Treatise*, II, 254.

The importance of this name is that it associates the Comanches with the Shoshonean family.

The Comanches called themselves the *Ne'me-ne* or *Nemosin* or, as Lewis and Clark wrote it, *Nimiousin*, which was probably from a French source. Even this had been abbreviated to Num. Since the name was not used extensively, it may not seem important except that it shows the pride of the Comanches. It meant not only "people" but the "principal people." This would make them as important as the Kiowas, whom they outnumbered. The Comanches were important, and their language was so well known by both Indians and whites that it was called the "court language of the plains."

Their superb horsemanship won for them several descriptive names. Harston's assumption that the Comanches got their horses from the Coronado expedition may be questioned. More logical is the statement made by Waldo Wedel who said: "Shortly after 1700, the Comanches moved out of the Rockies into the adjacent Southern Plains, took over the horse from the Río Grande settlements, and turned on the Apaches."[35] The Apaches called them "enemies on horses." Not only did the horse give the Comanches prestige over their enemies but also a tremendous advantage over the migrating buffalos. The Arapahos named them *Ca'tha*, "having many horses." The Utes and Navahos called them the "horse Indians." More flattering, however, were such names as "knights of the Plains," "lords of the Southern Plains," and "centaurs of the Plains." They were also called "American Arabs" and "Tartars of the desert," the "desert" being west of the 100th meridian.[36]

On the Oklahoma border, south of Kiowa County, is the Kansas county named Comanche. The county had been named before it was organized, but the name was already in use. The ranchers in the area, who were organized under the leadership of Jesse Evans to keep out nesters, called themselves the Comanche Pool or the Comanche County Cattle Pool.[37]

[35] Wedel, *Prehistoric Man on the Great Plains*, 289.

[36] Harston, *Comanche Land*, 35–48.

[37] Beachy, in *Kansas City Star*, July 5, 1950; Mary Einsel, "Some Notes on the Comanche Cattle Pool," *KHQ*, XXVI, 59–60.

Like a lot of other counties, Comanche County had a town taking the county name. A surveyer in 1886 recorded in his diary that he had surveyed a place called Nashville, later named Comanche City.[38] Its chief competitor was a post office named Avilla, but neither survived. The crossing of the Arkansas west of the Jornada has been called the "Comanch and Santa Fe trading trail."[39]

According to *The Montana Almanac* for 1959–60, a Montana town is named Comanche, not for the Comanche Indians but for the historical horse which was reportedly the only surviver of the Battle of the Little Big Horn. The stuffed horse has been preserved and may be seen in the University of Kansas museum at Lawrence.

In Kansas the Iatan name was given to a town north of Leavenworth. It had earlier been known as Dougherty's Landing for Major John Dougherty who laid out the town and who named the town Iatan. He named it for an "Ottoe" Indian chief, said George Remsburg.[40] H. M. Chittendon also referred to the Oto chief named Ietan who had earned his name in a battle against the "Comanches or Iatans."[41]

For a couple of years there was also a town named Ute in Sheridan County. The Kiowas called the Utes *K'opk-i'ago*, meaning "mountain people." This name may not have been very distinctive, but it certainly was appropriate since the Utes lived in the heart of the Rockies of Utah and Colorado. Others called them the "black people," *Sapa wichasha* in the language of the Sioux.[42] Most of the Shoshonean names in Kansas came from the Comanche Indians.

Although the Kiowas and Comanches were relatively late arrivals in Kansas, in western Kansas they became serious contenders for the railway routes, river valleys, and ranch lands of the High Plains. Friendly at first, they fought for their buffalo lands after

38 *Protection Post*, March 6 and March 21, 1947.

39 Greene, *The Kanzas Region*, 148.

40 Remsburg, *Scrapbook*, I, 173, and II, 28.

41 *The American Fur Trade of the Far West*, II, 859.

42 Pearl Toothaker, *A History of Sheridan County*, 2; Mooney, "Calendar History of the Kiowa Indians," *BAE Seventeenth Annual Report* (1895–96), 407.

it was too late to stem the white tide. At the Little Arkansas Treaty in 1865 they recognized the fact that their Kansas lands would be lost.[43] But whether they were friend or foe, Kansas has recognized their historical presence and honored them by adopting their names as place-names. Kiowa and Comanche counties, which have contiguous borders, are located in the Kiowa-Comanche country south of the Arkansas River.

One more Shoshonean name came to Kansas when a post office in the southeastern part of Edwards County was named Bannock. The Bannocks, who lived primarily in the Snake River country, were closely related to the Utes linguistically, but they were intermingled with the Washakie Shoshonis of Wyoming. Idaho has given their name to the town of Bannock, Bannock County, Bannock River, and the Bannock Range. In Montana the name is spelled Bannack. Kansas may have taken the name from these western sites, but the name came originally from the natives.

Hodge suggested that the Bannock Indians called themselves the *Panaiti*, but they were also called *Panak* which is closer to Bannock. Their name could have come from the tribal division called the *Penointikara*, "the honey eaters." Swanton spelled the name *Bana'kwut*. It was a simple matter for the Americans to make Bannock out of *Bana'kwut*. Early western travelers must have had trouble with the Bannocks since they called them the "robber Indians." Others found them digging for roots which gave them the accepted name of "diggers."

[43] Connelley, *Kansas and Kansans*, I, 220.

▲ XXV

Sitka to South America

SOME INDIAN NAMES do not fit the category of the indigenous tribal names of Kansas nor of the immigrant tribes. One name came all the way from Alaska, a most unlikely source; others came from California; and a few came from Mexico, the West Indies, and South America. It is quite likely that the popular histories of the *Conquest of Mexico* and the *Conquest of Peru* by William Hickling Prescott had made many Latin American Indian names familiar to the American public. This would certainly be true of a name such as Peru or Montezuma.

Few Indian names were as well known as that of Montezuma, the majestic and rich monarch of the Aztecs who was conquered by Cortez. Many Americans became familiar with the name of Montezuma from reading the story of *The Fair God* by Lew Wallace. Some have associated his name with wealth, and to them "montezuma" became a word which meant "money." To others, his name became a general term for "Indian." While crossing the Kansas plains in 1850, one traveler wrote to his mother about a companion who kept his musket loaded, "watching for old Montezuma who he expected to meet every day."[1]

Montezuma's name, as we know it today, is a simplification of the earlier names used by the Spaniards for Montezuma II, emperor of the Aztecs. J. García Icazbalceta, one of the distinguished students of native history, spelled the name Moteuczomatzin.[2] A little simpler was Moteuczoma, which in 1883 was said to be the

[1] *KHQ*, XVI, 325.
[2] H. H. Bancroft, *The Native Races*, II, 182.

correct spelling. In their writing the Aztecs developed signs which grew out of pictures, as others have done. Montezuma's name was a combination of signs for syllables, starting with a mousetrap for *montli*, an eagle for *quauhtli*, a lancet for *zo*, and a hand for *maith*. A combination of these with a few deletions made *Mon-quau-zo-ma*.[3] "Monctezuma" was supposed to be fairly near to the correct pronunciation. Some have spelled it Moctezuma, but the most popular modern spelling is Montezuma. Eleven states had places named Montezuma before there was a Montezuma in Kansas.

During the boom in western Kansas in the 1880's, promoted in part by Asa T. Soule's irrigation projects, a boom town in Gray County was named Montezuma. Whoever named it was fully aware of the historical characters of the Spanish conquest, since the streets of Montezuma were named for the Indians and Spaniards who participated. The main street was named Aztec Street, and other streets were named Mexitli, Texcoco, Quatemotzin, and Quivira. Mexitli was the Nahuatl name for a war god and a likely source for the name of Mexico. Texcoco was the name of one of the three leading tribes in the valley of Mexico. The name was also given to the large lake which surrounded the island on which Tenochtitlan or Mexico City was originally built. Much of the lake has now been drained, and the area has become an important part of Mexico City with the name of Tezcoco. Quatemotzin, the successor to Montezuma, was tragically killed by Cortez, who was on his way to Honduras to destroy a deserter. There were several ways to spell Quatemotzin, and one of the more common was Quahtemoc. Finally, Quivira Street was named for the land sought by Coronado in Kansas.

Montezuma in Kansas had county-seat trouble, railroad trouble, and drought. It declined, and was even declared dead, only to have a renaissance after 1912 when it was revived by the Santa Fe Railway.[4] Many of the street names were beyond the limits of the town and almost beyond recall. Some of the names associated with

[3] A. Hyatt Verrill, *Old Civilizations of the New World*, 164; T. N. Brocklehurst, *Mexico Today*, 174n.

[4] *KHC*, XII, 463.

Montezuma still remain, but they are intermingled with such common and prosaic names as Sunnyside and Johnson.

Toluca was once a town located north of Satanta in Haskell County and not far from Montezuma. For thirteen years it was a post office, but western Kansas was thinly populated, and Toluca is no more. In Mexico it is one of the flourishing market towns west of Mexico City. Toluca has been said to be a Nahuatl name, a Toltec name, and a Tarascan name. It could be the name of an Aztec god, Tolotzin or Tlotzin.[5]

South of Mexico City is the old mining town of Taxco, now famed for its silversmiths. It was originally an Indian village named Tlacho, subject to the Aztecs, and the name meant a "ball court." When the Spaniards conquered it, they called the place *Real de Taxco*; the *real* had reference to the mines which were owned by the crown. Then it was changed to *Taxco de Alarcón* to honor a great literary figure in Spain, Ruiz de Alarcón. One Mexican dictionary said that *algunos autores escriben Tasco.* And if some authors do write it Tasco, as the statement says, then surely when the name is used in Kansas, the Tasco spelling should be permissible. In Kansas, Tasco was located in Sheridan County where its name replaced that of Guy in 1923 and where it served as a post office for thirty years. It is still a station on the Union Pacific.[6]

Coyote is a familiar name, but it is not of English origin. The coyote was the prairie wolf. The name came from *coyotl*, a Nahuatl name from central Mexico. Those who used coyote as a place-name in Kansas were probably not aware of its Mexico origin. In Sherman County, Kansas, some men hid from Indians in a buffalo wallow which the early settlers knew as Coyote Gulch. The Coyote name was given to post offices in both Phillips County and Ellis County. There was a Coyote station on the Kansas and Pacific Railroad in Trego County, serving for a time as the "End-o-Track" station. Its seventeen citizens were mostly railroad workers, and the town was as untamed as its name implied. The Coyote post office

[5] Vogel, *Indian Place Names in Illinois*, 149.

[6] See "Taxco" in the *Encyclopedia Americana;* Alberto Leduc and Luis Lara y Pardo, *Diccionario de Geografía, Historia, y Biografía Mexicanas*, 945.

in Ellit County lasted only six months, then the name followed the tracks into the next county. The station which replaced Coyote was Collyer, named for the Rev. Robert Collyer of Chicago.[7]

There was once a place named Hurricane in Grant County, but it soon disappeared. It could have been named for the high winds in western Kansas, but the name-givers probably did not know that the name came from the West Indies where the natives referred to the Caribbean storms as *huracan* which meant an "evil spirit." Who else could cause or would cause such destructive storms!

Webster's New International Dictionary lists the origin of pawpaw as *papai*, an Otomac word from central Mexico, or *ababai*, a Carib word. It is, of course, the name of a popular fruit called papaya. Lewis and Clark rested at Kaw Point on their return trip in 1806, and there, said William Clark, "we gathered great quantities of pawpaws." These were not the tropical papayas, but a North American variety. In Elk County the name appeared three times; there was a Paw Paw post office, also spelled Paupaw, located on Paw Paw Creek in Paw Paw Township.[8]

After the Clayton-Bulwer Treaty of 1850, which denied Britain or the United States the exclusive right to a future canal across Nicaragua, that little volcanic country was much in the limelight. The bombardment of Greytown by the United States in 1854, the year of the Kansas-Nebraska Bill, might have diverted public opinion from the plight of Kansas; it certainly attracted attention to Nicaragua. It is not strange, therefore, that a town in Woodson County was named Nicaragua. It was established in 1857 near the present town of Rose.[9]

In Central America, Nicaragua was the name of a "wise" and "valiant" chief who was met by Gil Gonzales, the Spaniard who conquered the land. Nicaragua was also known as Mahomet's Paradise for its beauty and as Vulcan's Land for its volcanoes. How-

[7] John C. Jones and Winoma Jones, *The Prairie Pioneers of Western Kansas and Eastern Colorado*, 65; Blackmar, *Kansas*, I, 470; Montgomery, *KHC*, XVII, 225 and 248. Federal Writers' Project, *Kansas, A Guide*, 365.

[8] Burch, *Handbook of Elk and Chautauqua Counties*, 6; Andreas and Cutler, *History of Kansas*, cf. 1173; Federal Writers' Project, *Kansas, A Guide*, 207; *KHC*, XII, 106.

[9] "Extinct Geographical Locations," *KHC*, XII, 484.

ever, it must have been the Anglo-American rivalry and the talk of canals that aroused Kansas interest in that name.[10]

William H. Prescott's *Conquest of Peru* had made Peru a familiar name, and fourteen places in the United States had been named Peru before the name came to Kansas. Peru was an Inca *(Quechua)* name, first heard of by the Spaniards in Panama as the Land of Biru. Garcilaso de la Vega, son of a Spanish captain and an Inca princess, said that the name came from a Quechua word *pelu*, which meant "river." The Spaniards mistakenly thought that *pelu* referred to the country or land of the Incas.[11]

Out of the three places named Peru in Kansas, one still remains. First there was a post office named Peru in Allen County which was replaced by Xenia in Bourbon County. Then there was a Peru in Osborne County which was changed to Osborne. The third was in Howard County, the part which is now Chautauqua County. Settlers from the towns of Peru and La Salle in Illinois came to Howard County, and, in choosing a name for their town, they tied the votes between their home-town names of Peru and La Salle. This left the decision to E. R. Cutler, president of the town company. He could not forsake his "old home town of Peru," he said, so he broke the tie by voting for Peru. Even this was a second choice, since the name of Belleville had been proposed but was rejected by the Post Office Department because the name had already been pre-empted by Belleville in Republic County. The headline for the story in the *Sedan Times-Star* read: "Name of Belleville chosen for Peru Balked by Government."[12]

The capital of Peru is Lima, long the most famous city in South America and known for its viceregal headquarters as "The City of Kings." It got its name from the Rimac River. The story of the river is well told in Thornton Wilder's *The Bridge of San Luis Rey*. Lima, or *rimac* in the Quechua tongue, said William Prescott, meant "one who speaks." This had reference to the shrine of a famous oracle.[13]

[10] Bancroft, *Annals of Early Central America*, 486.
[11] Prescott, *The Conquest of Peru*, I, 52n.
[12] *Sedan Times-Star*, Jan. 3, 1935.
[13] *The Conquest of Peru*, II, 28.

There was once a post office in Clay County named Lima, but its name was changed to Wyoming Valley in 1873. The next year there was a Lima in Elk County, lasting until 1887. The Lima in Allen County had no post office, and it is listed only among the extinct towns of Kansas.[14] Three times the name of Lima came to Kansas, but none has survived.

From the capital of Ecuador, Butler County residents took the name of Quito for a town. Quito is associated with the same rich civilization as that of El Dorado. It was originally the name of a tribe known as the *Quitus*. This part of the Inca empire had been conquered by the great Tupac Pachacutec, whose name meant "he who changes the world." But Quito, which Mooney, historian of Butler County, referred to as "Key Toe," is no longer in Kansas.[15]

San Luis Potosí in Mexico and Potosí in upper Peru, now Bolivia, were both world-famous mining towns. The silver mines of Potosí produced enough silver to revolutionize the economic systems of the world. Followers of the Incas were directed to explore the mountain, when they heard a clap of thunder and a voice warning them to "go away from this place." They gave it the Quechua name of *Potojchi*, meaning "a loud voice" or "thunder." Other definitions, based probably on association or anticipation, would make it "source for silver." Another form was *Ppotocci*. But it became known from *Cerro de Potosí* as "the Hill" and, with greater feeling, "that accursed hill." Potosí, the name of the largest town in America during its boom, became, like El Dorado, a synonym for wealth.[16]

Potosi in Kansas was in a mining area, as was the original Potosí in Bolivia, as well as Potosi in Missouri. Missouri and Kansas must have adopted the name because of this association, although in Kansas it was coal, not silver, that was being mined. The name

[14] *KHC*, XII, 481; Baughman, *Kansas Post Offices*, 74.

[15] Taylor, *Names and their Histories*, 231; Volney Paul Mooney, *History of Butler County, Kansas*, 62.

[16] Gwendolin B. Cobb, "Potosi, A Mining Frontier," in *Greater America* (ed. by Adele Ogden and Engel Sluiter), 40; *Visit Bolivia*, pamphlet No. 16 in *Travel in America, issued by Pan American Union*, 21.

must have come to Kansas by word of mouth since it was spelled Petosi when first used. The town was incorporated twice and ended with the correct spelling of Potosi. It replaced a post office named Hillsborough, which even had a remote association with the Potosí in South America called "the Hill." Pleasanton nearby took over the post office, and Potosi remained only as a township name.[17]

The Far West was in the limelight after the opening of Oregon, the winning of the war with Mexico, and the gold rush to California. Like a tidal wave, the adventurers and speculators were swept to the West. Many forty-niners who could not afford the long sea voyage to California crossed Kansas while going overland to the gold fields. Many returned from the Far West, and after 1854 found Kansas open to settlement and attractive enough to encourage many to stay. Kansas caught them on the rebound. Governor Charles Robinson was one of them. New names from the Far West took on a special interest as these adventurers spun their exciting tales about California, Oregon, and Alaska. It might be Lodi or Coloma in California, Walla Walla in Washington, or Sitka in Alaska whose romantic aura aroused a popular interest in Kansas.

Alaska received a lot of publicity, much of it unfavorable, after Seward's purchase. It was ridiculed as "Seward's Folly," "Johnson's Polar Bear Garden," and "Seward's Icebox." It also attracted adventurers who returned with mixed emotions. One of these adventurers was R. B. Pratt, who, it was said, "came from Alaska with money . . . to build a city." He settled in Clark County, Kansas, where he started a store which was made the post office in 1886 and given the name of Sitka. According to local tradition, the town was founded on "a very cold day," and a man who came from Alaska said that it was as cold as his home town of Sitka. So the founders named their town Sitka.[18]

Sitka is an Indian name, but its meaning "seems to have been lost," said Stewart. According to Swanton and Hodge, it was the name

[17] Ramsay, *Missouri Place Names*, 28; "Extinct Geographical Locations," *KHC*, XII, 485; Baughman, *Kansas Post Offices*, 104.

[18] *Clark County Clipper*, June 22 and Nov. 2, 1939; Wayne E. Corley, "County and Community Names in Kansas" (mimeograph copy, 1962), 68.

of a Tlingit community on the island of Baranof or of the people who lived "on Shi."[19] Perhaps it is best to think of it by its modern nickname, the "Paris of the Pacific." But it was no Paris in Kansas where its business rose and fell with the vagaries of the cattle trade. Its chief hotel, the Sitka House, was occasionally deserted and became the source for chilling ghost stories.

Wallawalla is the name of an Indian tribe living on the Walla Walla River where there was once a Walla Walla Fort in what is now Walla Walla County, Washington. It is said to be an Indian descriptive name meaning "little river." The name was first brought to the attention of the Americans by the Lewis and Clark expedition. Sergeant John Ordway spelled the name Wal-a-wal-a. Sergeant Patrick Gass gave it a terpsichorean touch by spelling it Wal-a-Waltz. Americans have preserved the phonetic pronunciation from the French of Duflot de Mofras who spelled it *Oualla Oualla*.[20]

The Montague family, early residents in the Junction City area, had once visited Walla Walla in Washington Territory. They talked much about Walla Walla and loved the sound of its name. When they looked for a name for their Kansas community, Walla Walla was the answer. Those who objected to the repetition say that the second part is only an echo. The repetition in the name is not displeasing, and it need not be abbreviated. In a playful approach to the name, it has been suggested that Walla Walla may be used in a memory test for people with a memory so short that they cannot remember what comes after "Walla." In pioneer days this may not have been a problem since most writers combined the name into one word as Wallawalla. In Kansas, however, it was Walla Walla, the name of a town that soon disappeared. Only the schoolhouse has retained the name.[21]

Similar to Walla Walla was Wallowa and Wallula, well-known names in Washington and Oregon. These names evidently have the same source, and Swanton's reference to Walula was simply,

[19] Stewart, *Names on the Land*, 396; Hodge, *Handbook of American Indians*, II, 582.

[20] Hodge, *Handbook of American Indians*, II, 900; Thwaites, *Early Western Travels*, cf. index; *The Journals of Lewis and Ordway*, 347–50.

[21] *Junction City Union*, March 9, 1935; *KHC*, IV, 582.

"see Wallawalla." In Kansas there was once a Walula in Crawford County, and Wyandotte County had a place named Wallula which served intermittently as a post office from 1889 until 1942. Wallula is still there in the northwestern corner of the county.[22]

Strange Indian names in California became familiar names after the forty-niners and their followers found gold to arouse the interest of easterners. Among the California Indian names in Kansas were Coloma, Inyo, Mono, and Modoc. Coloma was a post office in northern Woodson County for thirty-seven years. In California it had been named for a Maidu Indian village in the vicinity of Sutter's Mill where the first great gold discovery was made. It may have been the name of a tribal band called *Kulomum* or *Koloma.* On an old print of the California town it was referred to as Calluma Valley, with the explanation that "Calluma was the Indian word for 'Beautiful Vale.' "[23]

In Kansas, Mono was once a place in Kingman County, but not a post office, and there was an Inyo in Harper County. Mono could have a Spanish source, but as the name of Mono Lake, east of the Sierra Nevada, it is possibly an abbreviation of the Indian word *Monache*, which referred to a division of the Shoshonean linguistic family. In California, Inyo is the name of a mountain range east of Owens Lake. When miners asked Chief George about the name, they were told that *Inyo* meant "dwelling place of the great spirit." Inyo County, with its dreadful Death Valley, was, no doubt, well known in Kansas.[24]

Modoc, named for the Modoc Indians of northern California and southern Oregon, became a familiar name during the Modoc War of the 1870's. John P. St. John, later governor of Kansas, had fought the Modocs and was twice wounded. Kansas became fully aware of the Modoc name when the Modocs were brought through Kansas on their way to a reservation in the Indian Territory. A few Modocs were held prisoners at Fort Leavenworth, and others were for a short time at Baxter Springs. While they were

[22] Seymour, *Indian Agents of the Old Frontier*, 152; *Kansas City Times*, Dec. 3, 1953.

[23] Gudde, *California Place Names*, 67; *Motorland*, LXXXVII, 5.

[24] Gudde, *California Place Names*, 143 and 196.

in Kansas, Chief "Scarfaced Charlie" had a cordial visit with Governor St. John, even though the Governor still carried in his body a Modoc arrow point.[25]

The Modoc name became so popular in Kansas that a male chorus in Topeka in 1875 called itself the Modoc Club.[26] There was a post office named Modoc in Jewell County in 1875, the year after the Modoc War. There is still a town named Modoc in Scott County, replacing the name of Plummer. The name came from *Klamath Módokni*, "southern people," or from *Moatokni*, "southerner," referring to a southern band of the Klamath.[27]

Another name that could have come from California was Tehama, the name of a county in California and once a post-office name in Cherokee County, Kansas. In Gudde's *California Place Names*, it is listed as the name of an Indian village or tribe. Its meaning was said to be "plains" or "prairies" or possibly "lowlands." It is a coincidence that *tehama* is also an Arabic word, meaning "hot lowlands." But the Tehama in Kansas most likely came from California.

In Doniphan County a town was planned in 1856 and given the name of Arizona. It remained a paper town. Before C. N. James named the town of Augusta for his Wisconsin wife, there had been an ephemeral town there with the modified Arizona name of Arizonia, also written Orizonia. In the northeastern corner of Breckenridge (Lyon) County there was an Arizona on a Kansas map for 1859. The name was originally given to a "place with small springs" or of "little waters" near Tucson which was in the Papago language *Arizonac*. It does not mean, as some say, an "arid land." The name was first used as *El Rancho de Arizona*, and then, referring to the mines near Tucson, as *Real de Arizona*.[28]

[25] I. O. Pickering, "The Administration of John P. St. John," *KHC*, IX, 380; Barnes, *KHQ*, XXVI, 289.

[26] *Topeka State Journal*, Oct. 30, 1935; Shawnee County Historical Society *Bulletin* (Dec., 1950), 59.

[27] Hodge, *Handbook of American Indians*, I, 918; Gudde, *California Place Names*, 195 and 316.

[28] Gray, *Doniphan County History*, II, 24; Andreas and Cutler, *History of Kansas*, 1439; Roscoe G. Willson, "The Origin of Arizona's Name," *Arizona Highways*, XXXI, 2–3.

There was once a Taos in Marshall County. It served as a post office for two years, 1883 to 1885, but the site is now marked only by the Salem Church. The Spaniards made the name Taos out of *Towih*, the Tewa name for these Pueblo Indians. It may have meant "of the people." The Taos, New Mexico, site had another name, *Yahlahaimubahutulbo*, which was said to mean "red-willow place." This name would never have reached Kansas without being mutilated beyond recognition. The Taos name was publicized by the Santa Fe trade and by men like Kit Carson, who had his home there. It might better have been located on the Santa Fe Trail than in Marshall County where it was near the California Trail.[29]

Yuma was the name of a linguistic group of Indians who lived on the lower Colorado River a short distance above its mouth. The name may have come from their neighbors, the Pimas or Papagos. The Yumas were in the limelight when they closed Captain Anza's land route to California and left California so sparsely populated that the United States was able to conquer the land in time for the gold rush of 1849. It was again in the limelight when the United States made the Gadsden Purchase to provide a railway route to California. Up to that time there was no Yuma in the United States.

The meaning of the name is in doubt although it could have come from a Spanish misunderstanding of a reference to *Yahmayo*, "son of the captain." Gannett said that it meant "sons of the river." It has been a popular place-name used in at least six states. In Kansas it was the name of a place in Cloud County where it served intermittently as a post office three times. It has been listed as one of the extinct towns of Kansas, but it is still a railway station west of Concordia.[30]

Even the name of the New World native race, "Indian," came from Spanish America. That the natives of America were called Indians was an error in the beginning, and it has been confusing ever since. The error was made by Columbus who did not know where

[29] Hodge, *Handbook of American Indians*, II, 688; Forter, *History of Marshall County*, 208.

[30] Hodge, *Handbook of American Indians*, II, 1010; Swanton, *The Indian Tribes of North America*, 369; Gannett, *American Names*, 333; *KHC*, XII, 490.

he was when he came to the New World, nor did he know where he had been when he returned. The country was called the Indies. The Indians of America might have been distinguished from the Indians of India if the descriptive name of Amerind for those in the New World had been accepted. The use of the generic term Indian has, however, been popular for place-names all over the United States.

Creeks, hills, rivers, or valleys where pioneers encountered Indians were named for the incidents. There were at least fourteen Indian Creeks in Kansas. In Bourbon County there is an old Indian camp near the mouth of Indian Creek which flows into the Osage River.[31] Two Indian Creeks became the names of post offices: the first one was in Linn County, and a later one was in Elk County. Linn County once had an Indian City near Prescott. Anderson County still has an Indian Creek Township, and in 1861 it had an Indian Valley post office.[32] Indian Guide Hill, east of Peabody, was on one of the buffalo trails. Indian Mound, west of Dodge City, is on the north side of the Arkansas River near Chouteau's Island. It was while camping at the foot of this mound that Major Riley, escorting a Santa Fe caravan, was attacked by Indians. Indian Mound became a landmark on the Santa Fe Trail.[33] Indian Hill in Dickenson County marks the site of an Indian battle. The name is now used for Indian Hill Cemetery of Chapman.[34] Popular though the name of Indian has been, post offices with the name of Indian have disappeared more completely than has the vanishing Indian.

Whenever Kansas named a town for a state, it was generally an indication of the source of its settlers. This could have been the origin of Indiana Township in Lincoln County. Indiana City in Osage County was promoted, strangely enough, in Kentucky. The Kentuckians hauled frames in from Louisville for the four houses which constituted the "town" of Indiana City. It was not a "City"

[31] Cory, *Place Names in Bourbon County*, 7.

[32] Baughman, *Kansas Post Offices*, 62; "Extinct Geographical Locations," *KHC*, XII, 480.

[33] Whittemore, *Historic Kansas*, 33; *Lakin Independent*, Aug. 9, 1935.

[34] *Abilene Reflector-Chronicle*, April 20, 1935.

nor did it become a town except in the liberal interpretation of imaginative promoters.[35]

The name of Indiana was possibly started by the Indiana Company, real-estate promoters from Pennsylvania. Stewart also mentioned the use of the name Indiana in a Spanish study called *La Monarquia Indiana*. The addition of a vowel at the end of Indian is not unlike the change of the word "nonchalant" to make it Nonchalanta for the name of a town in Ness County. Indianapolis was twice a post office in what was Lykens County, now Miami, in Kansas. It was a coined name which the Hoosiers had made for the name of their state capital.[36]

Indianola is an attractive name which had already been used in Illinois, Iowa, and Texas before it was adopted as a place-name in Kansas. Both Iowa and Kansas got the name from Indianola in Texas. In Iowa, town surveyors were eating a lunch which had been wrapped in a newspaper when one of them saw a reference to a town in Texas by the name of Indianola. He liked the name, and he then and there named the Iowa town Indianola.[37] Kansas also took the name from Texas but without the Iowa story. In 1854 the Kansas town was founded on Soldier Creek with the name of Loring, but it was generally called Buzzard's Town. Then the name was changed to Indianola by Colonel Thomas Fauntleroy who had been stationed in Indianola, Texas.[38] Being on the military road, Indianola was for a time a more active town than Topeka, but when it was bypassed by the railroad, the town moved to Topeka.

The name of Indianola was later revived for a town in Butler County where it replaced the name of Smithfield on Indianola Creek. There it lasted until 1902 as a post office, which had been its chief reason for existence.[39] In Butler County the Kansas turnpike still has a sign with directions to the Indianola Road.

[35] Andreas and Cutler, *History of Kansas*, 1531; *Peoples Herald*, April 29, 1948.
[36] Stewart, *Names on the Land*, 191 and 233.
[37] Federal Writers' Project, *Iowa, A Guide*, 390; *KHC*, XII, 429; Root, "First Day's Battle at Hickory Point," *KHQ*, I, 34n.
[38] Howes, Shawnee County Historical Society *Bulletin*, I, 29.
[39] Andreas and Cutler, *History of Kansas*, 1430.

Indianola is a combination name with a pleasing lilt. It has been suggested that "ola" at the end of the name is a diminutive and that the name could then mean "little Indian town." Another interpretation is given for Indianola in Oklahoma where it has been assumed that "ola" has a Choctaw origin. In Choctaw *olah* meant "this side of." The Choctaw origin is logical, but in Choctaw or Seminole, *ola* could also mean a "waterfall."[40] Indianola is a coined name, euphonious but not widely used.

Travelers and adventurers who explored the Far West and the romantic Spanish lands have cherished names which they liked or which brought back memories of adventure. These transplanted names have added color and variety to the place-names of Kansas. Sitka in Kansas may have nothing in common with Sitka in Alaska, except for its association with one man's experience. Some of the names were in the limelight during exciting historical events, especially wars. The Modoc name is a good example. Soldiers have been active name-givers, some for battles and others for reminders of home. Armies distribute names, for example, Omaha Beach in France was given the name of a Siouan tribe.

[40] Shirk, *Oklahoma Place Names*, 109; McKenney and Hall, *The Indian Tribes of North America*, II, 363.

XXVI

Literary and Legendary

OUT OF SONG AND STORY, poetry and prose, came Indian names which have been preserved as place-names because of their popular appeal. Such are the names of Juniata, Wauneta, and Ramona. Perhaps the best known of all the Indian names from American literature is Hiawatha from Longfellow's epic poem, and from the "Song of Hiawatha" came other names with a popular appeal for American place-names, such as Minnehaha, Nokomis, and Wenonah.

Juniata in Kansas was named for the Blue Juniata in Pennsylvania, but it could have become familiar from the song named "The Blue Juniata" which Sigmund Spaeth called an "enormously popular ditty." The lyric contains these words:

Wild roved the Indian girl, bright Alfarata,
Where sweeps the waters of the Blue Juniata.[1]

After the name of Juniata was replaced by other names in the Manhattan area of Kansas, it was revived as the name of a post office between Alamota and Dighton in Lane County. By 1886, Juniata had lost its status as a post office. Then the name was revived for a railway station on the Santa Fe line between Salina and Lincoln Center. Juanita has been used as a place-name for five locations in Pennsylvania, but Kansas was the first to make it a place-name outside the Keystone State.

Americans have spelled Juniata as if it were "Junietta" or even

[1] *A History of Popular Music in America*, 101; Kenneth W. Porter, "Holding Down a Kansas Claim," *KHQ*, XXII, 226.

"Juanita." What can be done with a relatively simple name like Juanita is illustrated by what happened to the name in Oklahoma. According to Charles N. Gould: "The settlers in Southwestern Pottawatomie County wished to name their post office Juanita after the old home town, but the man who sent the application to Washington could not spell Juanita. The nearest he could come to it was Wanette, and so the name is spelled today."[2] Another illustration of the confusion caused by the similarity of Juniata, Juanita, and Wauneta may be seen in the use of these names in Nebraska. When settlers in Chase County, Nebraska, chose the name of Juanita from the popular song of that name, they were informed that this name was too much like Juniata which was already the name of a Nebraska post office. The problem was solved by changing the spelling of Juanita to Wauneta. This was a solution in writing which could satisfy the Post Office Department, but it was no solution in speech since the two names were pronounced alike.[3]

In Chautauqua County, Kansas, there is a station on the Missouri Pacific Railroad by the name of Wauneta. It was named for an Indian girl. Mrs. Peter Calvert, the wife of the postmaster and village blacksmith, had been brought up by the friendly family of an Indian chief whose daughter was named Wauneta. Mrs. Calvert admired the Indian girl and suggested that the local post office change its name from Fulda to Wauneta, and in 1883 this was done.[4]

Henry Gannett gave the definition of Wauneta as "winter camp." This interpretation has been questioned and also rejected. Waneta, with a slight variation in spelling, was also the name of a Yankton Sioux chief. The source of this name was said to be *Wahnaataa* or *Wahnahton*, meaning the "Charger."[5] Major Long was impressed when he met Waneta. "We have never seen a nobler face," he said, "or a more impressive character, than that of Waneta, the Dacotah chief."

[2] *Oklahoma Place Names*, 87.

[3] Fitzpatrick, *Nebraska Place-Names*, 11 and 35.

[4] *Sedan Times-Star*, Aug. 14, 1941; Missouri Pacific, *The Empire that the Missouri Pacific Built*, 150.

[5] Hodge, *Handbook of American Indians*, II, 910; Gilmore, Nebraska State Historical Society *Publications*, XIX, 138; Ralph H. Gabriel, *The Lure of the Frontier* (vol. II in *Pageant of America*), 181.

One of the most stirring historical novels of the last half of the nineteenth century was Helen Hunt Jackson's *Ramona.* The author had already presented the tragic case of the destruction of the Indian civilizations in America in a serious and sympathetic study called *A Century of Dishonor.* A wider appeal was made, however, in the romantic story of Ramona. The plight of the heroine was told in a California setting, but its appeal was universal. Aside from its tragedy, the attractive name of Ramona seemed to be enshrined in romance. The novel was published in 1884, and three years later a post office in the northern part of Marion County was given the name of Ramona. It has been suggested that the name came "indirectly" from the novel.[6]

The "Song of Hiawatha" by Longfellow has made Hiawatha one of the great legendary characters in Indian literature. Longfellow's poem is largely fictional and contains legends from both the Iroquois and the Chippewas, with no clear-cut distinctions but with characteristics which have been colored by the poet's fertile imagination. J. B. N. Hewitt wrote of the original Hiawatha, an Iroquoian chief in the sixteenth century: "He was a noted reformer, statesman, legislator, and magician, justly celebrated as one of the founders of the League of the Five Nations."[7] In the forming of this League, Hiawatha worked closely with the Onondagas and the Oneidas, although he was most likely a Mohawk. He was considered to be a man of wisdom and peace.

Lewis Morgan wrote the name Ha-yo-went'ha, and he gave its meaning as "the man who combs," with the interpretation that it was he who combed the snakes from the hair of To-do-da'no, an Onondaga hero. This was a symbol of victory of good over evil. Hewitt's Haion-hwa'tha, not far from Longfellow's spelling, was interpreted to mean "he who makes rivers." Another has suggested that the name meant "a very wise man." Hiawatha was described as the "incarnation of human progress and civilization."[8] This

[6] Corley, "County and Community Names in Kansas" (mimeograph copy, 1962), 60.

[7] Hodge, *Handbook of American Indians,* I, 546.

[8] See "Hiawatha" in the *Encyclopedia Britannica* and in Morgan, *League of the Ho-de-no-sau-nee,* I, 60 and 64.

description would be appropriate either for the organizer of the Five Nations of the Iroquois or for the legendary Chippewa demigod named Manabozho with whom Longfellow's Hiawatha has also been associated.[9]

Longfellow's "Song of Hiawatha" was published in 1855, and fifty thousand copies were sold in less than two years. In 1858, Dr. Edwin H. Grant, who had been the editor of the *St. Joseph Democrat*, gave the name of Hiawatha to a Kansas town in Brown County.[10] The township in which it was located was also named Hiawatha. But Hiawatha is not a popular place-name, and the only one listed in a recent edition of Lippincott's world gazetteer is in Kansas. However, east of the Dinosaur National Monument on the Colorado side of the state border is a place named Hiawatha Camp.

Many other names were popularized by Longfellow, including Minnehaha, the name of the dark-eyed daughter of the Dakota Arrow-maker. Longfellow explained the meaning of the name of this beautiful girl who was loved by Hiawatha.

> *And he named her for the river,*
> *From the waterfall he named her,*
> *Minnehaha, Laughing Water.*

As a place-name, Minnehaha is another of those interesting Indian names which migrated from Minnesota to Kansas. Longfellow did not create the name; he merely made it romantic. Minnehaha had once been the name of the Little Falls near Fort Snelling. "The Indians call them Minnehaha, or 'Laughing Water,' " or, as Mrs. Eastman wrote in her *Dacotah Legends*, "Mine-hah-hah." Hodge even found some support for assuming that Minnehaha could mean "laughing waters," with *mini* for "water" and *haha*, which he made sound as if it were *cha-cha*, meaning "laughter." However, Minnehaha may be better translated as "cascade," "cataract," or "waterfall." As George Stewart has pointed out, the addition of "Falls"

[9] Vogel, *Indian Place Names in Illinois*, 34; Remsburg, *Scrapbook*, I, 188; Hodge, *Handbook of American Indians*, I, 546.

[10] Remsburg, *Scrapbook*, I, 188; *KHC*, VII, 479.

to the name Minnehaha makes it become "water-waterfalls-falls."[11]

The name of Minnehaha came to Kansas, but Longfellow's popular meaning of the name did not save it from abbreviation and deletion. The post office named Minnehaha or Minneha was located on the Little Osage Trail on the Sedgwick-Butler county border east of Wichita. The name appears to have been shortened to Minneha as the name of Sedgwick County post office in 1871. On the Butler County side the Minneha name was replaced by the name of Midland in 1872, only to be restored as the Minneha post office from 1873 to 1876. Then the name of Minneha was changed to Cloud, or, as Blackmar gave it, Cloud City. When a new influence from Andover, Massachusetts, came in, the name was changed to Andover, a name which came originally from England.[12]

In the meantime the name of Minneha remained fixed on a Sedgwick County township, and in the township was a little country schoolhouse called the Minneha School, replaced by a larger one after the population explosion around Beechcraft. The Minneha post-office name disappeared from Sedgwick County for a short time. In 1889 the name of Manchester was replaced by Minneha which served as a post office name until 1900. It is now the name for a whistle-stop station nearer Wichita than the first Minneha on the Frisco Road. There are those who would say that having lost one "ha" from Minnehaha or "Laughing Waters," the name in Kansas is only half as funny as the one in Minnesota.

Nekoma, which is considered a variation of Nekomis, is the name of a station on the Santa Fe Railway in Rush County. It is also a place-name in North Dakota, but in Saskatchewan it is spelled Nokomis. In Illinois there is both a Nekoma and a Nokomis. It is an attractive name, believed to be of Chippewa origin, meaning "grandmother." Vogel accepted this interpretation for both Nokomis and Nekoma in Illinois, since he had "not found a better explanation."[13] The origin of this name is also Longfellow's "Hiawatha." Nokomis was the mother of Wenonah and the grand-

[11] Hodge, *Handbook of American Indians*, I, 869; Stewart, *Names on the Land*, 291.

[12] Cf. Baughman, *Kansas Post Offices*, 4 and 64–65; Blackmar, *Kansas*, I, 77.

[13] *Indian Place Names in Illinois*, 87.

mother of Hiawatha. The name may have a Chippewa origin, but it also has the appearance of a Siouan name.

The popular name of Wenonah also came from Longfellow's poem:

> *Fair Nokomis bore a daughter*
> *And she called her name Wenonah,*
> *As the first-born of her daughters.*

In the Santee Sioux dialect, Wenonah is a name which means "the first-born child," if the child is a daughter, or it may mean literally "little woman."[14]

Although Wenonah was the name of the daughter of Nokomis and the mother of Hiawatha, only in Illinois is this form of the spelling followed. But there is also a Wenona in Illinois, which leaves the two names distinguished only by a silent "h." In Oklahoma the name is spelled Wynona. In Minnesota both a town and a county are named Winona, and the town is located on the site of an old Sioux village. Winona, as it is spelled in Minnesota, has been the accepted form for town names in Ontario, Arizona, and Kansas, and for lake names in both Indiana and Arkansas.

Twice the name of Winona has come to Kansas. There was first a Winona, also spelled Wenona, in Doniphan County. It had such great expectations of future growth and security that the legislature granted the town a charter for the establishment of a college. As a post office name, however, it lasted for only two years. But the name was attractive, and in western Kansas a station with the unattractive name of Gopher in Logan County had its name changed to Winona. Gopher must not only have had an unfortunate name, but it must also have been on the "wrong side of the tracks," since Winona was moved across the tracks. Small though it may be, Winona in Winona Township is still a reminder of Longfellow's epic poem.[15]

John C. Frémont, traveling on the Santa Fe Trail in 1842, intro-

[14] Hodge, *Handbook of American Indians*, II, 932 and 963; Leland, *Names*, I, 272.

[15] Gray, *Doniphan County History*, II, 23; *Logan County News*, July 1, 1937; *Winona Leader*, Jan. 19, 1961.

duced an elusive name when he wrote that his company had camped "on a small creek called by the Indians, Mishmagwi."[16] The resemblance between Mishmagwi and Mish-mokwa, the name of the big bear in Longfellow's poem, indicates that the two names may have had the same source. If so, the name must have been known before it was used by Longfellow. In the Osage dialect, the grizzly bear is called *mi'tsu*. The northern Sioux, according to Riggs's dictionary, called the grizzly *Ma-to-ho-ta*. Therefore, Frémont's Mishmagwi and Longfellow's Mish-mokwa appear to have the same source—the bear.

Other Indian names from "Hiawatha" became familiar to the reading public, and some of them, such as Wyoming Valley and Wabaunsee, became associated with Kansas. The "Valley of Wyoming" of Longfellow was the same Wyoming Valley in Pennsylvania from which Kansas got the names of Wyoming and Wyoming Valley. Wabaunsee, a name which means "dawn," is similar to Wabun, the east wind in the poem. Longfellow associates Wabun with the dawn:

> *Young and beautiful was Wabun;*
> *He it was that brought the morning,*
> *He it was whose silver arrows*
> *Chased the dark o'er hill and valley.*

Shawnee and Muscotah are other Kansas place-names that share a common source with names in "Hiawatha." Longfellow's Shawondasee, like Shawnee, was interpreted to mean "south" or "southerner," and Shawon is not unlike Shawanoe which was a common name for the Shawnee Indians. Muskoday has the same source as Muscotah, a place-name in Atchison County. Longfellow merely changed the meaning from prairie to meadow.

Many of the native names stand out boldly on the Kansas map. Modified though most of them have been to fit the ears and tongues of the white people, they still serve as a link and a record of a fading past. The immigrant Indians scarcely had time to become familiar with their homes in Kansas before they became emigrant Indians

[16] *The Exploring Expedition of the Rocky Mountains*, 8.

and moved southward into the Indian Territory of Oklahoma. However, even these Indians, whose residence was only a brief and troubled time on the Kansas prairies, have given color and character to the history of Kansas. Their names have been scattered freely over the land which was once all Indian. Even the names which are no longer on the map have a history, a meaning, and often a charm which stimulate the study of an important period in our civilization.

"Bury my heart at Wounded Knee," wrote Stephen Vincent Benét in his poem "American Names" in which he reflects on the appeal of names:

I have fallen in love with American names,
The sharp names that never get fat,
The snakeskin-titles of mining-claims,
The plumed war-bonnet of Medicine Hat,
Tucson and Deadwood and Lost Mule Flat. . . .

Bibliography

ABBREVIATIONS

BAE, Bureau of American Ethnology
KHC, Kansas State Historical Society
Transactions and Collections
KHQ, *Kansas Historical Quarterly*
KSHL, Kansas State Historical Society Library
KSHS, Kansas State Historical Society
WSU, Wichita State University

I. MANUSCRIPTS

Boyer, John A. Letter to author, Scott City, Kans., Aug. 25, 1961.

Corley, Wayne E. "County and Community Names in Kansas" (mimeographed), Denver, 1962.

Ingleman, Anna A. "Indian Place Names in Kansas," M.A. thesis, University of Kansas, Lawrence, 1929.

Lawson, Oliver S. "History of Scott County, Kansas," M.A. thesis, Colorado State College, Fort Collins, 1936. Also at KSHL, Topeka.

Michener, L. L. Letter to *Wichita Beacon*, June 9, 1929, Kansas Collection, WSU Library.

"Names," MS, KSHS Archives, Topeka.

Neeland, Mary A. "History of Elk County, Kansas," M.A. thesis, Wichita State University, Wichita, 1933.

Sorensen, Conner. "Ghost Towns in Greeley County," term paper, University of Kansas, Lawrence, 1966.

Wallace, Bernice Boyd. "History of Paola, Kansas, 1855 to 1955" (mimeographed), KSHL, Topeka, n.d.

II. GOVERNMENT PUBLICATIONS

Donaldson, Thomas. "The George Catlin Indian Gallery," *Annual Report* of the Board of Regents of the Smithsonian Institution to July 1885. Washington, 1886.

Dorsey, James O. "A Study of Siouan Cults," *BAE Eleventh Annual Report* (1889–90). Washington, 1894.

———. "Siouan Sociology," *BAE Fifteenth Annual Report* (1893–94). Washington, 1897.

Fletcher, Alice C., and Francis La Flesche. "The Omaha Tribe," *BAE Twenty-seventh Annual Report* (1905–1906). Washington, 1911.

Gannett, Henry. *A Gazetteer of Kansas*, United States Geological Survey *Bulletin 154*. Washington, 1898.

Hodge, Frederick W., ed. *Handbook of American Indians North of Mexico*, BAE *Bulletin 30*. 2 vols. Washington, 1907.

La Flesche, Francis. *A Dictionary of the Osage Language*, BAE *Bulletin 109*. Washington, 1932.

Laws of the State of Kansas, 1875. Topeka, 1875.

McCoy, Isaac. "Shawnee Baptist Mission," *Annual Register of Indian Affairs within the Indian Territory*. Washington, 1837.

———, to Secretary of War. 22 Cong., 1 sess., *Exec. Doc. 172*.

McGee, W. J. "The Siouan Indians," *BAE Fifteenth Annual Report* (1893–94). Washington, 1897.

Mooney, James. "Calendar History of the Kiowa Indians," *BAE Seventeenth Annual Report* (1895–96), Part I. Washington, 1898.

———. "Myths of the Cherokee," *BAE Nineteenth Annual Report* (1897–98), Part I. Washington, 1900.

———. *The Siouan Tribes of the East*, BAE *Bulletin 22*. Washington, 1894.

Powell, J. W. "Indian Linguistic Families of America North of Mexico," *BAE Seventh Annual Report* (1885–86). Washington, 1911.

Riggs, Stephen R. *A Dakota-English Dictionary*, 52 Cong., 1 sess., *House Misc. Doc.* Washington, 1892.

Schoolcraft, Henry R. *Archives of Aboriginal Knowledge*. 6 vols. Washington, 1860.

Statutes of Kansas Territory, 1855. Topeka, 1856.

Swanton, John R. *The Indian Tribes of North America*, BAE *Bulletin 145*. Washington, 1952.

Ten Kate, Herman F. C. "The Indian of Literature," *Annual Report* of the Board of Regents of the Smithsonian Institution (1921). Washington, 1922.

United States Board of Geographic Names *Sixth Report*. Washington, 1933.

Wedel, Waldo R. *An Introduction to Pawnee Archaeology*, BAE *Bulletin 112*. Washington, 1936.

III. NEWSPAPERS

Abilene Reflector-Chronicle.
Ashland Clipper.
Atchison Daily Globe.
Burlington Daily Republican.
Clark County Clipper.
Coffeyville Daily Journal.
Emporia Daily News.
Emporia Democratic News.
Emporia Times.
Garden City Evening Telegraph.
Gridley Light.
Gypsum Advocate.
Hill City Times.
Hoisington Dispatch.
Horton Headlight.
Humboldt Union.
Junction City Union.
Kansas City Star.
Kansas City Times.
Kansas Cosmos. Council Grove, Kansas.
Kingman Journal.
Lakin Independent.
Larned Chronoscope.
Leavenworth Post.
Leavenworth Times.
Little River Monitor.
Logan County News.
Luray Herald.
Manhattan Tribune News.
Marion Record-Review.
Milwaukee Daily Sentinel.
Natoma Independent.
Oskaloosa Independent.
Oswego Democrat.
Oswego Independent.
Peoples Herald. Lynden, Kansas.
Pratt Daily Tribune.
Protection Post.
Rooks County Record.
Rush County News.
Sabetha Herald.
St. Mary's Star.
St. Paul Journal.
Scott City News Chronicle.
Sedan Times-Star.
Seneca Courier-Tribune.
South Haven New Era.
South Kansas Tribune. Independence, Kansas.
Sumner County Press. Wellington, Kansas.
Sunflower. University of Wichita.
Tescott News.
Topeka Capital.
Topeka Daily Commonwealth.
Topeka State Journal.
Wamego Reporter.
Western Advocate. Mankato, Kansas.

Wichita Beacon.
Wichita Eagle.
Wichita Evening Eagle.
Wilson County Citizen.
Winona Leader.

IV. DIARIES, MEMOIRS, AND ORIGINAL WRITINGS

Bell, Captain John R. *The Journal of Captain John R. Bell.* Ed. by Harlin M. Fuller. Vol. VI in LeRoy R. Hafen, *Far West and the Rockies, q.v.*

Benét, Stephen Vincent. *Ballads and Poems, 1915–1930.* Garden City, 1931.

Bolton, Herbert E. *Athanase de Mézières and the Louisiana-Texas Frontier, 1768–1780.* 2 vols. Cleveland, 1914.

———, ed. *Spanish Explorations in the Southwest.* New York, 1916.

Boone, Captain Nathan. "Captain Nathan Boone's Journal" (ed. by W. Julian Fessler), *Chronicles of Oklahoma,* VII, 58–105.

Bradbury, John. *Travels in the Interior of America.* Vol. V in R. G. Thwaites, *Early Western Travels, q.v.*

Chase, Charles Monroe. "An Editor Looks at Early-Day Kansas" (ed. by Lela Barnes), *KHQ,* XXVI, 267–301.

Darnell, William. "Reminiscences of William Darnell" (ed. by George A. Root), *KHC,* XVII, 479–513.

De Smet, Pierre Jean. *Letters and Sketches.* Vol. XXVII in R. G. Thwaites, *Early Western Travels, q.v.*

Emerson, Ralph Waldo. *Complete Works.* 12 vols. New York, 1923–29.

Everett, John, and Sarah Everett. "Letters of John and Sarah Everett," *KHQ,* VIII, 3–34.

Farnham, Thomas J. *Travels in the Great Western Prairies.* Vols. XXVIII–XXIX in R. G. Thwaites, *Early Western Travels, q.v.*

Frémont, J. C. *The Exploring Expedition of the Rocky Mountains of Brevet Colonel, J. C. Frémont.* Auburn, 1854.

Gregg, Josiah. *Commerce of the Prairies.* Ed. by Max L. Moorhead. Norman, 1954.

Hafen, LeRoy R., ed. *Pike's Peak Gold Rush Guidebooks of 1859.* Vol. IX in *Southwest Historical Series.* Glendale, 1941.

Hammond, George P., and Agapito Rey, eds. *Oñate, Colonizer of New Mexico.* Vol. IV in *Coronado Cuarto Centennial Publications.* Albuquerque, 1953.

———, eds. *Narrative of the Coronado Expedition, 1540–1542.* 2 vols. Albuquerque, 1940.

Hildt, George H. "The Diary of George H. Hildt" (ed. by Martha B. Caldwell), *KHQ*, X, 260–98.

Holliday, Cyrus Kurtz. "Letters of Cyrus Kurtz Holliday" (ed. by Lela Barnes), *KHQ*, VI, 241–94.

Irving, Washington. *Works of Washington Irving.* 15 vols. New York, 1897.

James, Edwin. *Account of an Expedition . . . from Notes of S. H. Long.* Vols. XIV–XVII in R. G. Thwaites, *Early Western Travels, q.v.*

Kenton, Edna, ed. *Black Gowns and Redskins: Adventures and Travels of the Early Jesuit Missionaries in North America.* 2 vols. New York, 1927.

Le Page du Pratz, Antoine Simon. *History of Louisiana.* London, 1774.

Lewis, Meriwether, and John Ordway. *The Journals of Captain Meriwether Lewis and Sergeant John Ordway.* Ed. by Milo M. Quaife. Madison, 1965.

Longfellow, Henry W. *The Poetical Works of Henry Wadsworth Longfellow.* 3 vols. Boston, 1881.

———. *The Song of Hiawatha.* New York, 1901.

Lowery, Woodbury, ed. *The Spanish Settlements within the Present Limits of the United States, 1513–1561.* New York, 1959.

McCoy, Isaac. "Journal of Isaac McCoy for the Exploring Expedition of 1830" (ed. by Lela Barnes), *KHQ*, V, 339–77.

———. "Journal of Isaac McCoy for the Exploring Expedition of 1828" (ed. by Lela Barnes), *KHQ*, V, 227–77.

Mason, Philip P., ed. *Schoolcraft's Expedition to Lake Itasca.* East Lansing, 1958.

Morgan, Lewis Henry. *Lewis Henry Morgan: The Indian Journals, 1859–62.* Ed. by Leslie A. White. Ann Arbor, 1959.

Pichardo, José Antonio. *Pichardo's Treatise on the Limits of Louisiana and Texas.* Ed. by Charles W. Hackett. 4 vols. Austin, 1931–46.

Pike, Zebulon Montgomery. *The Expedition of Zebulon Montgomery Pike.* Ed. by Elliot Coues. 3 vols. New York, 1895.

Platt, Jeremiah E. "Circuit-Riding in Southwest Kansas in 1885 and 1886" (ed. by Louise Barry), *KHQ*, XII, 378–89.

Richardson, Albert D. "Letters on the Pike's Peak Gold Region" (ed. by Louise Barry), *KHQ*, XII, 14–57.

Sibley, George Champlin. "Extracts from the Diary of Major Sibley," *Chronicles of Oklahoma*, V, 196–218.

———. *The Road to Santa Fe: The Journal and Diaries of George Champlin Sibley*. Ed. by Kate L. Gregg. Albuquerque, 1952.

Smith, Captain John. *Travels and Works of Captain John Smith*. Ed. by Edwards Arber. 2 vols. Edinburgh, 1910.

Thwaites, Reuben Gold, ed. *Early Western Travels, 1748–1846*. 32 vols. Cleveland, 1904–1907.

———, ed. *Jesuit Relations and Allied Documents*. 73 vols. New York, 1959.

Tixier, Victor. *Tixier's Travels on the Osage Prairies*. Ed. by John F. McDermott. Norman, 1940.

Van Gundy, John C. *Reminiscences of Frontier Life on the Upper Neosho in 1855 and 1856*. Topeka, 1925.

Wolf, Captain Lambert Bowman. "Extracts from the Diary of Captain Lambert Bowman Wolf" (ed. by George A. Root), *KHQ*, I, 195–210.

Wright, R. M. "Personal Reminiscences of Frontier Life in Southwest Kansas," *KHC*, VII, 47–83.

V. PERIODICALS AND PUBLICATIONS OF LEARNED SOCIETIES

Abel, Anne Eloise. "Indian Reservations in Kansas and the Extinguishment of their Title," *KHC*, VIII, 72–109.

Adams, F. G. "Reminiscences of Frederick Chouteau," *KHC*, VIII, 423–34.

Anthony, W. P. "Republican City, Clay County," *KHC*, XII, 440–41.

Atlantic Monthly, "Contributor's Club," XLVII, 720–33.

Barnes, Lela. "Notes on Imprints from Highland," *KHQ*, VIII, 140–42.

Barry, Louise. "The Emigrant Aid Company Parties of 1854," *KHQ*, XII, 115–55.

———, ed. "Kansas Before 1854," *KHQ*, XXVIII, 25–59, 167–204, 317–69, 497–514; XXIX, 41–81, 143–89, 324–59, 429–86; XXX, 62–91, 209–44, 339–412, 492–559; XXXI, 138–99, 256–339; XXXII, 33–112, 210–82, 426–503; XXXIII, 13–64, 172–213, 377–405.

———, ed. "With the First U.S. Cavalry in Indian Country," *KHQ*, XXIV, 399–425.

Baskett, James N. "Prehistoric Kansas: A Study of the Route of Coronado between the Rio Grande and Missouri," *KHC*, XII, 219–52.

Beers, W. George. "The Canadian Mecca," *The Century Magazine*, XXIV, 1–16.

Berryman, Jerome C. "A Circuit Rider's Frontier Experiences," *KHC*, XVI, 177–226.

Betton, Frank H. "The Genesis of a State's Metropolis," *KHC*, VII, 114–20.

Birch, James H. "The Battle of Coon Creek," *KHC*, X, 409–13.

Bisby, J. M. "Pioneering in Wabaunsee County," *KHC*, XI, 594–613.

Blackman, E. E. "Sherman County and the H. U. A.," *KHC*, VIII, 50–62.

Bondi, August. "With John Brown in Kansas," *KHC*, VIII, 275–89.

Boldinger, Wallace S. "The Amateur Plans a City," *KHQ*, XII, 3–13.

Botkin, Theodore. "Among the Sovereign Squats," *KHC*, VII, 418–41.

Brewster, S. W. "The Reverend Paul M. Ponziglione," *KHC*, IX, 19–32.

Brown, George W. "Kansas Indian Wars" (ed. by William A. Connelley), *KHC*, XVII, 134–39.

Caldwell, Martha B., ed. "Records of the Squatter Association of Whitehead District, Doniphan County," *KHQ*, XIII, 16–35.

Campbell, C. W. "W. E. Campbell, Pioneer Kansas Livestockman," *KHQ*, XVI, 245–73.

Campbell, Charles E. "Down Among the Red Men," *KHC*, XVII, 623–91.

Campbell, Hortense B. "Camp Beecher," *KHQ*, III, 172–85.

Campbell, Marjorie W. "Canada's Dynamic Heartland, Ontario," *National Geographic Magazine*, CXXIV, 5–97.

Carey, James C. "Juniata: Gateway to Mid-Kansas," *KHQ*, XXI, 87–94.

Chappell, Phil E. "A History of the Missouri River," *KHC*, IX, 237–94.

Coffin, William H. "Settlement of the Friends in Kansas," *KHC*, VII, 322–61.

Cole, Fannie E. "Pioneer Life in Kansas," *KHC*, XII, 353–58.

Cone, William W. "On the Wakarusa," Shawnee County Historical Society *Bulletin 31* (Dec., 1958), 25–30.

Connelley, William E. "Characters and Incidents of the Plains," *KHC*, X, 111–19.

———. "The East Boundary Lines of Kansas," *KHC*, XI, 75–80.

———. "First Provisional Constitution of Kansas," *KHC*, VI, 97–113.

———. "Kansas City, Kansas: Its Place in the History of the State," *KHC*, XV, 181–91.

———. "Life and Adventures of George E. Brown," *KHC*, XVII, 98–134.
———. "Notes on the Early Indian Occupancy of the Great Plains," *KHC*, XIV, 438–70.
———. "Origin of the Name Topeka," *KHC*, XVII, 589–93.
———. "The Prairie Band of the Pottawatomie," *KHC*, XIV, 488–570.
———, ed. *The Provisional Government of Nebraska Territory*, Special Publication of the Nebraska Historical Society *Proceedings*, 2nd series, Vol. III, Lincoln, 1899.
———. "Religious Conceptions of the Modern Hurons," *KHC*, XV, 92–102.
Cory, Charles E. "Slavery in Kansas," *KHC*, VII, 229–42.
Cruise, John D. "Early Days on the Union Pacific," *KHC*, XI, 529–49.
Dale, Edward E. "Letters of the Two Boudinots," *Chronicles of Oklahoma*, VI, 328–47.
Dale, Kittie. "Story of Chetolah," *Salina Journal*, April 12, 1964.
Dallas, E. J. "Early-Day Post-Offices in Kansas," *KHC*, VII, 441–46.
Dick, Everett. "The Long Drive," *KHC*, XVII, 27–97.
Diller, Aubrey. "Origin of the Names of the Tributaries of the Kansas River," *KHQ*, XXI, 401–406.
Dolbee, Cora. "First Book on Kansas," *KHQ*, II, 139–89.
———. "The Fourth of July in Early Kansas," *KHQ*, VIII, 115–39.
———. "The Third Book on Kansas," *KHQ*, VIII, 238–78.
Doran, Thomas F. "Kansas Sixty Years Ago," *KHC*, XV, 482–501.
Douglas, Richard L. "A History of Manufactures in the Kansas District," *KHC*, XI, 81–215.
Dunbar, John B. "The White Man's Foot in Kansas," *KHC*, X, 54–98.
———. "The Pawnee Indians," *Magazine of American History*, IV, 241–81.
Einsel, Mary. "Some Notes on the Comanche Cattle Pool," *KHQ*, XXVI, 59–66.
Emmet, D. B. "Sedgwick County," in John P. Edwards, *Historical Atlas of Sedgwick County*, *q.v.*
Errett, Russell. "Indian Geographical Names," *Magazine of Western History*, II, 51–59, 238–46.
Ferris, Ida M. "Sauks and Foxes in Franklin and Osage Counties, Kansas," *KHC*, XI, 335–95.
Field, Thomas P. "The Indian Place-Names of Kentucky," *Names*, VII, 154–66.

Folmer, Henri. "Étienne Véniard de Bourgmont in the Missouri Country," *Missouri Historical Review*, XXXVI, 279–98.

———. "Mallet Expedition of 1739 through Nebraska, Kansas, and Colorado to Santa Fe," *The Colorado Magazine*, XVI, 161–73.

Foreman, Grant. "Historical Background of the Kiowa-Comanche Reservation," *Chronicles of Oklahoma*, XIX, 129–40.

Fowke, Gerard. "Some Notes on the Aboriginal Inhabitants of Missouri," Missouri Historical Society *Collections*, IV, 82–103.

Gaeddert, G. Raymond. "The First Newspapers in Kansas," *KHQ*, X, 380–411.

Garfield, Marvin H. "Defense of the Kansas Frontier," *KHQ*, I, 140–52.

———. "The Military Post as a Factor in the Frontier Defense of Kansas," *KHQ*, I, 50–62.

Giddens, Paul H. "Eastern Kansas in 1869–70," *KHQ*, IX, 371–83.

Gill, Helen G. "The Establishment of Counties in Kansas," *KHC*, VIII, 449–72.

Gilmore, Melvin R. "Some Indian Place Names in Nebraska," Nebraska Historical Society *Publications*, XIX, 130–39.

Godsey, Flora R. "The Early Settlement and Raid on the 'Upper Neosho,'" *KHC*, XVI, 451–63.

Goodnow, Isaac T. "Personal Reminiscences and Kansas Emigration, 1855," *KHC*, IV, 244–53.

Greene, Albert R. "The Kansas River–Its Navigation," *KHC*, IX, 317–58.

Grinnell, George Bird. "Bent's Old Fort and Its Builders," *KHC*, XV, 28–88.

———. "Cheyenne Stream Names," *American Anthropologist* (n.s.), VIII, 15–22.

———. "Some Indian Stream Names," *American Anthropologist* (n.s.), XV, 327–31.

Guthrie, John. "Primeval Heroes, Patriots and Priests," *The Agora*, III, 64–75.

Haas, Mary R. "Comments on the Name 'Wichita,'" *American Anthropologist* (n.s.), XLIV, 164–65.

Harger, Charles M. "Cattle Trails of the Prairies," *Scribner's Magazine*, XI, 732–42.

Harper, Elizabeth A. "The Taovayas Indians in the Frontier Trade and Diplomacy, 1719–1768," *Chronicles of Oklahoma*, XXXI, 268–89.

Haucke, Frank. "The Kaw or Kansa Indians," *KHQ*, XX, 36–60.
Hawley, L. F. "The Chadakoin River," *Names*, III, 32–33.
Hay, Robert. "Kaw and Kansas: A Monograph on the Name of the State," *KHC*, IX, 521–26.
Hickman, Russell. "The Vegetarian and Octagon Settlement Companies," *KHQ*, II, 377–85.
Hoffhaus, Charles E. "Fort de Cavagnial," *KHQ*, XXX, 425–54.
Holliday, Cyrus K. "The Cities of Kansas," *KHC*, III, 396–401.
Howes, Cecil. "General Forsyth at Beecher Island," *Kansas Teacher*, LVII (Sept., 1948), 46–48.
———. "Ghost Towns of Shawnee County," Shawnee County Historical Society *Bulletin*, I, 25–31.
———. "Indian Missions," *Kansas Teacher*, LVIII (March, 1950), 46–48.
———. "Largest Lake in Kansas," *Kansas Teacher*, LVIII (Feb., 1950), 38–40.
———. "Ninety Years for the Santa Fe," *Kansas Teacher*, LVIII (Sept., 1949), 46–48.
———. "What About the Name Topeka?" Shawnee County Historical Society *Bulletin*, I, 104–108.
Hutchinson, William. "Sketches of Kansas Pioneer Experience," *KHC*, VII, 390–410.
Jackson, Sheldon, ed. "English Quakers Tour Kansas in 1858," *KHQ*, XIII, 36–52.
Johnson, C. W. "Survey of the Northern Boundary Line of Kansas," *KHC*, VII, 318–22.
Kansas State Historical Society. "Bypaths of Kansas History: This Name 'Kansas,'" *KHQ*, XX, 450.
———. "Governor Shannon's Administration," *KHC*, V, 234–64.
———. "Origin of City Names," *KHC*, VII, 475–86.
———. "Origin of County Names," *KHC*, VII, 472–74.
Kelly, H. B. "Building the Sedan Courthouse," *KHC*, IX, 89–93.
King, Joseph B. "The Ottawa Indians in Kansas and Oklahoma," *KHC*, XIII, 373–78.
Langsdorf, Edgar. "The First Survey of the Kansas River," *KHQ*, XVIII, 146–58.
———. "A Review of Early Navigation on the Kansas River," *KHQ*, XVIII, 140–45.

Lapham, Amos S. "Looking Backward: Early History of Chanute," *KHC*, XVI, 504–14.
Lawrence, Frederick W. "The Origin of American State Names," *National Geographic Magazine*, XXXVIII, 105–43.
Leland, J. A. C. "Indian Names in Missouri," *Names*, I, 266–73.
Lester, H. N. "Colonization of the Upper Arkansas Valley in Kansas," *KHC*, IV, 262–65.
Lewis, Anna. "La Harpe's First Expedition in Oklahoma, 1718–1719," *Chronicles of Oklahoma*, II, 331–49.
Link, J. T. *The Origin of Place Names in Nebraska*, Nebraska Geological Survey *Bulletin* 7, 1933. Reprinted as Part II of Fitzpatrick's *Nebraska Place-Names*.
Lutz, J. J. "Methodist Missions Among the Indian Tribes in Kansas," *KHC*, IX, 160–235.
McCampbell, C. W. "W. E. Campbell, Pioneer Kansas Livestockman," *KHQ*, XVI, 245–73.
McCoy, John C. "Survey of Kansas Indian Lands," *KHC*, IV, 298–311.
McDermott, John F. "Glossary of French," Washington University *Studies in Language and Literature*, No. 12. St. Louis, 1941.
———, ed. "Isaac McCoy's Second Exploring Trip in 1828," *KHQ*, XIII, 400–62.
McDougal, H. C. "Historical Sketch of Kansas City, Missouri," *KHC*, XI, 581–89.
McMurtrie, Douglas C. "Pioneer Printing in Kansas," *KHQ*, I, 3–16.
———. "The Shawnee Sun," *KHQ*, II, 339–42.
Madden, John. "Along the Trail," *KHC*, VIII, 67–71.
Malin, James C. "The Kinsley Boom of the late Eighties," *KHQ*, IV, 23–49, 164–87.
Maloy, John. "History of Morris County," *Kansas Cosmos*, Council Grove, April 23, 1886.
Martin, George W., "The Boundary Lines of Kansas," *KHC*, XI, 53–74.
———. "Memorial Monuments and Tablets in Kansas," *KHC*, XI, 253–81.
———. "The Territorial and Military Combine at Fort Riley," *KHC*, VII, 361–90.
Mather, Frederick G. "The River of Gen-nis-he-yo," *Magazine of Western History*, III, 101–102.
Mead, Andrew J. "Reminiscences of Kansas," *KHC*, VII, 467–70.

Mead, James R. "Origin of Names of Kansas Streams," Kansas Academy of Science *Transactions*, XVIII, 215–16.
———. "The Little Arkansas," *KHC*, X, 7–14.
———. "The Saline River Valley," *KHC*, IX, 8–19.
———. "The Wichita Indians in Kansas," *KHC*, VIII, 171–77.
Merwin, Ray E. "The Wyandot Indians," *KHC*, IX, 73–88.
Miller, Nyle H. "Surveying the Southern Boundary Line of Kansas," *KHQ*, I, 104–39.
Moffatt, Isaac. "The Kansas Prairie, or Eight Days on the Plains," *KHQ*, VI, 147–74.
Montgomery, Mrs. Frank C. "Fort Wallace and its Relation to the Frontier," *KHC*, XVII, 189–283.
Moore, Ely, Jr. "A Buffalo Hunt with the Miamis," *KHC*, X, 402–409.
———. "The Naming of Osawatomie," *KHC*, XII, 338–46.
———. "The Story of Lecompton," *KHC*, XI, 463–80.
Morehouse, George P. "Along the Kaw Trail," *KHC*, VIII, 206–12.
———. "History of the Kansa or the Kaw Indians," *KHC*, X, 327–68.
Morrison, T. F. "The Osage Treaty of 1865," *KHC*, XVII, 692–708. (Also printed in St. Paul, Kansas, 1925.)
Morrow, Robert. "Emigration to Kansas in 1856," *KHC*, VIII, 302–15.
Motorland (AAA, California), LXXXVII (March–April, 1966), 5.
Myers, Debs. "The Exciting Story of Kansas," *Holiday*, IX, 53–63, 166–68.
Nicholson, William. "A Tour of Indian Agencies," *KHQ*, III, 289–326.
O'Bryant, Arch. "Punning 1910 Speech Suggests Marble Players Named Wichita," *Wichita Eagle*, Nov. 13, 1965.
Patrick, G. E. "The Great Spirit Spring," Kansas Academy of Science *Transactions*, VII, 22–26.
Peck, Robert M. "Recollections of Early Times in Kansas," *KHC*, VIII, 484–507.
Phillips, William. "Kansas History," *KHC*, IV, 351–59.
Pickering, I. O. "The Administration of John P. St. John," *KHC*, IX, 378–94.
Plank, Pryor. "The Iowa, Sac and Fox Indian Mission and its Missionaries," *KHC*, X, 312–25.
Porter, Kenneth W. "Holding Down a Kansas Claim," *KHQ*, XXII, 220–35.
Pound, Louise, ed. "Miscellany," *American Speech*, IX, 150–60.
Ramsay, Robert L. *Our Storehouse of Missouri Place Names, Bulletin*

53 of the University of Missouri College of Arts and Sciences, Columbia, 1952.

Ray, P. Orman. "The Genesis of the Kansas-Nebraska Act," American Historical Association *Annual Report* (1914). 2 vols. Washington, 1916.

Romig, Joseph. "The Chippewa and Munsee Indians of Franklin County," *KHC*, XI, 314–23.

Root, George A. "Ferries in Kansas," *KHQ*, II, 3–28, 115–38, 251–93, 343–76; III, 15–42, 115–44, 246–88, 339–42; IV, 3–22, 268–81; V, 319–24, 378–80; VI, 15–20, 132–46.

———. "First Day's Battle at Hickory Point," *KHQ*, I, 28–49.

———, ed. "No-ko-aht's Talk," *KHQ*, I, 153–59.

———, and Russell K. Hickman. "Pike's Peak Express Companies," *KHQ*, XIII, 485–526.

Ross, Edith Connelley. "The Old Shawnee Mission," *KHC*, XVII, 417–35.

———. "The Quivira Village," *KHC*, XVII, 514–34.

Sanborn, J. L. "American Town Names," *Kansas Magazine*, III, 158–67.

Scheffer, Theo. H. "Geographical Names in Ottawa County," *KHQ*, III, 227–45.

Schmidt, Henry. "Naming Southwestern Cities," *Dodge City Journal*, Jan. 8, 1948.

Schoewe, Walter H. "Political and Geographical Aspects of Territorial Kansas," *Territorial Kansas*, University of Kansas Publications, Lawrence, 1954.

Sheldon, Addison E. "The Otoe Indians," Nebraska Historical Society *Publications*, XXI, 175–81.

Shindler, Henry. "The First Capital of Kansas," *KHC*, XII, 331–37.

Smith, Alice Strieby. "Through the Eyes of my Father," *KHC*, XVII, 708–18.

Smith, William E. "The Oregon Trail," *KHC*, XVII, 435–64.

Snell, Joseph W., ed. "Diary of a Dodge City Buffalo Hunter, 1872–1873," *KHQ*, XXXI, 345–95.

Sopher, David E. "Arabic Place Names in Spain," *Names*, III, 8–9.

Spencer, Rev. Joab. "The Shawnee Indians: Their Customs, Traditions and Folk-Lore," *KHC*, X, 382–401.

Stearns, J. H. "Moneka," *KHC*, XII, 429–30.

Street, William D. "Cheyenne Indian Massacre on the Middle Fork of the Sappa," *KHC*, X, 368–73.

Taube, Edward. "Tribal Names Related to Algonkin," *Names*, III, 65–81.

Taylor, A. A. "Medicine Lodge Peace Council," *Chronicles of Oklahoma*, II, 98–118.

Thomas, Alfred B. "An Eighteenth Century Comanche Document," *American Anthropologist* (n.s.), XXXI, 289–98.

Thompson, Stith. "The Indian Legend of Hiawatha," Modern Language Association *Publications*, XXXVII, 128–43.

Thompson, Thomas E. "Early Days in 'Old Boston,'" *KHC*, XVI, 479–87.

Tilghman, Zoe A. "Origin of the Name Wichita," *American Anthropologist* (n.s.), XLI, 488–89.

Tooker, William T. "The Powhattan Name for Virginia," *American Anthropologist*, (n.s.), VIII, 23–28.

Veale, George W. "Coming In and Going Out," *KHC*, XI, 6-12.

Vincent, John R. "Midwest Indians and Frontier Photography," *Annals of Iowa*, XXXVIII, 3rd series, (Summer, 1965), 26–35.

Vizetelly, Frank H. "A Matter of Pronunciation," *Atlantic Monthly*, CXLVII, 148–51.

Vogel, Virgil J. "The Mystery of Chicago's Name," *Mid-America*, XL, 163–74.

———. "The Origin and Meaning of Missouri," Missouri Historical Society *Bulletin*, XVI, 213–22.

Wedel, Waldo R. "The Kansas Indians," Kansas Academy of Sciences, *Transactions*, XLIX, 1–35.

———. "Prehistory and Environment in Central Great Plains," Kansas Academy of Science *Transactions*, L, 1–18.

———. "Some Problems and Prospects in Kansas Prehistory," *KHQ*, VII, 115–32.

Wellman, Paul. "Some Famous Kansas Frontier Scouts," *KHQ*, I, 345–59.

Wharton, Clifton. "The Expedition of Major Wharton," *KHC*, XVI, 272–305.

Whitman, Walt. "An American Primer," *Atlantic Monthly*, XCIII, 460–70.

Willson, Roscoe G. "The Origin of Arizona's Name," *Arizona Highways*, XXXI, 2–5.

Wilson, Hill P. "Black Kettle's Last Raid—1868," *KHC*, VIII, 110–17.

Wilson, James Grant. "Arent Van Curler and his Journal of 1634–35,"

American Historical Association *Annual Report* (1895). Washington, 1896.

Wright, Muriel. "Some Geographical Names of French Origin," *Chronicles of Oklahoma*, VII, 188–93.

Wynkoop, Edward E. "Edward Wanshear Wynkoop," *KHC*, XIII, 71–79.

Zimmerman, Mark E. "Pawnee Americans," *KHC*, XVI, 463–75.

VI. GENERAL WORKS

Allen, Joseph W. *Cho-O-Nee to High Iron: The Hidden Years of the Town of Neodesha*. Neodesha, Kansas, 1962.

Andreas, Alfred T., and W. G. Cutler. *History of the State of Kansas*. Chicago, 1883.

Bancroft, H. H. *Annals of Early Central America*. New York, 1886.

———. *The Native Races*. 5 vols. San Francisco, 1886.

Banta, R. E. *The Ohio*. New York, 1949.

Barr, Elizabeth N. *Wabaunsee County Directory and History*. Topeka, 1907.

Barrington, F. H. *Kansas Day: Containing a Brief History of Kansas*. Topeka, 1892.

Baughman, Robert W. *Kansas in Maps*. Topeka, 1961.

Beadle, J. H. *The Undeveloped West, or Five Years in the Territories*. Philadelphia, 1873.

Beauchamp, W. M. *Indian Names in New York*. Fayetteville, N. Y., 1893.

Bentley, O. H., ed. *History of Sedgwick County*. 2 vols. Chicago, 1910.

Berthrong, D. J. *The Southern Cheyennes*, Norman, 1963.

Bird, J. S., ed. *Historical Plat Book of Jackson County*. Chicago, 1881.

Blair, Ed. *History of Johnson County, Kansas*. Lawrence, 1915.

Blanchard, Leola H. *Conquest of Southwest Kansas*. Wichita, 1931.

Bolton, Herbert E. "French Intrusion into New Mexico," in *Pacific Ocean in History* (ed. by H. Morse Stephens and H. E. Bolton). New York, 1917.

———. *Texas in the Middle Eighteenth Century*. New York, 1962.

Boynton, Rev. C. B., and T. B. Mason. *A Journey Through Kansas, with Sketches of Nebraska*. Cincinnati, 1885.

Bracke, William B. *Wheat Country*. New York, 1950.

Bright, John. *Kansas: The First Century*. 4 vols. New York, 1956.

Bristow, John T. *The Overland Trail, Old Military Road and Pony Express Route*. Horton, 1937.

Brocklehurst, T. N. *Mexico Today*. London, 1883.

Brown, A. Theodore. *Frontier Community: Kansas City to 1870*. Columbia, 1964.

Burch, C. S. *Handbook of Elk and Chautauqua Counties, Kansas*. Chicago, 1886.

Case, Nelson. *History of Labette County*, Kansas. Chicago, 1901.

Chase County Historical Society. *Chase County Historical Sketches*. 2 vols. Elmdale, Kansas, 1948.

Chittendon, Hiram M. *The American Fur Trade of the Far West*. 2 vols. New York, 1935.

Cobb, Gwendolin B. "Potosí, A Mining Frontier," in *Greater America* (ed. by Adele Ogden and Engel Sluiter). Berkeley, 1945.

Coblentz, Catherine C. *Sequoyah*. New York, 1946.

Connelley, William E. *A Standard History of Kansas and Kansans*. 5 vols. New York, 1918.

Cook, John R. *The Border and the Buffalo*. Topeka, 1907.

Cooper, James F. *The Last of the Mohicans*. Boston, 1896.

Cory, Charles E. *Place Names in Bourbon County, Kansas*. Fort Scott, Kansas, 1928.

Curtis, Natalie. *The Indian Book*. New York, 1935.

Cushman, Dan. *The Great North Trail*, New York, 1966.

Day, Arthur G. *Coronado's Quest*. Berkeley, 1940.

Deatherage, Charles P. *Greater Kansas City*. 2 vols. Kansas City, 1927.

Duncan, Lew Wallace. *History of Neosho and Wilson Counties, Kansas*. Fort Scott, Kansas, 1902.

Farley, Alan W. *The Delaware Indians in Kansas*. Kansas City, 1955.

Favour, Alpheus H. *Old Bill Williams, Mountain Man*. Chapel Hill, 1936.

Foreman, Grant. *Last Trek of the Indians*. Chicago, 1946.

———. *Sequoyah*. Norman, 1938.

Forter, Emma E. *History of Marshall County, Kansas*. Indianapolis, 1917.

Fortier, Alcée. *History of Louisiana*. 4 vols. New York, 1904.

French, Laura M. *History of Emporia and Lyons County*. Emporia, 1929.

Gabriel, Ralph H. *The Lure of the Frontier*. Vol. II in *Pageant of America*. New Haven, 1929.

Gaeddert, G. Raymond. *The Birth of Kansas*. Lawrence, 1940.
Garwood, Darrell. *Crossroads of America*. New York, 1948.
Gibson, A. M. *The Kickapoos: Lords of the Middle Border*. Norman, 1963.
Giles, F. W. *Thirty Years in Topeka: A Historical Sketch*. Topeka, 1886.
Goebel, Dorothy B., and Julius Goebel, Jr. *Generals in the White House*. New York, 1945.
Goodspeed Publishing Co. *Wyandotte County and Kansas City, Kansas*. Chicago, 1890.
Gould, Charles N. *Covered Wagon Geologist*. Norman, 1959.
———. *Oklahoma Place Names*. Norman, 1933.
Graves, William W. *History of the Kickapoo Mission and Parish*. St. Paul, Kansas, 1938.
———. *History of Neosho County*. 2 vols. St. Paul, Kansas, 1949–51.
Gray, Patrick L. *Doniphan County History*. 2 vols. Bendena, Kansas, 1905.
Greeley, Horace. *The Overland Journey from New York to San Francisco*. New York, 1860.
Green, Charles R. *Early Days in Kansas*. 5 vols. Olathe, Kansas, 1912–13.
Greene, Max. *The Kanzas Region: Forest, Prairie, Desert, Mountain, Vale and River*. New York, 1856.
Grinnell, George Bird. *Pawnee Hero Stories and Folk Tales*. New York, 1889.
———. *The Cheyenne Indians: Their History and Ways of Life*. 2 vols. New York, 1962.
Hafen, LeRoy R. *The Overland Mail, 1849–1869*. Cleveland, 1926.
———, and Carl C. Rister. *Western America*. New York, 1941.
Hagen, William T. *The Sac and Fox Indians*. Norman, 1958.
Hale, Edward Everett. *Kanzas and Nebraska*. Boston, 1854.
Hall, Jesse A., and Leroy T. Hand. *History of Leavenworth County, Kansas*. Topeka, 1921.
Hallowell, A Irving. *Culture and Experience*. Philadelphia, 1955.
Hans, Fred M. *The Great Sioux Nation*. Minneapolis, 1964.
Harrington, Grant W. *Historic Spots or Mile-stones in the Progress of Wyandotte County, Kansas*. Merriam, Kansas, 1935.
Harston, J. Emmor. *Comanche Land*. San Antonio, 1963.
Holloway, J. M. *History of Kansas*. Lafayette, 1868.

Houck, Louis. *A History of Missouri.* 3 vols. Chicago, 1908.
Hulbert, Archer B. *The Ohio River, A Course of Empire.* New York, 1906.
———. *Southwest on the Turquoise Trail.* Colorado Springs–Denver, 1933.
Hyde, George E. *Pawnee Indians.* Denver, 1951.
Ingalls, Sheffield. *History of Atchison County, Kansas.* Lawrence, 1916.
Jackson, Donald, ed. *Black Hawk.* Urbana, 1964.
Johnson, W. A. *The History of Anderson County, Kansas.* Garnett, Kansas, 1877.
Jones, Horace. *The Story of Early Rice County.* Lyons, Kansas, 1959.
Jones, John C., and Winoma C. Jones. *The Prairie Pioneers of Western Kansas and Eastern Colorado.* Boulder, 1956.
Jones, Paul A. *Coronado and Quivira.* Wichita, 1929.
Kenton, Edna, ed. *The Indians of North America.* 2 vols. New York, 1927.
King, James L. *History of Shawnee County, Kansas.* Topeka, 1905.
Lauvrière, Émile. *Histoire de la Louisiane Française, 1673–1939.* Baton Rouge, 1940.
McKenney, Thomas L., and James Hall. *The Indian Tribes of North America.* 3 vols. Edinburgh, 1933–34.
Masterson, V. V., *The Katy Railroad and the Last Frontier.* Norman, 1961.
Mathews, John J. *The Osages: Children of the Middle Waters.* Norman, 1961.
Mayhall, Mildred P. *The Kiowas.* Norman, 1962.
Maynard, Theodore. *De Soto and the Conquistadores.* London, 1930.
Mead, James R. "Meaning of the Word 'Wichita,'" in *History of Sedgwick County* (ed. by O. H. Bentley), *q.v.*
Mencken. H. L. *The American Language.* New York, 1938.
Millbrook, Minnie Dubbs. *Ness: Western County, Kansas.* Detroit, 1955.
Monaghan, James. *Civil War on the Frontier.* Boston, 1955.
Mooney, Volney Paul. *History of Butler County.* Lawrence, 1916.
Morgan, Lewis H. *League of the Ho-de-no-sau-nee or Iroquois.* 2 vols. New Haven, 1954.
Musick, John R. *Secession in the Real America in Romance.* 14 vols. New York, 1909.

Nasatir, A. P. *Before Lewis and Clark.* 2 vols. St. Louis, 1952.
Nelson, Edward G. *The Company and the Community.* Lawrence, 1956.
Newman, Tillie Karns. *Black Dog Trail.* Boston, 1957.
Nye, Wilbur S. *Bad Medicine and Good: Tales of the Kiowas.* Norman, 1962.
Paden, Irene D. *In the Wake of the Prairie Schooner.* New York, 1943.
Parker, Nathan H. *The Kansas and Nebraska Handbook for 1857–1858.* Boston, 1858.
Parkman, Francis. *The Conspiracy of Pontiac.* New York, 1913.
Paxson, Frederic L. *History of the American Frontier.* Boston, 1924.
Phillips, William. *The Conquest of Kansas by Missouri and her Allies.* Boston, 1856.
Plate, Robert. *The Dinosaur Hunters.* New York, 1964.
Prescott, William H. *The Conquest of Peru.* 2 vols. New York, 1898.
Richardson, Albert D. *Beyond the Mississippi.* Hartford, 1867.
Richardson, R. N. *The Comanche Barrier.* Glendale, 1933.
Rister, Carl Coke. *Southern Plainsman.* Norman, 1938.
Roenigh, Adolph. *Pioneer History of Kansas.* Lincoln, Kansas, 1933.
Root, Frank A., and William E. Connelley. *The Overland Stage to California.* Topeka, 1901.
Rydjord, John. "The Conquistadores Come to Kansas," in *Kansas: The First Century* (ed. by John Bright), *q.v.*
———. "French Frontier and the Indian Trade," in *Kansas: The First Century* (ed. by John Bright), *q.v.*
Sabin, Henry, and Edwin Sabin. *The Making of Iowa.* Chicago, 1900.
Sandoz, Mari. *Cheyenne Autumn.* New York, 1953.
Savage, Isaac O. *A History of Republic County, Kansas.* Beloit, Kansas, 1901.
Settle, Raymond W., and Mary L. Settle. *Empire on Wheels.* Stanford, 1949.
Seymour, Flora W. *Indian Agents of the Old Frontier.* New York, 1941.
Shackleton, Bernice C. *Handbook on the Frontier Days of Southeast Kansas.* Pittsburg, Kansas, 1961.
Spaeth, Sigmund G. *A History of Popular Music in America.* New York, 1948.
Spring, Leverett Wilson. *Kansas, the Period to the War for the Union.* Boston, 1887.

Stewart, George R. *Names on the Land*. Boston, 1958.
———. *U. S. 40: Cross Section of the United States of America*. Boston, 1953.
Stratford, Jesse Perry. *Butler County's Eighty Years, 1855–1935*. El Dorado, Kansas, 1934.
Thane, Eric. *High Border Country*. New York, 1942.
Thomas, Alfred B. *After Coronado*. Norman, 1935.
Tomlinson, William P. *Kansas in Eighteen Fifty-Eight*. New York, 1859.
Toothaker, Mrs. Pearl. *A History of Sheridan County*. Hoxie, Kansas, 1961.
Van Every, Dale. *Forth to the Wilderness*. New York, 1961.
Verrill, A. Hyatt. *Old Civilizations of the New World*. New York, 1938.
Vestal, Stanley. *Kit Carson*. Boston, 1928.
———. *The Missouri River*. New York, 1945.
———. *The Old Santa Fe Trail*. Boston, 1939.
Von Engeln, O. D., and Jane McElway Urquhart. *Story Key to Geographical Names*. New York, 1924.
Warren, William W. *History of the Ojibway Nation*. Minneapolis, 1957.
Webb, William E. *Buffalo Land*. Cincinnati, 1872.
Wedel, Waldo R. *Prehistoric Man on the Great Plains*. Norman, 1961.
Wheat, Carl I. *Mapping the Trans-Mississippi West, 1540–1861*. 5 vols., San Francisco, 1957–63.
Whitney, Mrs. Carrie. *Kansas City, Missouri*. 2 vols. Chicago, 1908.
Whittemore, Margaret. *Historic Kansas*. Lawrence, 1954.
Wiebe, David K. *They Seek a Country*. Hillsboro, Kansas, 1959.
Wilson, Robert R., and Ethel M. Sears. *History of Grant County, Kansas*. Wichita, 1950.
Woodman, Rea. *Wichitana, 1877–1897*. Wichita, 1948.
Woodward, Grace Steele. *The Cherokees*. Norman, 1963.
Wright, Muriel H. *A Guide to the Indian Tribes of Oklahoma*. Norman, 1951.

VII. GUIDES AND MISCELLANEOUS MATERIALS

Allen County Scrapbook (newspaper clippings). 2 vols. KSHL, Topeka.

Alsberg, Henry G., ed. *The American Guide: A Source Book and Complete Travel Guide for the United States.* New York, 1949.
Atchison, Topeka, and Santa Fe Railroad. *Along Your Way* (pamphlet).
Baughman, Robert W. *Kansas Post Offices.* Wichita, 1961.
Blackmar, Frank W. *Kansas: A Cyclopedia of State History.* 2 vols. Chicago, 1912.
Edwards, John P. *Atlas of Wilson County.* Philadelphia, 1882.
———. *Historical Atlas of Sedgwick County, Kansas.* Philadelphia, 1882.
Edwards Brothers. *An Illustrated Historical Atlas of Miami County.* Philadelphia, 1878.
Federal Writers' Project. *Florida, A Guide.* New York, 1939.
———. *A Guide to Salina.* Salina, Kansas, n.d.
———. *Iowa, A Guide.* New York, 1938.
———. *Kansas, A Guide.* New York, 1949.
———. *Michigan, A Guide.* New York. 1941.
———. *Wisconsin, A Guide.* New York, 1941.
Fitzpatrick, Lillian L. *Nebraska Place-Names.* Lincoln, 1960.
Franklin County Historical Society. *Reflections of Franklin County and Chautauqua Days.* Ottawa, Kansas, 1961.
Gannett, Henry. *American Names, A Guide.* Washington, 1905.
Griffith, George. "Chief Tonganoxie, 1794–1864" (ed. by Walt Neibarger), in *Sunflower Petals*, Tonganoxie, Kansas, 1938.
Gudde, Erwin G. *California Place Names.* Berkeley, 1949.
Holt, Alfred H. *American Place Names.* New York, 1938.
Isely, Bliss. In *Wichita Beacon*, April-Sept., 1929. Scrapbook, WSU Library.
Kane, Joseph Nathan. *The American Counties.* New York, 1962.
Kenny, Hamill Thomas. *The Origin and Meaning of Indian Place Names of Maryland.* Baltimore, 1961.
Kingman County Diamond Jubilee *Souvenir Historical Program.* Kingman, 1958.
Leduc, Alberto, and Luis Lara y Pardo. *Diccionario de Geografía, Historia, y Biografía Mexicanas.* Paris and Mexico, 1910.
Lippincott, Gramb & Co., *Gazetteer of the United States.* Philadelphia, 1853.
Missouri Pacific Railroad Co. *The Empire that the Missouri Pacific Built.* St. Louis, n.d.

Overman, William D. *Ohio Town Names.* Akron, 1958.
Pan American Union. "Visit Bolivia," in *Travel in America.* Washington, 1956.
Paullin, Charles O. *Atlas of the Historical Geography of the United States.* Milwaukee, 1934.
Remsburg, George J. *Scrapbook* (newspaper clippings). 4 vols. KSHL, Topeka.
Shankle, George Earle. *State Names, Flags, Seals, Songs, Birds, Flowers, and other Symbols.* New York, 1934.
Shirk, George H. *Oklahoma Place Names.* Norman, 1965.
Smith, Eldon C. *The Story of Our Names.* New York, 1950.
Taylor, Isaac. *Names and their Histories.* London, 1898.
Vogel, Virgil J. *Indian Place Names in Illinois.* Illinois State Historical Society Pamphlet Series No. 4. Springfield, 1963.

Index